Lefia DeForest.

from their Teacher.

Mrs. Hunter.

Gospel Hymns

Nos. 1 to 6.

BY

Ira D. Sankey

James McGranahan

AND ## Geo. C. Stebbins

(BREVIER EDITION)

PUBLISHED BY

THE BIGLOW & MAIN CO. | THE JOHN CHURCH CO.
New York. | Cincinnati.

MAY BE ORDERED OF BOOKSELLERS AND MUSIC DEALERS.

PREFACE.

GOSPEL HYMNS Nos. 1 and 2, by P. P. Bliss and Ira D. Sankey; Nos. 3, 4, 5, and 6, by Ira D. Sankey, James McGranahan and Geo. C. Stebbins, are now compiled in this volume under the title of

GOSPEL HYMNS Nos 1 to 6.

All duplicate pieces have been omitted and the Hymns re-numbered in consecutive order from 1 to 739.

In addition to the large number of Gospel Hymns and Sacred Songs in this collection there will also be found over 125 of the most useful and popular STANDARD HYMNS AND TUNES OF THE CHURCH.

GOSPEL HYMNS

NOS. 1 TO 6 COMPLETE.

———◉———

1

ALL people that on earth do dwell,
    Sing to the Lord with cheerful voice;
Him serve with mirth, His praise forth tell,
    Come ye before Him and rejoice.

2 Know that the Lord is God indeed;
    Without our aid He did us make:
We are His flock, He doth us feed,
    And for His sheep He doth us take.

3 O enter then His gates with praise,
    Approach with joy His courts unto:
Praise, laud, and bless His name always,
    For it is seemly so to do.

4 For why? the Lord our God is good,
    His mercy is for ever sure;
His truth at all times firmly stood,
    And shall from age to age endure.

———

2

DOXOLOGY. L. M.

PRAISE God, from whom all blessings flow;
    Praise Him, all creatures here below;
Praise Him above, ye heavenly host;
Praise Father, Son, and Holy Ghost.

GRACE.

May be sung before and after meat.

3   BLESSING INVOKED.

BE present at our table, Lord,
    Be here and everywhere adored;
These mercies bless, and grant that we
May feast in Paradise with Thee.

---

4   THANKS RETURNED.

WE thank Thee, Lord, for this our food,
    For life, and health, and every good:
Let manna to our souls be given,—
The Bread of Life sent down from heaven.

5

'TIS the promise of God, full salvation to give
    Unto him who on Jesus, His Son, will believe.

||: Hallelujah, 'tis done ! I believe on the Son;
  I am saved by the blood of the crucified One. :||

2 Tho' the pathway be lonely, and dangerous too,
  Surely Jesus is able to carry me through.
        Hallelujah, 'tis done! etc.

3 Many loved ones have I in yon heavenly throng,
  They are safe now in glory, and this is their song:
        Hallelujah, 'tis done ! etc.

4 Little children I see standing close by their King,
  And He smiles as their song of salvation they sing:
        Hallelujah, 'tis done! etc.

5 There are prophets and kings in that throng I behold,
  And they sing as they march through the streets of pure
        Hallelujah, tis done ! etc.   [gold.

6 There's a part in that chorus for you and for me,
  And the theme of our praises forever will be:
        Hallelujah, 'tis done! etc.

6   ---

SAFE in the arms of Jesus,
    Safe on His gentle breast,
There by His love o'ershaded,
Sweetly my soul shall rest.

Hark! 'tis the voice of angels,
  Borne in a song to me,
Over the fields of glory,
  Over the Jasper sea.

CHO.—Safe in the arms of Jesus,
    Safe on His gentle breast,
    There by His love o'ershaded,
    Sweetly my soul shall rest.

2 Safe in the arms of Jesus,
  Safe from corroding care,
Safe from the world's temptations,
  Sin cannot harm me there.
Free from the blight of sorrow,
  Free from my doubts and fears;
Only a few more trials,
  Only a few more tears!

3 Jesus, my heart's dear refuge,
  Jesus has died for me;
Firm on the Rock of Ages
  Ever my trust shall be.
Here let me wait with patience,
  Wait till the night is o'er;
Wait till I see the morning
  Break on the golden shore.

———

7

IN some way or other the Lord will provide:
  It may not be *my* way,
  It may not be *thy* way;
  And yet, in His *own* way,
  "The Lord will provide."

CHO.—Then, we'll trust in the Lord,
    And He will provide;
    Yes, we'll trust in the Lord,
    And He will provide.

2 At some time or other the Lord will provide;
  It may not be *my* time,
  It may not be *thy* time;
  And yet, in His *own* time,
  "The Lord will provide."

3 Despond then no longer: the Lord will provide;
   And this be the token—
   No word He hath spoken
   Was ever yet broken:
   "The Lord will provide."

4 March on then right boldly; the sea shall divide;
   The pathway made glorious,
   With shoutings victorious,
   We'll join in the chorus,
   "The Lord will provide."

8

WAND'RING afar from the dwellings of men,
   Hear the sad cry of the lepers—the ten;
"Jesus, have mercy!" brings healing divine;
One came to worship, but where are the nine?

  Cho.—||: Where are the nine? :||
    Were there not ten cleansed?
    Where are the nine?

2 Loudly the stranger sang praise to the Lord,
Knowing the cure had been wrought by His word,
Gratefully owning the Healer Divine;
Jesus says tenderly, "Where are the nine?"

3 "Who is this Nazarene?" Pharisees say;
"Is He the Christ? tell us plainly, we pray."
Multitudes follow him seeking a sign,
Show them His mighty works—where are the nine?

4 Jesus on trial to-day we can see,
Thousands deridingly ask, "Who is He?"
How they're rejecting Him, your Lord and mine!
Bring in the witnesses—where are the nine?

9

WHAT means this eager, anxious throng,
   Which moves with busy haste along,
These wondrous gatherings day by day?
What means this strange commotion, pray?
In accents hushed the throng reply:
"Jesus of Nazareth passeth by."

2 Who is this Jesus? Why should He
The city move so mightily?

A passing stranger, has He skill
To move the multitude at will?
Again the stirring notes reply:
"Jesus of Nazareth passeth by."

3 Jesus! 'tis He who once below
Man's pathway trod, 'mid pain and woe;
And burdened ones, where'er He came,
Brought out their sick, and deaf and lame,
The blind rejoiced to hear the cry—
"Jesus of Nazareth passeth by."

4 Again He comes! From place to place
His holy footprints we can trace.
He pauseth at our threshold—nay,
He enters—condescends to stay.
Shall we not gladly raise the cry—
"Jesus of Nazareth passeth by?"

5 Ho! all ye heavy-laden, come!
Here's pardon, comfort, rest, and home,
Ye wanderers from a Father's face,
Return, accept His proffered grace.
Ye tempted ones, there's refuge nigh,
"Jesus of Nazareth passeth by."

6 But if you still this call refuse,
And all His wondrous love abuse,
Soon will He sadly from you turn,
Your bitter prayer for pardon spurn.
"Too late! too late!" will be the cry—
"Jesus of Nazareth *has passed by.*"

10

THIS loving Saviour
Stands patiently;
Though oft rejected,
Calls again for thee.

CHO.—Calling now for thee, prodigal,
Calling now for thee;
Thou hast wandered far away,
But He's calling now for thee.

2 Oh, boundless mercy,
Free, free to all!
Stay, child of error,
Heed the tender call.

3 Though all unworthy,
    Come, now, come home—
Say, while he's waiting,
    "Jesus, dear, I come."

11

HO! my comrades, see the signal
    Waving in the sky!
Re-inforcements now appearing,
    Victory is nigh!

CHO.—"Hold the fort, for I am coming,"
        Jesus signals still,
    Wave the answer back to Heaven,—
        "By Thy grace we will."

2 See the mighty host advancing,
    Satan leading on:
Mighty men around us falling,
    Courage almost gone.

3 See the glorious banner waving,
    Hear the bugle blow;
In our Leader's name we'll triumph
    Over every foe.

4 Fierce and long the battle rages,
    But our Help is near;
Onward comes our Great Commander,
    Cheer, my comrades, cheer!

12

THERE is a gate that stands ajar,
    And through its portals gleaming,
A radiance from the Cross afar,
    The Saviour's love revealing.

REF.—Oh, depth of mercy! can it be
        That gate was left ajar for me?
    For me, for me?
    Was left ajar for me?

2 That gate ajar stands free for all
    Who seek through it salvation;
The rich and poor, the great and small,
    Of every tribe and nation,

3 Press onward then, though foes may frown,
   While mercy's gate is open:
Accept the cross, and win the crown,
   Love's everlasting token.

4 Beyond the river's brink we'll lay
   The cross that here is given,
And bear the crown of life away,
   And love Him more in heaven.

13

FREE from the law, oh, happy condition,
   Jesus hath bled, and *there* is remission,
Cursed by the law and bruised by the fall,
Grace hath redeemed us once for all.

Cho.—Once for all, oh, sinner receive it,
   Once for all, oh, brother believe it;
Cling to the Cross, the burden will fall,
Christ hath redeemed us once for all.

2 Now are we free—there's no condemnation,
   Jesus provides a perfect salvation;
"Come unto *Me*," oh, hear His sweet call,
Come, and He saves us once for all.

3 "Children of God," oh, glorious calling,
   Surely His grace will keep us from falling;
Passing from death to life at His call,
Blesséd salvation, once for all.

14

WORK, for the night is coming,
   Work thro' the morning hours;
Work while the dew is sparkling,
   Work 'mid springing flowers;
Work, when the day grows brighter,
   Work in the glowing sun;
Work, for the night is coming,
   When man's work is done.

Work, for the night is coming,
   Work through the sunny noon;
Fill brightest hours with labor,
   Rest comes sure and soon.

Give every flying minute,
  Something to keep in store;
Work, for the night is coming,
  When man works no more.

3 Work, for the night is coming,
    Under the sunset skies;
  While their bright tints are glowing,
    Work, for daylight flies,
  Work till the last beam fadeth,
    Fadeth to shine no more;
  Work while the night is darkening,
    When man's work is o'er.

15
————

I WILL sing you a song of that beautiful land,
    The far-away home of the soul,
Where no storms ever beat on the glittering strand,
  ||: While the years of eternity roll. :||
Where no storms ever beat on the glittering strand,
    While the years of eternity roll.

2 Oh, that home of the soul in my visions and dreams,
    Its bright, jasper walls I can see;
  Till I fancy but thinly the vail intervenes
    ||: Between the fair city and me. :|| Till I fancy, etc.

3 That unchangeable home is for you and for me,
    Where Jesus of Nazareth stands,
  The King of all kingdoms forever, is He,
    ||: And He holdeth our crowns in His hands. :|| The
      King of, etc.

4 Oh, how sweet it will be in that beautiful land,
    So free from all sorrow and pain;
  With songs on our lips and with harps in our hands,
    ||: To meet one another again. :|| With songs on, etc.

16
————

THERE is a land of pure delight,
    Where saints immortal reign;
Eternal day excludes the night,
    And pleasures banish pain.
There everlasting spring abides,
    And never-withering flowers;

Death, like a narrow sea, divides
This heavenly land from ours.

2 Sweet fields beyond the swelling flood,
  Stand dressed in living green,
So to the Jews old Canaan stood,
  While Jordan rolled between.
Could we but climb where Moses stood,
  And view the landscape o'er,
Not Jordan's stream, nor death's cold flood,
  Should fright us from the shore.

17

WE'RE going home,
    No more to roam,
No more to sin and sorrow;
    No more to wear
    The brow of care,
We're going home to-morrow.

CHO.—We're going home, we're going home
        to-morrow,
We're going home, we're going home
        to-morrow.

2 For weary feet
    Awaits a street
Of wondrous pave and golden;
    For hearts that ache,
    The angels wake
The story, sweet and olden.

3 For those who sleep,
    And those who weep,
Above the portals narrow,
    The mansions rise
    Beyond the skies—
We're going home to-morrow.

4 Oh, joyful song!
    Oh, ransomed throng!
Where sin no more shall sever;
    Our King to see,
    And, oh, to be
With Him at home forever!

18

I AM so glad that our Father in heaven
Tells of His love in the book He has given,
Wonderful things in the Bible I see;
This is the dearest, that Jesus loves me.

CHO.—I am so glad that Jesus loves me,
Jesus loves me, Jesus loves me,
I am so glad that Jesus loves me,
Jesus loves even me.

2 Though I forget Him and wander away,
Still He doth love me wherever I stray;
Back to His dear loving arms would I flee,
When I remember that Jesus loves me.

3 Oh, if there's only one song I can sing,
When in His beauty I see the Great King,
This shall my song in eternity be:
"Oh, what a wonder that Jesus loves me."

———

J ESUS loves me, and I know I love Him,
Love brought Him down my poor soul to
redeem;
Yes, it was love made Him die on the tree,
Oh, I am certain that Jesus loves me.

CHO.—I am so glad, etc.

2 If one should ask of me, how could I tell?
Glory to Jesus, I know very well:
God's Holy Spirit with mine doth agree,
Constantly witnessing—Jesus loves me.

3 In this assurance I find sweetest rest,
Trusting in Jesus, I know I am blest;
Satan dismayed, from my soul now doth flee,
When I just tell him that Jesus loves me.

———

19

R EJOICE and be glad!
The Redeemer has come!
Go look on His cradle, His cross, and His tomb.

CHO.—Sound His praises, tell the Story,
  Of Him who was slain;
  Sound His praises tell with gladness,
  He liveth again.

2 Rejoice and be glad !
  It is sunshine at last !
The clouds have departed, the shadows are past.

3 Rejoice and be glad !
  For the blood hath been shed;
Redemption is finished, the price hath been paid.

4 Rejoice and be glad !
  Now the pardon is free !
The Just for the unjust has died on the tree.

5 Rejoice and be glad !
  For the Lamb that was slain
O'er death is triumphant, and liveth again.

6 Rejoice and be glad !
  For our King is on high,
He pleadeth for us on His throne in the sky.

7 Rejoice and be glad!
  For He cometh again;
He cometh in glory, the Lamb that was slain.

CHO.—Sound His praises, tell the Story,
  Of Him who was slain;
  Sound His praises tell with gladness,
  He cometh again.

20

WE praise Thee, O God ! for the Son of Thy love,
  For Jesus who died, and is now gone above.

CHO.—Hallelujah ! Thine the glory, Hallelujah ! amen.
  Hallelujah ! Thine the glory, revive us again.

2 We praise Thee, O God ! for Thy Spirit of light,
Who has shown us our Saviour, and scattered our night.

3 All glory and praise to the Lamb that was slain,
 Who hath borne all our sins, and hath cleansed every stain.

4 All glory and praise to the God of all grace,
  Who has bought us; and sought us, and guided our ways.

5 Revive us again; fill each heart with Thy love;
  May ach soul be rekindled with fire from above.

21

ROCK of Ages, cleft for me,
  Let me hide myself in Thee;
Let the water and the blood,
From Thy riven side which flowed,
Be of sin the double cure,
Save me from its guilt and power.

2 Not the labor of my hands
  Can fulfil Thy law's demands;
Could my zeal no respite know,
Could my tears forever flow,
All for sin could not atone;
Thou must save, and Thou alone.

3 Nothing in my hand I bring,
  Simply to Thy cross I cling;
Naked, come to Thee for dress,
Helpless look to Thee for grace;
Foul, I to the fountain fly,
Wash me, Saviour, or I die.

4 While I draw this fleeting breath,
  While mine eyes shall close in death.
When I soar to worlds unknown,
See Thee on Thy judgment throne,
Rock of Ages, cleft for me,
Let me hide myself in Thee.

22

HAVE you on the Lord believed?
  Still there's more to follow;
Of His grace have you received?
  Still there's more to follow;
Oh, the grace the Father shows!
  Still there's more to follow,
Freely He His grace bestows,
  Still there's more to follow.

Cho.—More and more, more and more,
　　Always more to follow,
　　Oh, His matchless, boundless love!
　　Still there's more to follow.

2 Have you felt the Saviour near?
　　Still there's more to follow;
　Does His blesséd presence cheer?
　　Still there's more to follow;
　Oh, the love that Jesus shows!
　　Still there's more to follow,
　Freely He His love bestows,
　　Still there's more to follow.

3 Have you felt the Spirit's power?
　　Still there's more to follow;
　Falling like the gentle shower?
　　Still there's more to follow;
　Oh, the pow'r the Spirit shows!
　　Still there's more to follow,
　Freely He His power bestows,
　　Still there's more to follow.

23

H EAVENLY Father, bless me now;
　　At the cross of Christ I bow;
Take my guilt and grief away;
Hear and heal me now, I pray.

Ref.—Bless me now, bless me now,
　　Heavenly Father, bless me now.

2 Now, O Lord! this very hour,
　Send Thy grace and show Thy power;
　While I rest upon Thy word,
　Come and bless me now, O Lord!

3 Now, just now, for Jesus' sake,
　Lift the clouds, the fetters break;
　While I look, and as I cry,
　Touch and cleanse me ere I die.

4 Never did I so adore
　Jesus Christ, Thy Son, before;
　Now the time! and this the place!
　Gracious Father, show Thy grace.

24

WEARY gleaner, whence comest thou,
  With empty hands and clouded brow?
Plodding along thy lonely way,
Tell me, where hast thou gleaned to-day?
Late I found a barren field,
The harvest past my search revealed,
Others golden sheaves had gained,
Only stubble for me remained.

CHO.—Forth to the harvest field away!
    Gather your handfuls while you may;
    All day long in the field abide,
    Gleaning close by the reapers' side.

2 Careless gleaner, what hast thou here,
These faded flowers and leaflets sere?
Hungry and thirsty, tell me, pray,
Where, oh, where hast thou gleaned to-day?
All day long in shady bowers,
I've gaily sought earth's fairest flowers;
Now, alas! too late I see
All I've gathered is vanity.

3 Burdened gleaner, thy sheaves I see;
Indeed thou must a-weary be!
Singing along the homeward way,
Glad one, where hast thou gleaned to-day?
Stay me not, till day is done
I've gather'd handfuls one by one:
Here and there for me they fall,
Close by the reapers I've found them all.

——

25

AH, my heart is heavy-laden,
  Weary and oppressed!
"Come to me," saith One, "and coming,
  Be at rest!"

CHO.—"Come to me," saith One, "and coming,
    Be at rest!"

2 Hath He marks to lead me to Him,
  If He be my Guide?
"In His feet and hands are wound-prints,
  And His side."

3 Is there diadem, as monarch,
     That His brow adorns?
"Yes, a crown in very surety,
     But of thorns!"

4 If I find Him, if I follow,
     What's my portion here?
"Many a sorrow, many a conflict,
     Many a tear."

5 If I still hold closely to Him,
     What have I at last?
"Sorrow vanquished, labor ended,
     Jordan past!"

6 If I ask Him to receive me,
     Will he say me nay?
"Not till earth and not till heaven
     Pass away!"

26

O NE more day's work for Jesus,
     One less of life for me!
But heaven is nearer,
And Christ is dearer,
Than yesterday to me,
     His love and light
     Fill all my soul to-night.

CHO.—One more day's work for Jesus,
     One more day's work for Jesus,
     One more day's work for Jesus,
     One less of life for me.

2 One more day's work for Jesus;
     How glorious is my King!
'Tis joy, not duty,
To speak His beauty;
My soul mounts on the wing
     At the mere thought
     How Christ my life has bought.

3 One more day's work for Jesus;
     How sweet the work has been,
To tell the story,
To show the glory,

When Christ's flock enter in!
How it did shine
In this poor heart of mine!

4 One more day's work for Jesus—
Oh, yes, a weary day;
But heaven shines clearer,
And rest comes nearer,
At each step of the way;
And Christ in all—
Before His face I fall.

5 Oh, blesséd work for Jesus,
Oh, rest at Jesus' feet!
There toil seems pleasure,
My wants are treasure,
And pain for Him is sweet;
Lord, if I may,
I'll serve another day.

27

ONE there is above all others,
Oh, how He loves!
His is love beyond a brother's,
Oh, how He loves!
Earthly friends may fail or leave us,
One day soothe, the next day grieve us;
But this Friend will ne'er deceive us,
Oh, how He loves!

2 'Tis eternal life to know Him,
Oh, how He loves!
Think, oh think, how much we owe Him,
Oh, how He loves!
With His precious blood He bought us,
In the wilderness He sought us,
To his fold He safely brought us,
Oh, how He loves!

3 Blesséd Jesus! would you know Him,
Oh, how He loves!
Give yourselves entirely to Him,
Oh, how He loves!
Think no longer of the morrow,
From the past new courage borrow,

Jesus carries all your sorrow,
Oh, how He loves!

4 All your sins shall be forgiven,
Oh, how He loves!
Backward shall your foes be driven,
Oh, how He loves!
Best of blessings He'll provide you,
Nought but good shall o'er betide you,
Safe to glory He will guide you,
Oh, how He loves!

28

TELL me the Old, Old Story,
Of unseen things above,
Of Jesus and His glory,
Of Jesus and His love.
Tell me the Story simply,
As to a little child,
For I am weak and weary,
And helpless and defiled.

Cho.—Tell me the Old, Old Story,
Tell me the Old, Old Story,
Tell me the Old, Old Story,
Of Jesus and His love.

2 Tell me the Story slowly,
That I may take it in—
That wonderful redemption,
God's remedy for sin.
Tell me the Story often,
For I forget so soon,
The "early dew" of morning,
Has passed away at noon.

3 Tell me the Story softly,
With earnest tones, and **grave;**
Remember! I'm the sinner
Whom Jesus came to save;
Tell me that Story always,
If you would really be,
In any time of trouble,
A comforter to me.

4 Tell me the same old Story,
    When you have cause to fear
That this world's empty glory
    Is costing me too dear.
Yes, and when that world's glory
    Is dawning on my soul,
Tell me the Old, Old Story:
    "Christ Jesus makes thee whole."

29

THE Spirit, oh, sinner,
    In mercy doth move
Thy heart, so long hardened,
    Of sin to reprove;
Resist not the Spirit,
    Nor longer delay;
God's gracious entreaties, May end with to-day.

2 Oh, child of the kingdom,
    From sin-service cease:
Be filled with the Spirit,
    With comfort and peace.
Oh, *grieve* not the Spirit,
    Thy Teacher is He,
That Jesus, thy Saviour, May glorified be.

3 Defiled is the temple,
    Its beauty laid low,
On God's holy altar
    The embers faint glow.
By love yet rekindled,
    A flame may be fanned;
Oh, *quench* not the Spirit, *The Lord is at hand.*

30

I LOVE to tell the Story
    Of unseen things above,
Of Jesus and His Glory,
    Of Jesus and His Love!
I love to tell the Story!
    Because I know it's true;
It satisfies my longings,
    As nothing else would do.

Cho.—I love to tell the Story!
'Twill be my theme in glory,
To tell the Old, Old Story
Of Jesus and His love.

2 I love to tell the Story!
More wonderful it seems,
Than all the golden fancies
Of all our golden dreams.
I love to tell the Story!
It did so much for me!
And that is just the reason
I tell it now to thee.

3 I love to tell the Story!
'Tis pleasant to repeat
What seems, each time I tell it,
More wonderfully sweet.
I love to tell the Story;
For some have never heard
The message of salvation
From God's own Holy Word.

4 I love to tell the Story!
For those who know it best
Seem hungering and thirsting
To hear it, like the rest.
And when, in scenes of glory,
I sing the New, New Song,
'Twill be—the Old, Old Story
That I have loved so long.

31

H OLY Spirit, faithful Guide,
Ever near the Christian's side;
Gently lead us by the hand,
Pilgrims in a desert land;
Weary souls fore'er rejoice,
While they hear that sweetest voice
Whispering softly, "Wanderer, come!
Follow me, I'll guide thee home."

2 Ever present, truest Friend,
Ever near Thine aid to lend,
Leave us not to doubt and fear,
Groping on in darkness drear,

When the storms are raging sore,
Hearts grow faint, and hopes give o'er,
Whispering softly, "Wanderer, come!
Follow me, I'll guide thee home."

3 When our days of toil shall cease,
Waiting still for sweet release,
Nothing left but heaven and prayer,
Wondering if our names were there;
Wading deep the dismal flood,
Pleading nought but Jesus' blood;
Whispering softly, "Wanderer, come!
Follow me, I'll guide thee home!"

32

BENEATH the Cross of Jesus
   I fain would take my stand—
The shadow of a mighty Rock,
   Within a weary land.
A home within the wilderness,
   A rest upon the way,
From the burning of the noon-tide heat,
   And the burden of the day.

2 O safe and happy shelter,
   O refuge tried and sweet,
O trysting-place where Heaven's love,
   And Heaven's justice meet!
As to the Holy Patriarch
   That wondrous dream was given,
So seems my Saviour's cross to me,
   A ladder up to heaven.

3 There lies beneath its shadow,
   But on the further side,
The darkness of an awful grave
   That gapes both deep and wide;
And there between us stands the Cross,
   Two arms outstretched to save,
Like a watchman set to guard the way
   From that eternal grave.

4 Upon that Cross of Jesus,
   Mine eye at times can see
The very dying form of One,
   Who suffered there for me;

And from my smitten heart with tears,
Two wonders I confess,—
The wonders of His glorious love
And my own worthlessness.

5 I take, O Cross, thy shadow,
For my abiding place;
I ask no other sunshine
Than the sunshine of His face;
Content to let the world go by,
To know no gain nor loss,
My sinful self, my only shame,
My glory all the Cross.

33

WITH harps and with viols, there stands a great throng
In the presence of Jesus, and sing this new song:—

CHO.—Unto Him who hath loved us and washed us from sin,
Unto Him be the glory for ever.   Amen.

2 All these once were sinners, defiled in His sight,
Now arrayed in pure garments in praise they unite.

3 He maketh the rebel a priest and a king,
He hath bought us and taught us this new song to sing

4 How helpless and hopeless we sinners had been,
If He never had loved us till cleansed from our sin.

5 Aloud in His praises our voices shall ring,
So that others believing, this new song shall sing.

34

OH, bliss of the purified, bliss of the free,
I plunge in the crimson-tide opened for me;
O'er sin and uncleanness exulting I stand,
And point to the print of the nails in His hand.

CHO.—Oh, sing of His mighty love,
Sing of His mighty love,
Sing of His mighty love,
Mighty to save.

2 Oh, bliss of the purified, Jesus is mine,
No longer in dread condemnation I pine;
In conscious salvation I sing of His grace,
Who lifteth upon me the light of His face.

3 Oh, bliss of the purified! bliss of the pure!
  No wound hath the soul that His blood cannot cure;
  No sorrow-bowed head but may sweetly find rest,
  No tears but may dry them on Jesus' breast.

4 O Jesus the crucified! Thee will I sing;
  My blesséd Redeemer, my God and my King;
  My soul, filled with rapture, shall shout o'er the grave,
  And triumph in death in the "Mighty to Save."

35

GRACE! 'tis a charming sound,
      Harmonious to the ear;
Heaven with the echo shall resound,
    And all the earth shall hear.

REF.—Saved by grace alone,
        This is all my plea;
      Jesus died for all mankind,
        And Jesus died for me.

2 Grace first contrived a way
    To save rebellious man;
  And all the steps that grace display,
    Which drew the wondrous plan.

3 Grace taught my roving feet
    To tread the heavenly road;
  And new supplies each hour I meet,
    While pressing on to God.

4 Grace all the work shall crown,
    Through everlasting days;
  It lays in heaven the topmost stone,
    And well deserves our praise.

36

PRECIOUS promise God hath given
      To the weary passer by,
On the way from earth to heaven,
  "I will guide thee with mine eye."

REF.—I will guide thee, I will guide thee,
        "I will guide thee with mine eye;"
      On the way from earth to heaven,
        "I will guide thee with mine eye."

2 When temptations almost win thee,
  And thy trusted watchers fly,
Let this promise ring within thee,
  "I will guide thee with mine eye."

3 When thy secret hopes have perished,
  In the grave of years gone by,
Let this promise still be cherished,
  "I will guide thee with mine eye."

4 When the shades of life are falling,
  And the hour has come to die,
Hear thy trusty Pilot calling,
  "I will guide thee with mine eye."

37

DOWN life's dark vale we wander,
    Till Jesus comes;
We watch and wait and wonder;
    Till Jesus comes.

CHO.—All joy His loved ones bringing,
      When Jesus comes;
  All praise through heaven ringing,
      When Jesus comes.
  All beauty bright and vernal,
      When Jesus comes;
  All glory, grand, eternal,
      When Jesus comes.

2 Oh, let my lamp be burning
    When Jesus comes;
  For Him my soul be yearning,
    When Jesus comes.

3 No more heart-pangs nor sadness,
    When Jesus comes;
  All peace and joy and gladness,
    When Jesus comes.

4 All doubts and fears will vanish,
    When Jesus comes,
  All gloom His face will banish,
    When Jesus comes.

5 He'll know the way was dreary,
    When Jesus comes;
He'll know the feet grew weary,
    When Jesus comes.

6 He'll know what griefs oppressed me,
    When Jesus comes;
Oh, how His arms will rest me!
    When Jesus comes.

38

WHAT! "lay my sins on Jesus?"
    God's well-belovéd Son!
No! 'tis a truth most precious,
    That God e'en *that* has done.

CHO.—Hallelujah, Jesus saves me,
    He makes me " white as snow."
Hallelujah, Jesus saves me,
    He makes me " white as snow."

2 Yes, 'tis a truth most precious,
    To all who do believe,
God laid our sins on Jesus,
    Who did the load receive.

3 What? "bring our guilt to Jesus?"
    To wash away our stains;
The act is passed that freed us,
    And nought to do remains.

39

O CHRIST, what burdens bowed Thy head!
    Our load was laid on Thee;
Thou stoodest in the sinner's stead,
    Didst bear all ill for me.
A Victim led, Thy blood was shed;
    Now there's no load for me.

2 Death and the curse were in our cup—
    O Christ, 'twas full for Thee;
But Thou hast drained the last dark drop—
    'Tis empty now for me.
That bitter cup—love drank it up;
    Now blessings' draught for me.

3 Jehovah lifted up His rod—
O Christ, it fell on Thee!
Thou wast sore stricken of Thy God;
There's not one stroke for me.
Thy tears, Thy blood, beneath it flowed;
Thy bruising healeth me.

4 The tempest's awful voice was heard—
O Christ, it broke on Thee!
Thy open bosom was my ward,
It braved the storm for me.
Thy form was scarred, Thy visage marred;
Now cloudless peace for me.

5 Jehovah bade His sword awake—
O Christ, it woke 'gainst Thee!
Thy blood the flaming blade must slake;
Thy heart its sheath must be—
All for my sake, my peace to make;
Now sleeps that sword for me.

6 For me, Lord Jesus, Thou hast died,
And I have died in Thee;
Thou'rt risen: my bands are all untied,
And now Thou liv'st in me.
When purified, made white, and tried,
Thy GLORY then for me!

40
————

OH, to be over yonder!
In that land of wonder,
Where the angel voices mingle, and the angel harpers ring;
To be free from pain and sorrow,
And the anxious, dread to-morrow,
To rest in light and sunshine in the presence of the King.

2 Oh, to be over yonder!
My yearning heart grows fonder
Of looking to the east, to see the blesséd day-star bring
Some tidings of the waking,
The cloudless, pure day breaking;
My heart is yearning—yearning for the coming of the King.

3 Oh, to be over yonder!
Alas! I sigh and wonder
Why clings my poor, weak, sinful heart to any earthly thing;

Each tie of earth must sever,
      And pass away for ever;
But there's no more separation in the presence of the King

4 Oh, when shall I be dwelling
      Where angel voices, swelling
In triumphant hallelujahs, make the vaulted heavens ring?
      Where the pearly gates are gleaming,
      And the Morning Star is beaming?
Oh, when shall I be yonder in the presence of the King?

5 Oh, when shall I be yonder?
      The longing groweth stronger
To join in all the praises the redeemed ones do sing
      Within those heavenly places,
      Where the angels vail their faces,
In awe and adoration in the presence of the King.

6 Oh, I shall soon be yonder,
      And lonely as I wander,
Yearning for the welcome summer—longing for the bird's
            fleet wing,
      The midnight may be dreary,
      And the heart be worn and weary,
But there's no more shadow yonder, in the presence of the
            King.

41 ——————

FROM Greenland's icy mountains,
      From India's coral strand,
Where Afric's sunny fountains
      Roll down their golden sand;
From many an ancient river,
      From many a palmy plain,
They call us to deliver
      Their land from error's chain.

2 What though the spicy breezes
      Blow soft o'er Ceylon's isle,
Though every prospect pleases
      And only man is vile?
In vain, with lavish kindness,
      The gifts of God are strown:
The heathen, in his blindness,
      Bows down to wood and stone.

3 Shall we, whose souls are lighted
    By wisdom from on high,
Shall we to men benighted
    The light of life deny?
Salvation! oh, salvation!
    The joyful sound proclaim,
Till earth's remotest nation
    Has learned Messiah's name.

4 Waft, waft, ye winds, His story,
    And you, ye waters, roll,
Till, like a sea of glory,
    It spreads from pole to pole;
Till o'er our ransomed nature,
    The Lamb, for sinners slain,
Redeemer, King, Creator,
    In bliss returns to reign.

42

ALL the way my Saviour leads me;
    What have I to ask beside?
Can I doubt His tender mercy,
    Who through life has been my guide?
Heavenly peace, divinest comfort,
    Here by faith in Him to dwell?
For I know whate'er befall me,
    Jesus doeth all things well.

2 All the way my Saviour leads me;
    Cheers each winding path I tread;
Gives me grace for every trial,
    Feeds me with the living bread;
Though my weary steps may falter,
    And my soul a-thirst may be,
Gushing from the Rock before me,
    Lo! a spring of joy I see.

3 All the way my Saviour leads me;
    Oh, the fullness of His love!
Perfect rest to me is promised
    In my Father's house above;
When my spirit, clothed immortal,
    Wings its flight to realms of day,
This is my song through endless ages—
    Jesus led me all the way.

43

Go bury thy sorrow,
  The world hath its share;
Go bury it deeply,
  Go hide it with care;
Go think of it calmly,
  When curtain'd by night,
Go tell it to Jesus,
  And all will be right.

2 Go tell it to Jesus,
  He knoweth thy grief;
Go tell it to Jesus,
  He'll send thee relief;
Go gather the sunshine
  He sheds on the way;
He'll lighten thy burden,
  Go, weary one, pray.

3 Hearts growing a-weary
  With heavier woe
Now droop 'mid the darkness—
  Go comfort them, go !
Go bury thy sorrows,
  Let others be blest;
Go give them the sunshine;
  Tell Jesus the rest.

44

To the hall of the feast came the sinful and fair;
  She heard in the city that Jesus was there;
Unheeding the splendor that blazed on the board,
She silently knelt at the feet of the Lord.

2 The frown and the murmur went round thro' them all,
That one so unhallowed should tread in that hall;
And some said the poor would be objects more meet,
As the wealth of her perfume she shower'd on His feet.

3 She heard but the Saviour; she spoke but with sighs;
She dare not look up to the heaven of His eyes;
And the hot tears gush'd forth at each heave of her breast,
And her lips to His sandals were throbbingly pressed.

4 In the sky, after tempest, as shineth the bow,—
   In the glance of the sunbeam, as melteth the snow,
   He looked on that lost one: "her sins were forgiven,"
   And the sinner went forth in the beauty of heaven.

45

BRIGHTLY beams our Father's mercy
   From His light-house evermore;
But to us He gives the keeping
   Of the lights along the shore.

Cho.—Let the lower lights be burning !
   Send a gleam across the wave !
   Some poor fainting, struggling seaman,
   You may rescue, you may save.

2 Dark the night of sin has settled,
   Loud the angry billows roar;
   Eager eyes are watching, longing,
   For the lights along the shore.

3 Trim your feeble lamp, my brother:
   Some poor sailor tempest-tost,
   Trying now to make the harbor,
   In the darkness *may be lost.*

46

ALONG time I wandered in darkness and sin,
   And wondered if ever the light would shine in;
I heard Christian friends tell of rapture divine,
And wish'd, how I wish'd, that their Saviour were mine.

Cho.—I wish'd He were mine, yes, I wish'd He were mine,
   I wish'd, how I wish'd, that their Saviour were mine.

2 I heard the glad gospel of "good will to men;"
   I read "whosoever" again and again;
   I said to my soul, "Can that promise be thine ?"
   And then began hoping that Jesus was mine.

Cho.—I hoped He was mine, yes, I hoped He was mine;
   I then began hoping that Jesus was mine.

3 Oh, mercy surprising, He saves even me !
   "Thy portion forever," He says, "will I be,"

On His word I'm resting—assurance divine--
I'm "hoping" no longer—I know He is mine;

Cho.· I know He is mine, yes, I know He is mine;
I'm "hoping" no longer—I know He is mine!

47

TAKE the name of Jesus with you,
    Child of sorrow and of woe—
It will joy and comfort give you,
Take it then where'er you go.

Cho.—||: Precious name, O how sweet!
        Hope of earth and joy of heaven. :||

2 Take the name of Jesus ever,
    As a shield from every snare;
If temptations 'round you gather,
    Breathe that holy name in prayer.

3 Oh! the precious name of Jesus;
    How it thrills our souls with joy,
When His loving arms receive us,
    And His songs our tongues employ!

4 At the name of Jesus bowing,
    Falling prostrate at His feet,
King of kings in heaven we'll crown Him,
    When our journey is complete.

48

OH, to be nothing, nothing,
    Only to lie at His feet,
A broken and emptied vessel,
    For the Master's use made meet.
Emptied that He might fill me
    As forth to His service I go;
Broken, that so unhindered,
    His life through me might flow.

Cho.—Oh, to be nothing, nothing,
        Only to lie at His feet,
    A broken and emptied vessel,
        For the Master's use made meet,

2 Oh, to be nothing, nothing,
   Only as led by His hand;
A messenger at His gateway,
   Only waiting for His command;
Only an instrument ready
   His praises to sound at His will,
Willing, should He not require me,
   In silence to wait on Him still.

3 Oh, to be nothing, nothing,
   Painful the humbling may be,
Yet low in the dust I'd lay me
   That the world might my Saviour see.
Rather be nothing, nothing,
   To Him let our voices be raised,
He is the Fountain of blessing,
   He only is meet to be praised.

49

FULLY persuaded, Lord, I believe:
   Fully persuaded, Thy Spirit give;
   I will obey Thy call;
   Low at Thy feet I fall;
   Now I surrender all;
     Christ to receive.

2 Fully persuaded—Lord, hear my cry!
   Fully persuaded—pass me not by;
   Just as I am I come,
   I will no longer roam,
   O make my heart Thy home;
     Save, or I die!

3 Fully persuaded, no more opprest,
   Fully persuaded, now I am blest:
   Jesus is now my Guide,
   I will in Christ abide;
   My soul is satisfied
     In Him to rest!

4 Fully persuaded, Jesus is mine;
   Fully persuaded, Lord, I am Thine!
   O make my love to Thee
   Like Thine own love to me,
   So rich, so full and free,
     Saviour divine!

50

ONLY an armour-bearer, proudly I stand,
   Waiting to follow at the King's command;
Marching if "onward" shall the order be,
Standing by my Captain, serving faithfully.

CHO.—Hear ye the battle-cry! "Forward," the call!
    See! see the faltering ones! backward they fall.
    Surely the Captain may depend on me,
    Though but an armour-bearer I may be.

2 Only an armour-bearer, now in the field,
  Guarding a shining helmet, sword and shield,
  Waiting to hear the thrilling battle-cry,
  Ready then to answer, "Master, here am I."

3 Only an armour-bearer, yet may I share
  Glory immortal, and a bright crown wear:
  If, in the battle, to my trust I'm true,
  Mine shall be the honors in the Grand Review.

51

LIGHT in the darkness, sailor, day is at hand!
   See o'er the foaming billows fair Haven's land,
Drear was the voyage, sailor, now almost o'er,
Safe within the life-boat, sailor, pull for the shore.

CHO.—Pull for the shore, sailor, pull for the shore!
    Heed not the rolling waves, but bend to the oar,
    Safe in the life-boat, sailor, cling to self no more!
    Leave the poor old stranded wreck, and pull for the
      shore.

2 Trust in the life-boat, sailor, all else will fail,
  Stronger the surges dash and fiercer the gale,
  Heed not the stormy winds, though loudly they roar;
  Watch the "bright and morning star," and pull for the
    shore.

3 Bright gleams the morning, sailor, up lift the eye;
  Clouds and darkness disappearing, glory is nigh!
  Safe in the life-boat, sailor, sing evermore;
  "Glory, glory, hallelujah!" pull for the shore.

52

ONE offer of salvation,
    To all the world make known;
The only sure foundation
    Is Christ the Corner-Stone.

CHO.—No other name is given,
        No other way is known,
    'Tis Jesus Christ the First and Last,
        He saves, and He alone.

2 One only door of heaven
        Stands open wide to-day,
One sacrifice is given,
        'Tis Christ, the Living Way.

3 My only song and story
        Is—Jesus died for me;
My only hope of glory,
        The Cross of Calvary.

———

53

I LEFT it all with Jesus
        Long ago;
All my sins I brought Him,
        And my woe.
When by faith I saw Him
        On the tree,
Heard His small, still whisper,
    ' 'Tis for thee,'
From my heart the burden
Rolled away—Happy day!

2 I leave it all with Jesus,
        For He knows
How to steal the bitter
        From life's woes;
How to gild the tear-drop
        With His smile,
Make the desert-garden
        Bloom awhile;
When my weakness leaneth
On His might,   All seems light.

3 I leave it all with Jesus
    Day by day;
Faith can firmly trust Him
    Come what may.
Hope has dropped her anchor,.
    Found her rest
In the calm, sure haven
    Of His breast:
Love esteems it heaven
To abide   At His side.

4 Oh, leave it *all* with Jesus,
    Drooping soul !
Tell not *half* thy story,
    But the whole.
Worlds on worlds are hanging
    On His hand,
Life and death are waiting
    His command;
Yet His tender bosom
Makes *thee* room—Oh, come home !

54

OH, think of the home over there,
    By the side of the river of light,
Where the saints, all immortal and fair,
    Are robed in their garments of white.

REF.—Over there, over there,
        Oh, think of the home over there.
        Over there, over there, over there,
        Oh, think of the home over there.

2 Oh, think of the friends over there,
    Who before us the journey have trod,
Of the songs that they breathe on the air,
    In their home in the palace of God.

REF.—Over there, over there,
        Oh, think of the friends over there, etc.

3 My Saviour is now over there,
    There my kindred and friends are at rest;
Then away from my sorrow and care,
    Let me fly to the land of the blest

REF.—Over there, over there,
        My Saviour is now over there, etc.

4 I'll soon be at home over there,
   For the end of my journey I see
Many dear to my heart, over there,
   Are watching and waiting for me.

REF.—Over there, over there,
     I'll soon be at home over there, etc.

55

OH, come to the Saviour, believe in His name,
   And ask Him your heart to renew;
He waits to be gracious, O turn not away,
   For now there is pardon for you.

CHO.—||: Yes, there is pardon for you; :||
   For Jesus has died to redeem you,
   And offers full pardon to you.

2 The way of transgression that leads unto death,
   Oh, why will you longer pursue?
How can you reject the sweet message of love
   That offers full pardon for you?

3 Be warned of your danger; escape to the cross;
   Your only salvation is there;
Believe, and that moment the Spirit of grace
   Will answer your penitent prayer.

56

"GO work in My vineyard," there's plenty to do,
   The harvest is great and the laborers are few;
There's weeding and fencing, and clearing of roots,
And ploughing, and sowing, and gathering the fruits.
There are foxes to take, there are wolves to destroy,
All ages and ranks I can fully employ.
I've sheep to be tended, and lambs to be fed,
The lost must be gathered, the weary ones led.

CHO.—Go work, go work, go work in My vineyard; there's
     plenty to do;
   Go work, go work. The harvest is great, and the
     laborers are few.

2 "Go work in My vineyard," I claim thee as Mine,
With blood did I buy thee, and all that is thine;
Thy time and thy talents, thy loftiest powers,
Thy warmest affections, thy sunniest hours.

I willingly yielded My kingdom for thee,
The song of archangels—to hang on the tree;
In pain and temptation, in anguish and shame,
I paid thy full ransom; My purchase I claim.

3 "Go work in My vineyard;" oh, "work while 'tis day,"
The bright hours of sunshine are hastening away;
And night's gloomy shadows are gathering fast;
Then the time for our labor shall ever be past.
Begin in the morning, and toil all the day,
Thy strength I'll supply, and thy wages I'll pay;
And blessèd, thrice blessèd the diligent few,
Who finish the labor I've given them to do.

57

DEPTH of mercy! can there be
　　Mercy still reserved for me?
Can my God His wrath forbear?
Me, the chief of sinners, spare?

2 I have long withstood His grace;
Long provoked him to His face;
Would not hearken to His calls,
Grieved Him by a thousand falls.

3 Now, incline me to repent;
Let me now my sins lament;
Now my foul revolt deplore,
Weep, believe. and sin no more.

58

MY heart, that was heavy and sad,
　　Was made to rejoice and be glad,
And peace without measure I had,
　　When the Comforter came

REF.—Peace, sweet peace,
　　Peace when the Comforter came!
My heart that was heavy and sad,
Was made to rejoice and be glad,
And peace without measure I had,
　　When the Comforter came.

2 To sin and to evil inclined,
With darkness pervading my mind,
No rest I could anywhere find,
　　Till the Comforter came.

3 The voice of thanksgiving I raised,
  The Lord, my Redeemer, I praised;
  I was at His mercy amazed,
    When the Comforter came.

59

COME, sing the gospel's joyful sound,
  Salvation full and free;
Proclaim to all the world around,
  The year of jubilee!

CHO.—Salvation, Salvation,
      The grace of God doth bring;
    Salvation, Salvation,
      Through Christ our Lord and King.

2 Ye mourning souls, aloud rejoice;
  Ye blind, your Saviour see!
Ye prisoners, sing with thankful voice,
  The Lord hath made you free!

3 With rapture swell the song again,
  Of Jesus' dying love;
'Tis peace on earth, good will to men,
  And praise to God above.

60

ONWARD! upward! Christian soldier,
  Turn not back nor sheath thy sword,
Let its blade be sharp for conquest,
  In the battle for the Lord.
From the great white throne eternal,
  God Himself is looking down;
He it is who now commands thee,
  Take the cross and win the crown.

2 Onward! upward! doing, daring
  All for Him who died for thee;
Face the foe and meet with boldness
  Danger whatsoe'er it be.
From the battlements of glory,
  Holy ones are looking down,
Thou canst almost hear them shouting:
  "On! let no one take thy crown."

3 Onward! till thy course is finished,
  Like the ransomed ones before;

Keep the faith through persecution,
  Never give the battle o'er.
Onward! upward! till victorious,
  Thou shalt lay thy armor down,
And thy loving Saviour bids thee
  At His hand receive thy crown.

61

MORE love to Thee, O Christ!
  More love to Thee;
Hear Thou the prayer I make
  On bended knee;
This is my earnest plea,
More love, O Christ, to Thee,
  More love to Thee!

2 Once earthly joy I craved,
  Sought peace and rest;
Now Thee alone I seek,
  Give what is best:
This all my prayer shall be,
More love, O Christ, to Thee,
  More love to Thee!

3 Let sorrow do its work,
  Send grief or pain;
Sweet are Thy messengers,
  Sweet their refrain,
When they can sing with me,—
More love, O Christ, to Thee,
  More love to Thee!

4 Then shall my latest breath,
  Whisper Thy praise,
This be the parting cry
  My heart shall raise;
This still its prayer shall be:
More love, O Christ, to Thee,
  More love to Thee!

62

THINE, most gracious Lord,
  O make me wholly Thine—
Thine in thought, in word, and deed,
  For thou, O Christ, art mine.

REF.—Wholly Thine, wholly Thine;
　　　Thou hast bought me, I am Thine;
　　　Blesséd Saviour, Thou art mine;
　　　Make me wholly Thine.

2 Wholly Thine, my Lord,
　　To go when Thou dost call;
　Thine to yield my very self
　　In all things, great and small.

3 Wholly Thine, O Lord,
　　In every passing hour;
　Thine in silence, Thine to speak,
　　As Thou dost grant the power.

4 Wholly thine, O Lord,
　　To fashion as Thou wilt,—
　Strengthen, bless, and keep the soul
　　Which Thou hast saved from guilt.

5 Thine, Lord, wholly Thine,
　　For ever one with Thee—
　Rooted, grounded in Thy love,
　　Abiding, sure, and free.

63

ALL my doubts I give to Jesus!
　I've His gracious promise heard—
"I shall never be confounded"—
I am trusting in that word.

CHO.—||: I am trusting, fully trusting,
　　　Sweetly trusting in His word. :||

2 All my sin I lay on Jesus!
　　He doth wash me in His blood;
　He will keep me pure and holy,
　　He will bring me home to God.

3 All my fears I give to Jesus!
　　Rest my weary soul on Him;
　Though my way be hid in darkness,
　　Never can His light grow dim.

4 All my joys I give to Jesus!
　　He is all I want of bliss;
　He of all the worlds is Master—
　　He has all I need in this.

5 All I am I give to Jesus!
    All my body, all my soul,
All I have, and all I hope for,
    While eternal ages roll.

64

JESUS shall reign where'er the sun
    Does his successive journeys run;
His kingdom spread from shore to shore,
Till moons shall wax and wane no more.
From north to south the princes meet,
To pay their homage at His feet;
While western empires own their Lord,
And savage tribes attend His word.

2 To Him shall endless prayer be made,
And endless praises crown His head;
His name like sweet perfume shall rise
With every morning sacrifice.
People and realms of every tongue
Dwell on His love with sweetest song,
And infant voices shall proclaim
Their early blessings on His Name.

65

MY song shall be of Jesus,
    His mercy crowns my days,
He fills my cup with blessings,
    And tunes my heart to praise;
My song shall be of Jesus,
    The precious Lamb of God,
Who gave Himself my ransom,
    And bought me with His blood.

2 My song shall be of Jesus,
    When, sitting at His feet,
I call to mind His goodness,
    In meditation sweet;
My song shall be of Jesus,
    Whatever ill betide;
I'll sing the grace that saves me,
    And keeps me at His side.

3 My song shall be of Jesus,
    While pressing on my way

To reach the blissful region
Of pure and perfect day.
And when my soul shall enter
The gate of Eden fair,
A song of praise to Jesus
I'll sing forever there.

———

66

ONLY a step to Jesus!
Then why not take it now?
Come, and thy sin confessing,
To Him thy Saviour bow.

REF.—Only a step, only a step;
Come, He waits for thee;
Come, and, thy sin confessing,
Thou shalt receive a blessing;
Do not reject the mercy
He freely offers thee.

2 Only a step to Jesus!
Believe, and thou shalt live;
Lovingly now He's waiting,
And ready to forgive.

3 Only a step to Jesus!
A step from sin to grace;
What hast thy heart decided?
The moments fly apace.

4 Only a step to Jesus!
O why not come and say,
Gladly to Thee, my Saviour,
I give myself away.

———

67

THE sands of time are sinking,
The dawn of heaven breaks,
The summer morn I've sighed for—
The fair, sweet morn awakes.
Dark, dark hath been the midnight,
But day-spring is at hand,
And glory—glory dwelleth
In Immanuel's land.

2 I've wrestled on toward heaven.
  'Gainst storm and wind and tide,
Now, like a weary traveler
  That leaneth on his guide,
Amid the shades of evening,
  While sinks life's lingering sand,
I hail the glory dawning,
  From Immanuel's land.

3 Deep waters crossed life's pathway,
  The hedge of thorns was sharp;
Now these lie all behind me—
  O! for a well-tuned harp!
O, to join the hallelujah
  With yon triumphant band!
Who sing where glory dwelleth,
  In Immanuel's land.

68

DARK is the night, and cold the wind is blowing,
  Nearer and nearer comes the breakers' roar;
Where shall I go, or whither fly for refuge?
  Hide me, my Father, till the storm is o'er;

CHO.—With His loving hand to guide, let the clouds above
    me roll,
  And the billows in their fury dash around me.
I can brave the wildest storm, with His glory in my soul,
  I can sing amidst the tempest—Praise the Lord!

2 Dark is the night, but cheering is the promise;
  He will go with me o'er the troubled wave;
Safe He will lead me through the pathless waters,
  Jesus, the Mighty One, and strong to save.

3 Dark is the night, but lo! the day is breaking,
  Onward my bark, unfurl thy every sail;
Now at the helm I see my Father standing,
  Soon will my anchor drop within the vail.

69

LO! the day of God is breaking;
  See the gleaming from afar!
Sons of earth from slumber waking,
  Hail the Bright and Morning star.

Cho.—Hear the call! O gird your armour on,
 Grasp the Spirit's mighty Sword:
 Take the Helmet of salvation,
  Pressing on to battle for the Lord!

2 Trust in Him who is your Captain;
 Let no heart in terror quail;
Jesus leads the gathering legions,
 In His name we shall prevail,

3 Onward marching, firm and steady,
 Faint not, fear not Satan's frown,
For the Lord is with you always,
 Till you wear the victor's crown.

4 Conquering hosts with banners waving,
 Sweeping on o'er hill and plain,
Ne'er shall halt till swells the anthem,
 "Christ o'er all the world doth reign!"

70

I'VE found a joy in sorrow,
 A secret balm for pain,
A beautiful to-morrow
 Of sunshine after rain;
I've found a branch of healing
 Near every bitter spring,
A whispered promise stealing
 O'er every broken string.

2 I've found a glad hosanna
 For every woe and wail;
A handful of sweet manna
 When grapes of Eshcol fail;
I've found a Rock of Ages
 When desert wells are dry;
And after weary stages,
 I've found an Elim nigh.

3 An Elim with its coolness,
 Its fountains and its shade;
A blessing in its fulness,
 When buds of promise fade.
O'er tears of soft contrition
 I've seen a rainbow light;
A glory and fruition,
 So near!—yet out of sight.

4 My Saviour, Thee possessing,
   I have the joy, the balm,
The healing and the blessing,
   The sunshine and the psalm;
The promise for the fearful,
   The Elim for the faint;
The rainbow for the tearful,
   The glory for the saint!

71

I LOVE to think of the heavenly land
   Where white-robed angels are:
Where many a friend is gathered safe
   From fear and toil and care.

Ref.—‖: There'll be no parting, :‖
   There'll be no parting,
   There'll be no parting there.

2 I love to think of the heavenly land,
   Where my Redeemer reigns,
Where rapturous songs of triumph rise,
   In endless, joyous strains.

3 I love to think of the heavenly land,
   The saints eternal home,
Where palms, and robes, and crowns ne'er fade,
   And all our joys are one.

4 I love to think of the heavenly land,
   The greetings there we'll meet,
The harps—the songs forever ours—
   The walks—the golden streets.

5 I love to think of the heavenly land,
   That promised land so fair,
Oh, how my raptured spirit longs,
   To be forever there.

72

"CALL them in"—the poor, the wretched,
   Sin-stained wanderers from the fold;
Peace and pardon freely offer;
   Can you weigh their worth with gold?
"Call them in"—the weak, the weary,
   Laden with the doom of sin;

Bid them come and rest in Jesus;
He is waiting—"Call them in."

2 "Call them in "—the Jew, the Gentile;
Bid the stranger to the feast;
"Call them in"—the rich, the noble,
From the highest to the least:
Forth the Father runs to meet them,
He hath all their sorrows seen;
Robe, and ring, and royal sandals,
Wait the lost ones—"Call them in."

3 "Call them in "—the mere professors,
Slumbering, sleeping, on death's brink;
Nought of life are they possessors,
Yet of safety vainly think;
Bring them in—the careless scoffers,
Pleasure seekers of the earth:
Tell of God's most gracious offers,
And of Jesus' priceless worth.

4 "Call them in "—the broken-hearted,
Cowering 'neath the brand of shame;
Speak Love's message low and tender,
'Twas for sinners Jesus came:
See, the shadows lengthen round us,
Soon the day-dawn will begin;
Can you leave them lost and lonely?
Christ is coming—" Call them in."

73

I BRING my *sins* to Thee,
The sins I cannot count,
That all may cleansèd be
In Thy once opened Fount;
I bring them Saviour, all to Thee;
The burden is too great for me.

2 I bring my *grief* to Thee,
The grief I cannot tell;
No words shall needed be,
Thou knowest all so well;
I bring the sorrow laid on me,
O suffering Saviour, all to Thee.

3 My *joys* to Thee I bring,
    The joys Thy love has given,
That each may be a wing
    To lift me nearer heaven,
I bring them, Saviour, all to Thee,
Who hast procured them all for me.

4 My *life* I bring to Thee,
    I would not be my own;
O Saviour, let me be
    Thine ever, Thine alone,
My heart, my life, my all I bring
To Thee, my Saviour and my King.

74

I HAVE heard of a Saviour's love,
    And a wonderful love it must be;
But did He come down from above,
    Out of love and compassion for me, for me,
    Out of love and compassion for me?

CHO.—Yes, yes, yes, for me, for me,
    Yes, yes, yes, for me;
    Our Lord from above in His infinite love,
    On the cross died to save you and me.

2 I have heard how He suffered and bled,
    How He languished and died on the tree;
But then is it anywhere said,
    That He languished and suffered for me, for me,
    That He languished and suffered for me!

3 I've been told of a heaven on high,
    Which the children of Jesus shall see;
But is there a place in the sky
    Made ready and furnished for me, for me,
    Made ready and furnished for me?

4 Lord, answer these questions of mine,
    To whom shall I go but to Thee?
And say by Thy Spirit divine,
    There's a Saviour and heaven for me, for me,
    There's a Saviour and heaven for me.

75

A T the feet of Jesus,
  Listening to His word:
Learning wisdom's lesson
  From her loving Lord:
Mary, led by heavenly grace,
Chose the meek disciple's place.

Cho.—At the feet of Jesus is the place for me,
  There a humble *learner* would I choose to be.

2 At the feet of Jesus,
  Pouring perfume rare,
Mary did her Saviour,
  For the grave prepare:
And, from love the "good work" done,
She her Lord's approval won.

Cho.—At the feet of Jesus is the place for me,
  There in sweetest *service* would I ever be.

3 At the feet of Jesus,
  In that morning hour,
Loving hearts receiving
  Resurrection power:
Haste with joy to preach the Word:
"Christ is risen, Praise the Lord!"

Cho.—At the feet of Jesus, risen now for me,
  I shall sing His *praises* through eternity.

76

O H, for the peace that floweth as a river,
  Making life's desert-places bloom and smile;
Oh, for the faith to grasp "Heaven's bright forever,"
  Amid the shadows of earth's "little while."

2 "A little while" for patient vigil-keeping,
  To face the storm and wrestle with the strong;
"A little while" to sow the seed with weeping,
  Then bind the sheaves and sing the harvest song.

3 "A little while" the earthen pitcher taking,
  To wayside brooks, from far-off fountains fed;
Then the parched lip its thirst forever slaking
  Beside the fulness of the Fountain-head.

4 "A little while" to keep the oil from failing,
  "A little while" faith's flickering lamp to trim;
And then the Bridegroom's coming footsteps hailing,
  We'll haste to meet Him with the bridal hymn.

77

NOW just a word for Jesus;
    Your dearest Friend so true,
Come, cheer our hearts and tell us
    What He has done for you.

REF.—Now just a word for Jesus—
        'Twill help us on our way;
    One little word for Jesus,
        O speak, or sing, or pray.

2 Now just a word for Jesus;
    You feel your sins forgiven,
  And by His grace are striving
    To reach a home in heaven.

3 Now just a word for Jesus;
    A cross it cannot be
  To say, "I love my Saviour
    Who gave His life for me."

4 Now just a word for Jesus;
    Let not the time be lost;
  The heart's neglected duty
    Brings sorrow, to its cost.

5 Now just a word for Jesus;
    And if your faith be dim,
  Arise in all your weakness,
    And leave the rest to Him.

78

WE'RE marching on to Canaan with banner and song,
    We're soldiers enlisted to fight 'gainst the wrong,
But, lest in the conflict our strength should divide,
We ask, Who among us is on the Lord's side?

CHO.—||:Oh, who is there among us, the true and the tried,
    Who'll stand by his colors—who's on the Lord's side?:||

2 The sword may be burnished, the armor be bright,
  For Satan appears as an angel of light;
  Yet darkly the bosom may treachery hide,
  While the lips are professing, "I'm on the Lord's side."

3 Who is there among us yet under the rod,
  Who knows not the pardoning mercy of God?
  Oh, bring to Him humbly the heart in its pride;
  Oh, haste, while He's waiting and seek the Lord's side.

4 Oh, heed not the sorrow, the pain and the wrong,
  For soon shall our sighing be changed into song;
  So, bearing the cross of our Covenant Guide,
  We'll shout, as we triumph, *"I'm on the Lord's side."*

79

A LAS! and did my Saviour bleed?
    And did my Sovereign die?
Would He devote that sacred head
  For such a worm as I?

Cho.—Help me, dear Saviour, Thee to own,
    And ever faithful be;
  And when Thou sittest on Thy throne,
    O Lord, remember me.

2 Was it for crimes that I had done
    He groaned upon the tree?
  Amazing pity! grace unknown!
    And love beyond degree.

3 Well might the sun in darkness hide,
    And shut his glories in,
  When Christ, the mighty Maker died
    For man, the creature's sin.

4 Thus might I hide my blushing face,
    Whilst His dear cross appears,
  Dissolve my heart in thankfulness,
    And melt mine eyes to tears.

5 But drops of grief can ne'er repay
    The debt of love I owe;
  Here, Lord, I give myself away;
    'Tis all that I can do.

80

L OOK away to Jesus,
    Soul by woe oppressed;
'Twas for thee He suffered,
  Come to Him and rest,
All thy griefs He carried
  All thy sins He bore;
Look away to Jesus;
  Trust Him evermore.

2 Look away to Jesus,
  Soldier in the fight;
When the battle thickens
  Keep thine armor bright;
Though thy foes be many,
  Though thy strength be small,
Look away to Jesus;
  He shall conquer all.

3 Look away to Jesus,
  When the skies are fair;
Calm seas have their dangers;
  Mariner, beware!
Earthly joys are fleeting,
  Going as they came,
Look away to Jesus;
  Evermore the same.

4 Look away to Jesus,
  'Mid the toil and heat;
Soon will come the resting
  At the Master's feet;
For the guests are bidden,
  And the feast is spread;
Look away to Jesus,
  In His footsteps tread.

5 When, amid the music
  Of the endless feast,
Saints will sing His praises,
  Thine shall not be least;
Then, amid the glories
  Of the crystal sea,
Look away to Jesus,
  Through eternity.

81

OUR lamps are trimmed and burning,
  Our robes are white and clean,
We've tarried for the Bridegroom,
  Oh, may we enter in?
We know we've nothing worthy
  That we can call our own—
The light, the oil, the robes we wear,
  Are all from Him alone.

CHO.—Behold the Bridegroom cometh!
    And all may enter in,
      Whose lamps are trimmed and burning,
      Whose robes are white and clean.

2 Go forth, go forth to meet Him,
    The way is open now,
    All lighted with the glory
      That's streaming from His brow.
  Accept the invitation
    Beyond deserving kind;
  Make no delay, but take your lamps,
    And joy eternal find.

3 We see the marriage splendor
    Within the open door,
  We know that those who enter
    Are blest for evermore.
  We see He is more lovely
    Than all the sons of men,
  But still we know the door once shut
    Will never ope again.

82

L ORD Jesus, I long to be perfectly whole;
  I want Thee forever, to live in my soul;
Break down every idol, cast out every foe;
Now wash me, and I shall be whiter than snow.

CHO.—Whiter than snow, yes, whiter than snow;
    Now wash me, and I shall be whiter than snow.

2 Lord Jesus, look down from Thy throne in the skies
And help me to make a complete sacrifice;
I give up myself, and whatever I know—
Now wash me, and I shall be whiter than snow

3 Lord Jesus, for this I most humbly entreat;
I wait, blesséd Lord, at Thy crucified feet,
By faith, for my cleansing, I see Thy blood flow—
Now wash me, and I shall be whiter than snow.

4 Lord Jesus, Thou seest I patiently wait;
Come now, and within me a new heart create;
To those who have sought Thee, Thou never said'st No—
Now wash me, and I shall be whiter than snow.

83

FRESH from the throne of glory,
    Bright in its crystal gleam,
Bursts out the living fountain,
    Swells on the living stream;
Bless'd River,   Let me ever
    Feast my eyes on thee.

2 Stream full of life and gladness,
    Spring of all health and peace,
No harps by thee hang silent,
    Nor happy voices cease;
Tranquil River,   Let me ever
    Sit and sing by thee.

3 River of God, I greet thee,
    Not now afar, but near;
My soul to thy still waters
    Hastes in its thirstings here;
Holy River,   Let me ever
    Drink of only thee.

84

IN Zion's Rock abiding,
    My soul her triumph sings;
In His pavillion hiding,
    I praise the King of kings.

CHO.—My High Tower is He!
    To Him I will flee;
In Him confide,   In Him abide;
    My High Tower is He!

2 Wild waves are round me swelling,
    Dark clouds above I see;
Yet, in my Fortress dwelling,
    More safe I cannot be.

3 My Tower of strength can never
    In time of trouble fail;
No power of hell, forever,
    Against it shall prevail.

85

I STOOD outside the gate,
    A poor, wayfaring child;
Within my heart there beat
    A tempest loud and wild;

A fear oppressed my soul,
  That I might be *too late;*
And oh, I trembled sore,
  And prayed outside the gate.

2 Oh, "Mercy!" loud I cried,
    "Now give me rest from sin!"
  "I will," a voice replied;
    And Mercy let me in;
  She bound my bleeding wounds,
    And soothed my heart opprest.
  She washed away my guilt
    And gave me peace and rest.

3 In Mercy's guise I knew
    The Saviour long abused,
  Who often sought my heart,
    And wept when I refused;
  Oh! what a blest return
    For all my years of sin!
  I stood outside the gate,
    And Jesus let me in.

86

LET us gather up the sunbeams,
    Lying all around our path;
Let us keep the wheat and roses,
  Casting out the thorns and chaff,
Let us find our sweetest comfort
  In the blessings of to-day,
With a patient hand removing
  All the briers from the way.

CHO.—‖:Then scatter seeds of kindness, :‖
    Then scatter seeds of kindness,
      For our reaping by and by.

2 Strange we never prize the music
    Till the sweet-voiced bird is flown!
  Strange that we should slight the violets
    Till the lovely flowers are gone!
  Strange that summer skies and sunshine
    Never seem one half so fair,
  As when winter's snowy pinions
    Shake the white down in the air.

3 If we knew the baby fingers,
    Pressed against the window pane,
Would be cold and stiff to-morrow—
    Never trouble us again—
Would the bright eyes of our darling
    Catch the frown upon our brow?—
Would the prints of rosy fingers
    Vex us then as they do now?

4 Ah! those little ice-cold fingers,
    How they point our memories back
To the hasty words and actions
    Strewn along our backward track!
How those little hands remind us,
    As in snowy grace they lie,
Not to scatter thorns—but roses—
    For our reaping by and by.

87

O NWARD, Christian soldiers!
    Marching as to war,
With the cross of Jesus
    Going on before.
Christ the Royal Master
    Leads against the foe,
Forward into battle,
    See His banners go.

CHO.—Onward, Christian soldiers!
    Marching as to war,
With the Cross of Jesus
    Going on before.

2 Like a mighty army
    Moves the Church of God;
Brothers, we are treading
    Where the saints have trod;
We are not divided,
    All one body we;
One in hope and doctrine,
    One in charity.

3 Crowns and thrones may perish,
    Kingdoms rise and wane;
But the Church of Jesus
    Constant will remain;

Gates of hell can never
'Gainst that Church prevail;
We have Christ's own promise—
And that cannot fail.

4 Onward, then, ye faithful,
Join the happy throng,
Blend with ours your voices
In the triumph song;
Glory, laud, and honor,
Unto Christ the King.
This through countless ages
Men and angels sing.

88

OH, spirit, o'erwhelmed by thy failures and fears,
Look up to thy Lord, though with trembling and
tears:
Weak Faith, to thy call seem the heavens only dumb!
To thee is the message, "Hold fast till I come."

CHO.—‖: Hold fast till I come; :‖
A bright crown awaits thee;
Hold fast till I come.

2 Hold fast when the world would allure thee to sin;
Hold fast when the tempter assails from within;
In sunshine or sadness, in gain or in loss,
To falter were madness; Oh, cling to the Cross.

3 Thy Saviour is coming in tenderest love,
To make up His jewels and bear them above;
Oh, child, in thine anguish, despairing or dumb,
Remember the message, "Hold fast till I come."

89

TENDERLY the Shepherd,
O'er the mountains cold,
Goes to bring His lost one
Back to the fold.

CHO.—‖: Seeking to save, seeking to save,
Lost one, 'tis Jesus seeking to save.:‖

2 Patiently the owner
Seeks with earnest care,
In the dust and darkness
Her treasure rare.

3 Lovingly the Father
    Sends the news around:
"He once dead now liveth—
    Once lost is found.

90

HALLELUJAH, He is risen!
    Jesus is gone up on high!
Burst the bars of death asunder,
    Angels shout and men reply:
He is risen, He is risen,
    Living now, no more to die.

2 Hallelujah, He is risen!
    Our exalted Head to be;
Sends the witness of the Spirit
    That our advocate is He:
He is risen, He is risen,
    Justified in Him are we.

3 Hallelujah, He is risen!
    Death for aye hath lost his sting,
Christ, Himself the Resurrection,
    From the grave His own will bring:
He is risen, He is risen,
    Living Lord and coming King.

91

O CROWN of rejoicing that's waiting for me,
    When finished my course, and when Jesus I see,
And when from my Lord comes the sweet sounding
        word:
"Receive, faithful servant, the joy of thy Lord."

CHO.—O Crown of rejoicing, O wonderful song;
    O joy everlasting, O glorious throng;
    O beautiful home, my home can it be?
    O glory reserved for me!

2 O wonderful song that in glory I'll sing,
    To Him who redeemed me to Jesus my King;
All glory and honor to Him shall be given,
And praises unceasing forever in heaven.

3 O joy everlasting when heaven is won,
    Forever in glory to shine as the sun;

No sorrow nor sighing—these all flee away,
No night there, no shadows—'tis one endless day.

4 O wonderful name which the glorified bear,
The new name which Jesus bestows on us there;
To him that o'ercometh 'twill only be given,
Blest sign of approval, our welcome to heaven.

92

WHILE foes are strong and danger near,
   A voice falls gently on my ear;
My Saviour speaks, He says to me,
That as my days my strength shall be.

CHO.—His word a Tower to which I flee,
   For as my days my strength shall be.

2 With such a promise need I fear,
For all that now I hold most dear?
No, I will never anxious be,
For as my days my strength shall be.

3 And when at last I'm called to die,
Still on Thy promise I'll rely;
Yes, Lord, I then will trust in Thee,
That as my days my strength shall be.

93

IN the silent midnight watches,
   List—thy bosom's door!
How it knocketh, knocketh, knocketh,
   Knocketh ever more!
Say not 'tis thy pulse's beating.
   'Tis thy heart of sin;
'Tis thy Saviour knocks, and crieth,
   "Rise, and let me in!"

2 Death comes down with reckless footsteps,
   To the hall and hut;
Think you death will tarry knocking,
   When the door is shut?
Jesus waiteth, waiteth, waiteth;
   But the door is fast;
Grieved, away thy Saviour goeth,
   Death breaks in at last.

3 Then is't time to stand entreating
    Christ to let thee in;
At the gate of heaven beating,
    Wailing for thy sin?
Nay! alas, thou guilty creature!
    Hast thou, then, forgot?
Jesus waited long to know thee,
    Now He knows thee not!

94

WE shall sleep, but not forever,
    There will be a glorious dawn!
We shall meet to part, no, never,
    On the resurrection morn!
From the deepest caves of ocean,
    From the desert and the plain,
From the valley and the mountain,
    Countless throngs shall rise again.

CHO.—We shall sleep, but not forever,
        There will be a glorious dawn;
      We shall meet to part, no, never,
        On the resurrection morn!

2 When we see a precious blossom,
    That we tended with such care,
Rudely taken from our bosom,
    How our aching hearts despair!
Round its little grave we linger,
    Till the setting sun is low,
Feeling all our hopes have perished
    With the flower we cherished so.

3 We shall sleep, but not for ever,
    In the lone and silent grave;
Blesséd be the Lord that taketh,
    Blesséd be the Lord that gave.
In the bright, eternal city
    Death can never, never come:
In His own good time He'll call us
    From our rest, to Home, sweet Home.

95

WATCHMAN, tell me, does the morning
    Of fair Zion's glory dawn;
Have the signs that mark His coming,
    Yet upon my pathway shone?

Pilgrim, yes, arise, look round thee,
  Light is breaking in the skies;
Spurn the unbelief that bound thee,
  Morning dawns, arise, arise!

2 See the glorious light ascending
  Of the grand Sabbatic year,
Hark! the voices loud proclaiming
  The Messiah's kingdom near;
Watchman, yes; I see just yonder,
  Canaan's glorious heights arise;
Salem, too, appears in grandeur,
  Towering 'neath her sunlit skies.

3 Pilgrim, in that golden city,
  Seated in the jasper throne,
Zion's King, arrayed in beauty,
  Reigns in peace from zone to zone;
There, on verdant hills and mountains,
  Where the golden sunbeams play,
Purling streams, and crystal fountains,
  Sparkle in th'eternal day.

4 Pilgrim, see! the light is beaming
  Brighter still upon thy way;
Signs through all the earth are gleaming
  Omens of the coming day,
When the last loud trumpet sounding,
  Shall awake from earth to sea,
All the saints of God now sleeping,
  Clad in immortality.

38

GIVE me the wings of faith to rise,
    Within the vail, and see
The saints above, how great their joys,
  How bright their glories be.

JHO.—Many are the friends who are waiting to-day,
    Happy on the golden strand.
  Many are the voices calling us away,
    To join their glorious band.
  Calling us away,   Calling us away,
    Calling to the better land.

2 Once they were mourners here below,
  And poured out cries and tears;
They wrestled hard, as we do now,
  With sins, and doubts, and fears.

3 I asked them whence their victory came;
　　They, with united breath,
Ascribe their conquest to the Lamb,
　　Their triumph to His death.

97

MY latest sun is sinking fast,
　　My race is nearly run;
My strongest trials now are past,
　　My triumph is begun.

CHO.—O come, angel band,
　　Come and around me stand,
O bear me away on your snowy wings
　　To my immortal home.

2 I know I'm nearing the holy ranks
　　Of friends and kindred dear,
For I brush the dews on Jordan's banks,—
　　The crossing must be near.

3 I've almost gained my heavenly home;
　　My spirit loudly sings;
Thy holy ones, behold, they come!
　　I hear the noise of wings.

4 O, bear my longing heart to Him
　　Who bled and died for me;
Whose blood now cleanses from all sin,
　　And gives me victory.

98

THOU didst leave Thy throne, and Thy kingly crown
　　When Thou camest to earth for me;
But in Bethlehem's home there was found no room
　　For Thy nativity.

REF.—Oh, come to my heart, Lord Jesus!
　　There is room in my heart for Thee.
Oh, come to my heart Lord Jesus, come!
　　There is room in my heart for Thee.

2 Heaven's arches rang when the angels sang,
　　Of Thy birth and Thy royal degree;
But in lowly birth didst Thou come to earth,
　　And in greatest humility.

3 Foxes found their rest, and the birds had their nests,
   In the shade of the cedar tree;
But Thy couch was the sod, O Thou Son of God,
   In the deserts of Galilee.

4 Thou camest, O Lord, with Thy living word,
   That should set Thy people free;
But with mocking and scorn, and with crown of thorn,
   Did they bear Thee to Calvary.

5 Heaven's arches shall ring, and its choirs shall sing,
   At Thy coming to victory,
Thou wilt call me home, saying " yet there is room,"
   There is room at My side for thee.

99
————

"HOME at last " on heavenly mountains,
   Heard the " Come and enter in;"
Saved by life's fair flowing fountains,
   Saved from earthly taint and sin.

REF.—" Home, sweet home," our home forever;
   All the pilgrim-journey past;
Welcomed home to wander, never,
   Saved through Jesus—" Home at last."

2 Free at last from all temptation,
   No more need of watchful care;
Joyful in complete salvation,
   Given the victor's crown to wear.

3 Saved to greet on hills of glory
   Loved ones we have missed so long;
Saved to tell the sinner's story,
   Saved to sing redemption's song.

4 Welcomed at the pearly portal,
   Ever more a welcome guest;
Welcomed to the life immortal,
   In the mansions of the blest.

100
————

THE mistakes of my life have been many,
   The sins of my heart have been more,
And I scarce can see for weeping,
   But I'll knock at the open door.

CHO.—I know I am weak and sinful,
 It comes to me more and more;
  But when the dear Saviour shall bid me come in,
  I'll enter the open door.

2 I am lowest of those who love Him,
 I am weakest of those who pray;
  But I come as He has bidden,
  And He will not say me nay.

3 My mistakes His free grace will cover,
 My sins He will wash away,
  And the feet that shrink and falter
  Shall walk through the gates of day.

4 The mistakes of my life have been many,
 And my spirit is sick with sin,
  And I scarce can see for weeping,
  But the Saviour will let me in.

101

COME, for the feast is spread;
 Hark to the call!
Come to the Living Bread,
 Broken for all;
Come to His house of wine,
Low on His breast recline,
All that He hath is thine;
 Come, sinner, come.

2 Come where the fountain flows—
 River of life—
Healing for all thy woes,
 Doubting and strife;
Millions have been supplied,
No one was e'er denied;
Come to the crimson tide,
 Come, sinner, come.

3 Come to the throne of grace,
 Boldly draw near;
He who would win the race
 Must tarry here;
Whate'er thy want may be,
Here is the grace for thee,

Jesus thy only plea,
  Come, Christian, come.

4 Come to the Better Land,
  Pilgrim, make haste!
Earth is a foreign strand—
  Wilderness, waste!
Here are the harps of gold,
Here are the joys untold
Crowns for the young and old;
  Come, pilgrim, come.

5 Jesus, we come to Thee,
  Oh, take us in!
Set Thou our spirits free;
  Cleanse us from sin!
Then, in yon land of light,
Clothed in our robes of white
Resting not day nor night,
  Thee will we sing.

102

ONE sweetly solemn thought
  Comes to me o'er and o'er;
I'm nearer home to-day, to-day,
Than I have been before.

CHO.—‖: Nearer my home, :‖
  Nearer my home to-day, to-day,
  Than I have been before.

2 Nearer my Father's house.
  Where many mansions be;
Nearer the great white throne to-day
  Nearer the crystal sea.

3 Nearer the bound of life,
  Where burdens are laid down;
Nearer to leave the cross to-day,
  And nearer to the crown.

4 Be near me when my feet
  Are slipping o'er the brink;
For I am nearer home to-day,
  Perhaps, than now I think.

103

LIFT up, lift up thy voice with singing,
    Dear land, with strength lift up thy voice!
The kingdoms of the earth are bringing
    Their treasures to thy gates—rejoice!

CHO.—Arise and shine in youth immortal,
        Thy light is come, thy King appears!
    Beyond the Century's swinging portal,
        Breaks a new dawn—*the thousand years!*

2 And shall His flock with strife be riven?
    Shall envious lines His church divide,
When He, the Lord of earth and heaven,
    Stands at the door to claim His bride?

3 Lift up thy gates! bring forth oblations!
    One crowned with crowns, a message brings,
His word, a sword to smite the nations;
    His name—the Christ, the King of kings.

4 He comes! let all the earth adore Him;
    The path His human nature trod
Spreads to a royal realm before Him,
    The LIGHT of life, the WORD OF GOD!

104

I HAVE entered the valley of blessing,
    And Jesus abides with me there;
And His spirit and blood make my cleansing complete,
    And His perfect love casteth out fear.

CHO.—Oh, come to this valley of blessing,
        Where Jesus will fullness bestow—
    And believe, and receive, and confess Him,
        That all His salvation may know.

2 There is peace in the valley of blessing,
    And plenty the land doth impart,
And there's rest for the weary-worn traveler's feet,
    And joy for the sorrowing heart.

3 There is love in the valley of blessing,
    Such as none but the blood-washed may feel,
When heaven comes down redeemed spirits to greet,
    And Christ sets His covenant seal.

4 There's a song in the valley of blessing,
  That angels would fain join the strain,
As with rapturous praises we bow at His feet,
  Crying, Worthy the Lamb that was slain.

105

I'M a pilgrim and I'm a stranger;
  I can tarry, I can tarry but a night!
Do not detain me, for I am going
To where the streamlets are ever flowing.

CHO—I'm a pilgrim, and I'm a stranger;
  I can tarry, I can tarry but a night!

2 Of that city, to which I journey:
  My Redeemer, my Redeemer is the light;
There is no sorrow, nor any sighing,
  Nor any tears there, nor any dying:

3 There the sunbeams are ever shining,
  Oh, my longing heart, my longing heart is there;
Here in this country, so dark and dreary,
  I long have wandered forlorn and weary:

106

OH, what are you going to do, brother?
  Say, what are you going to do?
You have thought of some useful labor,
  But what is the end in view?
You are fresh from the home of your boyhood,
  And just in the bloom of youth!
Have you tasted the sparkling water
  That flows from the fount of truth?

CHO.—Is your heart in the Saviour's keeping?
  Remember He died for you!
    Then what are you going to do, brother?
      Say, what are you going to do?

2 Oh, what are you going to do, brother?
  The morning of youth is past;
The vigor and strength of manhood,
  My brother, are yours at last:
You are rising in worldly prospects,
  And prospered in worldly things;—
A duty to those less favored,
  The smile of your fortune brings.

Cho.—Go prove that your heart is grateful—
    The Lord has a work for you!
    Then what are you going to do, brother?
    Say, what are you going to do?

3 Oh, what are you going to do, brother?
    Your sun at its noon is high;
It shines in meridian splendor,
    And rides through a cloudless sky;
You are holding a high position,
    Of honor, and trust, and fame;—
Are you willing to give the glory
    And praise to your Saviour's Name?

Cho.—The regions that sit in darkness
    Are stretching their hands to you!
    Then what are you going to do, brother?
    Say, what are you going to do?

4 Oh, what are you going to do, brother?
    The twilight approaches now;—
Already your locks are silvered,
    And winter is on your brow:
Your talents, your time, and your riches,
    To Jesus, your Master, give;
Then ask if the world around you
    Is better because you live.

Cho.—You are nearing the brink of Jordan,
    But still there is work for you!
    Then what are you going to do, brother?
    Say, what are you going to do?

107

ART thou weary, art thou languid?
    Art thou sore distressed?
"Come to me," saith One, and coming,
    "Be at rest."

2 Hath He marks to lead me to Him
    If He be my guide?
"In His feet and hands are wound-prints,
    And His side."

3 Is there diadem as monarch,
    That His brow adorns?

"Yes, a crown in very surety,
    But of thorns!"

4 If I find Him, if I follow,
    What my future here?
"Many a sorrow, many a labor,
    Many a tear."

5 If I still hold closely to Him,
    What hath He at last?
"Sorrow vanquished, labor ended,
    Jordan past."

6 If I ask Him to receive me,
    Will He say me nay?
"Not till earth and not till heaven
    Pass away." AMEN.

108

SHALL we meet beyond the river,
    Where the surges cease to roll?
Where in all the bright forever
    Sorrow ne'er shall press the soul?

CHO.—Shall we meet, shall we meet,
    ||: Shall we meet beyond the river, :||
    Where the surges cease to roll?

2 Shall we meet in that blest harbor,
    When our stormy voyage is o'er?
Shall we meet and cast the anchor
    By the fair, celestial shore?

3 Shall we meet in yonder city,
    Where the towers of crystal shine?
Where the walls are all of jasper,
    Built by workmanship divine?—

4 Shall we meet with Christ our Saviour,
    When He comes to claim His own?
Shall we know His blessèd favor,
    And sit down upon His throne?

109

ALL glory to Jesus be given,
    That life and salvation are free;
And all may be washed and forgiven,
    And Jesus can save even me.

CHO.—Yes, Jesus is mighty to save,
        And all His salvation may know,
    On His bosom I lean,
    And His blood makes me clean,
        For His blood can wash whiter than snow.

2 From darkness and sin and despair,
        Out into the light of His love,
    He has brought me and made me an heir,
        To kingdoms and mansions above.

3 Oh, the rapturous heights of·His love,
        The measureless depths of His grace,
    My soul all His fullness would prove,
        And live in His loving embrace.

4 In Him all my wants are supplied,
        His love makes my heaven below,
    And freely His blood is applied,
        His blood that makes whiter than snow.

110

THERE'S a land that is fairer than day,
    And by faith we can see it afar;
For the Father waits over the way,
    To prepare us a dwelling-place there.

CHO.—||: In the sweet by-and-by,
        We shall meet on that beautiful shore. :||

2 We shall sing on that beautiful shore
    The melodious songs of the blest,
And our spirits shall sorrow no more,
    Not a sigh for the blessing of rest.

3 To our bountiful Father above,
    We will offer our tribute of praise,
For the glorious gift of His love,
    And the blessings that hallow our days.

111

OH, turn ye, oh, turn ye, for why will ye die?
    When God in great mercy is coming so nigh?
Now Jesus invites you, the Spirit says, "Come,"
And angels are waiting to welcome you home.

2 How vain the delusion, that while you delay,
Your hearts may grow better, your chains melt away;
Come guilty, come wretched, come just as you are,
All helpless and dying, to Jesus repair.

3 The contrite in heart He will freely receive,
Oh! why will you not the glad message believe?
If sin be your burden, why will you not come?
'Tis you He makes welcome; He bids you come home.

112

MUST Jesus bear the cross alone,
    And all the world go free?
No, there's a cross for every one,
    And there's a cross for me.

2 The consecrated cross I'll bear,
    Till death shall set me free;
And then go home my crown to wear,
    For there's a crown for me.

3 Upon the crystal pavement, down
    At Jesus' piercéd feet,
With joy I'll cast my golden crown,
    And His dear name repeat.

4 O precious cross! O glorious crown!
    O resurrection day!
Ye angels, from the stars come down,
    And bear my soul away.

113

THROUGH the valley of the shadow I must go,
    Where the cold waves of Jordan roll;
But the promise of my Shepherd will I know,
    Be the rod and the staff to my soul.
Even now down the valley as I glide,
    I can hear my Saviour say, "Follow me!"
And with Him I'm not afraid to cross the tide,
    There's a light in the valley for me.

CHO.—‖: There's a light in the valley, :‖
    There's a light in the valley for me,
    And no evil will I fear,
    While my Shepherd is so near,
    There's a light in the valley for me.

2 Now the rolling of the billows I can hear,
    As they beat on the turf-bound shore;
But the beacon light of love so bright and clear,
    Guides my bark, frail and lone safely o'er,
I shall find down the valley no alarms,
    For my Saviour's blessèd smile I can see;
He will bear me in His loving, mighty arms,
    There's a light in the valley for me.

114

'TIS a goodly pleasant land that we pilgrims journey
    through,
And our Father's constant blessings fall around us like
    the dew;
But its sunshine and its beauty to our hearts no joy can
    bring,
Like the splendors that await us in the palace of the King.
In this goodly pleasant land only strangers now are we,
For we seek a better country, and 'tis there we long
    to be;
Yes, we long to swell the anthem that for evermore shall
    ring,
From the pure in heart made perfect, in the palace of the
    King.

REF.—O the palace of the King, royal palace of the King;
        Where our Father in His mercy all the ransomed ones
          will bring;
        Where our sorrows and our trials like a dream will
          pass away,
        And our souls shall dwell forever in the realms ot
          endless day.

2 Our Redeemer is the King; what a sacrifice He made,
    When He purchased our redemption, and His blood the
        ransom paid;
In His cross shall be our glory, to that blessèd cross we'll
    cling,
Till we reach the gates that open to the palace of the
    King.
We shall see Him bye and bye, hallelujah to His name!
Through the blood of His atonement, life eternal we may
    claim;

We shall cast our crowns before Him and our songs of
victory sing,
When we enter in triumphant to the palace of the King.

115

THEY dreamed not of danger, those sinners of old,
    Whom Noah was chosen to warn;
By frequent transgressions their hearts had grown cold,
    They laughed his entreaties to scorn:
Yet daily he called them, "Oh, come, sinners, come,
    Believe and prepare to embark!
Receive ye the message, and know there is room
    For all who will come to the Ark."

Cho.—Then come, come, oh, come;
        There's refuge alone in the Ark,
        Receive ye the message, and know there is room
        For all who will come to the Ark.

2 He could not arouse them, unheeding they stood,
    Unmoved by His warning and prayer;
The prophet passed in from the oncoming flood,
    And left them to hopeless despair:
The flood-gates were opened, the deluge came on,
    The heavens as midnight grew dark,
Too late, then they turned, every foot-hold was gone,
    They perished in sight of the Ark.

3 O sinners, the heralds of mercy implore,
    They cry like a patriarch, "Come;"
The Ark of salvation is moored to your shore,
    Oh, enter while yet there is room!
The storm-cloud of Justice rolls dark over head,
    And when by its fury you're tossed,
Alas, of your perishing soul 'twill be said,
    "They heard—they refused—*and were lost!*"

116

WHEN my final farewell to the world I have said,
    And gladly lie down to my rest;
When softly the watchers shall say, "He is dead,"
    And fold my pale hands o'er my breast;

And when, with my glorified vision at last
    The walls of "That City" I see,
Will any one then at the beautiful gate,
    Be waiting and watching for me?

Cho.—||: Be waiting and watching,
        Be waiting and watching for me. :||

2 There are little ones glancing about in my path,
    In want of a friend and a guide;
There are dear little eyes looking up into mine,
    Whose tears might be easily dried.
But Jesus may beckon the children away
    In the midst of their grief and their glee—
Will any of them, at the beautiful gate,
    Be waiting and watching for me?

3 There are old and forsaken who linger awhile
    In homes which their dearest have left;
And a few gentle words or an action of love
    May cheer their sad spirits bereft.
But the Reaper is near to the long standing corn,
    The weary will soon be set free—
Will any of them, at the beautiful gate.
    Be waiting and watching for me?

4 Oh, should I be brought there by the bountiful grace
    Of Him who delights to forgive,
Though I bless not the weary about in my path,
    Pray only for self while I live,—
Methinks I should mourn o'er my sinful neglect,
    If sorrow in heaven can be,
Should no one I love, at the beautiful gate,
    Be waiting and watching for me!

117

O! WHAT shall I do to be saved
    From the sorrows that burden my soul?
Like the waves in the storm
    When the winds are at war,
Chilling floods of distress o'er me roll.
    What shall I do? what shall I do?
    O! what shall I do to be saved?

2 O! what shall I do to be saved,
When the pleasures of youth are all fled?
  And the friends I have loved,
  From the earth are removed
And I weep o'er the graves of the dead?
What shall I do? what shall I do?
O! what shall I do to be saved?

3 O! what shall I do to be saved,
When sickness my strength shall subdue?
  Or the world in a day,
  Like a cloud roll away,
And eternity opens to view?
What shall I do? what shall I do?
O! what shall I do to be saved?

4 O! Lord look in mercy on me,
Come, O come and speak peace to my soul:
  Unto whom shall I flee,
  Dearest Lord, but to Thee,
Thou canst make my poor, broken heart whole.
That will I do! that will I do!
To Jesus I'll go and be saved.

118

HOLY, Holy, Holy! Lord God Almighty!
  Early in the morning our song shall rise to Thee,
Holy, Holy, Holy! Merciful and Mighty!
God in three Persons, blessèd Trinity!

2 Holy, Holy, Holy! all the saints adore Thee,
Casting down their golden crowns around the glassy sea;
Cherubim and Seraphim falling down before Thee,
Which wert and art, and evermore shall be.

3 Holy, Holy, Holy! though the darkness hide Thee,
Though the eye of sinful man Thy glory may not see,
Only Thou art Holy, there is none beside Thee,
Perfect in power, in love and purity.

4 Holy, Holy, Holy! Lord God Almighty!
All Thy works shall praise Thy name in earth, and sky
  and sea;
Holy, Holy, Holy! Merciful and Mighty!
God in three Persons, blessèd Trinity! AMEN.

119

WHEN the storms of life are raging,
   Tempests wild on sea and land,
I will seek a place of refuge
   In the shadow of God's hand.

Cho.—He will hide me, He will hide me,
   Where no harm can e'er betide me;
   He will hide me, safely hide me
   In the shadow of His hand.

2 Though He may send some affliction,
   'Twill but make me long for home;
For in love and not in anger,
   All His chastenings will come.

3 Enemies may strive to injure,
   Satan all his arts employ;
He will turn what seems to harm me
   Into everlasting joy.

4 So, while here the cross I'm bearing,
   Meeting storms and billows wild,
Jesus, for my soul is caring,
   Naught can harm His Father's child.

120

THINE, Jesus, Thine,
   No more this heart of mine
Shall seek its joy apart from Thee;
The world is crucified to me,
   And I am Thine.

2 Thine, Thine alone,
   My joy, my hope, my crown;
Now earthly things may fade and die,
They charm my soul no more, for I
   Am Thine alone.

3 Thine, ever Thine,
   Forever to recline,
On love eternal, fixed and sure,
Yes, I am Thine for evermore,
   Lord, Jesus, Thine.

4 Thine, Jesus, Thine,
   Soon in Thy crown to shine

When from the glory Thou shalt come,
And with Thy saints shall take me home,
Lord, Jesus, come.

121

LONG in darkness we have waited,
    For the shining of the Light;
Long have felt the things we hated,
Sink us still in deeper night.

CHO.—Bless'd Jesus, loving Saviour!
    Tender, faithful, strong and true,
Break the fetters that have bound us,
    Make us in Thyself anew.

2 Now, at last, the Light appeareth,
    Jesus stands upon the shore;
And, with tender voice, He calleth,
    "Come to me and sin no more!"

3 Nothing have we, but our weakness,
    Naught but sorrow, sin and care;
All within, is loathsome vileness,
    All without, is dark despair.

4 All our talents we have wasted,
    All Thy laws have disobeyed;
But Thy goodness now we've tasted,
    In Thy robes we stand arrayed.

5 Thou hast saved us—do Thou keep us,
    Guide us by Thine eye divine;
Let the Holy Spirit teach us,
    That our light may ever shine.

CHO.—Bless'd Jesus, be Thou near us;
    Give us of Thy grace to-day;
While we're calling, do Thou hear us,
    Send us, now, Thy peace, we pray.

122

JESUS, gracious One, calleth now to thee,
    "Come, O sinner, come!"
Calls so tenderly, calls so lovingly,"
    "*Now,* O sinner, come."
Words of peace and blessing,
Christ's own love confessing;

REF.—Hear the sweet voice of Jesus,
        Full, full of love;
    Calling tenderly, calling lovingly,
        "Come, O sinner, come."

2 Still He waits for thee, pleading patiently,
    "Come, O come to Me!"
  "Heavy-laden one, I thy grief have borne,
    Come and rest in Me."
    Words with love o'erflowing,
    Life and bliss bestowing;

3 Weary, sin-sick soul, called so graciously,
    Canst thou dare refuse?
  Mercy offered thee, freely, tenderly,
    Wilt thou still abuse?
    Come, for time is flying,
    Haste, thy lamp is dying;

123

WE'VE journeyed many a day
    Upon an ocean wide,
Amid the mist and spray
    Of many a surging tide;
But, lo! the land is near!
    For just beyond the foam
I see it bright and clear,
    The light of home, sweet home.

REF.—There's a light upon the shore, brother,
        It flashes from the strand;
    The night is almost o'er, brother,
        The haven's just at hand.

2 We've had our storms of doubt,
    Our rains of bitter tears,
  Our fightings fierce without,
    Within our anxious fears;
  But, lo! the storms are past,
    They cannot reach us more;
  We've sighted land at last,
    The blessèd stormless shore.

3 O land of calmest rest,
    Where suns no more go down!

O haven of the blest,
  With bliss and glory crowned!
No more the storm, the dark,
  The breakers and the foam,
No more the wail, for hark!
  We hear the songs of home.

124

TAKE my life and let it be
    Consecrated, Lord, to Thee;
Take my hands and let them move
  At the impulse of Thy love.

CHO.—All to Thee, all to Thee,
    Consecrated, Lord, to Thee.

2 Take my feet and let them be
    Swift and beautiful for Thee;
  Take my voice and let me sing
    Always—only—for my King.

3 Take my lips and let them be
    Filled with messages from Thee;
  Take my silver and my gold,
    Not a mite would I withhold.

4 Take my moments and my days,
    Let them flow in endless praise;
  Take my intellect and use
    Every power as Thou shalt choose.

5 Take my will and make it Thine,
    It shall be no longer mine;
  Take my heart, it is Thine own,
    It shall be Thy royal throne.

6 Take my love, my God, I pour
    At Thy feet its treasure store;
  Take myself, and I will be
    Ever, only, all for Thee.

125

THE Gospel bells are ringing,
    Over land, from sea to sea:
Blesséd news of free salvation
  Do they offer you and me.

" For God so loved the world
　　That His only Son He gave,
Whosoe'er believeth in Him
　　Everlasting life shall have."

CHO.—Gospel bells, how they ring;
　　　Over land from sea to sea;
　　Gospel bells freely bring
　　　Blesséd news to you and me.

2 The Gospel bells invite us
　　To a feast prepared for all;
Do not slight the invitation,
　　Nor reject the gracious call.
" I am the bread of life;
　　Eat of Me, thou hungry soul,
Though your sins be red as crimson,
　　They shall be as white as wool."

3 The Gospel bells give warning,
　　As they sound from day to day,
Of the fate which doth await them
　　Who forever will delay.
" Escape ye, for thy life;
　　Tarry not in all the plain,
Nor behind thee look, oh, never,
　　Lest thou be consumed in pain."

4 The Gospel bells are joyful,
　　As they echo far and wide,
Bearing notes of perfect pardon,
　　Through a Saviour crucified.
" Good tidings of great joy
　　To all people do I bring,
Unto you is born a Saviour,
　　Which is Christ the Lord" and King.

126

———

JOY to the world! the Lord is come;
　　The mighty God, the Everlasting Father, and the
　　　Prince of Peace.
Let every heart prepare Him room,
The mighty God, the Everlasting Father, and the Prince of
　　Peace.

2 Joy to the world! the Saviour reigns,
The mighty God, the Everlasting Father, and the Prince of
Peace.
O praise Him, floods, rocks, hills and plains,
The mighty God, the Everlasting Father, and the Prince of
Peace.

3 He rules the world with truth and grace,
The mighty God, the Everlasting Father, and the Prince of
Peace.
And saves us by His righteousness,
The mighty God, the Everlasting Father, and the Prince of
Peace.

127

A RULER once came to Jesus by night,
  To ask Him the way of salvation and light;
The Master made answer in words true and plain.
" Ye must be born again."

CHO.—|: :" Ye must be born again, :||
        I verily, verily say unto thee,
        Ye must be born again."

2 Ye children of men, attend to the word
So solemnly uttered by Jesus, the Lord,
And let not this message to you be in vain,
" Ye must be born again."

3 O ye who would enter that glorious rest,
And sing with the ransomed the song of the blest;
The life everlasting if ye would obtain,
" Ye must be born again."

4 A dear one in heaven thy heart yearns to see,
At the beautiful gate may be watching for thee;
Then list to the note of this solemn refrain,
" Ye must be born again."

128

Justice.

C UT it down, cut it down,
   Spare not the fruitless tree!
It spreads a harmful shade around,
It spoils what else were useful ground,
No fruit for years on it I've found,
Cut it down! cut it down!

Mercy.   2 One year more, one year more,
        Oh, spare the fruitless tree!
        Behold its branches broad and green,
        Its spreading leaves have hopeless been,
        Some fruit thereon may yet be seen,
        One year more! one year more!

Justice.   3 Cut it down, cut it down,
        And burn the worthless tree!
        For other use the soil prepare,
        Some other tree will flourish there,
        And in my vineyard much fruit bear,
        Cut it down! cut it down!

Mercy.   4 One year more, one year more,
        For mercy spare the tree!
        Another year of care bestow,
        On its fair form some fruit may grow,
        If not—then lay the cumberer low,
        One year more! one year more!

        5 Still it stands, still it stands,
        A fair, but fruitless tree!
        The Master, seeking fruit thereon
        Has come—but, grieved at finding none,
        Now speaks to Justice—Mercy flown—
        Cut it down! cut it down!

129

COME near me, O my Saviour!
   Thy tenderness reveal;
O, let me know the sympathy
   Which Thou for me dost feel
I need Thee every moment;
   Thine absence brings dismay;
But when the tempter hurls his darts
   'Twere death with Thee away.

2 Come near me, my Redeemer,
   And never leave my side;
My bark, when tossed on trouble's sea,
   The storm cannot outride,
Unless Thy word of power
   Arrest the surging wave;
No voice but Thine its rage can quell,
   No arm but Thine can save.

3 Come near me, blesséd Jesus!
    I need Thee in my joy,
No less than when the direst ills
    My happiness destroy;
For when the sun shines o'er me
    And flowers strew my way,
Without Thy wise and guiding hand
    More easily I stray.

4 Be near me, mighty Saviour,
    When comes the latest strife;
For Thou thro' death's shadow passed,
    And ope'd the gates of life;
And when among the ransomed
    I stand with crown and palm,
To Thee, Divine, unfailing Friend,
    I'll raise eternal psalm.

130

WHY do you wait, dear brother,
    Oh, why do you tarry so long?
Your Saviour is waiting to give you
    A place in His sanctified throng.

CHO.—‖: Why not? why not?
    Why not come to Him now? :‖

2 What do you hope, dear brother,
    To gain by a further delay?
There's no one to save you but Jesus
    There's no other way but His way.

3 Do you not feel, dear brother,
    His Spirit now striving within?
Oh, why not accept His salvation,
    And throw off thy burden of sin?

4 Why do you wait, dear brother?
    The harvest is passing away;
Your Saviour is longing to bless you,
    There's danger and death in delay.

131

IS Jesus able to redeem
    A sinner lost, like me?
My sins so great, so many seem!
    O sinner, "come and see."

REF.—The blood that Jesus shed of old,
　　　Was shed for you and me:
　　　And there is room within the fold—
　　　O "come to Him and see."

2 Is Jesus willing to forgive
　A rebel child, like me?
Who would not in His favor live?
　O rebel, "come and see."

3 Is Jesus waiting to relieve
　A wanderer, like me,
Who chose the Father's House to leave?
　O wanderer, "come and see."

4 Is Jesus ready now to save
　A guilty one, like me,
Who brought Him to the cross and grave?
　Come, guilty one, and see.

132

O WHAT a Saviour that He died for me!
　From condemnation He hath made me free;
"He that believeth on the Son," saith He,
　"*Hath* everlasting life."

CHO.—"Verily, verily, I say unto you,
　　　Verily, verily," message ever new;
　　"He that believeth on the Son," 'tis true,
　　　"*Hath* everlasting life."

2 All my iniquities on Him were laid,
All my indebtedness by Him was paid;
All who believe on Him, the Lord hath said,
　"*Hath* everlasting life."

3 Though poor and needy, I can trust my Lord;
Though weak and sinful, I believe His word:
O glad message! every child of God,
　"*Hath* everlasting life."

4 Though all unworthy, yet I will not doubt,
For him that cometh, He will not cast out,
"He that believeth," O the good news shout,
　"HATH everlasting life."

133

IF never the gaze of sun and moon,
   On the blesséd home above,
From whence are its rays of wondrous noon?
   Oh! "The LAMB is the light thereof."

CHO.—They shall walk in white, there shall be no night
   In the fadeless home above;
And the shout shall ring as the ransomed sing,
   Oh! "The LAMB is the light thereof."

2 And thus saith the page of Holy Writ
   Of the land of song and love,
" The glory of God did lighten it,
   And the LAMB is the light thereof."

3 Then follow Him, till the eye grows dim,
   And the soul, as ark-freed dove,
Shall speed away to realms of day,
   Where "The LAMB is the light thereof."

134

OH, how happy are we,
   Who in Jesus agree,
And expect His return from above;
We sit 'neath His vine, and delightfully join
   In the praise of His excellent love.

CHO.—Oh, how happy are we
    Who in Jesus agree,
     How happy, how happy are we.

2 When united to Him,
   We partake of the stream
Ever flowing in peace from the throne,
We in Jesus believe, and the Spirit receive,
   That proceeds from the Father and Son.

3 We remember the word
   Of our crucified Lord,
When He went to prepare us a place,
"I will come in that day and will take you away,
   And admit to a sight of my face."

4 Come, Lord, from the skies
   And command us to rise
To the mansions of glory above;
With Thee to ascend and eternity spend,
   In a rapture of heavenly love.

135

BLESSÉD hope that in Jesus is given,
  In our sorrow to cheer and sustain,
That soon in the mansions of Heaven,
  We shall meet with our loved ones again.

CHO.—‖: Blesséd hope, blesséd hope,
    We shall meet with our loved ones again. :‖

2 Blesséd hope in the word God has spoken,
    All our peace by that word we obtain;
  And as sure as God's word was ne'er broken,
    We shall meet with our loved ones again.

3 Blesséd hope! how it shines in our sorrow,
    Like the star over Bethlehem's plain,
  That it may be, with Him, ere the morrow,
    We shall meet with our loved ones again.

4 Blesséd hope! the bright star of the morning
    That shall herald His coming to reign;
  Oh, the glory that waits its fair dawning,
    When we meet with our loved ones again.

136

TEMPTED and tried!
    Oh! the terrible tide
May be raging and deep, may be wrathful and wide!
    Yet its fury is vain,
    For the Lord shall restrain,
And forever and ever Jehovah shall reign.

CHO.—Tempted and tried,
      Yet the Lord at thy side,
    Shall guide thee, and keep thee,
      Though tempted and tried.

2 Tempted and tried,
      There is One at thy side,
And never in vain shall His children confide!
      He shall save and defend,
      For He loves to the end,
Adorable Master and glorious Friend!

3 Tempted and tried,
      Whate'er may betide,
In His secret pavilion His children shall hide,

'Neath the shadowing wing,
Of Eternity's King,
His children shall trust, and His servants shall sing.

4 Tempted and tried!
Yet the Lord will abide,
Thy faithful Redeemer, thy Keeper and Guide,
Thy Shield and thy Sword,
Thine exceeding Reward,
Then enough for the servant to be as his Lord.

5 Tempted and tried,
The Saviour who died,
Hath called thee to suffer and reign by His side;
His cross thou shall bear,
And His crown thou shalt wear,
And forever and ever His glory shalt share.

137

I CANNOT tell how precious
The Saviour is to me,
Since I have Him accepted,
And He hath made me free;
I cannot tell His goodness,
Enough to satisfy;
And if you'll only take Him,
You'll see the reason why.

CHO.—I cannot tell how precious
The Saviour is to me;
I only can entreat you
To come, and taste and see.

2 I cannot do for Jesus
As much as I should like;
But I will e'er endeavor
To work with all my might;
For, was not my dear Saviour
For sinners crucified?
For me, then, surely, Jesus
Hung on the cross and died.

3 Whene'er I think of Jesus,
I cannot but rejoice;
To me He's ever precious,
For Him I raise my voice:

I know He has in glory
A home prepared for me,
Where I shall live forever
So happy, and so free.

138

BEAUTIFUL valley of Eden!
Sweet is thy noon-tide calm;
Over the hearts of the weary,
Breathing thy waves of balm.

REF.—Beautiful valley of Eden,
Home of the pure and blest,
How often amid the wild billows
I dream of thy rest—sweet rest!

2 Over the heart of the mourner
Shineth thy golden day,
Wafting the song of the angels
Down from the far away.

3 There is the home of my Saviour;
There, with the blood-washed throng,
Over the highlands of glory
Rolleth the great new song.

139

FIERCE and wild the storm is raging
Round a helpless bark,
On to doom 'tis swiftly driving,
O'er the waters dark!

CHO.—Joy, behold the Saviour,
Joy, the message hear,
"I'll stand by until the morning,
I've come to save you, do not fear,"
Yes, I'll stand by until the morning,
I've come to save you, do not fear;

2 Weary, helpless, hopeless seamen
Fainting on the deck,
With what joy they hail their Saviour,
As He hails the wreck!

3 On a wild and stormy ocean,
Sinking neath the wave,
Souls that perish heed the message,
Christ has come to save!

4 Daring death thy soul to rescue,
  He in love has come;
Leave the wreck, and in Him trusting,
  Thou shalt reach thy home!

140

WE'RE saved by the blood
    That was drawn from the side
Of Jesus our Lord,
    When He languished and died.

REF.—Hallelujah to God,
      For redemption so free;
    Hallelujah, Hallelujah,
      Dear Saviour, to Thee.

2 O yes, 'tis the blood
    Of the Lamb that was slain;
  He conquered the grave,
    And He liveth again.

3 We're saved by the blood,
    We are sealed by its power;
  'Tis life to the soul,
    And its hope every hour.

4 That blood is a fount
    Where the vilest may go,
  And wash till their souls
    Shall be whiter than snow.

5 We're saved by the blood,
    Hallelujah again;
  We're saved by the blood;
    Hallelujah, Amen.

141

WHAT though clouds are hovering o'er me,
    And I seem to walk alone—
Longing 'mid my cares and crosses,
    For the joys that now are flown—
If I've Jesus, "Jesus only,"
    Then my sky will have a gem;
He's a Sun of brightest splendor,
    And the Star of Bethlehem.

2 What though all my earthly journey
    Bringeth naught but weary hours,
  And, in grasping for life's roses,
    Thorns I find instead of flowers—

If I've Jesus, "Jesus only,"
  I possess a cluster rare;
He's the "Lily of the Valley,"
  And the "Rose of Sharon" fair.

3 What though all my heart is yearning
  For the loved of long ago—
Bitter lessons sadly learning
  From the shadowy page of woe—
If I've Jesus, "Jesus only,"
  "He'll be with me to the end;
And, unseen by mortal vision,
  Angel bands will o'er me bend.

4 When I soar to realms of glory,
  And an entrance I await,
If I whisper, "Jesus only!"
  Wide will ope the pearly gate;
When I join the heavenly chorus,
  And the angel hosts I see,
Precious Jesus, "Jesus only,"
  Will my theme of rapture be.

142

WHOM have I, Lord, in heaven but Thee?
  None but Thee! None but Thee!
And this my song through life shall be,
  Christ for me! Christ for me!
He hath for me the wine-press trod,
He hath redeemed me "by His blood,"
And reconciled my soul to God,
  Christ for me! Christ for me!

2 I envy not the rich their joys,
  Christ for me! Christ for me!
I covet not earth's glittering toys,
  Christ for me! Christ for me!
Earth can no lasting bliss bestow,
"Fading" is stamped on all below;
Mine is a joy no end can know,
  Christ for me! Christ for me!

3 Though with the poor be cast my lot,
  Christ for me! Christ for me!
"He knoweth best,"—I murmur not,
  Christ for me! Christ for me!

Though "Vine and Fig-tree" blight assail,
The "labor of the Olive fail,"
And death o'er flocks and herds prevail,
Christ for me! Christ for me!

4 Though I am now on hostile ground,
Christ for me! Christ for me!
And sin beset me all around,
Christ for me! Christ for me!
Let earth her fiercest battles wage,
And foes against my soul engage,
Strong in His strength I scorn their rage,
Christ for me! Christ for me!

5 And when my life draws to its close,
Christ for me! Christ for me!
Safe in His arms I shall repose,
Christ for me! Christ for me!
When sharpest pains my frame pervade,
And all the powers of nature fade,
Still will I sing through death's cold shade,
Christ for me! Christ for me!

143

I HAVE heard of a land far away,
And its glories no tongue can declare;
But its beauty hangs over the way,
And with Jesus I long to be there.

REF.—‖: To be there, to be there,
And with Jesus I long to be there. :‖

2 There are fore-tastes of heaven below,
There are moments like joys of the blest;
But the splendors no mortal can know,
Of the land where the weary shall rest.

3 In that noon-tide of glory so fair,
In the gleam of the river of life,
There are joys that the faithful shall share;
O how sweetly they rest from the strife!

4 There the ransomed with Jesus abide
In the shade of the sheltering fold;
Evermore by Immanuel's side,
They shall dwell in the glory untold.

144

G LIDING o'er life's fitful waters,
   Heavy surges sometimes roll;
And we sigh for yonder haven,
   For the Home-land of the soul.

REF.—Blesséd Home-land, every fair !
      Sin can never enter there;
      But the soul, to life awaking,
      Everlasting bloom shall wear.

2 Oft we catch a faint reflection
   Of its bright and vernal hills;
And, though distant, how we hail it!
   How each heart with rapture thrills!

3 To our Father, and our Saviour,
   To the Spirit, Three in One,
We shall sing glad songs of triumph
   When our harvest work is done.

4 'Tis the weary pilgrim's Home-land,
   Where each throbbing care shall cease,
And our longings and our yearnings,
   Like a wave, be hushed to peace.

145

W OULD you lose your load of sin?
   Fix your eyes upon Jesus:
Would you know God's peace within?
   Fix your eyes upon Jesus.

CHO.—Jesus who on the cross did die,
      Jesus who *lives* and *reigns* on high,
      He alone can justify;
      Fix your eyes upon Jesus.

2 Would you calmly walk the wave?
   Fix your eyes upon Jesus;
Would you know His power to save ?
   Fix your eyes upon Jesus.

3 Would you have your cares grow light?
   Fix your eyes upon Jesus;
Would you songs have in the night?
   Fix your eyes upon Jesus.

4 Grieving, would you comfort know?
   Fix your eyes upon Jesus;

Humble be when blessings flow?
Fix your eyes upon Jesus.

5 Would you strength in weakness have?
Fix your eyes upon Jesus;
See a light beyond the grave?
Fix your eyes upon Jesus.

146

THERE is a land of pure delight,
Where saints immortal reign;
Eternal day excludes the night,
And pleasures banish pain.
There everlasting spring abides,
And never-fading flowers;
Death, like a narrow sea, divides
That heavenly land from ours.

2 Sweet fields, beyond the swelling flood,
Stand dressed in living green;
So to the Jews fair Canaan stood,
While Jordan rolled between.
But timorous mortals start and shrink
To cross this narrow sea,
And linger, trembling on the brink,
And fear to launch away.

3 O could we make our doubts remove,—
Those gloomy doubts that rise,—
And see the Canaan that we love,
With unbeclouded eyes,—
Could we but climb where Moses stood,
And view the landscape o'er—
Not Jordan's stream, nor death's cold flood,
Should fright us from the shore

147

OH, I am so happy in Jesus,
His blood has redeemed me from sin,
I weep and I sing in my gladness,
To know He is dwelling within.

CHO.—Oh, I am so happy in Jesus,
From sin and from sorrow so free,
So happy that He is my Saviour,
So happy that Jesus loves me.

2 Oh, I am so happy in Jesus,
   He taught me the *secret of faith*,
To rest in believing His promise,
   And *trust whatsoever He saith.*

3 Oh, I am so happy in Jesus,
   I lay my whole soul at His feet;
The love He has kindled within me
   Makes service and suffering sweet.

4 Oh, I am so happy in Jesus,
   If earth in His love is so blest,
What joy in His glorified presence,
   To sit at His feet as His guest.

148

THE gospel trumpet's sounding
   The year of jubilee,
And grace is all abounding,
   To set the bondmen free.

CHO.—Return, return, ye captives,
   Return unto your home,
||: The gospel trumpet's sounding,
   The jubilee is come ! :||

2 Forsake your wretched service,
   Your master's claims are o'er;
Avail yourselves of freedom,
   Be Satan's slaves no more.

3 A better Master's calling,
   In accents true and kind;
He asks a loving service,
   And claims a willing mind.

4 He offers you salvation,
   And points to joys above;
And, longing, waits to make you
   The objects of His love.

5 In living faith accept Him,
   Give up all else beside;
While grace is loudly calling,
   Look to the Crucified.

149

OH, the bitter pain and sorrow
　　That a time could ever be,
When I proudly said to Jesus
　　"All of self and none of Thee,"
||: All of self and none of thee, :||
When I proudly said to Jesus
　　"All of self and none of Thee."

2 Yet He found me; I beheld Him
　　Bleeding on th'accursèd tree,
And my wistful heart said faintly,
　　"Some of self, and some of Thee,"
||: Some of self, and some of Thee, :||
And my wistful heart said faintly,
　　"Some of self and some of Thee."

3 Day by day His tender mercy
　　Healing, helping, full and free,
Brought me lower, while I whispered,"
　　"Less of self and more of Thee,"
||: Less of self and more of Thee, :||
Brought me lower, while I whispered,
　　"Less of self and more of Thee."

4 Higher than the highest heavens,
　　Deeper than the deepest sea,
Lord, Thy love at last has conquered,
　　"*None* of self and *all* of Thee,"
||: *None* of self and *all* of Thee, :||
Lord, Thy love at last has conquered
　　"*None* of self and *all* of Thee."

150

CAN it be right for me to go
　　On in this dark, uncertain way?
Say, "I believe," and yet not know
　　Whether my sins are put away?

CHO.—I will no longer doubt Thee, O Lord!
　　I will forever rest in Thy word.

2 Can it be right in doubt to wait,
　　Wait for the day that tries the heart,
Ere I shall learn what is my state,
　　Fearing the Judge should say depart?

3 Can it be right such loads to bear,
    While He says "Come, I'll give you rest?"
Bidding me cast on Him my care,
    Leaning in love, upon His breast.

4 Can it be right to doubt His power,
    Both to forgive and vanquish sin?
Even in trials of darkest hour,
    Can not His love give peace within?

5 Can it be right no soul to seek,
    Lest I should prove unfit to guide?
Can He not teach my tongue to speak,
    Will He not ample strength provide?

6 Can it be right with *such* a Lord,
    Even to dread the hour of death?
Waiting in faith the great reward,
    Calmly I'll yield my dying breath.

151

From the riven Rock there floweth,
    Living water ever clear;
Weary pilgrim, journeying onward,
    Know you not that Fount is near?

Cho.—Jesus is the Rock of Ages—
    Smitten, stricken, lo! He dies;
From His side a living fountain,
    Know you not it satisfies?

2 "Without money, without merit,"
    Jesus calls, "Come unto me,"
Thirsty traveler, be encouraged,
    Know you not the Fount is free?

3 Fainting in the desert, dreary,
    Guilty sinner, hark! 'tis He!
'Tis the Saviour still entreating,
    Know you not He calleth thee?

152

Thou art coming, O my Saviour,
    Thou art coming! O my King,
Every tongue Thy name confessing,
    Well may we rejoice and sing;

Thou art coming! rays of glory,
　　Through the veil Thy death has rent,
Gladden now our pilgrim pathway,
　　Glory from Thy presence sent.

CHO.—Thou art coming, Thou art coming,
　　　We shall meet Thee on Thy way,
　　Thou art coming, we shall see Thee,
　　　And be like Thee on that day.
　　Thou art coming! Thou art coming!
　　　Jesus our belovéd Lord,
　　O the joy to see Thee reigning,
　　　Worshiped, glorified, adored.

2 Thou art coming, not a shadow,
　　Not a mist and not a tear,
Not a sin and not a sorrow,
　　On that sunrise grand and clear;
Thou art coming! Jesus Saviour,
　　Nothing else seems worth a thought,
Oh. how marvelous the glory,
　　And the bliss Thy pain hath bought.

3 Thou art coming, we are waiting
　　With a hope that cannot fail,
Asking not the day or hour,
　　Anchored safe within the veil;
Thou art coming! at Thy table
　　We are witnesses for this,
As we meet Thee in communion,
　　Earnest of our coming bliss.

153
　　　　　　　　　　———

O NLY trusting in my Saviour,
　　All to Him my soul would leave;
He has suffered to redeem me,
　　And His word I now believe.

REF.—Now to Christ alone I'm clinging.
　　　Though the tempest round me blow;
Heeding not the clouds above me,
　　Dreading not the waves below.

2 Only trusting, nothing doubting,
　　This is all that I can do;

Every trial that befalls me
    He will safely bring me through.

3 There are breakers in the distance,
    Yet no danger will I fear;
On the Rock my feet are resting,
    Naught of harm can reach me here.

4 Only trusting, only trusting,
    This is joy and life to me;
Thou wilt never leave me friendless
    While I cling, O Christ, to Thee.

154

IN my Father's house there is many a room,
    And my Lord has gone to prepare
A place for me; O can it be
    That I shall be with Him there?

CHO.—||: Forever with Jesus there;:||
        What grace divine, that He is mine!
And I shall be with Him there.

2 In my Father's house there is endless day,
    With no cloud of sorrow or care,
No tearful eyes, no groans or sighs,
    They know who are with Him there.

3 In my Father's house there's no want or woe,
    And there can be no more prayer;
For what beside can God provide,
    Since we shall be with Him there.

4 In my Father's house there is no more death,
    For the life of God we share;
No thought of sin can enter in,
    For we shall be with Him there.

5 In my Father's house there are blesséd Saints,
    Who His holy image bear;
They find in this their sweetest bliss,
    That they may be with Him there.

155

TEN thousand times ten thousand,
    In sparkling raiment bright,
The armies of the ransomed saints
    Throng up the steeps of light;

'Tis finished, all is finished,
  Their fight with death and sin;
Fling open wide the golden gates,
  And let the victors in.

CHO.—Hallelujah! Hallelujah
    To the Lamb who once was slain!
    Hallelujah! Hallelujah
    To Him who lives again!

2 What rush of hallelujahs
  Fill all the earth and sky!
What ringing of a thousand harps
  Bespeaks the triumph nigh!
O day, for which creation
  And all its tribes were made!
O joy, for all its former woes
  A thousand fold repaid!

3 O, then what raptured greetings
  On Canaan's happy shore!
What knitting severed friendships up,
  Where partings are no more?
Then eyes with joy shall sparkle,
  That brimmed with tears of late;
Orphans no longer fatherless,
  Nor widows desolate.

156

I FEEL like singing all the time,
  My tears are wiped away;
For Jesus is a friend of mine,
  I'll serve Him every day.

CHO.—I'm singing, singing,
    Singing all the time;
    Singing, singing,
    Singing all the time.

2 When on the cross my Lord I saw,
  Nailed there by sins of mine;
Fast fell the burning tears; but now,
  I'm singing all the time.

3 When fierce temptations try my heart,
  I sing, Jesus is mine;
And so, though tears at times may start,
  I'm singing all the time.

4 The wondrous story of the Lamb,
    Tell with that voice of thine,
Till others, with the glad new song
    Go singing all the time.

157

MINE! what rays of glory bright
    Now upon the promise shine!
I have found the Lord my light;
    I am His, and He is mine.

Cho.—Mine, oh, mine, mine, oh, mine,
    Jesus Christ, my Lord and Saviour,
    I am His and He is mine!

2 Mine! the promise often read,
    Now in living truth impressed,
Once acknowledged in the head,
    Now a fire within the breast.

3 Mine! the promise cannot change,
    Mine, though oft my eyes are dim;
Naught can from His love estrange,
    Those who place their trust in Him.

4 Mine! though oft my hand may fail,
    He is strong and holds me fast;
By His blood I shall prevail,
    He shall lead me home at last.

5 Mine! when death the bars shall break,
    'Mid those glories all divine.
"Satisfied" I shall awake,
    Clasp His feet, and call Him *mine*.

158

ETERNITY dawns on my vision to-day,
    Gather round me my loved ones to sing and to pray;
The shadows are past, and the veil is withdrawn,
Brightly now does the morn of eternity dawn.

Cho.—Hallelujah! Hallelujah! Hallelujah, we sing!
    Jesus conquered the grave, robbing death of its sting;
    Hosanna! again let the glad anthem ring,
    "Sing and pray! Eternity dawns!"

2 Eternity dawns! Oh, the glories that rise,
  How they burst on my soul in its blissful surprise;
  With rapture the gleam of the city I see,
  Where the crown and the mansion are waiting for me.

3 "Eternity dawns!" There will be no more night,
  I am nearing the gates of the city of light;
  The shadows of time are passing away,
  Tarry not, O my Saviour, come quickly, I pray.

4 "Eternity dawns!" Earth recedes from my view;
  Weeping friends, now farewell, I must bid you adieu;
  I'm resting in Jesus, His merits I plead,
  Fear ye not, "for my God shall supply all your need."

5 "Eternity dawns!" 'Tis a source of content,
  That in preaching salvation my life has been spent;
  'Tis "Jesus my All," and the Saviour of men,
  May His grace be upon you forever. Amen.

159

NOTHING, either great or small—
    Nothing, sinner, no;
Jesus died and paid it all,
    Long, long ago.

CHO.—"It is finished!" yes, indeed,
        Finished every jot;
      Sinner, this is all you need,
        Tell me, is it not?

2 When He, from His lofty throne,
    Stooped to do and die,
  Everything was fully done:
    Hearken to His cry!

3 Weary, working, burdened one,
    Wherefore toil you so?
  Cease your doing; all was done
    Long, long ago.

4 Till to Jesus' work you cling
    By a simple faith,
  "Doing" is a deadly thing—
    "Doing" ends in death.

5 Cast your deadly "doing" down—
    Down at Jesus' feet;
Stand in Him, in Him alone,
    Gloriously complete.

160

WE speak of the land of the blest,
    A country so bright and so fair,
And oft are its glories confest,
    But what must it be to be there?

REF.—‖: To be there, to be there,
    Oh, what must it be to be there? :‖

2 We speak of its pathways of gold,
    Its walls decked with jewels so rare,
Its wonders and pleasures untold,
    But what must it be to be there?

3 We speak of its peace and its love,
    The robes which the glorified wear,
The songs of the blessèd above,
    But what must it be to be there?

4 We speak of its freedom from sin,
    From sorrow, temptation and care,
From trials without and within,
    But what must it be to be there?

5 Do Thou, Lord, midst pleasure or woe,
    For heaven our spirits prepare,
Then shortly we also shall *know*,
    And *feel* what it is to be there!

161

OUR Master has taken His journey
    To a country that's far away,
And has left us the care of the vineyard,
    To work for Him day by day.

CHO.—There's a work for me and a work for you,
    Something for each of us now to do;
Yes, a work for me and a work for you,
    Something for each of us now to do.

2 In this "little while," doth it matter,
    As we work, and we watch, and we wait,

If we're filling the place He assigns us,
  Be its service small or great.

3 There's only one thing should concern us,
    To find just the task that is ours;
  And then, having found it, to *do* it
    With all our God-given powers.

4 Our Master is coming most surely,
    To reckon with every one;
  Shall we *then*, count our toil or our sorrow,
    If His sentence be, " Well done."

162

BE our joyful song to-day,
    Jesus, only Jesus;
  He who took our sins away,
    Jesus, only Jesus.
  Name with every blessing rife,
  Be our joy and hope through life,
  Be our strength in every strife,
    Jesus, only Jesus.

2 Once we wandered far from God,
    Knowing not of Jesus,
  Treading still the down-ward road,
    Leading far from Jesus;
  Till the Spirit taught us how,
  'Neath the Saviour's yoke to bow,
  And we fain would follow now,
    Jesus, only Jesus.

3 Be our trust through years to come,
    Jesus, only Jesus;
  Pass-word to the heavenly home,
    Jesus, only Jesus.
  When from sin and sorrow free,
  On through all eternity,
  This our theme and song shall be,
    Jesus, only Jesus.

163

HOW sweet the word of Christ the Lord,
    While on the cross He dies,
  A word to all who on Him call
    For life in paradise.

CHO.—From the cross the Saviour cries,
    Come with Me to paradise;
    Look to Me, believe and live,
    Accept the life I freely give.

2 The dying thief, in full belief,
    On Jesus fixed his eyes;
    His only plea, "Remember me,
    O Lord, in paradise."

3 By man condemned, without a friend,
    Will Jesus heed his cries?
    O blessèd Lord, how quick Thy word,
    "To-day in paradise."

4 Though vile as he, O sinner, flee
    While Jesus calls, be wise;
    His word believe, and now receive
    A life in paradise.

164

REJOICE with me, for now I'm free,
    I joy in a new pleasure:
From God above, the gift of love
    Is mine in fullest measure.

CHO.—Rejoice, rejoice, Christ is my choice,
    His cross alone my glory;
When life shall last, when death is past,
    I'll sing the joyful story.

2 Once vile with sin, Christ makes me clean,
    Gone is all condemnation;
For I believe and now receive
    A full and free salvation.

3 In Christ I live, and He doth give,
    Great joy where once was sadness;
And in this way, from day to day,
    My life is filled with gladness.

4 To all proclaim His wondrous name,
    Repeat the Old, old story;
Till work is done and heaven won,
    Then praise Him more in glory.

165

THE prize is set before us,
　　To win, His words implore us,
The eye of God is o'er us
　　From on high, from on high;
His loving tones are calling
While sin is dark, appalling,
'Tis Jesus gently calling,
　　He is nigh, He is nigh.

CHO.—By and by we shall meet Him,
　　By and by we shall greet Him,
　　And with Jesus reign in glory
　　　　By and by.

2 We'll follow where He leadeth,
　　We'll pasture where He feedeth,
　　We'll yield to Him who pleadeth
　　　　From on high, from on high;
　　Then naught from Him shall sever,
　　Our hope shall brighten ever,
　　And faith shall fail us never,
　　　　He is nigh, He is nigh.

3 Our home is bright above us,
　　No trials dark to move us,
　　But Jesus dear to love us
　　　　There on high, there on high;
　　We'll give Him best endeavor,
　　And praise His name forever,
　　His precious words can never,
　　　　Never die, never die.

166

I AM trusting Thee, Lord Jesus,
　　Trusting only Thee!
Trusting Thee for full salvation,
　　Great and free.

2 I am trusting Thee for pardon,
　　At Thy feet I bow;
For Thy grace and tender mercy
　　Trusting now.

3 I am trusting Thee for cleansing
　　In the crimson flood;
Trusting Thee to make me holy
　　By Thy blood.

4 I am trusting Thee to guide me,
    Thou alone shalt lead,
Every day and hour supplying
    All my need.

5 I am trusting Thee for power;
    Thine can never fail;
Words which Thou Thyself shalt give me
    Must prevail.

6 I am trusting Thee, Lord Jesus,
    Never let me fall!
I am trusting Thee forever
    And for all!

187

GOOD news from heaven, good news for thee,
    There flows a pardon, full and free,
To guilty sinners, through the blood
Of the Incarnate Son of God;
He paid the debt that thou didst owe,
He suffered death for thee below,
He bore the wrath divine for thee,
He groaned and bled on Calvary.

Cho.—Good news from heaven, good news for thee,
    There flows a pardon, full and free,
    To guilty sinners through the blood
    Of the Incarnate Son of God.

2 Good news from heaven, good news for thee,
The Saviour cries, " Come unto me
All ye who toil, with fears opprest;
Come, weary one, oh, come and rest:"
He loves thee with o'erflowing love,
He hears thy prayer in heaven above,
He all thy pasture shall prepare,
And lead thee with a shepherd's care.

3 Good news from heaven, good news for thee,
Has echoed from eternity;
And loud shall our hosannas ring,
When with the ransomed throng we sing.
" Worthy the lamb," whose precious blood
Has made us kings and priests to God;
Our harps we'll tune to noblest strains.
And glory give to Him who reigns.

168

SAVIOUR, breathe an evening blessing,
　Ere repose our spirits seal;
Sin and want we come confessing,
　Thou canst save and Thou canst heal.

2 Though destruction walk around us,
　Though the arrows past us fly;
Angel guards from Thee surround us,
　We are safe if Thou art nigh.

3 Though the night be dark and dreary,
　Darkness cannot hide from Thee;
Thou art He who, never weary,
　Watchest where Thy people be.

4 Should swift death this night o'ertake us,
　And our couch become our tomb,
May the morn in heaven awake us,
　Clad in bright and deathless bloom.

169

SOUND the high praises of Jesus our King,
　He came and He conquered, His victory sing;
Sing, for the power of the tyrant is broken,
　The triumph's complete over death and the grave;
Vain is their boasting, Jehovah hath spoken,
　And Jesus proclaimed Himself Mighty to Save.

CHO.—Sound the high praises of Jesus our King,
　He came and He conquered, His victory to sing.

2 Praise to the Conqueror!　Praise to the Lord,
　The enemy quailed at the might of His word;
In heaven He ascends and unfolds the glad story,
　The hosts of the blesséd exult in His fame;
In love He looks down from the throne of His glory,
　And rescues the ruined who trust in His name.

170

THIS is the day of toil,
　Beneath earth's sultry noon,
This is the day of service true,
　But resting cometh soon.

CHO.—||: Hallelujah! Hallelujah!
　There emains a rest for us. ;||

2 Spend and be spent would we,
   While lasteth time's brief day;
No turning back in coward fear,
   No lingering by the way.

3 Onward we press in haste,
   Upward our journey still;
Ours is the path the Master trod
   Through good report and ill.

4 The way may rougher grow,
   The weariness increase,
We gird our loins and hasten on,—
   The end, the end is peace.

171

THERE is joy among the angels,
   Singing round the throne above,
When repentant tears are flowing,
While the risen Lord is showing
   All the riches of His love,
||: All the riches of His love. :||

CHO.—There is joy, oh, there is joy,
   Joy that never can be told,
When a soul that long has wandered,
   Comes within the Saviour's fold.

2 There is joy among the angels,
   When a sinner heeds the call;
When he turns to Christ believing,
And from Him is love receiving,
   Grace that saves us one and all,
||: Grace that saves us one and all. :||

3 There is joy among the angels,
   When His cause is speeding on;
When the notes of praise are ringing,
That the gospel work is bringing,
   Precious sheaves for harvest morn,
||: Precious sheaves for harvest morn. :||

172

OVER the ocean wave, far, far away,
   There the poor heathen live, waiting for day;
Groping in ignorance, dark as the night,
No blessèd Bible to give them the light

CHO.—Pity them, pity them, Christians at home,
    Haste with the Bread of Life, hasten and come.

2 Here in this happy land we have the light
Shining from God's own word, free, pure and bright;
Shall we not send to them Bibles to read,
Teachers, and preachers, and all that they need?

3 Then, while the mission ships glad tidings bring,
List! as that heathen band joyfuly sing,
" Over the ocean wave, oh, see them come,
Bringing the bread of life, guiding us home."

———

173

WHEN we reach our Father's dwelling,
    On the Strong eternal hills,
And our praise to Him is swelling
    Who the vast creation fills,
Shall we then recall the sadness,
    And the clouds that hung so dim,
When our hearts were turned from hardness,
    And our feet from paths of sin?

CHO.—Yes, we surely shall remember,
    And His grace we'll freely own;
For the love so strong and tender,
    That redeemed and brought us home.

2 When the paths of prayer and duty;
    And affliction all are trod,
And we wake and see the beauty
    Of our Saviour and our God,
Shall we then recall the story
    Of our mortal griefs and tears,
When on earth we sought the glory
    Wrestling oft with doubts and fears?

3 And the way by which He brought us,
    All the grievings that He bore,
All the patient love that taught us,
    We'll remember evermore;
And His rest will be the dearer,
    As we think of weary ways,
And His light will be the clearer
    As we muse on cloudy days.

174

"MUST I go and empty-handed,"
    Thus my dear Redeemer meet?
Not one day of service give Him,
    Lay no trophy at His feet?

CHO.—"Must I go and empty-handed,"
    Must I meet my Saviour so?
Not one soul with which to greet Him,
    Must I empty-handed go?

2 Not at death I shrink nor falter,
    For my Saviour saves me now;
But to meet Him empty-handed,
    Thought of that now clouds my brow.

3 Oh, the years of sinning wasted,
    Could I but recall them now,
I would give them to my Saviour,
    To His will I'd gladly bow.

4 Oh, ye saints, arouse, be earnest,
    Up and work while yet 'tis day,
Ere the night of death o'ertakes thee,
    Strive for souls while still you may.

175

MY sin is great, my strength is weak,
    My path beset with snares,
But Thou, O Christ, hast died for me,
    And Thou wilt hear my prayers.

REF.—To Thee, to Thee, the Crucified,
    The sinner's only plea,
Relying on Thy promised grace,
    My faith still clings to Thee.

2 The world is dark without Thee, Lord,
    I turn me from its strife
To find Thy love a sweet relief;
    Thou art the Light of Life.

3 Temptations lure and fears assail
    My frail, inconstant heart;
But precious are Thy promises,
    And they new strength impart.

4 Unfold Thy precepts to my mind,
   And cleanse my blinded eyes;
Grant me to work for Thee on earth,
   Then praise Thee in the skies.

176

I'VE found the pearl of greatest price!
   My heart doth sing for joy;
And sing I must, for Christ is mine!
   Christ shall my song employ.

CHO.—I've found the pearl of greatest price!
   My heart doth sing for joy;
   And sing I must, for Christ is mine!
   Christ shall my song employ.

2 Christ is my Prophet, Priest, and King;
   My Prophet full of light,
My great High Priest before the throne,
   My King of heavenly might.

3 For He indeed is Lord of lords,
   And He the King of kings;
He is the Sun of Righteousness,
   With healing in His wings.

4 Christ is my peace; He died for me,
   For me He shed His blood;
And as my wondrous Sacrifice,
   Offered Himself to God.

5 Christ Jesus is my all in all,
   My comfort and my love;
My life below, and He shall be
   My joy and crown above.

177

"FAINT, yet pursuing," we press our way
   Up to the glorious gates of day;
Following Him who has gone before,
Over the path to the brighter shore.

CHO.—"Faint, yet pursuing," from day to day,
   Over the sure and the blood-marked way;
Strengthen and keep us, O Saviour, Friend,
Ever pursuing, unto life's end.

2 "Faint, yet pursuing," whate'er befall,
He who has died for us, died for all;
So should they come, as a mighty throng
Bearing His banner aloft with song.

3 "Faint, yet pursuing," till eventide,
Under the cross of the Crucified;
Knowing, when darkly are skies o'ercast,
Sorrow and sighing will end at last.

4 "Faint, yet pursuing," the eye afar
Sees through the darkness the Morning Star,
Shedding its ray for the weary feet,
Keeping the way to the golden street.

178

BESIDE the well at noontime,
I hear a sad one say:
"I want that living water,
Give me to drink, I pray;
The well is deep, O pilgrim,
But deeper is my need;
I thirst for life eternal,
The 'Gift of God' indeed."

CHO.—Ho, every one that thirsteth,
The living water buy!
Ye blesséd ones that hunger,
Take, eat and never die.

2 Beside the pool Bethesda,
I hear a mournful cry:
"No help, no hope is offered
To one so weak as I;"
Oh, cease thy sad complaining,
The gospel gives thee cheer;
Come to the house of mercy,
For Christ the pool is here.

CHO.—'Tis He, the great Physician,
Can cure the sin-sick soul;
Rise up and walk," He bids thee,
"Thy faith hath made thee whole."

3 While seated on the hill-side,
The hungry ones were fed

By Him who said most truly:
"I am the living bread;"
'Tis He, the heavenly manna,
Who doth our souls restore;
By faith, of Him partaking,
We live for evermore,

CHO.—Ho, every one that thirsteth,
The living water buy!
Ye blessèd ones that hunger,
Take, eat and never die.

179

O N Jordan's stormy banks I stand,
And cast a wishful eye
To Canaan's fair and happy land,
Where my possessions lie.

CHO.—We will rest in the fair and happy land
Just across on the evergreen shore,
Sing the song of Moses and the Lamb, by and by
And dwell with Jesus evermore.

2 O'er all those wide-extended plains
Shines one eternal day;
There God the Son forever reigns,
And scatters night away.

3 When shall I reach that happy place,
And be forever blest?
When shall I see my Father's face,
And in His bosom rest?

4 Filled with delight, my raptured soul
Would here no longer stay;
Though Jordan's waves around me roll,
Fearless I'd launch away,

180

O LAND of rest, for thee I sigh,
When will the moment come,
When I shall lay my armor by,
And dwell in peace at home?

CHO.—We'll work till Jesus comes,
||:We'll work till Jesus comes,:||
And we'll be gathered home.

2 No tranquil joys on earth I know,
    No peaceful sheltering dome:
This world's a wilderness of woe,
    This world is not my home.

3 To Jesus Christ I fled for rest;
    He bade me cease to roam,
And lean for succor on His breast,
    Till He conduct me home.

4 I sought at once my Saviour's side,
    No more my steps shall roam;
With Him I'll brave death's chilling tide,
    And reach my heavenly home.

181

I KNOW not what awaits me,
    God kindly veils mine eyes,
And o'er each step of my onward way
    He makes new scenes to rise;
And every joy He sends me, comes
    A sweet and glad surprise.

CHO.—Where He may lead I'll follow,
    My trust in Him repose;
||:And every hour in perfect peace
    I'll sing, He knows, He knows.:||

2 One step I see before me,
    'Tis all I need to see,
The light of heaven more brightly shines,
    When earth's illusions flee;
And sweetly through the silence, came
    His loving "Follow me."

3 O blissful lack of wisdom,
    'Tis blessèd not to know;
He holds me with His own right hand,
    And will not let me go,
And lulls my troubled soul to rest
    In Him who loves me so.

4 So on I go not knowing,
    I would not if I might;

I'd rather walk in the dark with God
Than go alone in the light;
I'd rather walk by faith with Him
Than go alone by sight.

CHO.—Where He may lead I'll follow,
My trust in Him repose;
||: And every hour in perfect peace
I'll sing, He knows, He knows. :||
He knows, He knows, He knows.

182

WHEN we get home from our sorrow and care,
And we stand with the angels of light,
Oh, what a meeting in heaven there'll be,
In that land without shadow or night;
Sorrow and care, tribulation and pain
We'll leave, when we pass through the tomb;
Clouds of despair, storms of trial and care
We shall leave for that beautiful home.

CHO.—When we get home, oh, when we get home,
Get home to glory land,
Praises we'll sing to Jesus, our King,
A ransomed, a glorified band.

2 When we get home to the mansions above,
With the loved ones gone over before,
Oh, who can tell what joy that will be
There, to live and rejoice evermore;
Angels will praise, the Redeemer will smile,
And loved ones we'll clasp by the hand;
Free from all pain, far beyond earthly stain,
We shall dwell in that beautiful land.

3 When we get home, when the morning is come
And forth from the city of gold
Angels of God, coming down, shall call home
All of those who belong to His fold;
Will you be there, brother, loved ones to greet,
Or will you forever be lost?
What is thy choice, fleeting pleasures of earth,
Or a home when death's river is crossed?

183

I HAVE read of a beautiful city,
    Far away in the kingdom of God;
I have read how its walls are of jasper,
    How its streets are all golden and broad.
In the midst of the street is life's river,
    Clear as crystal and pure to behold;
But not half of that city's bright glory
    To mortals has ever been told.

CHO.—||: Not half has ever been told; :||
        Not half of that city's bright glory
        To mortals has ever been told,

2 I have read of bright mansions in Heaven,
    Which the Saviour has gone to prepare;
And the saints who on earth have been faithful,
    Rest forever with Christ over there;
There no sin ever enters, nor sorrow,
    The inhabitants never grow old;
But not half of the joys that await them
    To mortals has ever been told.

3 I have read of white robes for the righteous,
    Of bright crowns which the glorified wear,
When our Father shall bid them " Come, enter,
    And my glory eternally share;"
How the righteous are evermore blessed
    As they walk through the streets of pure gold;
But not half of the wonderful story
    To mortals has ever been told.

4 I have read of a Christ so forgiving,
    That vile sinners may ask and receive
Peace and pardon from every transgression,
    If when asking they only believe.
I have read how He'll guide and protect us,
    If for safety we enter His fold;
But not half of His goodness and mercy
    To mortals has ever been told.

184

A RE you coming Home, ye wanderers,
    Whom Jesus died to win,
All foot-sore, lame and weary,
    Your garments stained with sin;

Will you seek the blood of Jesus
To wash your garments white;
Will you trust His precious promise,
Are you coming Home to-night?

CHO.—||: Are you coming Home to-night, :||
Are you coming Home to Jesus,
Out of darkness into light?
||: Are you coming Home to-night, :||
To your loving, heavenly Father,
Are you coming Home to-night?

2 Are you coming Home, ye lost ones?
Behold your Lord doth wait:
Come, then no longer linger,
Come ere it be too late;
Will you come and let Him save you,
O trust His love and might;
Will you come while He is calling,
Are you coming Home to-night?

3 Are you coming Home, ye guilty,
Who bear the load of sin;
Outside you've long been standing,
Come now and venture in;
Will you heed the Saviour's promise,
And dare to trust Him quite;
"Come unto me," saith Jesus;
Are you coming Home to night?

185
_____

SAY, where is thy refuge, poor sinner,
And what is thy prospect to-day?
Why toil for the wealth that will perish,
The treasures that rust and decay?
Oh! think of thy soul, that forever
Must live on eternity's shore,
When thou, in the dust art forgotten,
When pleasure can charm thee no more.

CHO.—'Twill profit thee nothing, but fearful the cost,
||: To gain the whole world if thy soul should be lost. :||

2 The Master is calling thee, sinner,
In tones of compassion and love,
To feel that sweet rapture of pardon,
And lay up thy treasure above:

Oh! kneel at the cross where He suffered,
    To ransom thy soul from the grave;
The arm of His mercy will hold thee,
    The arm that is mighty to save.

3 As summer is waning, poor sinner,
    Repent, ere the season is past;
God's goodness to thee is extended,
    As long as the day-beam shall last;
Then slight not the warning repeated
    With all the bright moments that roll,
Nor say, when the harvest is ended,
    That no one hath cared for thy soul.

186

BRIGHTLY gleams our banner,
    Pointing to the sky,
Waving wanderer's onward,
    To their home on high;
Journeying o'er the desert,
    Gladly thus we pray,
And with hearts united.
    Take our heavenward way.

Cho.—Brightly gleams our banner,
    Pointing to the sky,
Waving wanderers onward
    To their home on high.

2 Jesus, Lord and Master,
    At Thy sacred feet,
Here with hearts rejoicing,
    See Thy children meet;
Often have we left Thee,
    Often gone astray,
Keep us, mighty Saviour,
    In the narrow way.

3 All our days direct us,
    In the way we go,
Lead us on victorious
    Over every foe;
Bid Thine angels shield us,
    When the storm-clouds lower,
Pardon Thou and save us
    In the last dread hour.

4 Then with Saints and Angels
    May we join above,
Offering endless praises
    At Thy Throne of love;
When the toil is over,
    Then comes rest and peace,—
Jesus, in His beauty;—
    Songs that never cease.

187

HEAR ye the glad Good News from heaven?
    Life to a death-doomed race is given!
Christ on the cross for you and me
    Purchased a pardon full and free.

Cho.—He that believeth, he that believeth,
    He that believeth hath everlasting life.

2 When we were lost, the Son of God
    Made an atonement by His blood:
When we the glad Good News believe,
    Then the atonement we receive.

3 Why not believe the glad Good News?
    Why still the voice of God refuse?
Why not believe, when God hath said,
    All, *all* our guilt " on Him " was laid.

188

THE way is dark, my Father! ‖ Cloud upon cloud
    Is gathering thickly o'er my head, and loud
The thunders roar | a- | bove me, ‖ Yet see, I stand
Like one bewildered! Father, | take my | hand,
    And through the gloom lead safely home.
        Safely home, safely home,
        Lead safely home Thy child!

2 The day declines, my Father! ‖ and the night
    Is drawing darkly down. My faithless sight
Sees | ghostly | visions. ‖ Fears like a spectral band
Encompass me. O Father, | take my | hand,
    And from the night lead up to light,
        Up to light, up to light,
        Lead up to light Thy child!

3 The way is long, my Father! || and my soul
Longs for the rest and quiet | of the | goal; ||
While yet I journey through this weary land,
Keep me from wandering. Father, | take my | hand,
    And in the way to endless day,
        Endless day, endless day,
      Lead safely on Thy child!

4 The path is rough, my Father! || Many a thorn
Has pierced me! and my feet, all torn
And bleeding, | mark the | way. || Yet Thy command
Bids me press forward. Father, | take my | hand;
    Then safe and blest, O lead to rest,
        Lead to rest, lead to rest,
      O lead to rest Thy child!

5 The throng is great, my Father! || Many a doubt
And fear of danger compass me about;
And foes op- | press me | sore. || I cannot stand,
Or go, alone. O Father! | take my | hand;
    And through the throng, lead safe along,
        Safe along, safe along,
      Lead safe along Thy child.

6 The cross is heavy, Father! || I have borne
It long, and | still do | bear it. || Let my worn
And fainting spirit, rise to that bright land
Where crowns are given. Father, | take my | hand;
    And, reaching down, lead to the crown,
        To the crown, to the crown,
      Lead to the crown Thy child.

189

HEAVENLY Father, we beseech Thee,
    Grant Thy blessing ere we part;
Take us in Thy care and keeping,
    Guard from evil every heart.

CHO.—Bless the words we here have spoken,
      Offered prayer and cheerful strain;
    If Thy will, O Lord, we pray Thee,
      Grant we all may meet again.

2 Loving Saviour, go Thou with us,
    Be our comfort and our stay;

Grateful praise to Thee we render,
For the joy we feel to-day.

3 Holy Spirit, dwell within us,
May our souls Thy Temple be;
May we tread the path to glory,
Led and guided still by Thee.

4 Heavenly Father, Loving Saviour,
Holy Spirit, Three in One;
As among Thy saints and angels,
So on earth, Thy will be done.

190

THE gospel of Thy grace
My stubborn heart has won,
"For God so loved the world,
He gave His only Son,

REF.—"That whosoever will believe,
Shall everlasting life receive!"
"Shall everlasting life receive!"

2 The serpent "lifted up"
Could life and healing give,
So Jesus on the cross
Bids me to look and live;

REF.—For "Whosoever," etc,

3 "The soul that sinneth dies:"
My awful doom I heard;
I was forever lost,
But for Thy gracious word

REF.—"That whosoever," etc.

4 "Not to condemn the world"
The "Man of sorrows" came;
But that the world might have
Salvation through His name;

REF.—For "Whosoever," etc.

5 "Lord, help my unbelief!"
Give me the peace of faith,
To rest with child-like trust
On what Thy gospel saith,

REF.—"That whosoever," etc.

191

GLORY be to the Father and to the Son, and to the Holy
    Ghost,
As it was in the beginning, is now, and ever shall be, world
    without end. AMEN.

192

TELL it out among the nations that the Lord is King,
        Tell it out!   Tell it out!
Tell it out among the nations, bid them shout and sing;
        Tell it out!   Tell it out!
Tell it out with adoration that He shall increase,
That the mighty King of Glory is the King of Peace;
Tell it out with jubilation, let the song ne'er cease;
        Tell it out!   Tell it out!

2 Tell it out among the people that the Saviour reigns;
        Tell if out!   Tell it out!
Tell it out among the heathen, bid them break their chains;
        Tell it out!   Tell it out!
Tell it out among the weeping ones that Jesus lives,
Tell it out among the weary ones what rest He gives,
Tell it out among the sinners that He came to save;
        Tell it out !   Tell it out!

3 Tell it out among the people, Jesus reigns above;
        Tell it out !   Tell it out!
Tell it out among the nations that His reign is love;
        Tell it out !   Tell it out!
Tell it out among the highways and the lanes at home,
Let it ring across the mountains and the ocean's foam,
That the weary, heavy-laden, need no longer roam;
        Tell it out!   Tell it out!

193

LIGHT after darkness,
    Gain after loss,
Strength after weakness,
    Crown after cross;
Sweet after bitter,
    Hope after fears,
Home after wandering,
    Praise after tears.

2 Sheaves after sowing,
    Sun after rain,
Sight after mystery,
    Peace after pain;
Joy after sorrow,
    Calm after blast,
Rest after weariness,
    Sweet rest at last.

3 Near after distant,
    Gleam after gloom,
Love after loneliness,
    Life after tomb;
After long agony,
    Rapture of bliss,
Right was the pathway,
    Leading to this.

194

GLORY, glory be to Jesus,
    Glory to His precious name;
Sweet it is to sound His praises,
    Blest it is to spread His fame.

Cho.—Glory, glory, hallelujah!
    Glory be to Jesus' name,
Sweet it is to sound His praises,
    Blest it is to spread His fame.

2 In the place of His rejection,
    Where He suffered, where He died,
Bursts of holy praise ascending,
    Greets the glorious Crucified.

3 Here was marred His blesséd visage,
    Here His brow was wreathed with thorn,
Here the object of derision,
    Bitter taunt and mocking scorn.

4 Yes, triumphant hallelujahs
    Still arise to greet His name;
Sweet it is to sound His praises,
    Blest it is to spread His fame.

195

WHAT can wash away my stain?
    Nothing but the blood of Jesus;
What can make me whole again?
    Nothing but the blood of Jesus,

CHO.—Oh, precious is the flow
        That makes me white as snow;
    No other fount I know,
        Nothing but the blood of Jesus.

2 For my cleansing this I see—
    Nothing but the blood of Jesus;
For my pardon this my plea—
    Nothing but the blood of Jesus.

3 Nothing can for sin atone—
    Nothing but the blood of Jesus;
Naught of good that I have done—
    Nothing but the blood of Jesus.

4 This is all my hope and peace—
    Nothing but the blood of Jesus;
This is all my righteousness—
    Nothing but the blood of Jesus.

5 Now by this I'll overcome—
    Nothing but the blood of Jesus;
Now by this I'll reach my home—
    Nothing but the blood of Jesus.

6 Glory! glory! thus I sing—
    Nothing but the blood of Jesus;
All my praise for this I bring—
    Nothing but the blood of Jesus.

196

O CHRIST in Thee my soul hath found,
    And found in Thee alone,
The peace, the joy I sought so long,
    The bliss till now unknown.

CHO.—Now none but Christ can satisfy,
        None other name for me,
    There's love, and life, and lasting joy,
        Lord Jesus, found in Thee.

2 I sighed for rest and happiness,
   I yearned for them, not Thee;
But while I passed my Saviour by,
   His love laid hold on me.

3 I tried the broken cisterns, Lord,
   But ah! the waters failed!
E'en as I stooped to drink they fled,
   And mocked me as I wailed.

4 The pleasures lost I sadly mourned,
   But never wept for Thee,
Till grace my sightless eyes received,
   Thy loveliness to see.

197

O SOUL in the far away country,
   A-weary, and famished, and sad,
There's rest in the home of thy Father,
   His welcome will make thy heart glad.

Сно.—Come, come, prodigal, come,
   And wander no longer afar from home;
Come, come, prodigal, come,
   A welcome awaits in thy Father's home.

2 Arise! and come back to thy Father,
   He'll meet thee while yet on the way;
Assured of His tender compassion,
   O why wilt thou longer delay?

3 Although thou hast sinned against heaven
   And weak and unworthy may be;
He offers the full restoration,
   And pardon abundant and free.

198

WHEN the Lord from heaven appears,
   When are banished all our fears,
When the sleepers from the tomb,
   With the watchers reach their home,

Сно.—‖: Then, enthroned our Lord with Thee.
   We shall reign eternally. :‖

2 When our eyes the King shall see,
In His glorious Majesty,
When to Him we're called above,
Partners of His joy and love,

3 Debtors to His matchless grace,
At His feet our crowns will place,
And as ages roll along,
Still will sing the glad new song.

4 Let this hope now purify
Those who on Thy word rely;
Comfort to our hearts afford,
'Till the coming of the Lord.

199

COME. sing, my soul, and praise the Lord,
Who hath redeemed thee by His blood;
Delivered thee from chains that bound,
And brought thee to redemption ground.

CHO.—Redemption ground, the ground of peace,
Redemption ground, O wondrous grace;
Here let our praise to God abound,
Who saves us on redemption ground.

2 Once from my God I wandered far,
And with His holy will made war:
But now my songs to God abound;
I'm standing on redemption ground.

3 O joyous hour when God to me
A vision gave of Calvary:
My bonds were loosed, my soul unbound;
I sang upon redemption ground.

4 No works of merit now I plead,
But Jesus take for all my need;
No righteousness in me is found,
Except upon redemption ground.

5 Come, weary soul, and here find rest;
Accept redemption, and be blest:
The Christ who died, by God is crowned
To pardon on redemption ground.

200

R ISE up, and hasten! my soul, haste along !
And speed on thy journey with hope and with song;
Home, home is nearing, 'tis coming into view,
A little more of toiling and then to earth adieu.

CHO.—Come then, come, and raise the joyful song!
     Ye children of the wilderness, our time cannot be
        long.
     Home, home, home, oh, why should we delay?
     The morn of heaven is dawning, we're near the break
        of day.

2 Why should we linger when heaven lies before !
   While earth's fast receding, and soon will be no more;
   Pleasures and treasures which once here we knew,
   No more can they charm us with such a goal in view.

3 Loved ones in Jesus they've passed on before,
   Now resting in glory, they weary are no more;
   Toils all are ended, and nothing now but joy,
   And praises ascending, their ever glad employ,

4 No condemnation! how blesséd is the word,
   And no separation! forever with the Lord;
   He will be with us who loved us long before,
   And Jesus, our Jesus, is ours for evermore.

201

I THINK when I read that sweet story of old,
   When Jesus was here among men,
How He called little children, as lambs to His fold,
   I should like to have been with them then.

REF.—||: I should like to have been with them then,:||
     How He called little children as lambs to His fold,
     I should like to have been with them then.

2 I wish that His hands had been placed on my head,
     That His arm had been thrown around me,
   And that I might have seen His kind look when He said
     "Let the little ones come unto Me."

REF.—||: "Let the little ones come unto Me; ":||
     And that I might have seen His kind look when He
     "Let the little ones come unto Me."   [said,

3 Yet still to His foot-stool in prayer I may go,
   And ask for a share in His love;
And if I now earnestly seek Him below,
   I shall see Him and hear Him above.

REF.—||: I shall see Him and hear Him above; :||
   And if I now earnestly seek Him below,
   I shall see Him and hear Him above.

4 In that beautiful place He is gone to prepare,
   For all that are washed and forgiven;
And many dear children are gathering there,
   For "Of such is the kingdom of heaven."

REF.—||:For "Of such is the kingdom of heaven;":||
   And many dear children are gathering there,
   For "Of such is the kingdom of heaven."

202

JESUS I will trust Thee, trust Thee with my soul;
   Guilty, lost, and helpless, Thou canst make me whole.
There is none in heaven or on earth like Thee:
Thou hast died for sinners—therefore, Lord, for me.

CHO.—In Thy love confiding I will seek Thy face,
   Worship and adore Thee, for Thy wondrous grace.
   Jesus, I will trust Thee, trust Thee with my soul;
   Guilty, lost, and helpless, Thou canst make me whole.

2 Jesus, I can trust Thee, trust Thy written word,
Since Thy voice of mercy I have often heard,
When Thy Spirit teacheth, to my taste how sweet—
Only may I hearken, sitting at Thy feet.

3 Jesus, I do trust Thee, trust Thee without doubt:
"Whosoever cometh, Thou wilt not cast out,"
Faithful is Thy promise, precious is Thy blood—
These my soul's salvation, Thou my Saviour God!

203

"NOT my own," but saved by Jesus,
   Who redeemed me by His blood,
Gladly I accept the message,
   I belong to Christ the Lord.

CHO.—"Not my own!" Oh, "not my own!
    Jesus, I belong to Thee!
    All I have, and all I hope for,
      Thine for all eternity.

2 "Not my own!" to Christ, my Saviour,
    Believing, trust my soul;
  Everything to Him committed,
    While eternal ages roll.

3 "Not my own!" my time, my talent
    Freely all to Christ I bring,
  To be used in joyful service
    For the glory of my King.

4 "Not my own!" the Lord accepts me,
    One among the ransomed throng,
  Who in heaven shall see His glory
    And to Jesus Christ belong.

204

WITH His dear and loving care,
    Will the Saviour lead us on,
To the hills and valleys fair,
    Over Jordan?
Yes, we'll rest our weary feet
By the crystal waters sweet,
When the peaceful shore we greet
    Over Jordan.

CHO.—Over Jordan! Over Jordan!
  Yes, we'll rest our weary feet
  By the crystal waters sweet,
    Over Jordan, over Jordan,
  When the peaceful shore we'll greet,
    Over Jordan.

2 Through the rocky wilderness,
    Will the Saviour lead us on,
To the land we shall possess,
    Over Jordan?
Yes, by night the wondrous ray,
Cloudy pillar by the day,
They shall guide us on our way,
    Over Jordan.

3 With His strong and mighty hand,
 Will the Saviour lead us on,
 To that good and pleasant land
   Over Jordan?
 Yes, where vine and olive grow,
 And the brooks and fountains flow,
 Thirst nor hunger shall we know,
   Over Jordan.

4 In the Promised Land to be,
 Will the Saviour lead us on,
 Till fair Canaan's shore we see,
   Over Jordan?
 Yes, to dwell with Thee, at last,
 Guide and lead us, as Thou hast,
 Till the parted wave be passed,
   Over Jordan.

205

PRAISE ye the Lord; for it is good
   Praise to our God to sing:
 For it is pleasant, and to praise
 It is a comely thing.

Cho.—Praise the Lord, it is good,
   Praise to our God to sing:
   For it is pleasant, and to praise
   It is a comely thing.

2 Those that are broken in their heart,
   And troubled in their minds,
 He healeth, and their painful wounds,
   He tenderly upbinds.

3 He counts the number of the stars;
   He names them every one:
 Our Lord is great, and of great power,
   His wisdom search can none.

206

OH, I left it all with Jesus, long ago;
   All my sins I brought Him and my woe;
 When by faith I saw Him bleeding on the tree,
 Heard His still small whisper, "'Tis for thee!"

CHO.—‖: From my weary heart the burden rolled away,
　　　Happy day! happy day! :‖

2 Oh, I leave it all with Jesus, for He knows,
　How to steal the bitter from life's woes;
　How to gild the tear of sorrow with His smile,
　Make the desert garden bloom awhile.

CHO. —‖: Then with all my weakness leaning on His might,
　　　All is light! all is light! :‖

3 O, I leave it all with Jesus, day by day;
　Faith can firmly trust Him, come what may;
　Hope has dropped for aye her anchor, found her rest;
　In the calm, sure haven of His breast.

CHO.—‖: Love esteems it joy of heaven to abide
　　　At His side! at His side! :‖

4 Leave, oh, leave it all with Jesus, drooping soul;
　Tell not half thy story, but the whole;
　Worlds on worlds are hanging ever on His hand,
　Life and death are waiting His command.

CHO.—‖: Yet His tender, loving mercy makes thee room;
　　　Oh, come home! oh, come home! :‖

207

DEPTH of mercy! can there be
　　Mercy still reserved for me?
Can my God His wrath forbear?
Me, the chief of sinners, spare?

CHO.—God is love! I know, I feel;
　　Jesus lives, and loves me still;
　　　Jesus lives,
　　He lives, and loves me still.

2 I have long withstood His grace
　Long provoked Him to His face:
　Would not hearken to His calls;
　Grieved Him by a thousand falls.

3 Now incline me to repent;
　Let me now my sins lament;
　Now my foul revolt deplore,
　Weep, believe, and sin no more.

208

THE blood has always precious been,
    'Tis precious now to me;
Through it alone my soul has rest,
    From fear and doubt set free.

CHO.—Oh, wondrous is the crimson tide
    Which from my Saviour flowed;
And still in heaven my song shall be,
    The precious, precious blood.

2 I will remember now no more,
    God's faithful Word has said,
The follies and the sins of him
    For whom my Son has bled.

3 Not all my well-remembered sins
    Can startle or dismay;
The precious blood atones for all
    And bears my guilt away.

4 Perhaps this feeble frame of mine
    Will soon in sickness lie,
But resting on the precious blood
    How peacefully I'll die.

———

209

LORD, I care not for riches,
    Neither silver nor gold;
I would make sure of heaven,
    I would enter the fold.
In the book of Thy kingdom,
    With its pages so fair,
Tell me, Jesus, my Saviour,
    Is my name written there?

CHO.—Is my name written there,
        On the page white and fair?
    In the book of Thy kingdom,
        Is my name written there?

2 Lord, my sins they are many,
    Like the sands of the sea,
But Thy blood, oh, my Saviour!
    Is sufficient for me;

For Thy promise is written,
   In bright letters that glow,
"Though your sins be as scarlet,
   I will make them like snow."

3 Oh! that beautiful city,
   With its mansions of light,
With its glorified beings,
   In pure garments of white;
Where no evil thing cometh,
   To despoil what is fair;
Where the angels are watching,
   Yes, my name's written there.

210

HELPLESS I come to Jesus' blood
   And all myself resign;
I lose my weakness in that flood,
   And gather strength divine.

REF.—‖: My soul will overcome by the blood of the Lamb, :‖
‖: Overcome, :‖ overcome by the blood of the Lamb.

2 'Tis Jesus gives me life within,
   And nerves me for the fray;
He spoiled the hosts of death and sin,
   And took their power away.

3 Though clouds of conflict hide my view,
   And foes are fierce and strong,
In Jesus' name I'll struggle through,
   And enter heaven with song.

211

O SAVIOUR, precious Saviour,
   Whom, yet unseen, we love;
O Name of might and favor,
   All other names above.

CHO.—We worship Thee! we bless Thee!
   To Thee alone we sing!
We praise Thee and confess Thee,
   Our Saviour and our King!

2 O Bringer of salvation,
   Who wondrously hast wrought
Thyself the revelation
   Of love beyond our thought.

3 In Thee all fulness dwelleth,
   All grace and power divine;
The glory that excelleth,
   O Son of God, is Thine.

4 Oh, grant the consummation
   Of this our song, above,
In endless adoration
   And everlasting love.

CHO.—Than shall we praise and bless Thee!
        Where perfect praises ring!
      And evermore confess Thee,
        Our Saviour and our King!

212

TRUST on! trust on, believer!
   Though long the conflict be,
Thou yet shalt prove victorious;
   Thy God shall fight for thee.

CHO.—Trust on!   Trust on!
        Though dark the night and drear;
      Trust on!   Trust on!
        The morning dawn is near.

2 Trust on! trust on; thy failings
   May bow thee to the dust,
But in thy deepest sorrow,
   O give not up thy trust.

3 Trust on! the danger presses,
   Temptation strong is near,
Yet o'er life's dangerous rapids,
   He shall thy passage steer.

4 O Christ is strong to save us,
   He is a faithful Friend,
Trust on! trust on! believer,
   O trust Him to the end.

213

SHOULD the Death-angel knock at thy chamber,
   In the still watch of to-night,
Say, will your spirit pass into torment,
   Or to the land of delight

CHO.—Say, are you ready, O are you ready?
 If the Death-angel should call;
Say, are you ready? O are you ready?
 Mercy stands waiting for all.

2 Many sad spirits now are departing
 Into the world of despair;
Every brief moment brings your doom nearer;
 Sinner, O sinner, beware!

3 Many redeemed ones now are ascending
 Into the mansions of light;
Jesus is pleading, patiently pleading,
 O let Him save you to-night.

214

TRUSTING in the Lord thy God,
 Onward go! onward go!
Holding fast His promised word,
  Onward go!
Ne'er deny His worthy Name,
Though it bring reproach and shame;
Spreading still His wondrous fame,
  Onward go!

2 Has He called thee to the plough?
 Onward go! onward go!
Night is coming, serve Him now;
  Onward go!
Faith and love in service blend;
On His mighty arm depend;
Standing fast until the end,
  Onward go!

3 Has He given thee golden grain?
 Onward go! onward go!
Sow, and thou shalt reap again;
  Onward go!
To thy Master's gate repair,
Watching be and waiting there;
He will hear and answer prayer;
  Onward go!

4 Has He said the end is near?
    Onward go! onward go!
Serving Him with holy fear;
    Onward go!
Christ thy portion, Christ thy stay,
Heavenly bread upon the way,
Leading on to glorious day;
    Onward go!

5 In this little moment then,
    Onward go! onward go!
In thy ways acknowledge Him;
    Onward go!
Let His mind be found in thee:
Let His will thy pleasure be;
Thus in life and liberty,
    Onward go!

215

THE love that Jesus had for me,
    To suffer on the cruel tree,
That I a ransomed soul might be,
    Is more than tongue can tell.

CHO.—‖: His love is more than tongue can tell; :‖
    The love that Jesus had for me
    Is more than tongue can tell.

2 The many sorrows that He bore,
And oh, that crown of thorns He wore
That I might live for evermore,
    Is more than tongue can tell.

3 The peace I have in Him, my Lord,
Who pleads before the throne of God
The merit of His precious blood,
    Is more than tongue can tell.

4 The joy that comes when He is near,
The rest He gives so free from fear,
The hope in Him so bright and clear,
    Is more than tongue can tell.

216

ALL-seeing, gracious Lord—
My heart before Thee lies;
All sin of thought and life abhorred,
My soul to Thee would rise.

CHO.—Hear Thou my prayer, O God,
Unite my heart to Thee;
Beneath Thy love, beneath Thy rod,
From sin deliver me.

2 Thou knowest all my need,
My inmost thought dost see;
Ah, Lord! from all allurements freed,
Like Thee transformed I'd be.

3 Thou holy blessèd One,
To me, I pray, draw near;
My spirit fill, O heavenly Son,
With loving, Godly fear.

4 Bind Thou my life to Thine,
To me Thy life is given;
While I my all to Thee resign,
Thou art my all in heaven.

217

SAY, is your lamp burning, my brother?
I pray you look quickly and see;
For if it were burning, then surely
Some beam would fall brightly on me.
There are many and many around you,
Who follow wherever you go,
If you thought that they walked in the shadow,
Your lamp would burn brighter. I know.

CHO.—Say, is your lamp burning, my brother?
I pray you look quickly and see;
For if it were burning, then surely
Some beam would fall brightly on me!

2 Upon the dark mountains they stumble;
They are bruised on the rocks, and they lie
With white, pleading faces turned upward,
To the clouds and the pitiful sky.

There is many a lamp that is lighted--
  We behold them anear and afar;
But not many among them, my brother,
  Shine steadily on like a star.

3 If once all the lamps that are lighted
  Should steadily blaze in a line,
Wide over the land and the ocean,
  What a girdle of glory would shine!
How all the dark places would brighten!
  How the mists would roll up and away!
How the earth would laugh out in her gladness,
  To hail the millennial day!

218

OUR way is often rugged
  While here on earth we roam,
And thorns are in the pathway,
  But we are going home.

Cho.—We're going, going,
    Yes, we are going home;
  We soon shall cross the river,
    And be with Christ at home.

2 To Marah's bitter waters
  We oft have murmuring come,
But God the cup has sweetened,
  And so we're going home.

3 When of the desert weary,
  Our God His grace has shown,
By resting us at Elim,
  With sweet fore-tastes of home.

4 With hunger often fainting,
  We've made complaining moan;
But, fed by heavenly manna,
  We still are going home.

5 Some stand to-day on Nebo,
  The journey nearly done,
And some are in the valley,
  But all are going home.

219

BROTHER, art thou worn and weary,
   Tempted, tried, and sore oppressed?
Listen to the word of Jesus,
  "Come unto me, and rest!"

REF.—||:"Come unto me, and rest!":||
   Come, ye weary, heavy-laden,
  "Come unto me, and rest!"

2 Oh, He knows the dark forebodings
   Of the conscience-troubled breast;
And to such His word is given,
  "Come unto me, and rest!"

3 To the Lord bring all your burden,
   Put the promise to the test;
Hear Him say, your Burden-Bearer,
  "Come unto me, and rest!"

4 If in sorrow thou art weeping,
   Grieving for the loved ones missed,
Surely then to you He whispers,
  "Come unto me, and rest!"

5 Trust to Him for all thy future,
   He will give thee what is best;
Why then fear when He is saying,
  "Come unto me, and rest!"

———

220

THEY'RE gathering homeward from every land,
   One by one! one by one!
As their weary feet touch the shining strand,
   Yes, one by one!
They rest with the Saviour, they wait their crown,
Their travel-stained garments are all laid down;
They wait the white raiment the Lord shall prepare
For all who the glory with Him shall share.

REF.—Gathering home! gathering home!
   Fording the river one by one!
Gathering home! gathering home!
   Yes, one by one!

2 Before they rest they pass through the strife,
        One by one! one by one!
  Through the waters of death they enter life,
        Yes, one by one!
To some are the floods of the river still,
As they ford on their way to the heavenly hill;
The waves to others run fiercely and wild
Yet they reach the home of the undefiled.

3 We too must come to the riverside,
        One by one! one by one!
  We are nearer its waters each eventide,
        Yes, one by one!
We can hear the noise of a dashing stream,
Oft now and again, through our life's deep dream;
Some times the dark floods all the banks overflow,
Sometimes in ripples and small waves go.

4 Oh, Jesus, Redeemer, we look to Thee,
        One by one! one by one!
  We lift up our voices tremblingly,
        Yes, one by one!
The waves of the river are dark and cold,
But we know the place where our feet shall hold;
O Thou who didst pass through the deepest mid-
        night,
Now guide us, and send us the staff and light.

221

ONLY a little while
    Of walking with weary feet,
Patiently over the thorny way
    That leads to the golden street.

2 Suffer, if God shall will,
    And work for Him while we may,
From Calvary's cross to Zion's crown,
    Is only a little way.

3 Only a little while,
    For toiling a few short days,
And then comes the rest, the quiet rest,
    Eternity's endless praise.

222

I HEAR the words of Jesus,
    They speak of peace with God;
I see the lamb, Christ Jesus,
    Who bore my heavy load;
I trust the blood of Jesus,
    From sin it sets me free,
I love the name of Jesus,
    Who gave Himself for me.

2 His word divinely blesséd,
    It shows me what I am;
His cross it brings salvation,
    The victim was the Lamb;
His blood procureth pardon,
    And justifies the soul,
His name, how sweet and precious,
    It makes the sinner whole.

3 Oh! hear the words of Jesus,
    The tidings are for thee;
Oh! clasp the cross of Jesus,
    And there for refuge flee;
Oh! trust the blood of Jesus,
    Be saved this very hour;
Oh! love the name of Jesus,
    Blest name of wondrous power.

———

223

M Y soul is happy all day long—
    Jesus is my Saviour;
And all my life is full of song—
    Jesus died for me.

CHO.—Hallelujah! Hallelujah!
    To the loving Lamb for sinners slain
Hallelujah! Hallelujah!
    To the Lamb who lives again.

2 My heavy load of sin is gone—
    Jesus is my Saviour;
At His dear cross I laid it down—
    Jesus died for me.

3 I heard the voice of mercy call—
   Jesus is my Saviour;
 I simply trusted, that was all—
   Jesus died for me.

4 Now will I tell it all around—
   Jesus is my Saviour;
 How sweet a blessing I have found—
   Jesus died for me.

224

SAD and weary, lone and dreary,
   Lord, I would Thy call obey;
Thee believing, Christ receiving,
   I would come to Thee to-day.

CHO.—I am coming, I am coming,
      Coming, Saviour to be blessed;
   I am coming, I am coming,
      Coming, Lord, to Thee for rest.

2 Thou, the Holy, meek and lowly,
   Jesus, unto Thee I come;
Keep me ever, let me never
   From Thy blesséd keeping roam.

3 Here abiding, in Thee hiding,
   Seeks my weary soul to rest,
Till the dawning of the morning,
   When I wake among the blest.

4 Be Thou near me, keep and cheer me,
   Through life's dark and stormy way;
Turn my sadness into gladness,
   Turn my darkness into day.

225

I SAW a way-worn traveler
   In tattered garments clad,
And struggling up the mountain,
   It seemed that he was sad;
His back was laden heavy,
   His strength was almost gone,
Yet he shouted as he journeyed,
   Deliverance will come.

CHO.—Then palms of victory, crowns of glory,
Palms of victory I shall bear.

2 The summer sun was shining,
The sweat was on his brow,
His garments worn and dusty,
His steps seemed very slow;
But he kept pressing onward,
For he was wending home;
Still shouting as he journeyed,
Deliverance will come.

3 The songsters in the arbor,
That stood beside the way,
Attracted his attention,
Inviting his delay;
His watchword being "Onward!"
He stopped his ears and ran,
Still shouting as he journeyed,
Deliverance will come.

4 I saw him in the evening,
The sun was bending low,
He'd overtopped the mountain,
And reached the vale below;
He saw the golden city,—
His everlasting home,—
And shouted loud, Hosanna,
Deliverance will come!

5 While gazing on that city,
Just o'er the narrow flood,
A band of holy angels
Came from the throne of God:
They bore him on their pinions
Safe o'er the dashing foam;
And joined him in his triumph,—
Deliverance had come!

6 I heard the song of triumph
They sang upon that shore,
Saying, Jesus has redeemed us
To suffer nevermore:

Then, casting his eyes backward
On the race which he had run,
He shouted loud, Hosanna,
Deliverance has come!

226

JESUS, my Lord, to Thee I cry,
 Unless Thou help me I must die;
Oh, bring Thy free salvation nigh,
 And take me as I am.

Cho.—||: Take me as I am, :||
 Lord, I give myself to thee,
 Oh, take me as I am.

2 Helpless I am and full of guilt,
But yet for me Thy blood was spilt;
And Thou canst make me what Thou wilt,
 And take me as I am.

3 I bow before Thy mercy-seat,
Behold me, Saviour, at Thy feet;
Thy work begin, Thy work complete,
 And take me as I am.

4 If Thou hast work for me to do,
Inspire my will, my heart renew;
And work both in, and by me too,
 And take me as I am.

5 And when at last the work is done,
The battle fought, the victory won;
Still, still my cry shall be alone,
 Oh, take me as I am.

227

ONCE more we come, God's word to hear,
 The word so pure and holy;
Now grant us, Lord, a list'ning ear,
 A spirit meek and lowly;
For if we hear, and heed it not,
 We hear for condemnation;
For "doers of the word," we're taught,
 Are heirs of Christ's salvation.

2 The life of God is in the word;
 And whosoe'er believeth,

The record there of Christ the Lord
　Eternal life receiveth;
But if we hear, believing not,
　We hear for condemnation;
For "doers of the word," we're taught,
　Are heirs of Christ's salvation.

3 The word of God, by faith received,
　　Imparts regeneration;
And he who hath in Christ believed
　Lives out a new creation;
But if we hear, and do it not,
　We hear for condemnation;
For "doers of the word," we're taught,
　Are heirs of Christ's salvation.

4 So when the word of God we hear,
　　Let us be humbly pleading
The Holy Ghost to give us light,
　As we the word are heeding;
But if we hear, and feel it not,
　We hear for condemnation;
For "doers of the word," we're taught,
　Are heirs of Christ's salvation.

228

WE praise Thee and bless Thee,
　Our Father in heaven,
For the joy of salvation
　Thy gospel hath given.

CHO.—Hallelujah! we praise Thee
　Through Jesus our Lord;
Hallelujah! we bless Thee
　For the gift of Thy word!

2 We praise Thee and bless Thee:
　Once sinful and sad,
By the word thou hast given,
　To Christ we were led.

3 We praise Thee and bless Thee:
　The Spirit hath come
To dwell with, and teach us,
　And guide us safe home.

4 We praise Thee and bless Thee,
   For food by the way;
The manna from heaven
   Provided each day.

5 We praise Thee and bless Thee:
   Thy word hath gone forth,
That Christ shall be King and
   Reign over the earth,

6 We praise Thee and bless Thee,
   And wait His return
To fulfil every promise
   He made to his own.

7 We praise Thee and bless Thee:
   We'll reign with Him then,
To praise Thee and bless Thee
   For ever.   AMEN.

229

MY God and Father, while I stray
   Far from my home, on life's rough way,
Oh, teach me from my heart to say,
   "Thy will be done!"

REF.—||: Thy will be done! :||
   Oh, teach me from my heart to say,
   "Thy will be done!"

2 What though in lonely grief I sigh
   For friends beloved, no longer nigh,
Submissive still would I reply,
   "Thy will be done!"

REF.—||: Thy will be done! :||
   Submissive still would I reply,
   "Thy will be done!"

3 Let but my fainting heart be blest
   With Thy sweet Spirit for its guest,
My God, to Thee I leave the rest,
   "Thy will be done!"

REF.—||: Thy will be done! :||
   My God, to Thee I leave the rest,
   "Thy will be done!"

4 Renew my will from day to day;
　Blend it with Thine; and take away
　All now that makes it hard to say,
　　"Thy will be done!"

REF.—‖: Thy will be done! :‖
　All now that makes it hard to say,
　"Thy will be done!"

5 Then when on earth I breathe no more
　The prayer oft mixed with tears before,
　I'll sing upon a happier shore,
　　"Thy will be done!"

REF.—‖: Thy will be done! :‖
　I'll sing upon a happier shore,
　"Thy will be done!"

230

IN Thy cleft, O Rock of Ages,
　　Hide Thou me;
When the fitful tempest rages,
　　Hide Thou me;
Where no mortal arm can sever
From my heart Thy love forever,
Hide me, O Thou Rock of Ages,
　　Safe in Thee.

2 From the snare of sinful pleasure,
　　Hide Thou me;
Thou, my soul's eternal treasure,
　　Hide Thou me;
When the world its power is wielding,
And my heart is almost yielding,
Hide me, O Thou Rock of Ages,
　　Safe in Thee.

3 In the lonely night of sorrow,
　　Hide Thou me;
Till in glory dawns the morrow,
　　Hide Thou me;
In the sight of Jordan's billow,
Let Thy bosom be my pillow;
Hide me, O Thou Rock of Ages,
　　Safe in Thee.

231

WHEN the King in His beauty shall come to His throne,
And around Him are gathered His loved ones, His own;
There be some who will knock at His fair palace door,
To be answered within, "There is mercy no more."

Cho.—||: "I have never known you,":||
    "I have never, I have never,
      I have never known you."

2 They had known whence He came, and the grace which
    He brought;
  In their presence He healed, in their streets He had taught,
  They had mentioned His name and their friendship pro-
    fessed;
  But they never believed, for of them He confessed:

3 Now the righteous are reigning with Abraham there;
  But for these is appointed an endless despair:
  It is vain that they call: He once knocked at their gate,
  But they welcomed Him not; so now this is their fate:

4 O sinner, give heed to this story of gloom,
  For the hour is fast nearing that fixes your doom:
  Will you still reject mercy? still harden your heart?
  Oh, then, what will you do as the King cries—"Depart!"

232

I AM waiting for the morning
  Of the blessèd day to dawn,
When the sorrow and the sadness
  Of this changeful life are gone.

Cho.—I am waiting, only waiting,
    Till this weary life is o'er;
  Only waiting for my welcome,
    From my Saviour on the other shore.

2 I am waiting; worn and weary
    With the battle and the strife,
Hoping when the warfare's over
    To receive a crown of life.

3 Waiting, hoping, trusting ever,
    For a home of boundless love;

Like a pilgrim, looking forward
To the land of bliss above.

4 Hoping soon to meet the loved ones
Where the " many mansions " be;
Listening for the happy welcome
Of my Saviour calling me.

233

HEAVENLY Father, we Thy children,
Gathered round our risen Lord,
Lift our hearts in earnest pleading:
Oh, revive us by Thy word !

CHO.—Send refreshing, send refreshing
From Thy presence, gracious Lord!
Send refreshing, send refreshing,
And revive us by Thy word !

2 Gracious gales of heavenly blessing
In Thy love to us afford;
Let us feel Thy Spirit's presence,
Oh, revive us by Thy word!

3 Weak and weary in the conflict,
"Wrestling not with flesh and blood,"
Help us, Lord, as faint we falter;
Oh, revive us by Thy word !

4 With Thy strength, O Master, gird us,
Be our Guide and be our Guard;
Fill us with Thy holy Spirit,
Oh, revive us by Thy word!

234

JESUS is coming! sing the glad word!
Coming for those He redeemed by His blood,
Coming to reign as the glorified Lord !
Jesus is coming again!

CHO.—Jesus is coming, is coming again!
Jesus is coming again!
Shout the glad tidings o'er mountain and plain!
Jesus is coming again!

2 Jesus is coming! the dead shall arise,
  Loved ones shall meet in a joyful surprise,
  Caught up together to Him in the skies.
    Jesus is coming again.

3 Jesus is coming! His saints to release;
  Coming to give to the warring earth peace:
  Sinning, and sighing, and sorrow, shall cease.
    Jesus is coming again!

4 Jesus is coming! the promise is true;
  Who are the chosen, the faithful, the few,
  Waiting and watching, prepared for review?
    Jesus is coming again!

235

WE are children of a King,
    Heavenly King,   Heavenly King,
We are children of a King,
  Singing as we journey;
Jesus Christ our Guard and Guide,
  Bids us, nothing terrified,
Follow closely at His side,
  Singing as we journey.

2 We are traveling to our home,
    Blesséd home,   Blesséd home,
  We are traveling to our home,
    Singing as we journey;
  Toward a city out of sight,
    Where will fall no shade of night,
  For our Saviour is its light,
    Singing as we journey.

3 Full of joy we onward go,
    Heavenward go,   Heavenward go,
  Full of joy we onward go
    Singing as we journey;
  Singing all the journey through—
    Singing hearts are brave and true—
  Singing till our home we view,
    Singing as we journey.

236

WHO is on the Lord's side?
  Who will serve the King?
Who will be His helpers,
  Other lives to bring?
Who will leave the world's side?
  Who will face the foe?
Who is on the Lord's side?
  Who for Him will go?

CHO.—Who is on the Lord's side?
    Who will serve the King?
  Who will be His helpers,
    Other lives to bring?
  By Thy grand redemption,
    By Thy grace divine,
  We are on the Lord's side;
    Saviour, we are Thine.

2 Not for weight of glory,
    Not for crown and palm,
  Enter we the army,
    Raise the warrior-psalm;
  But for love that claimeth
    Lives for whom He died,
  He whom Jesus nameth
    Must be on His side.

3 Jesus, Thou hast bought us,
    Not with gold or gem,
  But with Thine own life-blood,
    For Thy diadem;
  With Thy blessing filling
    All who come to Thee,
  Thou hast made us willing,
    Thou hast made us free.

4 Fierce may be the conflict,
    Strong may be the foe,
  But the King's own army,
    None can overthrow;
  Round His standard ranging,
    Victory is secure,
  For His truth unchanging
    Makes the triumph sure.

237

TRAVELING to the better land,
  O'er the desert's scorching sand,
Father: let me grasp Thy hand;
  Lead me on, lead me on!

2 When at Marah, parched with heat,
  I the sparkling fountain greet,
Make the bitter waters sweet;
  Lead me on, lead me on!

3 When the wilderness is drear,
  Show me Elim's palm-groves near,
And her wells as crystal clear;
  Lead me on, lead me on!

4 Through the water, through the fire,
  Never let me fall or tire,
Every step brings Canaan nigher:
  Lead me on, lead me on!

5 Bid me stand on Nebo's height,
  Gaze upon the land of light,
Then transported with the sight,
  Lead me on, lead me on!

6 When I stand on Jordan's brink,
  Never let me fear or shrink;
Hold me, Father, lest I sink;
  Lead me on, lead me on!

7 When the victory is won,
  And eternal life begun,
Up to glory lead me on!
  Lead me on, lead me on!

238

LOOK unto Me and be ye saved,
  I heard the Just One say;
And as by faith on Him I gazed,
  My burden rolled away.

Cho.—I've passed the cross at Calvary,
  I'm on the Heaven side;
‖: The world is crucified to me,
  Since Christ my ransom died. :‖

2 By His atonement reconciled,
   My Father's face I see;
   The empty tomb now intervenes
   Between the world and me.

3 Oh, glorious height of vantage ground!
   Oh, blest victorious hour!
   In Him to trust and fully know
   His resurrection power.

239

NO works of law have we to boast,
   By nature ruined, guilty, lost;
Condemned already, but Thy hand
Provided what Thou didst demand.

CHO.—‖: We take the guilty sinner's name,
      The guilty sinner's Saviour claim. :‖

2 No faith we bring, 'tis Christ alone,
   'Tis what He is—what He has done;
   He is for us as given by God,
   It was for us He shed His blood.

3 We do not *feel* our sins are gone,
   We know it by Thy word alone;
   We know that there our sins didst lay
   On Him who has put sin away.

4 Because we know our sins forgiven,
   We happy feel—our home is heaven;
   O help us now as sons of God,
   To tread the path that Jesus trod.

240

THERE is love, true love, and the heart grows warm,
   When the Lord to Bethany comes.
And the word of life has a wondrous charm,
   When the Lord to Bethany comes.
There is joy, glad joy, and a feast is spread,
   When the Lord to Bethany comes;
For His heavenly voice brings to life the dead,
   When the Lord to Bethany comes.

CHO.—'Twas a happy, happy day in the olden time,
 When the Lord to Bethany came,
 Open wide the door, let Him enter now!
 For His love is ever the same!
||: His love is ever the same! :||
 Open wide the door, let Him enter now!
 For His love is ever the same!

2 There is peace, sweet peace, and the life grows calm,
 When the Lord to Bethany comes;
And the trusting soul sings a sweet, soft psalm,
 When the Lord to Bethany comes.
There is faith, strong faith, and our home seems near
 When the Lord to Bethany comes;
And the crown more bright, and the cross more dear,
 When the Lord to Bethany comes.

241

CHILD of sin and sorrow,
 Filled with dismay,
Wait not for to-morrow,
 Yield thee to-day:
Heaven bids thee come,
 While yet there's room;
Child of sin and sorrow,
 Hear and obey.

2 Child of sin and sorrow,
 Why wilt thou die?
Come while thou canst borrow
 Help from on high;
Grieve not that love
 Which from above,
Child of sin and sorrow,
 Would bring thee nigh.

242

LORD, my trust I repose in Thee;
 O how great is Thy love to me!
Thou the strength of my life shalt be;
 This I know, this I know.

REF.—Thine, Thine, and only Thine,
 Now and ever Thine;
Thou dost love me, Saviour mine;
 This I know, this I know.

2 Thou dost lead with a sweet command,
    Thou dost lead with a gentle hand;
On the rock of Thy Truth I stand;
    This I know, this I know.

3 I shall rise to a world of light,
    I shall rest in a mansion bright;
Then my faith shall be lost in sight;
    This I know, this I know.

243

NOT what these hands have done,
    Can save this guilty soul;
Not what this toiling flesh has borne,
    Can make my spirit whole.

Ref.—Thy work alone, my Saviour,
    Can ease this weight of sin;
Thy blood alone, O Lamb of God,
    Can give me peace within.

2 Not what I feel or do,
    Can give me peace with God;
Not all my prayers, nor sighs, nor tears,
    Can ease my awful load,

3 Thy love to me, O God,
    Not mine, O Lord, to Thee,
Can rid me of this dark unrest,
    And set my spirit free.

4 No other work save Thine,
    No meaner blood will do;
No strength, save that which is divine,
    Can bear me safely through.

5 I praise the God of grace,
    I trust His love and might;
He calls me His, I call Him mine,
    My God, my joy, my light!

244

MY life flows on in endless song;
    Above earth's lamentation,
I hear the sweet, though far-off, hymn
    That hails a new creation:

Through all the tumult and the strife
  I hear the music ringing;
It finds an echo in my soul—
  How can I keep from singing?

2 What though my joys and comfort die?
  The Lord my Saviour liveth;
What though the darkness gather round?
  Songs in the night He giveth;
No storm can shake my inmost calm
  While to that refuge clinging,
Since Christ is Lord of heaven and earth,
  How can I keep from singing?

3 I lift my eyes; the cloud grow thin;
  I see the blue above it;
And day by day this pathway smooths,
  Since first I learned to love it;
The peace of Christ makes fresh my heart,
  A fountain ever springing;
All things are mine since I am His—
  How can I keep from singing?

245

ONCE again the Gospel message
  From the Saviour you have heard;
Will you heed the invitation?
  Will you turn and seek the Lord?

CHO.—||: Come believing! come believing!
  Come to Jesus, look and live! :||

2 Many summers you have wasted,
  Ripened harvests you have seen;
Winter snows by Spring have melted,
  Yet you linger in your sin.

3 Jesus for your choice is waiting;
  Tarry not: at once decide!
While the Spirit now is striving,
  Yield, and seek the Saviour's side.

4 Cease of fitness to be thinking;
  Do not longer try to feel;
It is *trusting* and not *feeling*,
  That will give the Spirit's seal.

5 Let your will to God be given,
    Trust in Christ's atoning blood;
Look to Jesus now in heaven,
    Rest on His unchanging word.

246

SOUND the alarm! let the watchman cry!—
   "Up! for the day of the Lord is nigh;
Who will escape from the wrath to come?
Who have a place in the soul's bright home?"

REF.—Sound the alarm, watchman, sound the alarm!
    For the Lord will come with a conquering arm;
    And the hosts of sin, as their ranks advance,
    Shall wither and fall at His glance.

2 Sound the alarm! let the cry go forth,
Swift as the wind, o'er the realms of earth;
Flee to the Rock where the soul may hide!
Flee to the Rock! in its cleft abide.

3 Sound the alarm on the mountain's brow!
Plead with the lost by the wayside now;
Warn them to come and the truth embrace;
Urge them to come and be saved by grace,

4 Sound the alarm in the youthful ear,
Sound it aloud that the old may hear;
Blow ye the trump while the day-beams last!
Blow ye the trump till the light is past!

247

BEAUTIFUL morning! Day of hope,
    Dawn of a better life;
Now in thy peaceful hours we rest,
    Far from earth's noise and strife.

CHO.—Morning of resurrection joy,
    Day when the Saviour rose,
    Singing shall greet thy opening hour,
    Singing shall mark thy close.

2 Beautiful morning! All the week
    Waiteth thy welcome light,
Since the first dawning, calm and clear,
    Out of the darkest night.

3 Beautiful morning!   Grief and pain,
　　Weeping before the tomb,
　Fly at thy dawning, Jesus rose,
　　Jesus dispelled the gloom.

248

'TWILL not be long our journey here,
　　Each broken sigh and falling tear
　Will soon be gone, and all will be
　A cloudless sky, a waveless sea.

REF.—Roll on, dark stream,
　　　We dread not thy foam;
　　The Pilgrim is longing
　　　For home, sweet home.

2 'Twill not be long the yearning heart
　　May feel its every hope depart,
　And grief be mingled with its song;
　We'll meet again, 'twill not be long.

3 Though sad we mark the closing eye,
　Of those we loved in days gone by,
　Yet sweet in death their latest song—
　We'll meet again, 'twill not be long.

4 These checkered wilds, with thorns o'erspread,
　Through which our way so oft is led—
　This march of time, with truth so strong,
　Will end in bliss, 'twill not be long.

249

'TIS known on earth, in heaven too,
　　'Tis sweet to me because 'tis true;
　The "old, old story" is ever new;
　　Tell me more about Jesus.

CHO.—‖: "Tell me more about Jesus!" :‖
　　　Him would I know who loved me so;
　　"Tell me more about Jesus!"

2 Earth's fairest flowers will droop and die,
　Dark clouds o'erspread yon azure sky;
　Life's dearest joys flit fleetest by;
　　Tell me more about Jesus.

3 When overwhelmed with unbelief,
  When burdened with a blinding grief,
  Come kindly then to my relief;
    Tell me more about Jesus.

4 And when the Glory-land I see,
  And take the "place prepared" for me,
  Through endless years my song shall be—
    "Tell me more about Jesus."

250

THE word of God is given
  To all who serve Him here,
That when the Lord from heaven
  In glory shall appear,
We then shall be delivered
  From sorrow, sin, and pain;
And if for Christ we suffer,
  With Him we then shall reign.

CHO.—We are going home to Jesus!
    Going home to Jesus!
    Going to the mansions
      He's preparing there on high!
    We are going home to Jesus!
    Going home to Jesus!
    And we'll gather there in glory,
      By and by!

2 Once in our sin we wandered
    Far, far away from God,
  And precious hours we squandered
    Upon the downward road;
  But God in grace hath called us,
    And given us to share
  The purchase of our Saviour,
    A mansion bright and fair.

3 Now with this hope to cheer us,
    And with the Spirit's seal,
  That all our sins were pardoned,
    Through Him whose stripes did heal;
  As "strangers" and as "pilgrims,"
    No place on earth we own,
  But work and watch as "servants,"
    Until our Lord shall come.

251

TO Him who for our sins was slain,
  To Him for all His dying pain.

REF.—Hallelujah, hallelujah,
    Hallelujah to His name.

2 To Him, the Lamb, our Sacrifice,
Who gave His life the ransomed price.

3 To Him who died that we might die
To sin and live with Him on high.

4 To Him who rose that we might rise,
And reign with Him beyond the skies.

5 To Him who now for us doth plead,
And helpeth us in all our need.

6 To Him who doth prepare on high,
Our home in immortality.

7 To Him be glory evermore!
Ye heavenly hosts, your Lord adore.

252

THE sands of time are sinking,
  The dawn of heaven breaks,
The summer morn I've sighed for—
  The fair, sweet morn awakes:
Dark, dark hath been the midnight,
  But day-spring is at hand,
And glory, glory dwelleth
  In Immanuel's land.

2 I've wrestled on toward heaven,
  'Gainst storm and wind and tide,
Now, like a weary traveler
  That leaneth on his guide;
Amid the shades of evening,
  While sinks life lingering sand,
I hail the glory dawning
  From Immanuel's land.

3 Deep waters crossed life's pathway,
  The hedge of thorns was sharp;
Now these lie all behind me—
  O! for a well-tuned harp!

O, to join the hallelujah
With yon triumphant band!
Who sing where glory dwelleth
In Immanuel's land.

253

I KNOW that my Redeemer lives!
 What comfort this sweet message gives!
He lives, who once was dead;
He lives, all-glorious in the sky;
He lives, exalted there on high,
 My everlasting Head.

Cho.—‖ He lives! He lives!
 I know that my Redeemer lives! :‖

2 He lives, to bless me with His love;
He lives, to plead for me above,
 My hungry soul to feed;
He lives, to grant me rich supply;
He lives, to guide me with His eye,
 To help in time of need.

3 He lives, triumphant from the grave;
He lives, eternally to save;
 And while He lives I'll sing;
He lives, my ever faithful Friend;
He lives, and loves me to the end,
 My Prophet, Priest, and King!

4 He lives, my mansion to prepare;
He lives to bring me safely there;
 My Jesus still the same:
What joy this blest assurance gives!
"I know that my Redeemer lives:"
 All glory to His name!

254

"A LITTLE while!" and He shall come;
 The hour draws on apace,
The blesséd hour, the glorious morn,
 When we shall see His face:
How light our trials then will seem!
How short our pilgrim way!
Our life on earth a fitful dream,
 Dispelled by dawning day!

Cho.—Then come, Lord Jesus, quickly come,
　　　In glory and in light!
　　　Come, take Thy longing children home,
　　　And end earth's weary night!

2 "A little while!" with patience, Lord,
　　I fain would ask, "How long?"
　For how can I with such a hope
　　Of glory and of home,
　With such a joy awaiting me,
　　Not wish the hour were come?
　How can I keep the longing back,
　　And how suppress the groan?

3 Yet peace, my heart! and hush, my tongue!
　　Be calm, my troubled breast!
　Each passing hour is hastening on
　　The everlasting rest:
　Thou knowest well—the time thy God
　　Appoints for thee is best:
　The morning star will soon arise;
　　The glow is in the East.

255

PRECIOUS Saviour, may I live,
　　Only for Thee!
Spend the powers Thou dost give,
　　Only for Thee!
Be my spirit's deep desire,
　　Only for Thee!
May my intellect aspire,
　　Only for Thee!

Cho.—Only Christ who died for me
　　　Paid the price and made me free,
　　　Now, and through eternity,
　　　　Only for Thee!

2 In my joys may I rejoice
　　　Only for Thee!
　In my choosing make my choice,
　　　Only for Thee!
　Meekly may I suffer grief,
　　　Only for Thee!
　Gratefully accept relief,
　　　Only for Thee!

3 Be my smiles and be my tears,
  Only for Thee!
Be my young and riper years,
  Only for Thee!
Be my peace and be my strife,
  Only for Thee!
Be my love and be my life,
  Only for Thee!

256

ONLY waiting till the shadows
  Are a little longer grown;
Only waiting till the glimmer
  Of the day's last beam is flown;
Till the night of death has faded
  From the heart once full of day;
Till the stars of heaven are breaking
  Through the twilight soft and gray.

2 Only waiting till the reapers
  Have the last sheaf gathered home;
For the summer time has faded
  And the autumn winds have come.
Quickly, reapers! gather quickly,
  All the ripe hours of my heart;
For the bloom of life is withered,
  And I hasten to depart.

3 Only waiting till the angels
  Open wide the pearly gate,
At whose portals long I've lingered,
  Weary, poor, and desolate:
Even now I hear their footsteps,
  And their voices far away;
If they call me, I am waiting,
  Only waiting to obey.

4 Waiting for a brighter dwelling
  Than I ever yet have seen,
Where the tree of life is blooming,
  And the fields are ever green:
Waiting for my full redemption,
  When my Saviour shall restore
All that sin has caused to wither;
  Age and sorrow come no more.

257

ONCE more, my soul, thy Saviour, through the
Word,
Is offered full and free;
And now, O Lord, I must, I must decide;
Shall I accept of Thee?

CHO.—I will! I will! I will, God helping me,
I will, I will be Thine!
Thy precious blood was shed to purchase me—
I will be wholly Thine!

2 By grace I will Thy mercy now receive,
Thy love my heart hath won;
On Thee, O Christ, I will, I will believe,
And trust in Thee alone!

3 Thou knowest, Lord, how very weak I am,
And how I fear to stray;
For strength to serve I look to Thee alone—
The strength Thou must supply!

4 And now, O Lord, give all with us to-day
The grace to join our song;
And from the heart to gladly with us say:
"I WILL to Christ belong!"

5 To all who came, when Thou wast here below,
And said, "O Lord, wilt Thou?"
To them "I will!" was ever Thy reply;
We rest upon it now.

258

IT'S a bonnie, bonnie warl' that we're livin' in the noo,
An sunny is the lan' that noo we aften traiv'll throo;
But in vain we look for something here to which oor
hearts may cling,
For its beauty is as naething tae the palace o' the King.
We like the gilded simmer, wi' its merry, merry tread,
An' we sigh when hoary winter lays its beauties wi' the
dead;   [ter's wing,
For tho' bonnie are the snawflakes, an' the doon on Win-
It's fine to ken it daurna touch the palace o' the King.

2 Then again, I've juist been thinkin' that when a'thing
here's sae bright,   [licht,
The sun in a' its grandeur, an' the mune wi' quiverin'

The ocean i' the simmer; or the woodland i' the spring,
What maun it be up yonner i' the palace o' the King.
It's here we hae oor trials, an' it's here that He prepares
His chosen for the raiment which the ransomed sinner
    wears.
An' its here that He wad hear us 'mid oor tribulations
    sing,
"We'll trust oor God wha' reigneth i' the palace o' the
    King.

3 Oh! its honor heaped on honor that His courtiers should
    be ta'en
Frae the wand'rin' anes He died for i' this warl' o' sin an'
    pain.
An' its fu'est love an' service that the Christians aye
    should bring
To the feet o' Him wha reigneth i' the palace o' the King.
The time for sawin' seed, it is a wearin', wearin' dune;
An' the time for winnin' souls will be ower vera sune.
Then lat us a' be active, if a fruitfu' sheaf we'd bring
To adorn the Royal table i' the palace o' the King.

4 Then let us trust Him better than we've ever dune afore,
For the King will feed His servants frae His ever boun-
    teous store:
Lat us keep a closer grip o' Him, for time is on the wing,
An' sune He'll come an' tak' us tae the palace o' the King.
It's iv'ry halls are bonnie upon which the rainbows
    shine,
An' its Eden bow'rs are trellised wi' a never fadin' Vine;
An' the pearly gates o' Heaven, do a glorious radiance
    fling,
On the starry floor that shimmers i' the palace o' the
    King.

5 Nae nicht shall be in Heaven, an' nae desolatin' sea,
And nae tyrant hoofs shall trample i' the city o' the free;
There's an everlastin' daylicht, an' a never fadin' spring,
Where the Lamb is a' the glory i' the palace o' the King.
We see our freen's await us ower yonner at His gate;
Then lat us a' be ready, for ye ken its gettin' late;
Let oor lamps be brichtly burnin'; let us raise oor voice
    and sing,
For sune we'll meet, to pairt nae mair, i' the palace o' the
    King.

259

"REDEEMED!" "redeemed!"
 Oh, sing the joyful strain!
Give praise; give praise
 And glory to His name;
Who gave His blood our souls to save,
||: And purchased freedom for the slave!:||

CHO.—"Redeemed!" redeemed from sin and all its woe!
"Redeemed!" redeemed eternal life to know!
"Redeemed!" redeemed by Jesus' blood,
"Redeemed!" redeemed! Oh, praise the Lord!

2 What grace! what grace!
   That He who calmed the wave,
  Should stoop, my soul,
   My guilty soul to save!
  That He the curse should bear for me,
||: A sinful wretch, His enemy! :||

3 "Redeemed!" redeemed!
   The word has brought repose,
  And joy, and joy
   That each redeemed one knows,
  Who sees his sins on Jesus laid,
||: And knows His blood the ransom paid. :||

4 "Redeemed!" redeemed?
   O joy, that I should be
  In Christ, in Christ,
   From sin forever free!
  Forever free to praise His name,
||: Who bore for me the guilt and shame! :||

260

———

GOD is great, and God is good,
 And we thank Him for this food:
By His hand must all be fed,
Give us, Lord, our daily bread.

261

———

MASTER, the tempest is raging!
 The billows are tossing high!
The sky is o'ershadowed with blackness,
 No shelter or help is nigh;

"Carest Thou not that we perish?"—
How canst Thou lie asleep,
When each moment so madly is threatening
A grave in the angry deep?

CHO.—The winds and the waves shall obey My will,
"Peace, be still!"
Whether the wrath of the storm-tossed sea,
Or demons, or men, or whatever it be,
No water can swallow the ship where lies
The Master of ocean and earth and skies;
||: They all shall sweetly obey My will;
"Peace, be still!" :||

2 Master, with anguish of spirit
I bow in my grief to-day;
The depths of my sad heart are troubled;
Oh, waken and save, I pray!
Torrents of sin and of anguish
Sweep o'er my sinking soul;
And I perish! I perish! dear Master;
Oh! hasten, and take control.

3 Master, the terror is over,
The elements sweetly rest;
Earth's sun in the calm lake is mirrored,
And heaven's within my breast;
Linger, O blesséd Redeemer,
Leave me alone no more;
And with joy I shall make the blest harbor,
And rest on the blissful shore.

262

O WHAT shall I do to be saved?
The gathering storm I behold,
Exposed to the wrath of my God;
||: Is there no sheltering fold? :||

CHO.—||: I am the door, by me if any man enter in,
He shall be saved, he shall be saved. :||

2 O what shall I do to be saved?
No light, no hope, can I see,
No help in myself can I find;
||: Is there no mercy for me? :||

3 O what shall I do to be saved?
    So vile, so burdened with sin,
O how to the fold may I come,
    ||: How may I enter therein? :||

4 I enter the wide open door,
    In Christ I *now* have believed;
I'm cleansed from my sins by His **blood;**
    ||: I trust and *now* I am saved! :||

263

JESUS, I my cross have taken,
    All to leave and follow Thee;
Naked, poor, despised, forsaken,
    Thou from hence my all shalt be.
Perish every fond ambition,
    All I've sought, or hoped, or **known,**
Yet how rich is my condition,
    God and heaven are still my own.

2 Let the world despise and leave me,
    They have left my Saviour too;
Human hearts and looks deceive me—
    Thou art not, like them, untrue;
Oh! while Thou dost smile upon me,
    God of wisdom, love, and might,
Foes may hate, and friends disown **me—**
    Show Thy face, and all is bright.

3 Haste thee on from grace to glory,
    Armed by faith, and winged by prayer!
Heaven's eternal day's before thee,
    God's own hand shall guide thee there:
Soon shall close thy earthly mission,
    Soon shall pass thy pilgrim days,
Hope shall change to glad fruition,
    Faith to sight, and prayer to praise.

264

ALONG the River of Time we glide,
    Along the River, along the River,
The swiftly flowing, resistless tide,
    The swiftly flowing, the swiftly flowing,
And soon, ah, soon, the end we'll see,
    Yes, soon 'twill come and we will be

CHO.—‖: Floating, floating,
    Out on the sea of eternity! :‖

2 Along the River of Time we glide,
    Along the River, along the River,
A thousand dangers its currents hide,
    A thousand dangers, a thousand dangers,
And near our course the rocks we see,
Oh, dreadful thought! a wreck to be,

3 Along the River of Time we glide,
    Along the River, along the River,
Our Saviour only our bark can guide,
    Our Saviour only, our Saviour only,
But with Him we secure may be,
No fear, no doubt, but joy to be

265

"TILL *He come!*"—oh, let the words
    Linger on the trembling chords;
Let "the little while" between
In their golden light be seen;
Let us think, how heaven and home
Lie beyond that *"Till He come."*

3 When the weary ones we love
Enter on their rest above,
When the words of love and cheer
Fall no longer on our ear,
Hush! be every murmur dumb!
It is only *"Till He come."*

3 Clouds and darkness round us press,
Would we have one sorrow less?
All the sharpness of the cross,
All that tells the world is loss.
Death, and darkness, and the tomb,
Pain us only *"Till He come."*

3 See the feast of love is spread,
Drink the wine and eat the bread:
Sweet memorials,—till the Lord
Call us round His heavenly board;
Some from earth, from glory some,
Severed only *"Till He come."*

166

OH, to be over yonder,
In that land of wonder,
Where the angel voices mingle, and the angel harpers ring;
To be free from pain and sorrow,
And the anxious, dread to-morrow,
To rest in light and sunshine in the presence of the King.

Cho.—Oh! to be over yonder,
In that land of wonder,
There to be forever
In the presence of the King.

2 Oh, to be over yonder!
My yearning heart grows fonder
Of looking to the east, to see the blesséd day-star bring
Some tidings of the waking,
The cloudless, pure day breaking!
My heart is yearning—yearning for the coming of the King.

3 Oh, to be over yonder!
Alas! I sigh and wonder—
Why clings my poor, weak, sinful heart to any earthly thing?
Each tie of earth must sever,
And pass away forever:
at there's no more separation in the presence of the King.

4 Oh, when shall I be dwelling
Where angel voices, swelling
In triumphant hallelujahs, make the vaulted heavers ring—
Where the pearly gates are gleaming,
And the Morning Star is beaming?
Oh, when shall I be yonder in the presence of the King.

5 Oh, I shall soon be yonder,
Though lonely here I wander,
Yearning for the welcome summer—longing for the bird's
fleet wing;
The midnight may be dreary,
And the heart be worn and weary,
But there's no more shadow yonder in the presence of the
King.

267

COME, thou weary, Jesus calls thee
　　To His wounded side;
"Come to me," saith He, "and ever
　　Safe abide."

2 Seeking Jesus? Jesus seeks thee—
　　Wants thee as thou art;
He is knocking, ever knocking
　　At thy heart.

3 If thou let Him, He will save thee—
　　Make thee all His own;
Guide thee, keep thee, take thee, dying,
　　To His throne.

4 Wilt thou still refuse His offer?
　　Wilt thou say Him nay?
Wilt thou let Him, grieved, rejected,
　　Go away?

4 Dost thou feel thy life is weary?
　　Is thy soul distressed?
Take His offer, wait no longer;
　　Be at rest!

268

MY Saviour's praises I will sing,
　　And all His love express;
Whose mercies each returning day,
　　Proclaim His faithfulness.

CHO.—||: "Every day will I bless Thee!" :||
　　And I will praise, will praise, Thy name
　　Forever and ever!

2 Redeemed by His almighty power,
　　My Saviour and my King;
My confidence in Him I place,
　　To Him my soul would cling.

3 On Thee alone, my Saviour, God,
　　My steadfast hopes depend;
And to Thy holy will my soul,
　　Submissively would bend.

4 Oh, grant Thy Holy Spirit's grace,
　　And aid my feeble powers;
　　That gladly I may follow Thee
　　Through all my future hours.

269

"ONWARD, upward, homeward!"
　　　Joyfully I flee
From this world of sorrow,
　　With my Lord to be;
Onward to the glory,
　　Upward to the prize,
Homeward to the mansions,
　　Far above the skies.

REF.—Onward to the glory,
　　　Upward to the prize,
　　Homeward to the mansions,
　　　Far above the skies.

2 "Onward, upward, homeward!"
　　Here I find no rest;
Treading o'er the desert
　　Which my Saviour pressed;
"Onward, upward, homeward!"
　　I shall soon be there,
Soon its joys and pleasures,
　　I, through grace, shall share.

3 "Onward, upward, homeward!"
　　Come along with me;
Ye who love the Saviour,
　　Bear me company;
"Onward, upward, homeward!"
　　Press with vigor on;
Yet a little moment
　　And the race is won,

270

OH, soul-tossed on the billows, afar from friendly land,
　　Look up to Him who holds thee in "The hollow of
　　His hand."

CHO.—In "The hollow of His hand,"
　　　In the hollow of His hand,
　　O how safe are all who trust Him,
　　　In "The hollow of His hand."

2 Though raging winds may drive thee, a wreck upon the
    strand,
  Still cling to Him who holds thee in "The hollow of His
    hand."

3 When strength is spent in toiling, and wearily you stand,
  Then rest in Him who holds thee in "The hollow of His
    hand."

4 When by the swelling Jordan, your feet in sinking sand,
  Remember still He holds thee in "The hollow of His
    hand."

5 And when at last we're gathered, with all the ransomed
    band,
  We'll praise our God who holds us in "The hollow of
    His hand."

271

Praise Him! praise Him! Jesus, our blesséd Redeemer!
  Sing, O earth—His wonderful love proclaim!
Hail Him! hail Him! highest arch-angels in glory;
  Strength and honor give to His holy name!
Like a shepherd, Jesus will guard His children,
  In His arms He carries them all day long;
Praise Him! praise Him! tell of His excellent greatness,
  Praise Him! praise Him! ever in joyful song!

2 Praise Him! praise Him! Jesus, our blesséd Redeemer!
  For our sins He suffered, and bled, and died;
He our rock, our hope of eternal salvation,
  Hail Him! hail Him! Jesus, the crucified.
Sound His praises! Jesus who bore our sorrows,
  Love unbounded, wonderful, deep and strong;
Praise Him! praise Him! tell of His excellent greatness,
  Praise Him! praise Him! ever in joyful song!

3 Praise Him! praise Him! Jesus, our blesséd Redeemer!
  Heavenly portals, loud with hosannas ring!
Jesus, Saviour, reigneth for ever and ever:
  Crown Him! crown Him! Prophet, and Priest, and King!
Christ is coming! over the world victorious,
  Power and glory unto the Lord belong;
Praise Him! praise Him! tell of His excellent greatness,
  Praise Him! praise Him! ever in joyful song!

272

I KNOW not why God's wondrous grace
  To me He hath made known,
Nor why—unworthy—Christ in love
Redeemed me for His own.

CHO.—But "I know whom I have believed,
      And am persuaded that he is able
      To keep that which I've committed
        Unto him against that day."

2 I know not how this saving faith
    To me He did impart,
Nor how believing in His word
Wrought peace within my heart.

3 I know not how the Spirit moves,
    Convincing men of sin,
Revealing Jesus, through the word,
Creating faith in Him.

4 I know not what of good or ill
    May be reserved for me,
Of weary ways or golden days,
Before His face I see.

5 I know not when my Lord may come,
    At night or noonday fair,
Nor if I'll walk the vale with Him,
Or "meet Him in the air."

273

BEHOLD a Fountain deep and wide,
  Behold its onward flow;
'Twas opened in the Saviour's side,
‖: And cleanseth "white as snow." :‖

CHO.—Come to this Fountain,
      'Tis flowing to-day;
And all who will may freely come,
And wash their sins away.

2 From Calvary's cross, where Jesus died
    In sorrow, pain, and woe,
Burst forth the wondrous crimson tide
‖: That cleanseth "white as snow." :‖

3 O may we all the healing power
  Of that bless'd Fountain know;
Trust only in the precious blood
  ‖: That cleanseth " white as snow." :‖

4 And when at last the message comes,
  And we are called to go,
Our trust shall still be in the blood
  ‖: That cleanseth "white as snow." :‖

274

COME with thy sins to the fountain,
  Come with thy burden of grief;
Bury them deep in its waters,
  There thou wilt find a relief.

CHO.—Haste thee away, why wilt thou stay?
  Risk not thy soul on a moment's delay;
  Jesus is waiting to save thee,
  Mercy is pleading to-day.

2 Come as thou art to the fountain,
  Jesus is waiting for thee;
What though thy sins are like crimson,
  White as the snow they shall be.

3 These are the words of the Saviour;
  They who repent and believe,
They who are willing to trust Him,
  Life at His hand shall receive.

4 Come and be healed at the fountain,
  List to the peace-speaking voice;
Over a sinner returning
  Now let the angels rejoice.

275

O CHILD of God, wait patiently
  When dark thy path may be,
And let thy faith lean trustingly
  On Him who cares for Thee;
And though the clouds hang drearily
  Upon the brow of night,
Yet in the morning joy will come,
  And fill thy soul with light.

2 O child of God, He loveth thee,
  And thou art all His own;
With gentle hand He leadeth thee,
  Thou dost not walk alone;
And though thou watchest wearily
  The long and stormy night,
Yet in the morning joy will come,
  And fill thy soul with light.

3 O child of God, how peacefully
  He calms thy fears to rest,
And draws thee upward tenderly,
  Where dwell the pure and blest;
And He who bendeth silently
  Above the gloom of night,
Will take thee home where endless joy
  Shall fill thy soul with light.

276

O WONDERFUL words of the gospel!
    O wonderful message they bring,
Proclaiming a blesséd redemption
  Through Jesus our Saviour and King.

CHO.—Believe, oh, believe in His mercy
      That flows like a fountain so free;
    Believe, and receive the redemption
      He offers to you and to me.

2 He came from the throne of His glory,
    And left the bright mansions above,
  The world to redeem from its bondage;
    So great His compassion and love.

3 O come to this wonderful Saviour,
    Come weary and sorrow-oppressed;
  Behold on the cross how He suffered,
    That you in His kingdom might rest.

4 There's no other refuge but Jesus,
    No shelter where lost ones may fly;
  And now, while He's tenderly calling:
    O " turn ye," " for why will ye die?"

277

C LOSER, Lord, to Thee I cling,
    Closer still to Thee;
Safe beneath Thy sheltering wing
    I would ever be;
Rude the blast of doubt and sin,
Fierce assaults without, within,
Help me, Lord, the battle win;—
    Closer, Lord, to Thee.

2 Closer yet, O Lord, my Rock,
    Refuge of my soul;
Dread I not the tempest shock,
    Though the billows roll?
Wildest storm cannot alarm,
For, to me, can come no harm,
Leaning on Thy loving arm;—
    Closer, Lord, to Thee.

3 Closer still, my Help, my Stay,
    Closer, closer still;
Meekly there I learn to say,
    "Father, not my will;"
Learn that in affliction's hour,
When the clouds of sorrow lower,
Love directs Thy hand of power;—
    Closer, Lord, to Thee.

4 Closer, Lord, to Thee I come,
    Light of life Divine;
Through the ever Blessèd Son,
    Joy and peace are mine;
Let me in Thy love abide,
Keep me ever near Thy side,
In the " Rock of Ages " hide,
    Closer, Lord, to Thee.

278

R EJOICE in the Lord, O let His mercy cheer,
    He sunders the bands that enthrall;
Redeemed by His blood, why should we ever fear
    Since Jesus is our ' all in all.'

CHO.—If God be for us, if God be for us, if God be for us,
    Who can be against us, who, who, who,
    Who can be against us, against us?

2 Be strong in the Lord, rejoicing in His might,
   Be loyal and true, day by day;
When evils assail, be valiant for the right,
   And He will be our strength, our stay.

2 Confide in His word, His promises so sure.
   In Christ, they are "yea, and amen;"
Though earth pass away, they ever shall endure,
   'Tis written o'er and o'er again.

4 Abide in the Lord, secure in His control,
   'Tis life everlasting begun;
To pluck from His hand the weakest, trembling soul,
   It never, never can be done.

279

"GOD is Love!—His word proclaims it,
   Day by day the truth we prove;
Heaven and earth with joy are telling,
   Ever telling, "God is Love!"

Cho.—Hallelujah! tell the story,
   Sung by angel choirs above;
   Sounding forth the mighty chorus—
   "God is Light, and God is Love!"

2 "God is Love!"—Oh, tell it gladly,
   How the Saviour from above
Came to seek and save the lost ones,
   Showing thus the Father's love.

3 "God is Love!"—Oh, boundless mercy—
   May we all its fullness prove!
Telling those who sit in darkness,
   "God is Light, and God is Love!"

280

JESUS, my Saviour, to Bethlehem came,
   Born in a manger to sorrow and shame;
Oh, it was wonderful—blest be His name!
   Seeking for me, for me!

Ref.—‖: Seeking for me!   Seeking for me! :‖
   Oh, it was wonderful—blest be His name!
   Seeking for me, for me!

2 Jesus, my Saviour, on Calvary's tree,
   Paid the great debt, and my soul He set free;
Oh, it was wonderful—how could it be?
   Dying for me, for me!

REF.—||: Dying for me!   Dying for me! :||
   Oh, it was wonderful—how could it be?
     Dying for me, for me!

3 Jesus, my Saviour, the same as of old,
   While I was wandering afar from the fold,
Gently and long did He plead with my soul,
   Calling for me, for me!

REF.—||: Calling for me!   Calling for me! :||
   Gently and long did He plead with my soul,
     Calling for me, for me!

4 Jesus, my Saviour, shall come from on high—
   Sweet is the promise as weary years fly;
Oh, I shall see Him descending the sky,
   Coming for me, for me!

REF.—||: Coming for me!   Coming for me! :||
   Oh, I shall see Him descending the sky,
     Coming for me, for me!

281

OUT of my bondage, sorrow and night,
   Jesus, I come, Jesus, I come;
Into Thy freedom, gladness and light,
   Jesus, I come to Thee;
Out of my sickness into Thy health,
Out of my want and into Thy wealth,
Out of my sin and into Thyself,
   Jesus, I come to Thee.

2 Out of my shameful failure and loss,
   Jesus, I come, Jesus, I come;
Into the glorious gain of Thy cross,
   Jesus, I come to Thee;
Out of earth's sorrows into Thy balm,
Out of life's storms and into Thy calm,
Out of distress to jubilant psalm,
   Jesus, I come to Thee.

3 Out of unrest and arrogant pride,
    Jesus, I come, Jesus, I come;
Into Thy blesséd will to abide,
    Jesus, I come to Thee;
Out of myself to dwell in Thy love,
Out of despair into raptures above,
Upward for àye on wings like a dove,
    Jesus, I come to Thee.

4 Out of the fear and dread of the tomb,
    Jesus, I come, Jesus, I come;
Into the joy and light of Thy home,
    Jesus, I come to Thee;
Out of the depths of ruin untold,
Into the peace of Thy sheltering fold,
Ever Thy glorious face to behold,
    Jesus, I come to Thee.

282

GLORY ever be to Jesus,
    God's own well-belovéd Son;
By His grace He hath redeemed us,
    "It is finished," all is done.

CHO.—Saved by grace through faith in Jesus,
    Saved by His own precious blood,
    May we in His love abiding,
    Follow on to know the Lord.

2 Oh the weary days of wandering,
    Longing, hoping for the light;
These at last lie all behind us,
    Jesus is our strength and might.

3 In His safe and holy keeping,
    'Neath the shadow of His wing,
Gladly in His love confiding,
    May our souls His praises sing.

283

WHO came down from heaven to earth?
    Jesus Christ our Saviour;
Came a child of lowly birth?
    Jesus Christ our Saviour.

Cho.—Sound the chorus loud and clear,
    He hath brought salvation near.
    None so precious, none so dear,
      Jesus Christ our Saviour.

2 Who was lifted on the tree?
    Jesus Christ our Saviour;
   There to ransom you and me?
    Jesus Christ our Saviour.

3 Who hath promised to forgive?
    Jesus Christ our Saviour;
   Who hath said, 'Believe and live?
    Jesus Christ our Saviour.

4 Who is now enthroned above?
    Jesus Christ our Saviour;
   Whom should we obey and love?
    Jesus Christ our Saviour.

5 Who again from heaven shall come?
    Jesus Christ our Saviour;
   Take to glory all His own?
    Jesus Christ our Saviour.

284

WE have heard the joyful sound:
    Jesus saves! Jesus saves!
Spread the tidings all around:
    Jesus saves! Jesus saves!
Bear the news to every land,
   Climb the steeps and cross the waves
Onward!—'tis our Lord's command:
    Jesus saves! Jesus saves!

2 Waft it on the rolling tide:
    Jesus saves! Jesus saves!
Tell to sinners far and wide:
    Jesus saves! Jesus saves!
Sing, ye islands of the sea,
   Echo back, ye ocean caves;
Earth shall keep her jubilee:
    Jesus saves! Jesus saves!

3 Sing above the battle strife,
　　Jesus saves! Jesus saves!
By His death and endless life,
　　Jesus saves! Jesus saves!
Sing it softly through the gloom,
　　When the heart for mercy craves;
Sing in triumph o'er the tomb,—
　　Jesus saves! Jesus saves!

4 Give the winds a mighty voice:
　　Jesus saves! Jesus saves!
Let the nations now rejoice,—
　　Jesus saves! Jesus saves!
Shout salvation full and free,
　　Highest hills and deepest caves;
This our song of victory,—
　　Jesus saves! Jesus saves!

285

HE is coming, the "Man of Sorrows,"
　　Now exalted on high;
He is coming with loud hosannas,
　　In the clouds of the sky,

CHO.—Hallelujah! Hallelujah!
　　　He is coming again;
　　And with joy we shall gather round Him,
　　　At His coming to reign.

2 He is coming, our loving Saviour,
　　Blesséd Lamb that was slain;
In the glory of God the Father,
　　On the earth He shall reign.

3 He is coming, our Lord and Master,
　　Our Redeemer and King;
We shall see Him in all His beauty,
　　And His praise we shall sing.

4 He shall gather His chosen people,
　　Who are called by His name;
And the ransomed of every nation,
　　For His own He shall claim.

286

WHEREVER we may go, by night or day,
    A loving voice within doth gently say:
My son, from every way of sin depart;
    Be Satan's slave no more, "Give me thy heart!"

Cho.—"Give Me thy heart, give me thy heart;
    O weary, wandering child, give me thy heart."

2 Slight not that voice so kind, but gladly hear,
    And choose the Lord to day, while He is near;
He will His pardoning love to thee impart;
    Oh, hear Him calling still, "Give me thy heart!"

3 We may have chosen long from Him to roam,
    Yet He will welcome us, if we but come;
Oh, may we not delay, but quickly start—
    While Jesus sayeth still, "Give me thy heart!"

287

O LIST to the voice of the Prophet of old,
    Proclaiming in language divine,
The wonderful, wonderful message of truth
    That "They that be wise shall shine."

Cho.—They shall shine as bright as the stars,
    In the firmament jeweled with light;
And they that turn many to righteousness
    As the stars forever bright.

2 Though rugged the path where our duty may lead,
    O! why should we ever repine?
When faithful and true, is the promise to all
    That "They that be wise shall shine."

3 The grandeur of wealth, and the temples of fame,
    Where beauty and splendor combine,
Will perish, forgotten and crumble to dust,
    But "They that be wise shall shine."

4 Then let us go forth to the work yet to do,
    With zeal that shall never decline,
Be strong in the Lord, and the promise believe
    That "They that be wise shall shine."

288

I BELIEVED in God's wonderful mercy and grace,
  Believed in the smile of His reconciled face,
Believed in His message of pardon and peace;
  I believed, and I keep on believing.

CHO.—Believe! and the feeling may come or may go,
  Believe in the word, that was written to show
That all who believe, their salvation may know;
  Believe, and keep right on believing.

2 I believed in the work of my crucified Lord,
  Believed in redemption alone through His blood,
Believed in my Saviour by trusting His word:
  I believed, and I keep on believing.

3 I believed in the heart that was opened for me,
  Believed in the love flowing blesséd and free,
Believed that my sins were all nailed to the tree;
  I believed, and I keep on believing.

4 I believed in Himself, as the true Living One,
  Believed in His presence on high on the throne,
Believed in His coming in glory full soon;
  I believed, and I keep on believing.

289

MEET me there! Oh, meet me there!
  In the heavenly world so fair,
Where our Lord has entered in,
And there comes no taint of sin;
With our friends of long ago,
Clad in raiment white as snow,
Such as all the ransomed wear,—
Meet me there! Yes, meet me there!

2 Meet me there! Oh, meet me there!
  Far beyond this world of care;
When this troubled life shall cease,
Meet me where is perfect peace;
Where our sorrows we lay down
For the kingdom and the crown,
Jesus doth a home prepare,—
Meet me there! Yes, meet me there!

3 Meet me there! Oh, meet me there!
No bereavements we shall bear;
There no sighings for the dead,
There no farewell tear is shed:
We shall, safe from all alarms.
Clasp our loved ones in our arms,
And in Jesus' glory share,—
Meet me there! Yes, meet me there!

290

A RE you ready, are you ready for the coming of the Lord?
Are you living as He bids you in His word?
Are you walking in the light?
Is your hope of heaven bright?
Could you welcome Him to-night?
Are you ready?

CHO.—Therefore be ye also ready, be ye also ready.
Therefore be ye also ready,
For in such an hour, in such an hour as ye think not,
The Son of man cometh.

2 Are you waiting, are you waiting for the coming of the King?
Have you bundles of the golden grain to bring?
Can you lay at Jesus' feet
Any gathered sheaves of wheat,
There your blessèd Lord to greet?
Are you ready?

3 Have you risen, have you risen from the heavy midnight
Have you risen from your slumber long and deep? [sleep?
Are your garments washed from sin,
Are you cleansed and pure within?
Are you ready for the King?
Are you ready?

291

P RAISE the Saviour, ye who know Him;
Who can tell how much we owe Him?
Gladly let us render to Him
All we are and have.

2 Jesus is the name that charms us;
He for conflict fits and arms us;
Nothing moves and nothing harms us,
When we trust in Him.

3 Trust in Him, ye saints, for ever;
   He is faithful, changing never;
   Neither force nor guile can sever
     Those He loves from Him.

4 Keep us, Lord, oh, keep us cleaving
   To Thyself, and still believing,
   Till the hour of our receiving
     Promised joys in heaven.

5 Then we shall be where we would be,
   Then we shall be what we should be;
   Things which are not now, nor could be,
     Then shall be our own.

292

SHINE on, O Star of beauty,
   Thou Christ enthroned above;
Reflecting in Thy brightness,
   Our Father's look of love.

Cho.—‖: Shine on, shine on,
     Thou bright and beautiful Star.:‖

2 Shine on, O Star of glory,
   We lift our eyes to Thee;
   Beyond the clouds that gather,
   Thy radiant light we see.

3 Shine on, O star unchanging,
   And guide our pilgrim way,
   Until we see the dawning
   Of heaven's eternal day.

4 And when, with Thy redeemed ones,
   We reach the heavenly shore,
   May we with Thee in glory
   Shine on for evermore.

293

FAR, far away in heathen darkness dwelling,
   Millions of souls for ever may be lost;
Who, who will go salvation's story telling,
   Looking to Jesus, heeding not the cost?

Cho.—‖: " All power is given unto me, :‖
Go ye into all the world and preach the gospel, and lo,
     I am with you alway."

2 See o'er the world the open doors inviting,
   Soldiers of Christ, arise and enter in!
Brethren, awake! our forces all uniting,
   Send forth the gospel, break the chains of sin.

3 "Why will ye die?" the voice of God is calling,
   "Why will ye die?" re-echo in His name;
Jesus hath died to save from death appalling,
   Life and salvation therefore go proclaim.

4 God speed the day when those of every nation
   "Glory to God" triumphantly shall sing;
Ransomed, redeemed, rejoicing in salvation,
   Shout "Hallelujah for the Lord is King."

294

I KNOW I love Thee better, Lord,
   Than any earthly joy;
For Thou hast given me the peace
   Which nothing can destroy.

Cho.—The half has never yet been told,
   Of love so full and free!
The half has never yet been told,
   The blood—it cleanseth me!

2 I know that Thou art nearer still
   Than any earthly throng;
And sweeter is the thought of Thee
   Than any lovely song.

3 Thou hast put gladness in my heart;
   Then may I well be glad!
Without the secret of Thy love
   I could not but be sad.

4 O Saviour, precious Saviour, mine!
   What will Thy presence be,
If such a life of joy can crown
   Our walk on earth with Thee?

295

O PRECIOUS word that Jesus said!
   The soul that comes to Me,
I will in no wise cast Him out,
   Whoever he may be.

REF.—||: Whoever he may be, :||
    I will in no wise cast him out,
    Whoever he may be.

2 O precious word that Jesus said!
    Behold, I am the Door;
    And all who enter in by Me
    Have life for evermore.

REF.—||: Have life for evermore, :||
    And all who enter in by Me
    Have life for evermore.

3 O precious word that Jesus said!
    Come, weary souls oppressed,
    Come take My yoke and learn of Me
    And I will give you rest.

REF.—||: And I will give you rest, :||
    Come take My yoke and learn of Me,
    And I will give you rest.

4 O precious word that Jesus said!
    The world I overcame;
    And they who follow where I lead
    Shall conquer in My name.

REF.—||: Shall conquer in My name, :||
    And they who follow where I lead
    Shall conquer in My name.

296

WEARY gleaner in the field, poor or plenty be the yield,
    Labor on for the Master, nothing fearing,
There's a promise of reward, at the coming of the Lord,
    Unto all them that love His appearing.

CHO.—O the crown, the glory crown,
    O the day, the happy day is nearing,
When the crown of rich reward shall be given by the Lord,
    Unto all them that love His appearing.

2 Jesus now has gone above to complete His work of love;
    His return, day by day, is surely nearing,
When His own He will receive, and a welcome He will give,
    Unto all them that love His appearing.

3 O how light will seem the grief, and the toilsome way
 how brief,
When a crown in the glory we are wearing,
O the rapture who can tell, as for ever there we dwell,
With redeemed ones that loved His appearing.

297

WE lift our songs to Thee,
 Our Saviour and our guide;
O make us from our burdens free,
 And keep us near Thy side.

2 We lift our prayers to Thee,
 Who only heareth prayer;
They who on earth do thus agree,
 Shall find Thy blessing there.

3 We lift our faith to Thee,
 Increased by grace divine;
Help us, O Lord, Thy footsteps see
 And on Thy help recline.

4 We lift our all to Thee,
 For all things, Lord, are Thine;
Take us, and all we have, and see
 Thy likeness in us shine.

298

I KNOW that my Redeemer lives,
 And has prepared a place for me,
And crowns of victory He gives
 To those who would His children be.

CHO.—Then ask me not to linger long
 Amid the gay and thoughtless throng,
||: For I am only waiting here
 To hear the summons: "Child, come home!"

2 I'm trusting Jesus Christ for all,
 I know His blood now speaks for me,
I'm listening for the welcome call,
 To say: " The Master waiteth thee!"

3 I'm now enraptured with the thought,
 I stand and wonder at His love—
That He from heaven to earth was brought,
 To die, that I may live above.

4 I know that Jesus soon will come,
    I know the time will not be long,
'Till I shall reach my heavenly home,
    And join the everlasting song.

299

N OT far, not far from the Kingdom,
    Yet in the shadow of sin;
How many are coming and going!—
    How few there are entering in!

REF.—||: How few there are entering in! :||
      How many are coming and going!—
      How few there are entering in!

2 Not far, not far from the Kingdom,
    Where voices whisper and wait;
Too timid to enter in boldly,
    So linger still outside the gate.

3 Away in the dark and the danger,
    Far out in the night and the cold;
There Jesus is waiting to lead you
    So tenderly into His fold.

4 Not far, not far from the Kingdom,
    'Tis only a little space;
But oh, you may still be forever
    Shut out from yon heavenly place!

300

O NLY a beam of sunshine,
    But oh, it was warm and bright;
The heart of a weary traveler
    Was cheered by its welcome sight.
Only a beam of sunshine
    That fell from the arch above,
And tenderly, softly whispered
    A message of peace and love.

CHO.—Only a word for Jesus,
      Only a whispered prayer
      Over some grief-worn spirit
      May rest like a sunbeam fair.

2 Only a beam of sunshine
　　That into a dwelling crept,
Where over a fading rosebud,
　　A mother her vigil kept.
Only a beam of sunshine
　　That smiled through her falling tears,
And showed her the bow of promise,
　　Forgotten perhaps for years.

3 Only a word for Jesus!
　　Oh, speak it in His dear name;
To perishing souls around you
　　The message of love proclaim.
Go, like the faithful sunbeam,
　　Your mission of joy fulfil;
Remember the Saviour's promise,
　　That He will be with you still.

301

A WAKE, my soul! to sound His praise,
　　Awake my harp! to sing;
Join, all my powers! the song to raise,
　　And morning incense bring.

2 Among the people of His care,
　　And through the nations round,
Glad songs of praise will I prepare,
　　And there His name resound.

3 Be Thou exalted, O my God!
　　Above the starry train;
Diffuse Thy heavenly grace abroad,
　　And teach the world Thy reign.

4 So shall Thy chosen sons rejoice,
　　And throng Thy courts above;
While sinners hear Thy pardoning voice,
　　And taste redeeming love.

302

M Y Father is rich in houses and lands,
　　He holdeth the wealth of the world in His hands!
Of rubies and diamonds, of silver and gold,
His coffers are full,—He has riches untold.

CHO.—I'm the child of a King!
　The child of a King!
　With Jesus my Saviour,
　I'm the child of a King!

2 My Father's own Son, the Saviour of men,
Once wandered o'er earth as the poorest of them;
But now He is reigning forever on high,
And will give me a home in heaven by and by.

3 I once was an outcast stranger on earth,
A sinner by choice, an alien by birth!
But I've been adopted, my name's written down,—
An heir to a mansion, a robe, and a crown!

4 A tent or a cottage, why should I care?
They're building a palace for me over there!
Though exiled from home, yet still I may sing:
All glory to God, I'm the child of a King!

SONGS of gladness, never sadness,
　Sing the ransomed ones in heaven;
Anthem swelling, ever telling
　Of the joy of souls forgiven.

REF.—Sweetest music ever swelling
　　Through the courts of heaven above;
　　Ever singing, ever saying,
　　God is Life, and God is Love!

2 Ever sunshine, never shadow,
　Calm, mild, clear celestial day;
Ever summer in its brightness,
　Never winter or decay.

3 Ever gazing, loving, praising
　With the angel hosts above;
One eternal Hallelujah,
　One eternal song of love.

4 Never sighing, never sinning;
　No distrust, nor doubt, nor fears,
Through the long unending ages,
　Through the long eternal years.

304

BLESSED assurance, Jesus is mine!
O, what a foretaste of glory divine!
Heir of salvation, purchase of God,
Born of His Spirit, washed in His blood.

CHO.—‖: This is my story, this is my song,
Praising my Saviour all the day long. :‖

2 Perfect submission, perfect delight,
Visions of rapture now burst on my sight.
Angels descending, bring from above
Echoes of mercy, whispers of love.

3 Perfect submission, all is at rest,
I, in my Saviour, am happy and blest.
Watching and waiting, looking above
Filled with His goodness, lost in His love.

305

ALAS! and did my Saviour bleed,
And did my Sovereign die?
Would He devote that sacred head
For such a worm as I?

CHO.—At the cross, at the cross, where I first saw the light,
And the burden of my heart rolled away,
It was there by faith I received my sight,
And now I am happy all the day.

2 Was it for crimes that I have done,
He groaned upon the tree?
Amazing pity, grace unknown,
And love beyond degree!

3 But drops of grief can ne'er repay
The debt of love I owe;
Here, Lord, I give myself away,
'Tis all that I can do!

306

IN the shadow of His wings
There is rest, sweet rest;
There is rest from care and labor,
There is rest for friend and neighbor.

In the shadow of His wings
There is rest, sweet rest,
In the shadow of His wings
There is rest, *sweet rest*.

CHO. —‖: There is rest, there is peace, there is joy
In the shadow of His wings. :‖

2 In the shadow of His wings
There is peace, sweet peace,
Peace that passeth understanding,
Peace, sweet peace that knows no ending;
In the shadow of His wings
There is peace, sweet peace,
In the shadow of His wings
There is peace, *sweet peace*.

3 In the shadow of His wings
There is joy, glad joy,
There is joy to tell the story,
Joy exceeding, full of glory;
In the shadow of His wings,
There is joy, glad joy,
In the shadow of His wings
There is joy, *glad joy*.

307

JESUS, Thy name I love,
All other names above,
Jesus, my Lord!
Oh, Thou art all to me!
Nothing to please I see,
Nothing apart from Thee,
Jesus, my Lord!

2 Thou, blesséd Son of God,
Hast bought me with Thy blood,
Jesus, my Lord!
Oh, how great is Thy love,
All other loves above,
Love that I daily prove,
Jesus, my Lord!

3 When unto Thee I flee,
Thou wilt my Refuge be,
Jesus, my Lord!

What need I now to fear?
What earthly grief or care,
Since Thou art ever near,
    Jesus, my Lord!

4 Soon Thou wilt come again!
I shall be happy then,
    Jesus, my Lord!
Then Thine own face I'll see,
Then I shall like Thee be,
Then ever more with Thee,
    Jesus, my Lord!

308

JESUS is tenderly calling thee home—
    Calling to-day, calling to-day;
Why from the sunshine of love wilt thou roam
    Farther and farther away?

REF.—Calling to-day, calling to-day,
    Jesus is calling, is tenderly calling to-day.

2 Jesus is calling the weary to rest—
    Calling to-day, calling to-day;
Bring Him thy burden, and thou shalt be blest;
    He will not turn thee away.

3 Jesus is waiting, oh, come to Him now—
    Waiting to-day, waiting to-day;
Come with thy sins, at His feet lowly bow;
    Come, and no longer delay.

4 Jesus is pleading, oh, list to His voice—
    Hear Him to-day, hear Him to-day;
They who believe on His name shall rejoice;
    Quickly arise and away.

309

SOME one will enter the pearly gate
    By and by, by and by,
Taste of the glories that there await,
    Shall you? shall I?
Some one will travel the streets of gold,
Beautiful visions will there behold,
Feast on the pleasures so long foretold:
    Shall you? shall I?

2 Some one will gladly his cross lay down
    By and by, by and by,
Faithful, approved, shall receive a crown,
    Shall you? shall I?
Some one the glorious King will see,
Ever from sorrow of earth be free,
Happy with Him through eternity:
    Shall you? shall I?

3 Some one will knock when the door is shut
    By and by, by and by,
Hear a voice saying, "I know you not,"
    Shall you? shall I?
Some one will call and shall not be heard,
Vainly will strive when the door is barred.
Some one will fail of the saint's reward:
    Shall you? shall I?

4 Some one will sing the triumphant song
    By and by, by and by,
Join in the praise with the blood-bought throng,
    Shall you? shall I?
Some one will greet on the golden shore
Loved ones of earth who have gone before,
Safe in the glory for evermore:
    Shall you? shall I?

310

OH, wondrous Name, by prophets heard
    Long years before His birth;
They saw Him coming from afar,
    The Prince of Peace on earth.

CHO.—The Wonderful! The Counsellor!
    The Great and Mighty Lord!
The everlasting Prince of Peace!
    The King, the Son of God!

2 Oh, glorious Name the angels praise,
    And ransomed saints adore,—
The Name above all other names,
    Our Refuge evermore.

3 Oh, precious Name, exalted high,
    To Him all power is given:
Through Him we triumph over sin,
    By Him we enter heaven.

311

LET us sing of the love of the Lord,
　As now to the cross we draw nigh;
Let us sing to the praise of the God of all grace,
For the love that gave Jesus to die.

REF.—O the love that gave Jesus to die,
　The love that gave Jesus to die;
　Praise God, it is mine, this love so divine,
　The love that gave Jesus to die.

2 O how great was the love that was shown
　To us—we can never tell why—
Not to angels, but *men;* let us praise Him again
　For the love that gave Jesus to die.

3 Now this love unto all God commends,
　Not one would His mercy pass by;
" Whosoever shall call," there is pardon for all
　In the love that gave Jesus to die.

4 Who is he that can separate those
　Whom God doth in love justify;
Whatsoever we need He includes in the deed,
　In the love that gave Jesus to die.

312

O BROTHER, life's journey beginning,
　With courage and firmness arise;
Look well to the course thou art choosing,
　Be earnest, be watchful, and wise;
Remember, two paths are before thee,
　And both, thy attention invite;
But one leadeth on to destruction,—
　The other to joy and delight.

CHO.—God help you to follow His banner,
　And serve Him wherever you go;
　And when you are tempted, my brother,
　God give you the grace to say " No."

2 O brother, yield not to the tempter,
　No matter what others may do;
Stand firm in the strength of the Master,
　Be loyal, be faithful, and true;

Each trial will make you the stronger,
    If you, in the name of the Lord,
Fight manfully under your Leader,
    Obeying the voice of His word.

3 O brother, the Saviour is calling;
    Beware of the danger of sin;
Resist not the voice of the Spirit,
    That whispers so gently within;
God calls you to enter His service,—
    To live for Him here, day by day,
And share by and by in the glory
    That never shall vanish away.

313

O GOD, our help in ages past,
    Our hope for years to come,
Our shelter from the stormy blast,
    And our eternal home:—

2 Under the shadow of Thy throne
    Still may we dwell secure;
Sufficient is Thine arm alone,
    And our defence is sure.

3 Before the hills in order stood,
    Or earth received her frame,
From everlasting Thou art God,
    To endless years the same.

4 A thousand ages, in Thy sight,
    Are like an evening gone;
Short as the watch that ends the night,
    Before the rising sun.

314

FEAR not! God is thy shield,
    And He thy great reward;
His might has won the field:
    Thy strength is in the Lord!

REF.—Fear not! 'tis God's own voice
    That speaks to thee this word;
Lift up your head: rejoice
    In Jesus Christ thy Lord!

2 Fear not! for God has heard
   The cry of thy distress;
The water of His word
   Thy fainting soul shall bless.

3 Fear not! be not dismayed!
   He evermore will be
With thee, to give His aid,
   And He will strengthen thee.

4 Fear not! ye little flock;
   Your Shepherd soon will come,
Give water from the rock,
   And bring you to His home!

315

"THERE shall be showers of blessing:"
   This is the promise of love;
There shall be seasons refreshing,
   Sent from the Saviour above.

CHO.—Showers of blessing,
   Showers of blessing we need;
Mercy-drops round us are falling,
   But for the showers we plead.

2 "There shall be showers of blessing"—
   Precious reviving again;
Over the hills and the valleys,
   Sound of abundance of rain.

3 "There shall be showers of blessing;"
   Send them upon us, O Lord;
Grant to us now a refreshing,
   Come, and now honor Thy word.

4 "There shall be showers of blessing:"
   Oh, that to-day they might fall,
Now as to God we're confessing,
   Now as on Jesus we call!

316

WHEN we gather at last over Jordan,
   And the ransomed in glory we see,
As the numberless sands of the sea-shore,
   What a wonderful sight that will be!

CHO.—Numberless as the sands of the sea-shore!
Numberless as the sands of the shore!
Oh, what a sight 'twill be,
When the ransomed host we see,
As numberless as the sands of the sea-shore!

2 When we see all the saved of the ages,
Who from sorrow and trials are free,
Meeting there with a heavenly greeting—
What a wonderful sight that will be!

3 When we stand by the beautiful river,
Neath the shade of the life-giving tree,
Gazing over the fair land of promise—
What a wonderful sight that will be!

4 When at last we behold our Redeemer,
And His glory transcendent we see,
While as King of all kingdoms He reigneth—
What a wonderful sight that will be!

317

ABIDE with me! Fast falls the eventide,
    The darkness deepens—Lord, with me abide!
When other helpers fail, and comforts flee,
Help of the helpless, oh, abide with me!

2 Swift to its close ebbs out life's little day;
Earth's joys grows dim, its glories pass away;
Change and decay in all around I see;
O Thou, who changest not, abide with me!

3 I need Thy presence every passing hour,
What but Thy grace can foil the tempter's power?
Who, like Thyself, my guide and stay can be?
Through cloud and sunshine, oh, abide with me!

4 Hold Thou Thy cross before my closing eyes;
Shine through the gloom, and point me to the skies;
Heaven's morning breaks and earth's vain shadows flee!
In life, in death, O Lord, abide with me!

318

O PRAISE the Lord with heart and voice,
    With God's own word your doubts destroy,
Let those that trust in Him rejoice,
    Yea, let them shout for joy.

CHO. —Rejoice, rejoice in the Lord, rejoice in the Lord alway;
　　Rejoice, rejoice in the Lord, and again I say, Rejoice!

2 My life is hid with Thine, O Lord,
　　And sheltered from the world's alarm;
　Why should I sink beneath my load,
　　When leaning on Thine arm?

3 For nothing anxious I shall be,
　　But trusting Thee in every thing,
　With thanks for every gift from Thee,
　　My troubles all take wing.

4 The joys that memory turns to pain,
　　I leave for joys that never end;
　My loss I count my richest gain,
　　For Christ His joy doth send.

319

O LAND of the blesséd! thy shadowless skies
　　Sometimes in my dreaming I see;
I hear the glad songs that the glorified sing,
　　Steal over Eternity's sea;
Though dark are the shadows that gather between,
　I know that thy morning is fair:
I catch but a glimpse of thy glory and light,
　　And whisper: "Would God I were there!"

2 O land of the blesséd! thy hills of delight
　　Sometimes to my vision unfold;
Thy mansions celestial, thy palaces bright,
　　Thy bulwarks of jasper and gold;
Dear voices are chanting thy chorus of praise,
　Their forms in thy sunlight are fair;
I look from the valley of shadows below,
　　And whisper: "Would God I were there!"

3 Dear home of my Father, thou City of peace,
　　No shadow of changing can mar;
How glad are the souls that have tasted thy joy!
　How blest thine inhabitants are!
When weary of toiling, I think of the day—
　Who knows if its dawning be near?—
When He who doth love me shall call me away
　From all that hath burdened me here?

320

" NEARER the cross!" my heart can say,
    I am coming nearer;
Nearer the cross from day to day,
    I am coming nearer;
Nearer the cross where Jesus died,
Nearer the fountain's crimson tide,
Nearer my Saviour's wounded side,
    ||: I am coming nearer. :||

2 Nearer the Christian's mercy seat,
    I am coming nearer;
Feasting my soul on manna sweet,
    I am coming nearer;
Stronger in faith, more clear I see
Jesus who gave Himself for me;
Nearer to Him I still would be:
    ||: Still I'm coming nearer. :||

3 Nearer in prayer my hope aspires,
    I am coming nearer;
Deeper the love my soul desires,
    I am coming nearer;
Nearer the end of toil and care,
Nearer the joy I long to share,
Nearer the crown I soon shall wear:
    ||: I am coming nearer. :||

321

THE Lord's our Rock, in Him we hide,
    A shelter in the time of storm;
Secure whatever ill betide,
    A shelter in the time of storm.

CHO.—Oh, Jesus is a Rock in a weary land,
    A weary land, a weary land;
Oh, Jesus is a Rock in a weary land,
    A shelter in the time of storm.

2 A shade by day, defence by night,
    A shelter in the time of storm;
No fears alarm, no foes affright,
    A shelter in the time of storm.

3 The raging storms may round us beat,
    A shelter in the time of storm;

We'll never leave our safe retreat,
A shelter in the time of storm.

4 O Rock divine, O Refuge dear!
A shelter in the time of storm;
Be Thou our helper ever near,
A shelter in the time of storm.

322

OH, who is this that cometh
From Edom's crimson plain,
With wounded side; with garments dyed?
Oh, tell me now Thy name.
"I that saw thy soul's distress,
A ransom gave;
I that speak in righteousness,
Mighty to save!"

Cho.—‖: Mighty to save! :‖
Lord, I'll trust Thy wondrous love,
"Mighty to save!"

2 Oh, why is Thine apparel
So very deeply dyed?—
Like them that tread the wine-press red?
Oh, why this crimson tide?
"I the wine-press trod alone,
'Neath sorrow's wave;
Of the people there was none
Mighty to save!"

3 O bleeding Lamb, my Saviour,
How couldst Thou bear this shame?
With mercy fraught, Thine arm has brought
Salvation in Thy name!
"I the victory have won,
Conquered the grave:
Now the year of joy has come,
Mighty to save!"

323

LOW in the grave He lay—
Jesus, my Saviour!
Waiting the coming day—
Jesus, my Lord!

Cho.—Up from the grave He arose,
　　　With a mighty triumph o'er His foes:
　　　He arose a Victor from the dark domain,
　　　And He lives for ever with His saints to reign;
　　　　　He arose! He arose!
　　　　　Hallelujah! Christ arose!

2 Vainly they watched His bed—
　　　Jesus, my Saviour!
　　Vainly they seal the dead—
　　　Jesus, my Lord!

3 Death cannot keep his prey—
　　　Jesus, my Saviour!
　　He tore the bars away—
　　　Jesus, my Lord!

324

SOFTLY and tenderly Jesus is calling,
　　Calling for you and for me;
See on the portals He's waiting and watching,
　　Watching for you and for me.

Cho.—Come home, come home,
　　　Ye who are weary, come home;
　　Earnestly, tenderly, Jesus is calling,
　　　Calling, O sinner, come home!

2 Why should we tarry when Jesus is pleading,
　　　Pleading for you and for me?
　　Why should we linger and heed not His mercies,
　　　Mercies for you and for me?

3 Time is now fleeting, the moments are passing,
　　　Passing from you and from me;
　　Shadows are gathering, death-beds are coming,
　　　Coming for you and for me.

4 Oh, for the wonderful love He has promised,
　　　Promised for you and for me;
　　Though we have sinned He has mercy and pardon,
　　　Pardon for you and for me.

325

O WANDERING souls, why will you roam
　　Away from God, away from home;
The Saviour calls, O hear Him say,
Whoever will may come to-day.

REF.—Whoever will, whoever will,
  ||: Whoever will may come to-day, :||
    And drink of the water of life.

2 Behold His hands extended now,
    The dews of night are on His brow;
    He knocks, He calls, He waiteth still;
    Oh, come to Him, whoever will.

3 In simple faith His word believe,
    And His abundant grace receive,
    No love like His the heart can fill,
    Oh, come to Him, whoever will.

4 The "Spirit and the Bride say, Come!"
    And find in Him sweet rest, and home;
    Let Him that heareth, echo still,
    The blesséd *whosoever will*.

326

AFFLICTIONS, though they seem severe,
    In mercy oft are sent;
They stopped the prodigal's career,
    And caused him to repent.

CHO.—"I'll not die here for bread,
    I'll not die here for bread," he cries;
    "Nor starve in foreign lands;
    My father's house has large supplies,
    And bounteous are his hands."

2 "What have I gained by sin," he said,
    "But hunger, shame, and fear?"
    My father's house abounds in bread,
    While I am starving here!

3 "I'll go and tell him all I've done,
    Fall down before his face;
    Unworthy to be called his son,
    I'll seek a servant's place."

4 His father saw him coming back;
    He saw, he ran, he smiled,
    And threw his arms around the neck
    Of his rebellious child!

5 "O father, I have sinned—forgive!"
    "Enough," the father said;
  "Rejoice, my house; my son's alive
    For whom I mourned as dead!"

6 'Tis thus the Lord His love reveals,
    To call poor sinners home;
  More than a father's love He feels,
    And welcomes all that come.

327

HOW sweet, my Saviour, to repose
    On Thine almighty power!
To feel Thy strength upholding me,
    Through every trying hour!

CHO.—‖: Casting all your care upon Him,;‖
    Casting all your care upon Him,
    For He careth, He careth for you."

2 It is Thy will that I should cast
    My every care on Thee;
  To Thee refer each rising grief,
    Each new perplexity;

3 That I should trust Thy loving care,
    And look to Thee alone,
  To calm each troubled thought to rest,
    In prayer before Thy throne.

4 Why should my heart then be distrest
    By dread of future ill?
  Or why should unbelieving fear
    My trembling spirit fill?

328

IN the harvest field there is work to do,
    For the grain is ripe, and the reapers few;
And the Master's voice bids the workers true
    Heed the call that He gives to-day.

CHO.—Labor on! labor on!
    Keep the bright reward in view;
    For the Master has said,
    He will strength renew;
    Labor on till the close of day!

2 Crowd the garner well with its sheaves all bright,
Let the song be glad, and the heart be light;
Fill the precious hours, ere the shades of night
    Take the place of the golden day.

3 In the gleaner's path may be rich reward,
Though the time seems long, and the labor hard;
For the Master's joy, with His chosen shared,
    Drives the gloom from the darkest day.

4 Lo! the Harvest Home in the realms above
Shall be gained by each who has toiled and strove,
When the Master's voice, in its tones of love,
    Calls away to eternal day.

329

"FOR God so loved!" Oh, wondrous theme!
  Oh! wondrous key to wondrous scheme!
A Saviour sent to sinful men—
    Glory to God the Father!

Cho.—||: Glory to God the Father! :||
    Glory, glory,
    Glory to God the Father!

2 In love God gave, in love Christ came,
That man might know the Father's name,
And in the Son salvation claim—
    Glory to God the Father!

3 As man He tarried here below,
The power and love of God to show;
To help and heal all human woe—
    Glory to God the Father!

4 Upon the cross His life He gave,
His people from their sins to save;
For them descended to the grave—
    Glory to God the Father!

5 By God exalted from the dead,
He reigns on high the living head
Of every soul for whom He bled—
    Glory to God the Father!

330

O TROUBLED heart, there is a home,
   Beyond the reach of toil and care;
A home where changes never come;
   Who would not fain be resting there?

CHO.—‖: O wait, meekly wait, and murmur not; :‖
    O, wait, O, wait,
    O, wait, and murmur not.

2 Yet when bowed down beneath the load
   By heaven allowed, thine earthly lot;
Look up! thou'lt reach that blest abode,
   Wait, meekly wait, and murmur not.

3 If in thy path some thorns are found,
   O, think who bore them on His brow;
If grief thy sorrowing heart has found,
   It reached a holier than thou.

4 Toil on, nor deem, though sore it be,
   One sigh unheard, one prayer forgot;
The day of rest will dawn for thee;
   Wait, meekly wait, and murmur not.

———

331

SINNERS Jesus will receive:
   Sound this word of grace to all
Who the heavenly pathway leave,
   All who linger, all who fall.

REF.—Sing it o'er and o'er again:
    Christ receiveth sinful men;
    Make the message clear and plain:
    Christ receiveth sinful men.

2 Come, and He will give you rest;
   Trust Him, for His word is plain;
He will take the sinfulest:
   Christ receiveth sinful men.

3 Now my heart condemns me not,
   Pure before the law I stand;
He who cleansed me from all spot,
   Satisfied its last demand.

4 Christ receiveth sinful men,
　Even me with all my sin;
Purged from every spot and stain,
　Heaven with Him I enter in.

332

THERE'S a Stranger at the door;
　Let Him in!
He has been there oft before;
　Let Him in!
Let Him in ere He is gone;
Let Him in, the Holy one,
Jesus Christ, the Father's Son;
　Let Him in!

2 Open now to Him your heart;
　Let Him in!
If you wait He will depart;
　Let Him in!
Let Him in; He is your Friend;
And your soul He will defend,
He will keep you to the end;
　Let Him in!

3 Hear you now His loving voice?
　Let Him in!
Now, oh, now make Him your choice;
　Let Him in!
He is standing at the door;
Joy to you He will restore,
And His name you will adore;
　Let Him in!

4 Now admit the heavenly Guest;
　Let Him in!
He will make for you a feast;
　Let Him in!
He will speak your sins forgiven,
And when earth-ties all are riven,
He will take you home to heaven;
　Let Him in!

333

I LOOKED to Jesus in my sin,
My woe and want confessing;
Undone and lost, I came to Him,
I sought and found a blessing.

CHO.—"I looked to Him, to Him I looked,"
'Tis true, His " Whosoever; "
" He looked on me, on me He looked,
And we were one for ever."

2 I looked to Jesus on the cross,
For me I saw Him dying;
God's word believed, that all my sins
Were there upon Him lying.

3 I looked to Jesus there on high,
From death upraised to glory;
I trusted in His power to save,
Believed the old, old story.

4 He looked on me; O look of love!
My heart by it was broken;
And, with that look of love, He gave
The Holy Spirit's token.

5 Now one with Christ, I find my peace
In Him to be abiding,
And in His love for all my need,
In child-like faith confiding.

334

A LL hail the power of Jesus' name!
Let angels prostrate fall;
Bring forth the royal diadem,
And crown Him Lord of all.

CHO.—Let us crown Him, let us crown Him,
Let us crown the great Redeemer Lord of all;
Let us crown Him, let us crown Him,
Let us crown Him Lord of all.

2 Let every kindred, every tribe,
On this terrestrial ball,
To Him all majesty ascribe,
And crown Him Lord of all.

3 O that with yonder sacred throng
  We at His feet may fall;
We'll join the everlasting song,
  And crown Him Lord of all.

———

335

JESUS, my Lord, to Thee I cry;
  Unless Thou help me I must die:
Oh, bring Thy free salvation nigh,
  And take me as I am.

  CHO.—||: And take me as I am. :||
    My only plea—Christ died for me!
    Oh, take me as I am.

2 Helpless I am, and full of guilt;
  But yet for me Thy blood was spilt,
And Thou canst make me what Thou wilt,
  And take me as I am.

3 No preparation can I make,
  My best resolves I only break,
Yet save me for Thine own name's sake,
  And take me as I am.

4 Behold me, Saviour, at Thy feet,
  Deal with me as Thou seest meet;
Thy work begin, Thy work complete,
  And take me as I am.

———

336

SOULS of men, why will ye scatter
  Like a crowd of frightened sheep?
Foolish hearts! why will ye wander
  From a love so true and deep?
Was there ever kinder Shepherd,
  Half so gentle, half so sweet,
As the Saviour who would have us
  Come and gather round His feet?

2 It is God! His love *looks* mighty,
  But *is* mightier than it seems:
'Tis our Father. and His fondness
  Goes far out beyond our dreams.

There's a wideness in God's mercy,
   Like the wideness of the sea;
There's a kindness in His justice,
   Which is more than liberty.

3 There is no place where earth's sorrows
   Are more felt than up in heaven;
There is no place where earth's failings
   Have such kindly judgment given.
There is welcome for the sinner,
   And more graces for the good;
There is mercy with the Saviour;
   There is healing in His blood.

4 But we make His love too narrow,
   By false limits of our own;
And we magnify His strictness
   With a zeal He will not own.
There is plentiful redemption
   In the blood that has been shed;
There is joy for all the members
   In the sorrows of the Head.

5 If our love were but more simple
   We should take Him at His word;
And our lives would all be sunshine
   In the sweetness of our Lord.
For the love of God is broader
   Than the measures of man's mind;
And the heart of the Eternal
   Is most wonderfully kind.

337

IN the land of strangers,
   Whither thou art gone,
Hear a far voice calling,
   "My son! my son!"

CHO.—"Welcome! wanderer, welcome!
   Welcome back to home!
Thou hast wandered far away:
   Come home! come home!"

2 "From the land of hunger,
   Fainting, famished lone;
Come to love and gladness,
   My son! my son!"

3 "Leave the haunts of riot,
    Wasted, woe-begone,
Sick at heart and weary,
    My son! my son!"

4 "See the door still open!
    Thou art still my own;
Eyes of love are on thee,
    My son! my son!"

5 "Far off thou hast wandered;
    Wilt thou farther roam?
Come, and all is pardoned,
    My son! my son!"

6 "See the well-spread table,
    Unforgotten one!
Here is rest and plenty,
    My son! my son!"

7 "Thou art friendless, homeless,
    Hopeless, and undone;
Mine is love unchanging,
    My son! my son!"

338   ———

ON that bright and golden morning, when the Son of
    man shall come,
And the radiance of His glory we shall see;
When from every clime and nation He shall call His
    people home,
What a gathering of the ransomed that will be.

CHO.—What a gathering, what a gathering,
        What a gathering of the ransomed in the summer
            land of love;
    What a gathering, what a gathering,
        Of the ransomed in that happy home above.

2 When the blest who sleep in Jesus, at His bidding shall
        arise
    From the silence of the grave, and from the sea,
And with bodies all celestial they shall meet Him in the
        skies,
    What a gathering and rejoicing there will be.

3 When our eyes behold the city, with its many mansions
      bright,
  And its river, calm and restful, flowing free;
When the friends that death has parted shall in bliss
      again unite,
  What a gathering and a greeting there will be.

4 O the King is surely coming, and the time is drawing
      nigh,
  When the blessèd day of promise we shall see;
Then the changing "in a moment," "in the twinkling of
      an eye,"
  And forever in His presence we shall be.

339

O HEAR my cry, be gracious now to me,
  Come, Great Deliverer, come;
My soul bowed down is longing now for Thee,
  Come, Great Deliverer, come.

REF.--I've wandered far away o'er mountains cold,
  I've wandered far away from home;
O take me now, and bring me to Thy fold,
  Come, Great Deliverer, come.

2 I have no place, no shelter from the night,
  Come, Great Deliverer, come;
One look from Thee would give me life and light,
  Come, Great Deliverer, come.

3 My path is lone, and weary are my feet,
  Come, Great Deliverer, come;
Mine eyes look up Thy loving smile to meet,
  Come, Great Deliverer, come.

4 Thou wilt not spurn contrition's broken sigh,
  Come, Great Deliverer, come;
Regard my prayer, and hear my humble cry,
  Come, Great Deliverer, come.

340

G OD be with you till we meet again!--
  By His counsels guide, uphold you,
With His sheep securely fold you;
God be with you till we meet again!

CHO.—Till we meet!   Till we meet!
 Till we meet at Jesus' feet;
 Till we meet!   Till we meet!
 God be with you till we meet again!

2 God be with you till we meet again!—
 'Neath His wings protecting hide you,
 Daily manna still divide you;
 God be with you till we meet again!

3 God be with you till we meet again!—
 When life's perils thick confound you,
 Put His arms unfailing round you;
 God be with you till we meet again!

4 God be with you till we meet again!—
 Keep love's banner floating o'er you,
 Smite death's threatening wave before you;
 God be with you till we meet again!

341

I MUST walk through the valley and the shadow,
 But I'll journey in a loving Saviour's care;
He hath said He will never, never leave me,
 With His Staff He will comfort me there.

CHO.—Through the valley, through the valley,
 Through the valley and the shadow I must go,
But the dark waves of Jordan will not harm me,
 There is peace in the valley, I know.

2 When I walk through the valley and the shadow,
 All the weary days of toiling will be o'er;
For the strong arms of Jesus will enfold me,
 And with Him I shall sorrow no more.

3 Though I walk through the valley and the shadow,
 Yet the glory of the dawning I shall see;
I shall join in the anthems over Jordan,
 Where the loved ones are waiting for me.

4 I shall walk through the valley and the shadow,
 I shall follow where my Lord has gone before;
Through the mists of the valley He will lead me,
 Till I rest on the Evergreen Shore.

342

GOD'S almighty arms are round me,
    Peace, peace is mine;
Judgment scenes need not confound me,
    Peace, peace is mine.
Jesus came Himself and sought me!
Sold to Death, He found and bought me!
Then my blesséd freedom taught me,
    Peace, peace is mine.

2 While I hear life's rugged billows?
    Peace, peace is mine;
Why suspend my harp on willows?
    Peace, peace is mine.
I may sing with Christ beside me,
Though a thousand ills betide me;
Safely He hath sworn to guide me
    Peace, peace is mine.

3 Every trial draws Him nearer,
    Peace, peace is mine;
All His strokes but make Him dearer,
    Peace, peace is mine.
Bless I then the hand that smiteth
Gently, and to heal delighteth;
'Tis against *my sins* He fighteth,
    Peace, peace is mine.

4 Welcome every rising sunlight,
    Peace, peace is mine;
Nearer home each rolling midnight,
    Peace, peace is mine.
Death and hell cannot appal me;
Safe in Christ whate'er befall me;
Calmly wait I till He call me,
    Peace, peace is mine.

343

"LOOK unto me, and be ye saved,"
    O hear the blest command,
Salvation full! salvation free!
    Proclaim through every land.

Cho.—"Look unto me, and be ye saved,
    All the ends of the earth,

For I am God, there is none else.
Look unto me, and be ye saved."

2 " Look unto me," upon the cross,
O weary, burdened soul,
'Twas there on Me thy sins were laid,
Believe and be made whole.

3 " Look unto me," thy risen Lord,
In dark temptation's hour,
The needful grace I'll freely give,
To keep from Satan's power.

4 " Look unto me," and not *within*,
No help is *there* for thee;
For pardon, peace, and all thy need,
Look only unto Me.

344

AS I wandered 'round the homestead,
Many a dear familiar spot
Brought within my recollection
Scenes I'd seemingly forgot;
There, the orchard—meadow, yonder—
Here, the deep, old-fashioned well,
With its old, moss-covered bucket,
Sent a thrill no tongue can tell.

2 Though the house was held by strangers,
All remained the same within;
Just as when a child I rambled
Up and down, and out and in;
To the garret dark ascending—
Once a source of childish dread—
Peering through the misty cobwebs,
Lo! I saw my trundle bed.

3 Quick I drew it from the rubbish,
Covered o'er with dust so long:
When, behold, I heard in fancy
Strains of one familiar song,
Often sung by my dear mother
To me in that trundle bed;
" Hush, my dear, lie still and slumber!
Holy angels guard thy bed!"

4 While I listen to the music
   Stealing on in gentle strain,
I am carried back to childhood—
   I am now a child again:
'Tis the hour of my retiring,
   At the dusky eventide;
Near my trundle bed I'm kneeling,
   As of yore, by mother's side.

5 Hands are on my head so loving,
   As they were in childhood's days;
I, with weary tones, am trying
   To repeat the words she says;
'Tis a prayer in language simple
   As a mother's lips can frame:
"Father, Thou who art in heaven,
   Hallowed, ever, be Thy name."

6 Prayer is over: to my pillow
   With a "good-night!" kiss I creep,
Scarcely waking while I whisper,
   "Now I lay me down to sleep."
Then my mother, o'er me bending,
   Prays in earnest words, but mild:
"Hear my prayer, O heavenly Father,
   Bless, oh bless my precious child!"

7 Yet I am but only dreaming:
   Ne'er I'll be a child again;
Many years has that dear mother
   In the quiet churchyard lain;
But the mem'ry of her counsels
   O'er my path a light has shed,
Daily calling me to heaven,
   Even from my trundle bed.

345

OH, wonderful, wonderful Word of the Lord!
   True wisdom its pages unfold;
And though we may read them a thousand times o'er,
   They never, no never, grow old!
Each line hath a treasure, each promise a pearl,
   That all if they will may secure;
And we know that when time and the world pass away,
   God's Word shall for ever endure.

2 Oh, wonderful, wonderful Word of the Lord!
   The lamp that our Father above
So kindly has lighted to teach us the way
   That leads to the arms of His love!
Its warnings, its counsels are faithful and just;
   Its judgments are perfect and pure;
And we know that when time and the world **pass away,**
   God's Word shall for ever endure.

3 Oh, wonderful, wonderful Word of the Lord!
   Our only salvation is there;
It carries conviction down deep in the heart,
   And shows us ourselves as we are.
It tells of a Saviour, and points to the cross,
   Where pardon we now may secure;
For we know that when time and the world pass **away,**
   God's Word shall for ever endure.

4 Oh, wonderful, wonderful Word of the Lord!
   The hope of our friends in the past;
Its truth, where so firmly they anchored their trust,
   Through ages eternal shall last.
Oh, wonderful, wonderful Word of the Lord!
   Unchanging, abiding and sure;
For we know that when time and the world pass **away,**
   God's Word shall for ever endure.

346

THERE is no name so sweet on earth,
   No name so sweet in heaven;
The name, before His wondrous birth,
   To Christ the Saviour given.

REF.—We love to sing of Christ our King,
   And hail Him blesséd Jesus!
For there's no word ear ever heard
   So dear, so sweet, as "Jesus!"

2 And when He hung upon the tree,
   They wrote this name above Him
That all might see the reason we
   For evermore must love Him.

3 So now, upon His Father's throne—
   Almighty to release us
From sin and pain—He ever reigns,
   The Prince and Saviour, Jesus.

4 O Jesus! by that matchless Name
   Thy grace shall fail us never,
To-day as yesterday the same,
   Thou art the same for ever!

347

OUR life is like a stormy sea
   Swept by the gales of sin and grief,
While on the windward and the lee
   Hang heavy clouds of unbelief;
But o'er the deep a call we hear,
   Like Harbor bell's inviting voice,
It tells the lost that hope is near,
   And bids the trembling soul rejoice.

CHO.—This way, this way, O heart oppressed,
   So long by storm and tempest driven;
This way, this way, lo, here is rest,
   Rings out the Harbor bell of heaven.

2 O let us now the call obey,
   And steer our bark for yonder shore,
Where still that voice directs the way,
   In pleading tones for evermore;
A thousand life wrecks strew the sea;
   They're going down at every swell;
"Come unto me," "Come unto me,"
   Rings out th'assuring Harbor bell.

3 O tempted one, look up, be strong;
   The promise of the Lord is sure,
That they shall sing the victor's song,
   Who faithful to the end endure;
God's Holy Spirit comes to thee,
   Of His abiding love to tell;
To blissful port, o'er stormy sea,
   Calls heaven's inviting Harbor bell.

4 Come, gracious Lord, and in Thy love
   Conduct us o'er life's stormy wave;
O guide us to the home above,
   The blissful home beyond the grave;
There safe from rock, and storm, and flood,
   Our song of praise shall never cease,
To Him who bought us with His blood,
   And brought us to the port of peace.

348

OH, to have no Christ, no Saviour!
No Rock, no Refuge nigh!
When the dark days 'round thee gather,
When the storms sweep o'er the sky!

CHO.—Oh, to have no hope in Jesus!
No Friend, no light in Jesus!
Oh, to have no hope in Jesus!
How dark this world must be!

2 Oh, to have no Christ, no Saviour!
How lonely life must be!
Like a sailor, lost and driven,
On a wide and shoreless sea.

3 Oh, to have no Christ, no Saviour!
No hand to clasp thine own!
Through the dark, dark vale of shadows,
Thou must press thy way alone.

4 Now, we pray thee, come to Jesus;
His pard'ning love receive;
For the Saviour now is calling,
And He bids thee turn and live.

CHO.—Come to Jesus, He will save you;
He is the Friend of sinners;
Then, when thou hast found the Saviour,
How bright this world will be!

349

THERE is a land which lies afar,
Where grief is all unknown;
A land wherein the angels sing
Around the heavenly throne.

REF.—O 'twill be sweet when we shall meet
Upon that distant shore,
Whereon the glorious sun ne'er sets,
||: But shines for evermore. :||

2 We are but pilgrims on the earth,
And brief our sojourn here;
But well we know when hence we go,
There is a brighter sphere.

3 There is a realm of boundless love,
   A goal for hearts distrest,
 Where all may find for endless years
   A home among the blest.

350

HE dies! He dies! the lowly Man of sorrows,
   On whom were laid our many griefs and woes;
Our sins He bore, beneath God's awful billows,
And He hath triumphed over all our foes.

Cho.—" ||:I am he that liveth, that liveth and was dead; :||
   And, behold, I am alive for evermore;
   Behold, I am alive for evermore;
   I am he that liveth, that liveth and was dead;
   And, behold, I am alive for evermore."

2 He lives! He lives! what glorious consolation!
   Exalted at His Father's own right hand,
 He pleads for us, and by His intercession,
   Enables all His saints by grace to stand.

3 He comes! He comes! O blest anticipation!
   In keeping with His true and faithful word:
 To call us to our heavenly consummation—
   Caught up, to be *"forever with the Lord."*

351

OH, weary pilgrim, lift your head:
   For joy cometh in the morning!
 For God in His own Word hath said
   That joy cometh in the morning!

Cho.—||: Joy cometh in the morning! :||
   Weeping may endure for a night;
   But joy cometh in the morning!

2 Ye trembling saints, dismiss your fears:
   For joy cometh in the morning!
 Oh, weeping mourner, dry your tears:
   For joy cometh in the morning!

3 Let every burdened soul look up:
   For joy cometh in the morning!
 And every trembling sinner hope:
   For joy cometh in the morning!

4 Our God shall wipe all tears away:
    For joy cometh in the morning!
Sorrow and sighing flee away:
    For joy cometh in the morning!

352

REJOICE, rejoice, believer,
    And let thy joy and glory ever be
In Him, the Great Deliverer,
Who gave Himself a sacrifice for thee.

    CHO·—Rejoice, believer,
        Rejoice and sing
           Of Him who lives forever,
        Thy great High Priest and King.

2 Rejoice in thy Redeemer,
Thou hast a place that nothing can remove;
He bids thee dwell in safety,
And rest beneath the shadow of His love.

3 Rejoice, rejoice, believer,
A home on high is waiting now for thee;
    And there, in all His beauty,
The King of saints with wonder thou shalt see.

4 Rejoice, rejoice, believer,
Press on to join the happy, happy throng;
    Where soon thy Lord will call thee
To realms of joy and everlasting song.

353

"COME unto me," It is the Saviour's voice,
    The Lord of life, who bids thy heart rejoice;
O weary heart, with heavy cares oppressed,
"Come unto me," and I will give you rest.

REF.—"Come unto me, come unto me,
    Come unto me, and I will give you rest,
    ||: I will give you rest." :||

2 Weary with life's long struggle full of pain,
O doubting soul, thy Saviour calls again;
Thy doubts shall vanish and thy sorrows cease,
"Come unto me," and I will give you peace.

3 Oh, dying man, with guilt and sin dismayed,
  With conscience wakened, of thy God afraid;
  Twixt hopes and fears—oh, end the anxious strife,
  " Come unto me," and I will give you life.

4 Rest, peace, and life, the flowers of deathless bloom
  The Saviour gives us, not beyond the tomb—
  But here, and now, on earth, some glimpse is given
  Of joys which wait us through the gates of heaven.

354

SAFE home, safe home in port!
  Rent cordage, shattered deck,
Torn sails, provisions short,
  And only not a wreck:
But, oh! the joy, upon the shore,
To tell our voyage perils o'er.

2 The prize, the prize secure!
  The wrestler nearly fell;
Bare all he could endure,
  And bare not always well:
But he may smile at troubles gone
Who sets the victor-garland on!

3 No more the foe can harm!
  No more of leaguered camp,
And cry of night alarm,
  And need of ready lamp:—
And yet how nearly had he failed—
How nearly had that foe prevailed!

4 The exile is at home!
  Oh, nights and days of tears!
Oh, longings not to roam!
  Oh, sins and doubts and fears!
What matters now grief's darkest day,
When God has wiped all tears away!

355

ON Calvary's brow my Saviour died,
  'Twas there my Lord was crucified:
'Twas on the cross He bled for me,
And purchased there my pardon free.

CHO.—O Calvary! dark Calvary!
 Where Jesus shed His blood for me;
  O Calvary! blest Calvary!
   'Twas there my Saviour died for me.

2 'Mid rending rocks and darkening skies,
 My Saviour bows his head and dies;
  The opening vail reveals the way
  To heaven's joys and endless day.

3 O Jesus, Lord, how can it be,
 That Thou shouldst give Thy life for me,
  To bear the cross and agony,
  In that dread hour on Calvary?

356

HOLD Thou my hand; so weak I am, and helpless,
 I dare not take one step without Thy aid;
Hold Thou my hand; for then, O loving Saviour,
 No dread of ill shall make my soul afraid.

2 Hold Thou my hand, and closer, closer draw me
 To Thy dear self—my hope, my joy, my all;
Hold Thou my hand, lest haply I should wander,
 And, missing Thee, my trembling feet should fall.

3 Hold Thou my hand; the way is dark before me
 Without the sunlight of Thy face divine;
But when by faith I catch its radiant glory,
 What heights of joy, what rapturous songs are mine!

4 Hold Thou my hand, that when I reach the margin
 Of that lone river Thou didst cross for me,
A heavenly light may flash along its waters,
 And every wave like crystal bright shall be.

357

"BE ye strong in the Lord and the power of His might,"
 Firmly standing for the truth of His word;
He shall lead you safely through the thickest of the fight,
 You shall conquer in the name of the Lord.

CHO.—Firmly stand for the right,
 On to victory at the King's command;
For the honor of the Lord, and the triumph of His word,
 In the strength of the Lord firmly stand.

2 "Be ye strong in the Lord and the power of His might,"
　　Never turning from the face of the foe;
He will surely by you stand, as you battle for the right,
　　In the power of His might onward go,

3 "Be ye strong in the Lord and the power of His might,"
　　For His promises shall never, never fail;　　[right,
By thy right hand He'll hold thee while battling for the
　　Trusting Him thou shalt for evermore prevail.

358

O N the Resurrection morning,
　　Soul and body meet again,
No more sorrow, no more weeping,
　　No more pain.

2 Here awhile they must be parted,
　　And the flesh its Sabbath keep,
Waiting in a holy stillness,
　　Wrapped in sleep.

3 For a space the tired body
　　Waits in peace the morning's dawn,
When there breaks the last and brightest
　　Easter morn.

4 On that happy Easter morning
　　All the graves their dead restore,
Father, mother, sister, brother,
　　Meet once more.

5 Soul and body, reunited,
　　Henceforth nothing shall divide,
Waking up in Christ's own likeness,
　　Satisfied.

359

S ONS of God, beloved in Jesus!
　　O the wondrous word of grace;
In His Son the Father sees us,
　　And as sons He gives us place.

CHO.—"Belovéd, now are we the sons of God,
　　And it doth not yet appear what we shall be:
But ‖: we know that, when he shall appear, :‖
　　‖: We shall be like him, :‖
　　For we shall see him as he is."

2 Blessèd hope now brightly beaming,
    On our God we soon shall gaze;
And in light celestial gleaming,
    We shall see our Saviour's face.

3 By the power of grace transforming,
    We shall then His image bear;
Christ His promised word performing,
    We shall then His glory share.

360

THERE is a name I love to hear;
    I love to sing its worth:
It sounds like music in mine ear—
    The sweetest Name on earth.

2 It tells me of a Saviour's love
    Who died to set me free;
It tells me of His precious blood—
    The sinner's perfect plea.

3 It tells of One whose loving heart
    Can feel my smallest woe—
Who in each sorrow bears a part
    That none can bear below.

4 It bids my trembling soul rejoice,
    And dries each rising tear;
It tells me in a "still small voice,"
    To trust, and not to fear.

361

BLESSÈD be the Fountain of blood,
    To a world of sinners revealed;
Blessèd be the dear Son of God:
    Only by His stripes we are healed.
Though I've wandered far from His fold,
    Bringing to my heart pain and woe,
Wash me in the Blood of the Lamb,
    And I shall be whiter than snow.

Cho.—‖: Whiter than the snow. :‖
    Wash me in the Blood of the Lamb,
    And I shall be whiter than snow.

2 Thorny was the crown that He wore,
    And the cross His body o'ercame;
Grievous were the sorrows He bore,
    But He suffered thus not in vain.
May I to that Fountain be led,
    Made to cleanse my sins here below;
Wash me in the Blood that He shed,
    And I shall be whiter than snow.

3 Father, I have wandered from Thee,
    Often has my heart gone astray;
Crimson do my sins seem to me—
    Water can not wash them away.
Jesus to that Fountain of Thine,
    Leaning on Thy promise I go:
Cleanse me by Thy washing divine,
    And I shall be whiter than snow.

362

NOW the day is over,
    Night is drawing nigh,
Shadows of the evening
    Steal across the sky.

2 Jesus, give the weary
    Calm and sweet repose;
With Thy tenderest blessing,
    May our eyelids close.

3 Through the long night-watches
    May Thine angels spread
Their white wings above us,
    Watching round each bed.

4 When the morning wakens,
    Then may I arise
Pure, and fresh, and sinless
    In Thy holy eyes.

5 Glory to the Father,
    Glory to the Son,
And to Thee, blest Spirit,
    Whilst all ages run.   Amen.

363

IN the secret of His presence how my soul delights to
  hide!
Oh, how precious are the lessons which I learn at Jesus'
  side!
Earthly cares can never vex me, neither trials lay me low,
For when Satan comes to tempt me, to the secret place I
  go, to the secret place I go.

2 When my soul is faint and thirsty, 'neath the shadow of
   His wing
There is cool and pleasant shelter, and a fresh and crys-
  tal spring;
And my Saviour rests beside me, as we hold communion
  sweet:
If I tried, I could not utter what He says when thus we
  meet, what He says when thus we meet.

3 Only this I know: I tell Him all my doubts, my grief and
   fears;
Oh, how patiently He listens! and my drooping soul He
  cheers:
Do you think He ne'er reproves me? what a false friend
  He would be,
If He never, never told me of the sins which He must see,
  of the sins which He must see.

4 Would you like to know the sweetness of the secret of the
   Lord?
Go and hide beneath His shadow: this shall then be your
  reward;
And whene'er you leave the silence of that happy meeting
  place,
You must mind and bear the image of the Master in your
  face, of the Master in your face.

364

"TILL *He come!*"—oh, let the words
    Linger on the trembling chords,
Let the "little while" between
In their golden light be seen;
Let us think how heaven and home
Lie beyond that, "*Till He come.*"

2 When the weary ones we love
   Enter on their rest above,
When their words of love and cheer
   Fall no longer on our ear,
Hush! be every murmur dumb!
   It is only *"Till He come."*

3 Clouds and darkness round us press:
   Would we have one sorrow less?
All the sharpness of the cross,
   All that tells the world is loss.
Death, and darkness, and the tomb,
   Pain us only *"Till He come."*

4 See, the feast of love is spread,
   Drink the wine and eat the bread:
Sweet memorials, till the Lord
   Calls us round His heavenly board,
Some from earth, from glory some.
   Severed only *"Till He come."*

365

O NWARD, Christian soldiers!
   Marching as to war,
With the cross of Jesus
   Going on before.
Christ, the Royal Master,
   Leads against the foe;
Forward into battle,
   See His banners go.

CHO.—Onward, Christian soldiers,
   Marching as to war,
With the cross of Jesus,
   Going on before.

2 Like a mighty army
   Moves the Church of God:
Brothers, we are treading
   Where the saints have trod;
We are not divided,
   All one body we—
One in hope and doctrine,
   One in charity.

3 Crowns and thrones may perish,
　Kingdoms rise and wane;
But the Church of Jesus
　Constant will remain:
Gates of hell can never
　'Gainst that Church prevail:
We have Christ's own promise,
　And that cannot fail.

4 Onward, then, ye faithful,
　Join our happy throng,
Blend with ours your voices,
　In the triumph-song:
Glory, laud, and honor,
　Unto Christ the King:
This through countless ages
　Men and angels sing.

366

JESUS, Saviour, pilot me,
　Over life's tempestuous sea;
Unknown waves before me roll,
Hiding rock and treacherous shoal,
Chart and compass come from Thee.
Jesus, Saviour, pilot me.

2 As a mother stills her child,
Thou canst hush the ocean wild;
Boisterous waves obey Thy will
When thou say'st to them "Be still!"
Wondrous Sovereign of the sea,
Jesus, Saviour, pilot me.

3 When at last I near the shore,
And the fearful breakers roar
'Twixt me and the peaceful rest,
Then, while leaning on Thy breast,
May I hear Thee say to me,
"Fear not, I will pilot thee!"

367

I'VE found a friend in Jesus,—He's everything to me;
　He's the fairest of ten thousand to my soul!
The "Lily of the Valley," in Him alone I see,
　All I need to cleanse and make me fully whole:

In sorrow He's my comfort, in trouble He's my stay;
  He tells me every care on Him to roll;
He's the "Lily of the Valley," the Bright and Morning
  He's the fairest of ten thousand to my soul !   [Star;

Cho.—In sorrow He's my comfort, in trouble He's my stay;
  He tells me every care on Him to roll;
  He's the "Lily of the Valley," the Bright and Morn-
    ing Star;
    He's the fairest of ten thousand to my soul !

2 He all my grief has taken, and all my sorrows borne;
  In temptation He's my strong and mighty tower;
I've all for Him forsaken, I've all my idols torn
  From my heart, and now He keeps me by His power.
Though all the world forsake me, and Satan tempts me
    sore,
  Through Jesus I shall safely reach the goal;
He's the "Lily of the Valley," the Bright and Morning
    Star;
  He's the fairest of ten thousand to my soul !

3 He'll never, never leave me, nor yet forsake me here,
  While I live by faith, and do His blesséd will;
A wall of fire about me, I've nothing now to fear:
  With His manna He my hungry soul shall fill.
When crowned at last in glory, I'll see His blesséd face,
  Where rivers of delight shall ever roll;
He's the "Lily of the Valley," the Bright and Morning
    Star;
  He's the fairest of ten thousand to my soul !

368

Jesus, the very thought of Thee,
  With sweetness fills my breast;
But sweeter far Thy face to see,
  And in Thy presence rest.

2 Nor voice can sing, nor heart can frame,
  Nor can the memory find
A sweeter sound than Thy blest name,
  O Saviour of mankind!

3 Oh, hope of every contrite heart!
  Oh, joy of all the meek!

To those who fall, how kind Thou art!
How good to those who seek.

4 And those who find Thee, find a bliss
Nor tongue nor pen can show;
The love of Jesus, what it is
None but His loved ones know.

5 Jesus! our only joy be Thou,
As Thou our prize wilt be:
Jesus! be Thou our glory now,
And through eternity.

369

LIKE wandering sheep o'er mountains cold,
Since all have gone astray;
To "Life" and peace within the fold,
How may I find the way?

CHO.—‖: "I am the way, the truth, and the life:
No man cometh unto the Father, but by me.":‖

2 Bewildered oft with doubt and care,
To God I fain would go;
While many cry "Lo here! lo there!"
The Truth how may I know?

3 To Christ the WAY, the TRUTH, the LIFE,
I come, no more to roam;
He'll guide me to my "Father's house,"
To my Eternal home.

370

HAVE faith in God; what can there be
For Him too hard to do for thee?
He gave His Son; now all is free;
Have faith, have faith in God.

2 Have faith thy pardon to believe,
Let God's own word thy fears relieve;
Have faith the Spirit to receive;
Have faith, have faith in God.

3 Have faith in God, and Trust His might
That He will conquer as you fight,
And give the triumph to the right;
Have faith, have faith in God.

4 Have faith in God; press near His side;
  Thy troubled soul trust Him to guide;
  In life, in death, whate'er betide,
    Have faith, have faith in God.

371

WE shall reach the summer-land,
    Some sweet day, by and by;
We shall press the golden strand,
    Some sweet day, by and by;
Oh, the loved ones watching there,
By the tree of life so fair,
Till we come their joy to share,
    Some sweet day, by and by.

REF.—By and by, some sweet day,
      We shall meet our loved ones gone,
      Some sweet day, by and by.

2 At the crystal river's brink,
    Some sweet day, by and by;
We shall find each broken link,
    Some sweet day, by and by;
Then the star that, fading here,
Left our hearts and homes so drear,
We shall see more bright and clear,
    Some sweet day, by and by.

3 Oh, these parting scenes will end,
    Some sweet day, by and by;
We shall gather friend with friend,
    Some sweet day, by and by;
There before our Father's throne,
When the mists and clouds have flown,
We shall know as we are known,
    Some sweet day, by and by.

372

MY Jesus, as Thou wilt;
    Oh, may Thy will be mine;
Into Thy hand of love
  I would my all resign;
Through sorrow or through joy,
  Conduct me as Thine own,
And help me still to say,
  My Lord, Thy will be done.

2 My Jesus, as Thou wilt;
    Though seen through many a tear,
Let not my star of hope
    Grow dim or disappear:
Since Thou on earth hast wept,
    And sorrowed oft alone,
If I must weep with Thee,
    My Lord, Thy will be done.

3 My Jesus, as Thou wilt;
    All shall be well for me;
Each changing future scene
    I gladly trust with Thee:
Straight to my home above
    I travel calmly on,
And sing, in life or death,—
    My Lord, Thy will be done.

373

OH, what will you do with Jesus?
    The call comes low and sweet;
As tenderly He bids you
    Your burdens lay at His feet;
Oh soul, so sad and weary,
    That sweet voice speaks to thee;
Then what will you do with Jesus?
    Oh, what shall the answer be?

REF.—||: What shall the answer be? :||
    What will you do with Jesus?
    Oh, what shall the answer be?

2 Oh, what will you do with Jesus?
    The call comes loud and clear;
The solemn words are sounding
    In every listening ear;
Immortal life's in the question,
    And joy through eternity:
Then what will you do with Jesus?
    Oh, what shall the answer be?

3 Oh, think of the King of Glory—
    From heaven to earth come down,
His life so pure and holy;
    His death, His cross, His crown;

Of His divine compassion,
  His sacrifice for thee:
Then what will you do with Jesus?
  Oh, what shall the answer be?

374

L ABORERS of Christ, arise,
    And gird you for the toil;
The dew of promise from the skies
  Already cheers the soil.

2 Go where the sick recline,
    Where mourning hearts deplore;
And where the sons of sorrow pine,
  Dispense your hallowed lore.

3 Be faith, which looks above,
    With prayer, your constant guest;
And wrap the Saviour's changeless love
  A mantle round your breast.

4 So shall you share the wealth
    That earth may ne'er despoil,
And the blest gospel's saving health
  Repay your arduous toil.

375

G OD calling yet! shall I not hear?
    Earth's pleasures shall I still hold dear?
Shall life's swift passing years all fly,
And still my soul in slumber lie?

CHO.—||: Calling, oh, hear Him, :||
God is calling yet, oh, hear Him calling, calling,
  ||: Calling, oh, hear Him, :||
God is calling yet, oh, hear Him calling yet.

2 God calling yet! shall I not rise?
  Can I His loving voice despise,
And basely His kind care repay?
  He calls me still; can I delay?

3 God calling yet! and shall He knock,
  And I my heart the closer lock?
He still is waiting to receive.
  And shall I dare His Spirit grieve?

4 God calling yet! and shall I give
 No heed, but still in bondage live?
I wait, but He does not forsake;
 He calls me still; my heart, awake!

5 God calling yet! I cannot stay;
 My heart I yield without delay:
Vain world, farewell, from thee I part;
 The voice of God has reached my heart.

376

OH cease, my wandering soul,
 On restless wing to roam;
All this wide world, to either pole,
 Hath not for thee a home.

2 Behold the ark of God!
 Behold the open door!
Oh, haste to gain that dear abode.
 And rove, my soul, no more.

3 There safe thou shalt abide,
 There sweet shall be thy rest;
And every longing satisfied,
 With full salvation blest.

4 Ah, yes! I all forsake,
 My all to Thee resign;
Gracious Redeemer, take, oh take
 And seal me ever Thine!

377

GOD loved a world of sinners,
 For them He gave His Son;
And whosoe'er receives Him,
 He saves them, every one;
He came to bring salvation,
 To bear our sins away,
That we with Him in glory
 Might live through endless day.

CHO.—||: "How shall we escape if we neglect so great
 salvation? :||
 Neglect so great salvation?"

2 Behold the bleeding Saviour
   Upon the cruel tree,—
The Just, condemned, forsaken—
   He dies for you and me:
The "Son of God" belovéd,
   For us a curse was made;
That we might have redemption,
   The awful price He paid.

3 God loves the vilest sinner,
   But hates the smallest sin;
Then who shall see His Kingdom?
   Or who can enter in?
'The precious blood of Jesus'—
   Let every creature know—
Can make the " chief of sinners "
   Full whiter than the snow.

4 Return to God, O wanderer,
   Thy purchased pardon take;
Thy sins He'll not remember,
   For thy Redeemer's sake;
He'll cast them all behind Him,
   Or 'neath the deepest sea,
And love us ever freely
   Throughout Eternity.

372

COME to Jesus! come away!
   Forsake thy sins—Oh, why delay?
His arms are open night and day;
   He waits to welcome thee!

2 Come to Jesus! all is free;
   Hark! how He calls, " Come unto **Me!**
I cast out none, I'll pardon thee,"
   Oh, thou shalt welcome be!

3 Come to Jesus! cling to Him;
   He'll keep thee far from paths of **sin;**
Thou shalt at last a victory win,
   And He will welcome thee!

4 Come to Jesus!—Lord, I come!
   Weary of sin, no more I'd roam,

But with my Saviour be at home;
I know He'll welcome me!

379

AT the feast of Belshazzar and a thousand of His lords,
While they drank from golden vessels, as the Book
of Truth records—
In the night, as they revelled in the royal palace hall,
They were seized with consternation,—'twas the Hand
upon the wall!

CHO.—‖: 'Tis the hand of God on the wall! :‖
Shall the record be?—"Found wanting!"
Or shall it be?—"Found trusting!"
While that hand is writing on the wall?

2 See the brave captive, Daniel, as he stood before the
throng,
And rebuked the haughty monarch for his mighty deeds
of wrong;
As he read out the writing—'twas the doom of one and all,
For the kingdom now was finished—said the Hand upon
the wall!

3 See the faith, zeal, and courage, that would dare to do the
right,
Which the Spirit gave to Daniel—'twas the secret of his
might,
In his home in Judea, or a captive in the hall,
He understood the writing of his God upon the wall!

4 So our deeds are recorded—there's a Hand that's writing
now;
Sinner, give your heart to Jesus, to His royal mandates
bow;
For the day is approaching—it must come to one and all,
When the sinners' condemnation will be written on the
wall!

380

JERUSALEM! my happy home!
Name ever dear to me!
When shall my labors have an end,
In joy, and peace, in thee!

2 Oh, when, thou city of my God,
    Shall I thy courts ascend,
Where congregations ne'er break up,
    And Sabbaths have no end?

3 Jerusalem! my happy home!
    My soul still pants for thee;
Then shall my labors have an end,
    When I thy joy shall see.

381

THERE'S a royal banner given for display
    To the soldiers of the King;
As an ensign fair we lift it up to-day,
    While as ransomed ones we sing,

Cho.—Marching on! Marching on!
        For Christ count everything but loss;
    And to crown Him King, we'll toil and sing,
        'Neath the banner of the cross

2 Though the foe may rage and gather as the flood,
    Let the standard be displayed;
And beneath its folds, as soldiers of the Lord,
    For the truth be not dismayed!

3 Over land and sea, wherever man may dwell,
    Make the glorious tidings known;
Of the crimson banner now the story tell,
    While the Lord shall claim His own!

4 When the glory dawns—'tis drawing very near—
    It is hastening day by day—
Then before our King the foe shall disappear,
    And the Cross the world shall sway,

382

I WAS once far away from the Saviour,
    And as vile as a sinner could be;
And I wondered if Christ the Redeemer
    Could save a poor sinner like me.

2 I wandered on in the darkness,
    Not a ray of light could I see;
And the thought filled my heart with sadness,
    There's no hope for a sinner like me.

3 And then, in that dark lonely hour,
   A voice sweetly whispered to me,
Saying, Christ the Redeemer has power
   To save a poor sinner like thee.

4 I listened: and lo! 'twas the Saviour
   That was speaking so kindly to me;
I cried, "I'm the chief of sinners,
   Thou canst save a poor sinner like me!"

5 I then fully trusted in Jesus;
   And oh, what a joy came to me!
My heart was filled with His praises,
   For saving a sinner like me.

6 No longer in darkness I'm walking,
   For the light is now shining on me;
And now unto others I'm telling
   How He saved a poor sinner like me.

7 And when life's journey is over,
   And I the dear Saviour shall see,
I'll praise Him for ever and ever,
   For saving a sinner like me.

383

THERE is a calm beyond life's fitful fever,
   A deep repose, an everlasting rest;
Where white-robed angels welcome the believer
   Among the blest, among the blest:
There is a Home, where all the soul's deep yearnings,
   And silent prayers shall be at last fulfilled;
Where strife and sorrow, murm'rings and heart-burnings,
   At last are stilled, at last are stilled.

2 There is a Hope, to which the Christian clinging,
   Is lifted high above life's surging wave;
Finds life in death, and fadeless flowers springing
   From the dark grave, from the dark grave:
There is a Crown prepared for those who love Him,
   The Christian sees it in the distance shine,
Like a bright beacon glittering above him,
   And whispers, "Mine!" and whispers, "Mine!"

3 There is a spotless robe of Christ's own weaving;
   Will you not wrap it round your sin-stained soul?
Poor wandering child, upon thy past life grieving,
   Christ makes thee whole! Christ makes thee whole!
There is a Home, a Harp, a Crown in Heaven;—
   Alas! that any should Thy gift refuse!—
The awful choice of life and death is given—
   Which wilt thou choose? which wilt thou choose?

384

THERE is a stream, whose gentle flow
   Supplies the city of our God;
Life, love, and joy, still gliding through,
   And watering our divine abode.

2 That sacred stream, Thy holy Word,
   Supports our faith, our fears controls;
Sweet peace Thy promises afford,
   And give new strength to fainting souls.

3 Loud may the troubled ocean roar;
   In sacred peace our souls abide;
While every nation, every shore,
   Trembles, and dreads the swelling tide.

385

A GUILTY soul, by Pharisees of old,
   Was brought accused, alone,
But Jesus said, "Let him without a sin,
   Be first to cast a stone."

Cho.—"There is none righteous, no, not one:
   All, all have sinned,
There is none righteous, for all have sinned,
And come short of the glory, the glory of God,
||: Come short of the glory, :|| of the glory of God."

2 A learned Master, Ruler of the Jews,
   God's kingdom could not gain,
With all the lore and culture of the age,
   He "must be born again."

3 "Good Master," pray, can aught be lacking yet?
   Thy laws I do obey;
"Go sell and *give*, then come and follow me,"
   But sad he turned away.

386

JESUS bids us shine with a clear, pure light,
Like a little candle burning in the night;
In the world is darkness; so we must shine,
You in your corner and I in mine.

2 Jesus bids us shine first of all for Him,
Well He sees and knows it if our light is dim;
He looks down from heaven, He sees us shine,
You in your corner and I in mine.

3 Jesus bids us shine then for all around,
Many kinds of darkness in the world are found;
Sin and want and sorrow; so we must shine,
You in your corner and I in mine.

387

WHOEVER receiveth the Crucified One,
Whoever believeth on God's only Son,
A free and a perfect salvation shall have:
For He is abundantly able to save.

CHO.—My brother, the Master is calling for thee;
His grace and His mercy are wondrously free;
His blood as a ransom for sinners He gave,
And He is abundantly able to save.

2 Whoever receiveth the message of God,
And trusts in the power of the soul-cleansing blood,
A full and eternal redemption shall have:
For He is both able and willing to save.

3 Whoever repents and forsakes every sin,
And opens his heart for the Lord to come in,
A present and perfect salvation shall have:
For Jesus is ready this moment to save.

388

COME, come to Jesus!
He waits to welcome thee,
O wanderer! eagerly
Come, come to Jesus!

2 Come, come to Jesus!
He waits to ransom thee,
O slave! so willingly;
Come, come to Jesus!

3 Come, come to Jesus!
   He waits to lighten thee,
O burdened ! trustingly
   Come, come to Jesus!

4 Come, come to Jesus!
   He waits to give to thee,
O blind! a vision free;
   Come, come to Jesus!

5 Come, come to Jesus!
   He waits to shelter thee,
O weary! blessedly
   Come, come to Jesus!

6 Come, come to Jesus!
   He waits to carry thee,
O lamb! so lovingly
   Come, come to Jesus!

89

SITTING by the gateway of a palace fair,
   Once a child of God was left to die;
By the world neglected, wealth would nothing share;
   See the change awaiting there on high.

CHO.—Carried by the angels to the land of rest
   Music sweetly sounding through the skies;
Welcomed by the Saviour to the heavenly feast,
   Gathered with the loved in Paradise.

2 What shall be the ending of this life of care?
   Oft the question cometh to us all;
Here upon the pathway hard the burdens bear,
   And the burning tears of sorrow fall.

3 Follower of Jesus, scanty though thy store,
   Treasures, precious treasures wait on high;
Count the trials joyful, soon they'll all be o'er;
   O the change that's coming bye and bye.

4 Upward, then, and onward! onward for the Lord;
   Time and talent all in His employ;
Small may seem the service, sure the great reward;
   Here the cross, but there the crown of joy.

390

O CHRISTIAN traveler, fear no more
    The storms which round thee spread·
Nor yet the noontide's sultry beams
    On thy defenceless head.

Cho.—‖: "Fear thou not, for I am with thee:
    Be not dismayed, for I am thy God." :‖

2 Thy Saviour, who upon the cross
    Thy full redemption paid,
Will not from thee, His ransomed one,
    Withhold His promised aid.

3 A safe retreat and hiding-place
    Thy Saviour will provide;
And sorrow cannot fill thy heart,
    While sheltered at His side.

4 No; in thy darkest days on earth,
    When every joy seems flown,
Believer, thou shalt never tread
    The toilsome way alone.

—————

391

H AVE our hearts grown cold since the day of old?
    Have we left our souls' "first love?"
Neither cold nor hot. God commends us not,
    Nor our lukewarm ways approve.

Cho.—Repent ye, repent ye, repent ye!
    'Tis the call of God to every land;
Repent ye, repent ye, repent ye!
    For the kingdom of heaven is at hand.

2 Has the God above our supreme true love?
    Have we bowed to Him alway?
Do we own His claim and revere His name,
    And observe His holy day?

3 Do we honor those who have soothed our woes?
    Have we rendered good for ill?
Are we pure in heart, doing *all* our part
    To fulfil the Saviour's will?

4 Are we always true in the thing we do,
   In our words, our works, our ways?
Are we quite content with the blessings sent,
   Giving God alone the praise?

5 Dare a mortal say—for a single day—
   "I have kept Thy law, O God!
Undefiled by sin, I am pure within,
   And I need no cleansing blood?"

392

CLING to the Bible, though all else be taken;
   Lose not its promises precious and sure;
Souls that are sleeping its echoes awaken,
   Drink from the fountain, so peaceful, so pure.

Cho.—||: Cling to the Bible! :|| Cling to the Bible,
     Our Lamp and Guide.

2 Cling to the Bible, this jewel, this treasure
   Brings to us honor and saves fallen man;
Pearl whose great value no mortal can measure,
   Seek and secure it, O soul, while you can.

3 Lamp for the feet that in by-ways have wandered,
   Guide for the youth that would otherwise fall;
Hope for the sinner whose best days are squandered,
   Staff for the aged, and best book of all.

393

HARK! hark, my soul! Angelic songs are swelling
   O'er earth's green fields, and ocean's wave-beat
     shore;
How sweet the truth those blesséd strains are telling
   Of that new life when sin shall be no more.

Cho.—Angels, sing on! your faithful watches keeping;
   Sing us sweet fragments of the songs above,
Till morning's joy shall end the night of weeping,
   And life's long shadows break in cloudless love.

2 Far, far away, like bells at evening pealing,
   The voice of Jesus sounds o'er land and sea,
And laden souls, by thousands meekly stealing,
   Kind Shepherd, turn their weary steps to Thee.

3 Onward we go, for still we hear them singing,
 "Come, weary souls, for Jesus bids you come;"
And through the dark, its echoes sweetly ringing,
 The music of the Gospel leads us home.

394

GUIDE me, O Thou great Jehovah,
 Pilgrim through this barren land;
I am weak, but Thou art mighty;
 Hold me with Thy powerful hand:
Bread of heaven,   Bread of heaven,
 Feed me till I want no more.

2 Open now the crystal fountain,
 Whence the healing waters flow;
Let the fiery, cloudy pillar
 Lead me all my journey through:
Strong Deliverer,   Strong Deliverer,
 Be Thou still my strength and shield.

3 When I tread the verge of Jordan,
 Bid my anxious fears subside;
Bear me through the swelling current,
 Land me safe on Canaan's side:
Songs of praises,   Songs of praises
 I will ever give to Thee.

395

WE bow our knees unto the Father
 Of Christ the Lord of earth and heaven,
That riches of His grace and glory
 And power for service may be given.

CHO.—We are waiting for the promise of the Father—
 For the Holy Spirit's power;
O our Father, for Thy Spirit we are waiting, even
  now, this very hour.
 ||: We are waiting for His coming,:|
 For the Holy Spirit's power;
O our Father, for Thy Spirit we are waiting, even
  now, this very hour.

2 O fill the inward man with power,
 As Christ within our hearts doth dwell;
Our root in Him, though storms may lower,
 Victorious love we still shall tell.

3 The love that passeth knowledge give us,
    Its height and depth and breadth and length:
  Abundantly beyond our asking,
    Beyond our thought give us Thy strength.

4 Thy power it is that worketh in us,
    O multiply it here to-day,
  And Christ, our Lord, shall have the glory
    Within His church through endless day.

396

COME, praise the Lord, exalt His name,
    Our Saviour and our King;
  'Tis meet we should His praise proclaim,
    And hallelujah sing.

2 How great, how precious is His name,
    How poor the praise we bring;
  His people still should own His claim,
    And hallelujah sing.

3 A day will come, its dawn we greet,
    When heaven itself shall ring,
  And all the saints with joy shall meet,
    And hallelujah sing.

397

SOMETIMES I catch sweet glimpses of His face,
    But that is all;
  Sometimes He looks on me and seems to smile,
    But that is all;
  Sometimes He speaks a passing word of peace,
    But that is all;
  Sometimes I think I hear His loving voice
    Upon me call.

2 And is this all He meant when first He said,
    "Come unto me?"
  Is there no deeper, more enduring rest
    In Him for thee?
  Is there no steadier light for thee in Him?
    O come and see;
  Is there no deeper, more enduring rest
    In Him for thee?

3 Nay, do not wrong Him by thy heavy thoughts,
But trust His love;
Do thou full justice to His tenderness,
His mercy prove;
Take Him for what He is, O take Him all,
And look above;
And do not wrong Him by thy heavy thoughts,
But trust His love.

4 Christ and His love shall be thy blesséd all
For evermore;
Christ and His light shall shine on all thy ways
For evermore;
Christ and His peace shall keep thy troubled soul
For evermore;
Christ and His love shall be thy blesséd all
For evermore.

398

CHRISTIAN, walk *carefully*, danger is near;
On in thy journey with trembling and fear,
Snares from without and temptations within,
Seek to entice thee once more into sin.

CHO.—||: Christian, walk *carefully*, :||
Christian, walk *carefully*, danger is near.

2 Christian, walk *cheerfully* through the fierce storm,
Dark though the sky with its threats of alarm:
Soon will the clouds and the tempest be o'er,
Then with thy Saviour thou'lt rest ever more.

CHO.—||: Christian, walk *cheerfully*, :||
Christian, walk *cheerfully*, through the fierce storm.

3 Christian, walk *prayerfully*, oft wilt thou fall,
If thou forget on thy Saviour to call;
Safe thou shalt walk through each trial and care,
If thou art clad in the armor of prayer.

CHO.—||: Christian, walk *prayerfully*, :||
Christian, walk *prayerfully*, fear lest thou fall.

4 Christian, walk *hopefully*, sorrow and pain
　Cease when the haven of rest thou shalt gain;
　Then from the lips of the Judge, thy reward:
　"Enter thou into the joy of thy Lord."

　　CHO.—||: Christian, walk *hopefully*, :||
　　Christian, walk *hopefully*, rest thou shalt gain.

399

H E holds the key of all unknown,
　　And I am glad;
If other hands should hold the key,
Or, if He trusted it to me,
I might be sad,   I might be sad.

2 What if to-morrow's cares were here
　　　Without its rest?
　I'd rather He unlocked the day,
　And, as the hours swing open, say,
　" My will is best,"   " My will is best."

3 The very dimness of my sigh.
　　　Makes me secure;
　For, groping in my misty way,
　I feel His hand; I hear Him say,
　" My help is sure,"   " My help is sure."

4 I cannot read His future plans,
　　　But this I know:
　I have the smiling of His face,
　And all the refuge of His grace,
　While here below,   While here below.

5 Enough: this covers all my wants,
　　　And so I rest;
　For what I cannot, He can see,
　And in His care I safe shall be,—
　Forever blest,   Forever blest.

400

T HE cross it standeth fast,
　　Hallelujah! hallelujah!
Defying every blast,
　　Hallelujah! hallelujah!

The winds of hell have blown,
The world its hate hath shown,
Yet it is not overthrown,
  Hallelujah for the cross!

Cho.—‖: Hallelujah, hallelujah, hallelujah for the cross,
  Hallelujah, hallelujah, it shall never suffer loss. :‖

2 It is the old cross still,
    Hallolujah! hallelujah!
  Its triumph let us tell,
    Hallelujah! hallelujah!
  The grace of God here shone,
  Through Christ the blesséd Son,
  Who did for sin atone,
    Hallelujah for the cross!

3 'Twas here the debt was paid,
    Hallelujah! hallelujah!
  Our sins on Jesus laid,
    Hallelujah! hallelujah!
  So round the cross we sing,
  Of Christ our offering,
  Of Christ our living King,
    Hallelujah for the cross!

———

401

YOU'RE starting, my boy, on life's journey,
    Along the grand highway of life;
You'll meet with a thousand temptations—
    Each city with evil is rife.
This world is a stage of excitement,
    There's danger wherever you go;
But if you are tempted in weakness,
    Have courage, my boy, to say No!

Cho.—‖: Have courage, my boy, to say No! :‖
    ‖: Have courage, my boy, :‖
  Have courage, my boy, to say No!

2 In courage, my boy. lies your safety,
    When you the long journey begin;
  Your trust in a heavenly Father
    Will keep you unspotted from sin.

Temptations will go on increasing,
  As streams from a rivulet flow;
But if you'd be true to your manhood,
  Have courage, my boy, to say No!

3 Be careful in choosing companions,
  Seek only the brave and the true;
And stand by your friends when in trial,
  Ne'er changing the old for the new;
And when by false friends you are tempted
  The taste of the wine cup to know,
With firmness, with patience and kindness,
  Have courage, my boy, to say No!

402

CHOOSE I must, and soon must choose
  Holiness, or heaven lose;
While what heaven loves, I hate,
Shut for me is heaven's gate.

2 Endless sin means endless woe;
Into endless sin I go
If my soul, from reason rent,
Takes from sin its final bent.

3 As the stream its channel grooves,
And within that channel moves,
So doth habit's deepest tide
Groove its bed, and there abide.

4 Light obeyed increaseth light,
Light resisted bringeth night;
Who shall give me will to choose,
If the love of light I lose?

5 Speed, my soul; this instant yield;
Let the Light its sceptre wield:
While thy God prolongeth grace,
Haste thee toward His holy face!

403

SOME day we say, and turn our eyes
  Tow'rd the fair hills of Paradise:
Some day, some time, a sweet new rest
Shall blossom, flower-like, in each breast;

‖: Some day, some time, our eyes shall see
The faces kept in memory; :‖
Some day their hands shall clasp our hand,
‖: Just over in the morning land; :‖
Some day their hands shall clasp our hand,
Just over in the morning land;
O morning land!   O morning land!

2 Some day our ears shall hear the song
Of triumph over sin and wrong;
Some day, some time, but oh! not yet;
But we will wait and not forget,
‖: That some day all these things shall be,
And rest be given to you and me; :‖
So wait, my friends, though years move slow,
‖: That happy time will come, we know; :‖
So wait, my friends, though years move slow,
That happy time will come, we know,
O morning land!   O morning land!

404

COME to the Saviour, hear His loving voice,
    Never will you find a Friend so true;
Now He is waiting, trust Him and rejoice,
Tenderly He calleth you.

CHO.—O, what a Saviour standing at the door,
    Haste while He lingers, pardon now implore;
Still He is waiting, grieve His love no more,
    Tenderly He calleth you.

2 Blest words of comfort, gently now they fall,
    Jesus is the Life, the Truth, the Way;
Come to the fountain, there is room for all,
    Jesus bids you come to-day.

3 Softly the Spirit whispers in the heart,
    Do not slight the Saviour's offered grace;
Gladly receive Him, let Him not depart,
    Happy they who seek His face.

4 Light in the darkness, joy in any pain,
    Refuge for the weary and oppressed;
Still He is waiting, calling yet again,
    Come, and He will give you rest.

405

O GOLDEN day, O day of God,
   When sinless souls the garden trod!
In bliss supreme, 'neath sunny skies,
In Eden fair, in Paradise.

CHO.—O Paradise, sweet Paradise,
   From scenes of earth we long to rise;
   O Paradise, bright Paradise,
   Where Jesus reigns beyond the skies.

2 The fatal fall, the sin, the shame,
   The death, the doom, the sword aflame,
   The curse, the crime beyond disguise,
   The earth no more is Paradise.

3 The beaded brow, the silvered hair,
   The aching heart, the vacant chair,
   The grassy graves, the broken ties,
   Are not the scenes of Paradise.

4 To Christ the Lord upon the tree,
   A sinner cries:—" Remember me!"
   "To-day shalt thou," the Lord replies,
   " Be with me there in Paradise."

5 O golden day when Christ descends,
   The curse removes and sorrow ends;
   All glory-clad, the ransomed rise
   To reign with Him in Paradise.

406

I WILL sing the wondrous story
   Of the Christ who died for me;
How He left His home in glory,
   For the cross on Calvary.

CHO.—Yes, I'll sing the wondrous story
   Of the Christ who died for me;
   Sing it with the saints in glory,
   Gathered by the crystal sea.

2 I was lost, but Jesus found me,
   Found the sheep that went astray;
Threw His loving arms around me,
   Drew me back into His way.

3 I was bruised, but Jesus healed me,
   Faint was I from many a fall,
Sight was gone, and fears possessed me,
   But He freed me from them all.

4 Days of darkness still come o'er me,
   Sorrow's paths I often tread,
But the Saviour still is with me,
   By His hand I'm safely led.

5 He will keep me till the river
   Rolls its waters at my feet;
Then He'll bear me safely over,
   Where the loved ones I shall meet.

407

AWAKE, my soul, to joyful lays,
   And sing thy great Redeemer's praise
He justly claims a song from me,
His loving-kindness, oh, how free!
Loving-kindness, loving-kindness,
His loving-kindness, oh, how free!

2 He saw me ruined by the fall,
   Yet loved me notwithstanding all;
He saved me from my lost estate,
His loving-kindness, oh, how great!
Loving kindness, loving-kindness,
His loving-kindness, oh, how great!

3 Though numerous hosts of mighty foes,
   Though earth and hell my way oppose,
He safely leads my soul along,
His loving-kindness, oh, how strong!
Loving-kindness, loving-kindness,
His loving-kindness, oh, how strong!

4 When trouble, like a gloomy cloud,
   Has gathered thick, and thundered loud,
He near my soul has always stood,
His loving-kindness, oh, how good!
Loving-kindness, loving-kindness,
His loving-kindness, oh, how good!

408

WELL, wife, I've found the model church,
    And worshipped there to-day;
It made me think of good old times,
    Before my hair was gray;
The meeting house was finer built
    Than they were years ago;
But then I found when I went in,
    It was not built for show.

2 The sexton did not set me down,
    Away back by the door;
He knew that I was old and deaf,
    And saw that I was poor;
He must have been a Christian man—
    He led me boldly through
The crowded aisle of that grand church,
    To find a pleasant pew.

3 I wish you'd heard the singing, wife,
    It had the old-time ring;
The preacher said with trumpet voice,
    Let all the people sing:
"Old Coronation," was the tune;
    The music upward rolled,
Until I thought the angel-choir
    Struck all their harps of gold.

4 My deafness seemed to melt away,
    My spirit caught the fire;
I joined my feeble, trembling voice
    With that melodious choir;
And sang, as in my youthful days,
    "Let angels prostrate fall;
‖: Bring forth the royal diadem,
    And crown Him Lord of all." :‖

5 I tell you, wife, it did me good
    To sing that hymn once more;
I felt like some wrecked mariner
    Who gets a glimpse of shore;
I almost want to lay aside
    This weather-beaten form,
And anchor in the blessèd port,
    Forever from the storm.

6 'Twas not a flowery sermon, wife,
  But simple gospel truth;
It fitted humble men like me;
  It suited hopeful youth;
To win immortal souls to Christ,
  The earnest preacher tried;
He talked not of himself, or creed,
  But Jesus crucified.

7 Dear wife, the toil will soon be o'er,
  The victory soon be won;
The shining land is just ahead,
  Our race is nearly run:
We're nearing Canaan's happy shore,
  Our home so bright and fair;
Thank God, we'll never sin again;
  ||: "There'll be no sorrow there, :||
In heaven above, where all is love,
  There'll be no sorrow there."

409

THE Spirit and the bride say, "Come!
  And take the water of life!"
O blesséd call! Good news to all
  Who tire of sin and strife.

CHO·—||: The Spirit says, "Come!"
  The bride says, "Come!"
  And take of the water of life freely. :||

2 Let every one who hears, say "Come!"
  And joyful witness give;
I heard the sound,   The stream I found,
  I drank, and now I live!

3 Ye souls who are athirst, forsake
  Your broken cisterns first;
Then come, partake,   One draught will slake
  Your soul's consuming thirst.

4 Yea, whosoever will may come,
  Your longings Christ can fill;
The stream is free   To you and me,
  And whosoever will.

410

WHILE Jesus whispers to you,
    Come, sinner, come!
While we are praying for you,
    Come, sinner, come!
Now is the time to own Him,
    Come, sinner, come!
Now is the time to know Him,
    Come, sinner, come!

2 Are you too heavy laden?
    Come, sinner, come!
Jesus will bear your burden,
    Come, sinner, come!
Jesus will not deceive you,
    Come, sinner, come!
Jesus will now receive you,
    Come, sinner, come!

3 Oh, hear His tender pleading,
    Come, sinner, come!
Come and receive the blessing,
    Come, sinner, come!
While Jesus whispers to you,
    Come, sinner, come!
While we are praying for you,
    Come, sinner, come!

411

WHEN the mists have rolled in splendor
    From the beauty of the hills,
And the sunlight falls in gladness
    On the river and the rills,
We recall our Father's promise
    In the rainbow of the spray:
We shall know each other better
    When the mists have rolled away.

CHO.—We shall know as we are known,
    Never more to walk alone,
In the dawning of the morning
    Of that bright and happy day:
We shall know each other better
    When the mists have rolled away.

2 Oft we tread the path before us
    With a weary-burdened heart;
Oft we toil amid the shadows,
    And our fields are far apart:
But the Saviour's "Come, ye blesséd,"
    All our labor will repay,
When we gather in the morning
    Where the mists have rolled away.

3 We shall come with joy and gladness,
    We shall gather round the throne;
Face to face with those that love us,
    We shall know as we are known:
And the song of our redemption,
    Shall resound through endless day,
When the shadows have departed,
    And the mists have rolled away.

412

SAVIOUR, again to Thy dear name we raise
    With one accord our parting hymn of praise;
Once more we bless Thee ere our worship cease,
Then, lowly kneeling, wait Thy word of peace.

2 Grant us Thy peace upon our homeward way;
With Thee begun, with Thee shall end the day;
Guard Thou the lips from sin, the hearts from shame
That in this house have called upon Thy name.

3 Grant us Thy peace, Lord, through the coming night,
Turn Thou for us its darkness into light;
From harm and danger keep Thy children free,
For dark and light are both alike to Thee.

4 Grant us Thy peace throughout our earthly life,
Our balm in sorrow, and our stay in strife;
Then, when Thy voice shall bid our conflict cease.
Call us, O Lord, to Thine eternal peace.

413

CHRIST has for sin atonement made,
    What a wonderful Saviour!
We are redeemed! the price is paid!
    What a wonderful Saviour!

CHO.—What a wonderful Saviour is Jesus, my Jesus!
　　　What a wonderful Saviour is Jesus, my Lord!

2 I praise Him for the cleansing blood,
　　　What a wonderful Saviour!
　That reconciled my soul to God;
　　　What a wonderful Saviour!

3 He cleansed my heart from all its sin,
　　　What a wonderful Saviour!
　And now He reigns and rules therein;
　　　What a wonderful Saviour!

4 He walks beside me in the way,
　　　What a wonderful Saviour!
　And keeps me faithful day by day;
　　　What a wonderful Saviour!

5 He gives me overcoming power,
　　　What a wonderful Saviour!
　And triumph in each trying hour;
　　　What a wonderful Saviour!

6 To Him I've given all my heart,
　　　What a wonderful Saviour!
　The world shall never share a part;
　　　What a wonderful Saviour!

414

A MIGHTY fortress is our God,
　　A bulwark never failing;
Our Helper He, amid the flood
　Of mortal ills prevailing.
　　For still our ancient foe
　　Doth seek to work his woe:
　　His craft and power are great,
　　And armed with cruel hate—
　　On earth is not his equal.

2 Did we in our own strength confide,
　Our striving would be losing;
Were not the right man on our side,
　The man of God's own choosing.
　　Doth ask who that may be?
　　Christ Jesus, it is He;

Lord Sabaoth is His name,
From age to age the same;
And He must win the battle.

3 And though this world, with devils filled,
Should threaten to undo us;
We will not fear, for God hath willed,
His truth to triumph through us.
Let goods and kindred go,
This mortal life also;
The body they may kill;
God's truth abideth still,
His kingdom is forever.

415

BENEATH the glorious throne above,
The crystal fountain springing,
A river full of life and love,
Is joy and gladness bringing.

CHO.—O glorious fountain, now flowing so free,
O fountain of cleansing, opened wide to me.

2 Through all my soul its waters flow,
Through all my nature stealing;
And deep within my heart I know
The consciousness of healing.

3 The barren wastes are fruitful lands,
The desert blooms with roses;
And He, the glory of all lands,
His lovely face discloses.

4 My sun no more goes down by day,
My moon no more is waning;
My feet run swift the shining way,
The heavenly portals gaining.

5 Oh, depth of mercy! breadth of grace!
Oh, love of God unbounded!
My soul is lost in sweet amaze,
By wondrous love confounded.

416

HEAR us, O Saviour, while we pray,
    Humbly our need confessing;
Grant us the promised showers to-day,
    Send them upon us, O Lord.

REF.—Send showers of blessing;
        Send showers refreshing;
        Send us showers of blessing;
        Send them, Lord, we pray.

2 Knowing Thy love, on Thee we call,
    Boldly Thy throne addressing;
Pleading that showers of grace may fall,—
    Send them upon us, O Lord.

3 Trusting Thy word that cannot fail,
    Master, we claim Thy promise;
Oh that our faith may now prevail,—
    Send us the showers, O Lord.

417

I'VE learned to sing a glad new song
    Of praise unto our King!
And now with all my ransomed powers
    His praises I will sing.

CHO.—His praises I will sing,
        He is my Lord and King;
        And now with all my ransomed powers
        His praises I will sing.

2 I've learned to sing the song of peace,
    'Tis sweeter every day,
Since Jesus calmed my troubled soul,
    And bore my sins away.

3 I sing the song of perfect love,
    It casteth out all fear!
O breadth, O length, O depth, O height!
    O love so full of cheer!

4 I've learned to sing the song of joy,
    My cup is running o'er,
With blessings full of peace and love,
    And still there's more and more!

5 Soon I shall sing the new, new song
Of Moses and the Lamb,
With all the sainted hosts above,
Before the great I AM!

418

HOPE on, hope on, O troubled heart,
If doubts and fears o'ertake thee,
Remember this—the Lord hath said,
He never will forsake thee;
Then murmur not, still bear thy lot,
Nor yield to care or sorrow;
Be sure the clouds that frown to-day
Will break in smiles to-morrow.

2 Hope on, hope on, though dark and deep
The shadows gather o'er thee;
Be not dismayed; thy Saviour holds
The lamp of life before thee;
And if He will that thou to-day
Shouldst tread the vale of sorrow;
Be not afraid, but trust and wait;
The sun will shine to-morrow.

3 Hope on, hope on, go bravely forth
Through trial and temptation,
Directed by the worth of truth,
So full of consolation;
There is a calm for every storm,
A joy for every sorrow,
A night from which the soul shall wake
To hail an endless morrow.

419

WHY do you linger, why do you stay
In the broad road, that most dangerous way—
While right before you, narrow and strait,
Is the bright pathway to heaven's pearly gate?

REF.—||: Narrow and strait, :||
Is the bright pathway to heaven's pearly gate.

2 Do you find pleasures, lasting and pure,
In the gay scenes that the thoughtless allure,—
While your Redeemer, with love so great,
Points to the way that is narrow and strait?

3 Come then, belovéd, no longer stay;
　　Leave the broad highway, O leave it to-day;
　　Make your decision, oh, do not wait;
　　Take thou the pathway so narrow and strait.

420

M Y soul at last a rest hath found,
　　　A rest that will not fail;
A sure and certain anch'rage-ground
　　In Christ within the vail.

CHO.—O Rock of Ages cleft for me,
　　　In Thee my soul securely hide;
　　　My tower of strength, I fly to Thee,
　　　And safely there abide.

2 I'll hide me in this refuge strong,
　　From every stormy blast;
And sit and sing until the waves
　　Of wrath are overpast.

3 Ye comfortless and tempest-tost,
　　By sins and woes opprest,
Ye tempted, troubled, ruined, lost,
　　Come find in Christ your rest.

4 Ye thirsty, from this smitten Rock
　　Life's crystal waters spring;
There hide from every stormy shock,
　　And rest, and drink, and sing.

421

J ESUS saves! O blesséd story,
　　　Full of love and peace divine,
Bursting from the realms of glory,
　　Echoing through this world of time.

CHO.—Jesus saves! O glory! glory!
　　　　Shout the tidings o'er and o'er;
　　　Tell to all the earth the story,
　　　　Jesus saves for evermore.

2 Jesus saves! O, who can fathom
　　All the fulness of His love?

He once died for our redemption,
Now He waits for us above.

3 Jesus saves! O sinner, hearken
To the call of love to-day;
There's no other way to heaven,
Jesus is the only way.

422

HOW sweet the joy that fills my soul:
Christ is my Redeemer;
His precious blood has made me whole:
Christ is my Redeemer;
My sins were all upon Him laid,
A full atonement He hath made,
For me He hath the ransom paid:
Christ is my Redeemer.

2 Though Satan oft my way oppose,
Christ is my Redeemer;
With this I boldly meet my foes:
Christ is my Redeemer;
'Twas this that gave me life and light,
'Tis this that nerves me for the fight,
'Tis this my hope that shines so bright:
Christ is my Redeemer.

3 When trials come I still confess,
Christ is my Redeemer;
He gives me grace each care to bless:
Christ is my Redeemer;
He guides and keeps me day by day,
He closer comes when dark the way,
He doth with this my fears allay;
Christ is my Redeemer.

4 The victory by this I gain,
Christ is my Redeemer:
By this I break sin's galling chain:
Christ is my Redeemer;
And if He tarry and I sleep,
My dying hour this hope shall keep,
That when He comes the grave to reap,
Christ is my Redeemer.

423

LEAD to the shadow of the Rock of Refuge
        My weary feet;
Give me the water from the life stream flowing
        Clear, pure and sweet.

CHO.—There from the billows and the tempest hiding,
        Under the shelter of Thy love abiding,
        Safe in the shadow of the " Rock of Ages,"
                Joy shall be mine.

2 Lead to the shadow of the Rock Eternal
        My heart oppressed;
There in the secret of Thy holy presence,
        Calm shall I rest.

3 Lead to the shadow of the "Rock of Ages,"
        O keep thou me
Safe from the arrows of the world's temptations,
        Close, close to Thee.

424

JESUS, I come to Thee for light,
        Restore to me my blinded sight,
And from my soul dispel the night—
        ‖: Jesus, to Thee I come! :‖

2 Jesus, I come—I cannot stay
        From Thee another precious day;
I would Thy word at once obey—
        ‖: Jesus, to Thee I come! :‖

3 Jesus, I come—" just as I am,"
        To Thee, the holy, spotless Lamb;
Thou wilt my troubled spirit calm—
        ‖: Jesus, to Thee I come! :‖

425

RIDE on! ride on in majesty!
        Hark! all the tribes hosanna cry!
O Saviour meek, pursue Thy road
With palms and scattered garments strewed.

CHO.—Ride on, ride on in majesty!
        In lowly pomp, ride on to die.

2 Ride on! ride on in majesty!
  The angel armies of the sky
  Look down with sad and wondering eyes
  To see the approaching Sacrifice.

3 Ride on! ride on in majesty!
  The last and fiercest strife is nigh;
  The Father on His sapphire throne
  Awaits His own annointed Son.

4 Ride on! ride on in majesty!
  In lowly pomp ride on to die;
  Bow Thy meek head to mortal pain,
  Then take, O God, Thy power and reign.

426

O UR Saviour will descend again,
    Earth's buried millions raising;
With Him will come a glorious train,
  Adoring Him and praising.

Cho.—Raise high the song that loud and long
       Before Him ceaseth never,
     Till, casting down each golden crown,
       We worship Him forever.

2 And though these bodies lie in dust
  Before that glad appearing,
Yet shall they stand among the just,
  Our Saviour's image wearing.

3 What though earth's gathering tempests lower,
  And ages pass in sadness?
Yet we may see that glorious hour,
  And hail the dawn with gladness.

4 Then, safe at last, this blesséd throng,
  Set free from tribulation,
Shall ever praise in holy song
  The God of their salvation.

427

'T IS a true and faithful saying,
    Jesus died for sinful men;
Though we've told the story often,
  We must tell it o'er again.

CHO.—O glad and glorious Gospel!
    With joy we now proclaim
A full and free salvation,
    Through faith in Jesus' name.

2 He has made a full atonement,
    Now His saving work is done;
He has satisfied the Father,
    Who accepts us in His Son.

3 Still upon His hands the nail prints,
    And the scars upon His brow,
Our Redeemer, Lord and Saviour
    In the glory standeth now.

4 But remember this same Jesus
    In the clouds will come again,
And with Him His blood-bought people
    Evermore shall live and reign.

428

WHILE we pray, and while we plead,
    While you see your soul's deep need,
While your Father calls you home,
Will you not, my brother, come?

CHO.—||: Why not now? why not now?
    Why not come to Jesus now? :||

2 You have wandered far away;
    Do not risk another day;
Do not turn from God your face,
But, to-day, accept His grace.

3 In the world you've failed to find
    Aught of peace for troubled mind;
Come to Christ, on Him believe,
Peace and joy you shall receive.

4 Come to Christ, confession make;
    Come to Christ and pardon take;
Trust in Him from day to day,
He will keep you all the way.

429

CONQUERING now and still to conquer,
    Rideth a King in His might,
Leading the host of all the faithful
    Into the midst of the fight;
See them with courage advancing,
    Clad in their brilliant array,
Shouting the name of their Leader,
    Hear them exultingly say:

CHO.—" Not to the strong is the battle,
        Not to the swift is the race,
    Yet to the true and the faithful
        Vict'ry is promised through grace."

2 Conquering now and still to conquer:
    Who is this wonderful King?
Whence all the armies which He leadeth,
    While of His glory they sing?
He is our Lord and Redeemer,
    Saviour and Monarch divine,
They are the stars that forever
    Bright in His kingdom will shine.

3 Conquering now and still to conquer,
    Jesus, Thou Ruler of all,
Thrones and their scepters all shall perish,
    Crowns and their splendor shall fall;
Yet shall the armies Thou leadest,
    Faithful and true to the last,
Find in Thy mansions eternal,
    Rest when their warfare is past.

430

HOLY Ghost, with light divine,
    Shine upon this heart of mine;
Chase the shades of night away,
Turn my darkness in to-day.

2 Holy Ghost, with power divine,
    Cleanse this guilty heart of mine;
Long hath sin, without control,
Held dominion o'er my soul.

3 Holy Ghost, with joy divine,
Cheer this saddened heart of mine;
Bid my many woes depart,
Heal my wounded, bleeding heart.

4 Holy Spirit, all divine,
Dwell within this heart of mine;
Cast down every idol-throne,
Reign supreme—and reign alone.

431

REJOICE! ye saints, again rejoice!
And sing with one accord;
Rejoice with all your heart and voice,
In Christ your risen Lord.

CHO.—Rejoice, rejoice in the Lord!
Rejoice in the Lord alway;
Rejoice, rejoice in the Lord!
And again I say, rejoice!

2 Rejoice! rejoice! lift up your head,
And praise the living God,
That for your souls the Saviour shed
His own most precious blood.

3 Rejoice! rejoice! let praise abound
Before Jehovah's throne,
For dead ones raised, and lost ones found,
And prodigals brought home.

4 Rejoice! rejoice! the Lord will come,
According to His word,
And gather all His ransomed home,
"For ever with the Lord."

432

NEVER shone a light so fair,
Never fell so sweet a song,
As the chorus in the air
Chanted by the angel-throng:
Every star took up the story,
Christ has come, the Prince of glory,
Come in humble hearts to dwell
God with us, God with us,
God with us, Immanuel.

2 Still that Jubilee of song
   Breaks upon the rising morn;
While the anthem rolls along,
   Floods of light the earth adorn;
Old and young take up the story:
   Christ has come, etc.

3 Welcome now the blesséd day
   When we praise the Lord our King;
When we meet to praise and pray,
   And His love with gladness sing;
Let the world take up the story:
   Christ has come, etc.

433

O BRETHREN, rise and sing,
   Make hallelujahs ring
To our Almighty King,
   And bless His name.

CHO.—‖: Hallelujah, hallelujah,
   Hallelujah, bless His name! :‖

2 He wins for us the fight,
   He makes our darkness light;
All dreary doubts take flight
   When He appears.

3 No lack or want have they
   Who make the Lord their stay;
New strength for every day
   His grace supplies.

4 O trust Him then to guide,
   And for His own provide;
Should weal or woe betide,
   Trust to the end.

434

O NE day the Shepherd passed, and turning, said,
   "Come, follow me;"
What wonder that in haste I rose,
   So kind was He!

2 He led me through green pasture land,
        By waters still;
With such a Guide, who would not follow,
        Go where He will?

3 From out no other eye had ever beamed
        Such love on me;
Good Shepherd, lead, and I will follow
        Hard after Thee.

4 Black clouds were gathering on a blacker sky, the
        World all so drear;
Upon the night-wind rose the cry of
        One in great fear.

5 Dear Lord, the darkness falls upon me,
        I cannot see;
My feet are stumbling on the mountains;
        Oh! succor me.

6 And soon there came a loving call in answer,
        "Be not afraid;
Mine eyes shall guide the blind ones, and the weary
        Mine arm shall aid."

7 None ever perished following Jesus fully,
        No, never one;
The weakest lambs are carried in His bosom, and
        Brought safely home.

———

O WANDERING souls, why longer roam
        Away from God, away from home?
The Saviour calls, O hear Him say,—
Whoever will may come to-day.

CHO.—All praise and glory be unto Jesus,
        For He hath purchased a full salvation:
        Behold how wondrous the proclamation.
        "Whosoever will may come!"

    2 Behold His hands extended now,
        The dews of night are on His brow,
        He knocks, He calls, He waiteth still.
        Oh, come to Him, whoever will.

3 In simple faith His word believe,
And His abundant grace receive;
No love like His the heart can fill;
Oh, come to Him, whoever will.

4 The "Spirit and the Bride say, come!"
And find in Him sweet rest and home;
Let Him that heareth echo still,
The blesséd " *whosoever will.*"

436

HEAR me, blesséd Jesus,
Bid all fear depart;
Let Thy Spirit whisper
Peace within my heart.

CHO.—Then, whate'er Thou sendest,
Happy shall I be,
Jesus, my Redeemer,
Looking unto Thee.

2 Let me fully trust Thee,
Resting on Thy Word;
Let me still with patience
Wait on Thee, O Lord.

3 Hiding in the shadow
Of Thy sheltering wings,
I shall rest confiding
In the King of kings.

437

YES, we'll meet again in the morning,
In the dawn of a fairer day;
When the night of watching and waiting,
With its darkness has passed away.
Where no shadows veil the sunshine,
Over there in the heavenly land,
And the crystal waves of the river,
Ever flow o'er the golden sand.

2 Where our precious ones now are dwelling,
Free from toil and from every care;
With their garments spotless and shining,
Like the robes that the angels wear.

When our pilgrimage completed,
    And our footsteps no longer roam,
By the pearly gates gladly waiting,
    They will give us a welcome home.

3 O what joy when all shall be over,
    And the journey on earth we close,
And the angels homeward shall bear us,
    Where the life-stream forever flows.
We shall see the King of glory,
    We shall praise Him with harp and voice;
We shall sing the grace that redeemed us,
    While our hearts in His love rejoice.

438

GIRD on the sword and armor!
    Go raise the banner high!
The Captain of Salvation
    To thee is ever nigh.

CHO.—Then wave the glorious banner!
    Press forward in His name;
And soon thy Guide and Captain
    Will victory proclaim.

2 Gird on the sword and armor!
    Let faith be thy strong shield;
His promise shall sustain thee
    On every battle field.

3 Gird on the sword and armor!
    Press on the foe to fight;
No enemy can harm thee,
    For God sustains the right.

439

HOW do I know my sins forgiven?
    My Saviour tells me so!
That now I am an heir of heaven?
    My Saviour tells me so!

CHO.—Away with doubt, away with fear,
    When this by faith I know;
God's word shall stand for evermore:
    My Saviour tells me so.

2 By trusting Christ the witness came,
  My Saviour tells me so!
The pardon's free in Jesus' name:
  My Saviour tells me so.

3 Believe and thou shalt surely live:
  My Saviour tells me so!
The Spirit's witness God will give:
  My Saviour tells me so.

4 Though rough the way, I shall endure;
  My Saviour tells me so!
His sheep are ever kept secure:
  My Saviour tells me so.

5 How do I know I'll live again?
  My Saviour tells me so!
With Christ in glory I shall reign,
  My Saviour tells me so.

440

HIDE me, O my Saviour, hide me
    In Thy holy place;
Resting there beneath Thy glory,
  O let me see Thy face.

CHO.—Hide me, hide me!
    O blesséd Saviour, hide me;
    O Saviour, keep me
    Safely, O Lord, with Thee.

2 Hide me, when the storm is raging
    O'er life's troubled sea;
Like a dove on ocean's billows,
    O let me fly to Thee.

3 Hide me, when my heart is breaking
    With its weight of woe;
When in tears I seek the comfort
    Thou canst alone bestow.

441

THROW out the Life-Line across the dark wave,
    There is a brother whom some one should save;
Somebody's brother! oh, who then, will dare
To throw out the Life-Line, his peril to share?

CHO.—‖: Throw out the Life-Line! :‖
Some one is drifting away;
‖: Throw out the Life-Line! :‖
Some one is sinking to-day.

2 Throw out the Life-Line with hand quick and strong:
Why do you tarry, why linger so long?
See! he is sinking; oh, hasten to-day—
And out with the Life-Boat! away, then, away!

3 Throw out the Life-Line to danger-fraught men,
Sinking in anguish where you've never been;
Winds of temptation and billows of woe
Will soon hurl them out where the dark waters flow.

4 Soon will the season of rescue be o'er.
Soon will they drift to eternity's shore,
Haste then, my brother, no time for delay,
But throw out the Life-Line and save them to-day.

442

O WORSHIP the King, all-glorious above!
And gratefully sing His wonderful love;
Our Shield and Defender, the Ancient of days,
Pavilioned in splendor, and girded with praise.

2 O tell of His might, and sing of His grace,
Whose robe is the light, whose canopy space;
His chariots of wrath the deep thunder-clouds form,
And dark is His path on the wings of the storm.

3 Thy bountiful care, what tongue can recite?
It breathes in the air, it shines in the light;
Its streams from the hills, it descends to the plain,
And sweetly distills in the dew and the rain.

4 Frail children of dust, and feeble as frail,
In Thee do we trust, nor find Thee to fail—
Thy mercies, how tender! How firm to the end,
Our Maker, Defender, Redeemer, and Friend.

443

HOLY Spirit, Teacher Thou,
At the throne of grace we bow;
Come, perform Thine office now,
Teach us evermore.

Ref.—Holy Spirit, teach us ever,
  Comfort, guide, and leave us **never;**
  Dwell within us, we implore,
  Now and evermore.

2 Comforter indeed Thou art,
  Giving strength to every heart;
  Let Thy presence ne'er depart,
  Comfort evermore.

3 Sent to be our Guide to-day,
  Keep us in the narrow way;
  Grant that we may never stray,
  Guide us evermore.

4 Teacher, Comforter, and Guide,
  In our hearts do Thou abide;
  And in life, whate'er betide,
  Help us evermore.

444

PREACH the gospel, sound it forth,
  Tell of free and full salvation;
Spread the tidings o'er the earth,
  Go to every tribe and nation.

Cho.—Spread the joyful tidings in anthem and story,
Jesus hath redeemed us, O give Him the glory.

2 Preach the gospel full of joy,
  While on grace and mercy dwelling;
Heart and soul in full employ,
  As the story you are telling,

3 Preach the gospel, make it clear,
  By the blood of Christ remission;
Give the message, make them hear,
  This alone is our commission.

4 Preach the gospel full of love,
  Christ's compassion fully knowing;
Seek the power from above,
  While His great compassion showing.

5 Preach the gospel as if God
  Sinners lost through you were seeking;
His salvation through the word,
  Speak as if the Lord were speaking.

445

I AM trusting Thee, Lord Jesus,
　　Trusting only Thee!
Trusting Thee for full salvation,
　　Great and free.

Cho.—I am trusting,
　　　Trusting only Thee!
　　　I am trusting, trusting,
　　　Trusting only Thee.

2 I am trusting Thee for pardon,
　　At Thy feet I bow;
For Thy grace and tender mercy,
　　Trusting now.

3 I am trusting Thee for cleansing
　　In the crimson flood;
Trusting Thee to make me holy
　　By Thy blood.

4 I am trusting Thee for power,
　　Thine can never fail;
Words which Thou Thyself shalt give me,
　　Must prevail.

5 I am trusting Thee, Lord Jesus.
　　Never let me fall;
I am trusting Thee for ever,
　　And for all.

446

A FTER the toil and trouble,
　　There cometh a day of rest;
After the weary conflict,
　　Peace on the Saviour's breast;
After the care and sorrow,
　　The glory of light and love;
After the wilderness journey,
　　The Father's bright home above.

2 After the night of darkness,
　　The shadows all flee away;
After the day of sadness,
　　Hope sheds her brightest ray;

After the strife and struggle,
 The victory is won;
After the work is over,
 The Master's own word, "Well done."

3 After the hours of chastening,
 The spirit made pure and bright;
After the earth's dark shadow,
 Clear in the light of Light;
After the guiding counsel,
 Communion full and sweet;
After the willing service,
 All laid at the Saviour's feet.

4 After the pain and sickness,
 The tears are all wiped away;
After the flowers are gathered,
 No more of earth's decay;
After the deep heart-sorrow,
 An end of every strife;
After the daily crosses,
 A glorious crown of life.

447

SIN no more! thy soul is free,
 Christ has died to ransom thee;
Now the power of sin is o'er,
Jesus bids thee "sin no more."

Cho.—Sin no more! thy soul is free,
 Christ has died to ransom thee;
 Sing the message o'er and o'er,
 Christ forgives thee, sin no more.

2 Sin no more! but closely keep
 Near the Hand that guards the sheep;
Shun the snares that lured before,
Trembling go, and sin no more.

3 Sin no more! His blood hath bought,
 Think on what His love hath wrought;
Think of what for thee He bore,
Weeping go, and sin no more.

4 Sin no more! O sin no more!
  Jesus lives to keep thee pure;
  If o'ertaken He'll restore,
  Saying, "Go, and sin no more."

448

TAKE time to be holy,
    Speak oft with thy Lord;
Abide in Him always,
    And feed on His Word;
Make friends of God's children;
    Help those who are weak,
Forgetting in nothing
    His blessing to seek.

2 Take time to be holy,
    The world rushes on;
Spend much time in secret
    With Jesus alone;
By looking to Jesus,
    Like Him thou shalt be;
Thy friends in thy conduct
    His likeness shall see.

3 Take time to be holy,
    Let Him be thy Guide;
And run not before Him,
    Whatever betide;
In joy or in sorrow
    Still follow thy Lord,
And, looking to Jesus,
    Still trust in His Word.

4 Take time to be holy,
    Be calm in thy soul;
Each thought and each **motive**
    Beneath His control:
Thus led by His Spirit
    To fountains of love,
Thou soon shalt be **fitted**
    For service above.

449

THE Lord is coming by and by:
  Be ready when He comes!
He comes from His fair home on high:
  Be ready when He comes;
He is the Lord our Righteousness,
And comes His chosen ones to bless,
And at His Father's throne confess:
  Be ready when He comes!

CHO.—‖: Will you be ready when the Bridegroom comes? :‖
Will your lamps be trimmed and bright,
Be it morning, noon or night?
Will you be ready when the Bridegroom comes?

2 He soon will come to earth again:
  Be ready when He comes!
Begin His universal reign:
  Be ready when He comes!
With Hallelujahs heaven will ring,
When Jesus does redemption bring;
O trim your lamps to meet your King!
  Be ready when He comes!

3 Behold! He comes to one and all:
  Be ready when He comes!
He quickly comes with trumpet call:
  Be ready when He comes!
To judgment called at His command,
Drawn thither by His mighty hand,
Before His throne we all must stand;
  Be ready when He comes!

———

450

BEHOLD a Stranger at the door,
  He gently knocks, has knocked before;
Has waited long,—is waiting still;
You treat no other friend so ill.

2 O lovely attitude! He stands
With melting heart and laden hands;
O matchless kindness! and He shows
This matchless kindness to His foes.

3 But will He prove a Friend indeed?
He will—the very Friend you need;
The Friend of sinners, yes, 'tis He,
With garments dyed on Calvary.

4 Rise, touched with gratitude divine;
Turn out His enemy and thine,
That soul-destroying monster, Sin;
And let the heavenly Stranger in.

451

WE praise Thee, we bless Thee,
Our Saviour divine,
All power and dominion
Forever be Thine;
We sing of Thy mercy
With joyful acclaim:
‖: For Thou hast redeemed us;
All praise to Thy name. :‖

2 All honor and praise to
Thine excellent name;
Thy love is unchanging,
Forever the same;
We bless and adore Thee,
O Saviour and King;
‖: With joy and thanksgiving
Thy praises we sing. :‖

3 The strength of the hills, and
The depths of the sea,
The earth and its fulness,
Belong unto Thee;
And yet to the lowly
Thou bendest Thine ear,
‖: So ready their humble
Petitions to hear. :‖

4 Thine infinite goodness
Our tongues shall employ;
Thou givest us richly
All things to enjoy;
We'll follow Thy footsteps,
We'll rest in Thy love,
‖: And soon we shall praise Thee
In mansions above. :‖

452

"IT is finished!" what a gospel!
    Nothing has been left to do,
But to take with grateful gladness
    What the Saviour did for you.

Cho.—||: "It is finished," Hallelujah! :||
    Christ the work has fully done; Hallelujah!
All who will may have their pardon
    Through the blood of God's own Son.

2 "It is finished!" what a gospel!
    Bringing news of victory won,
Telling us of peace and pardon
    Through the blood of God's dear Son.

3 "It is finished!" what a gospel!
    Hear each weary, laden breast,
That accepts God's gracious offer,
    Enters into perfect rest.

4 "It is finished!" what a gospel!
    Jesus died to save your soul;
Have you taken His salvation?
    Have you let Him make you whole?

453

THERE is a Paradise of rest
    On yonder tranquil shore;
Beyond the shadow and the gloom of night,
    Where toil and tears are o'er.

Cho.—Meet me there! oh, meet me there!
At the dawning of that morning bright and fair;
    Meet me there! oh, meet me there!
In the land beyond the river, meet me there.

2 There is a City crowned with light,
    Its joys no tongue can tell;
For they who enter shall behold the King,
    And in His presence dwell.

3 There is a crown laid up on high,
    That Christ the Lord will give
To those who patiently His coming wait,
    And for His glory live.

4 Oh, then be faithful unto death,
   Press on the heavenly way,
That we may enter through the Gates of Life
   To realms of endless day.

454

L EAD, kindly Light, amid th'encircling gloom,
      Lead Thou me on;
The night is dark, and I am far from home,
      Lead Thou me on;
Keep Thou my feet; I do not ask to see
The distant scene; one step enough for me.

2 I was not ever thus, nor prayed that Thou
         Shouldst lead me on;
I loved to choose and see my path; but now
      Lead Thou me on:
I loved the garish day; and, spite of fears,
Pride ruled my will: remember not past years.

3 So long Thy power hath blest me, sure it still
         Will lead me on
O'er moor and fen, o'er crag and torrent, till
      The night is gone,
And with the morn those angel faces smile,
Which I have loved long since, and lost awhile.

455

W HEN God the way of life would teach
      And gather all His own,
He placed them safe beyond the reach
   Of death, by blood alone.

CHO.—It is His word, God's precious word,
      It stands forever true:
When I, the Lord, shall see the blood,
   I will pass over you.

2 By Christ, the sinless Lamb of God,
   The precious blood was shed,
When He fulfilled God's holy word,
   And suffered in our stead.

3 O soul, for thee salvation thus
 By God is freely given;
The blood of Christ atones for sin,
 And makes us meet for heaven.

4 The wrath of God that was our due,
 Upon the Lamb was laid;
And by the shedding of His blood,
 The debt for us was paid.

5 How calm the judgment hour shall pass
 To all who do obey
The word of God about the blood,
 And make that word their stay.

456

O UT on the mountain, sad and forsaken,
  Lost in its mazes, no light can'st thou see;
Yet in His mercy, full of compassion,
 Lo! the Good Shepherd is calling to thee.

Cho.—Calling to thee, calling to thee;
  Jesus is calling, "Come unto me;"
  Calling to thee, calling to thee,
  Hear the Good Shepherd calling to thee.

2 Far on the mountain, why wilt thou wander?
 Deeper in darkness thy pathway will be;
Turn from thy roaming, fly from its dangers,
 While the Good Shepherd is calling to thee.

3 Flee from thy bondage, Jesus will help thee,
 Only believe Him, and thou shalt be free;
Wonderful mercy, boundless compassion:
 Still the Good Shepherd is calling to thee.

457

I DO not ask for earthly store,
  Beyond a day's supply;
I only covet, more and more,
 The clear and single eye,
To see my duty face to face,
 And trust the Lord for daily grace.

CHO.—Then shall my heart keep singing,
    While to the cross I cling;
    For rest is sweet at Jesus' feet,
‖: While home-ward faith keeps winging.:‖

2 I care not for the empty show
    That thoughtless worldlings see;
I crave to do the best I know,
    And leave the rest with Thee;—
Well satisfied that sweet reward
Is sure to those who trust the Lord.

3 Whate'er the crosses mine shall be,
    I will not dare to shun;
I only ask to live for Thee,
    And that Thy will be done;
Thy will, O Lord, be mine each day,
While pressing on my homeward way.

4 And when at last, my labor o'er,
    I cross the narrow sea,
Grant, Lord, that on the other shore
    My soul may dwell with Thee;
And learn what here I cannot know,
Why Thou hast ever loved me so.

458

TRAVELING to the better land,
    O'er the desert's scorching sand,
Father, do Thou hold my hand,
    And lead me on.

2 When at Marah, parched with heat,
I the sparkling fountain greet,
Make the bitter waters sweet,
    And lead me on.

3 When the wilderness is drear,
Show me Elim's palm-groves near,
With its wells, as crystal clear,
    And lead me on.

4 Through the water and the fire,
This, O Lord, my one desire:
With Thy love my heart inspire,
    And lead me on.

5 When I stand on Jordan's brink,
   Do not let me fear or shrink;
Hold me, Father, lest I sink,
   And lead me on.

459

'TIS only a little way on to my home,
   And there in its sunshine forever I'll roam;
While all the day long I journey with song:
O beautiful Eden-land, thou art my home.

REF.—'Tis only a little way, only a little way,
   'Tis only a little way on to my home.

2 'Tis only a little way farther to go,
   O'er mountain and valley where dark waters flow?
My Saviour is near with blessings to cheer;
His word is my guiding-star—why should I fear?

3 'Tis only a little way; there I shall see
   The friends that in glory are waiting for me;
Their voices from home now float on the air—
They're calling me tenderly, calling me there.

460

I WILL praise the Lord my Glory,
   I will praise the Lord my Light;
He my cloud by day to cover,
   He my fire to guide by night.

CHO.—I will praise Thee with my whole heart, will praise
         Thee, O Lord;
I will be glad and rejoice in Thee, O Thou most high.

2 I will praise the Lord my Prophet,
   Holy Priest and Righteous King;
With the angels who adore Him,
   "Holy, holy," I will sing.

3 I will praise the Lord my Shepherd,
   Keeper, Pasture, Door and Fold;
O'er the lonely hills He sought me,
   When the night was dark and cold.

4 I will praise the Lord my Father,
   Saviour, Brother, Guide and Friend;
He thus far in life hath led me,
   He will lead me to the end.

5 I will love Him, I will trust Him,
    All the remnant of my days;
And will sing through endless ages,
    Only my Redeemer's praise.

———

461

NOT saved are we by trying,
    From self can come no aid;
'Tis on the blood relying,
    Once for our ransom paid;
'Tis looking unto Jesus,
    The holy One and Just;
'Tis His great work that saves us,
    It is not Try, but Trust.

CHO.—‖: It is not Try, but Trust; :‖
        'Tis His great work that saves us;
        It is not Try, but Trust.

2 'Twas vain for Israel bitten
    By serpents on their way,
To look to their own doing,
    That awful plague to stay;
The only way for healing,
    When humbled in the dust,
Was of the Lord's revealing,
    It was not Try, but Trust.

3 No deeds of ours are needed
    To make Christ's merit more;
No frames of mind, or feelings,
    Can add to His great store;
'Tis simply to receive Him,
    The holy One and Just,
'Tis only to believe Him,
    It is not Try, but Trust.

———

462

COME, Holy Spirit,
    Like a dove descending,
Rest Thou upon us
    While we meet to pray;

Show us the Saviour,
All His love revealing;
Lead us to Him,
　　The Life, the Truth, the Way.

2 Come, Holy Spirit,
Every cloud dispelling,
Fill us with gladness,
　　Through the Master's name;
Bring to our memory
Words that He hath spoken,
Then shall our tongues
　　His wondrous grace proclaim.

3 Come, Holy Spirit,
Sent from God the Father—
Thou Friend and Teacher,
　　Comforter and Guide—
Our thoughts directing,
Keep us close to Jesus,
And in our hearts
　　For evermore abide.

463

" JESUS of Nazareth!"　O what a name!
　　Let us rejoice and His glory proclaim!
Saviour and Keeper, for ever the same,
　　Shepherd, Redeemer and Lord.

Cho.—Jesus of Nazareth! once crucified,
　　Jesus of Nazareth! now glorified,
　　Jesus of Nazareth! throned at God's side,
　　Glory and praise to His name.

2 Jesus of Nazareth! truly a man,
Low in a cradle His life He began,
Lived before God, both in pattern and plan,
　　Righteous, obedient One.

3 Jesus of Nazareth! nailed to the tree,
Dying, that we by His death might be free,
Bearing the curse all for you and for me,
　　Dying a ransom for all.

4 Jesus of Nazareth! raised from the dead,
  Spotless and holy, and still in our stead,
  Made for us ever our glorified Head,
      Raised from the dead for us all.

5 Jesus of Nazareth! seated on high,
  Sending the Spirit of grace to apply
  Life through the word unto men far and nigh,
      Offering salvation to all.

6 Jesus of Nazareth! earth's coming King,
  Peace to the warring world soon He shall bring,
  Nations of saved ones His praises shall sing;
      All shall bow down at His name.

464

I BELONG to Jesus;
    I am not my own;
  All I have and all I am,
    Shall be His alone.

2 I belong to Jesus;
    He is Lord and King,
  Reigning in my inmost heart,
    Over everything.

3 I belong to Jesus;
    What can hurt or harm,
  When He folds around my soul
    His almighty Arm?

4 I belong to Jesus;
    Blessèd, blessèd thought.
  With His own most precious blood
    Has my soul been bought.

5 I belong to Jesus;
    He has died for me;
  I am His and He is mine,
    Through eternity.

6 I belong to Jesus;
    He will keep my soul,
  When the deathly waters dark
    Round about me roll.

7 I belong to Jesus;
   And ere long I'll stand
With my precious Saviour there,
   In the glory-land.

465

O COME to the Saviour while now He is calling.
   O come while there's mercy and pardon so free;
O trust in His grace, He will keep thee from falling,
And strength to o'ercome He offers to thee.

Cho.—O come, come to the Saviour,
    O come, come while you may;
    O come, come to the Saviour,
    He's tenderly calling to-day.

2 There's no other name among men that is given,
   There's no other way to be saved but His way;
O trust in His mercy; too long hast thou striven
With sin and with self; O come while you may.

3 The door of His mercy is now standing open;
   O hasten and enter, for "Yet there is room;"
For if you reject Him, this word He hath spoken,
That where He now is "Ye never can come.'

4 And he that believeth, the promise is written,
   Is saved through the blood of the Crucified One;
The Spirit is pleading; O will you not hasten,
And find in His love a refuge and home.

466

QUIET, Lord, my froward heart;
   Make me teachable and mild,
Upright, simple, free from art;
   Make me as a little child—
From distrust and envy free,
Pleased with all that pleases Thee.

2 What thou shalt to-day provide,
   Let me as a child receive;
What to-morrow may betide,
   Calmly to Thy wisdom leave;
'Tis enough that Thou wilt care;
Why should I the burden bear?

3. As a little child relies
   On a care beyond its own,
Being neither strong nor wise,
   Fears to take a step alone—
Let me thus with Thee abide,
As my Father, Friend, and Guide.

467

HOLY, holy, holy is the Lord!
   Sing, O ye people, gladly adore Him;
Let the mountains tremble at His word,
   Let the hills be joyful before Him;
Mighty in wisdom, boundless in mercy,
   Great is Jehovah, King over all.

CHO.—Holy, holy, holy is the Lord!
   Let the hills be joyful before Him.

2 Praise Him, praise Him, shout loud for joy,
   Watchman of Zion, herald the story;
Sin and death His kingdom shall destroy,
   All the earth shall sing of His glory;
Praise Him, ye angels, ye who behold Him
   Robed in His splendor, matchless, divine.

3 King eternal, blesséd be His name!
   So may His children gladly adore Him;
When in heaven we join the happy strain,
   When we cast our bright crowns before Him;
There in His likeness joyful awaking,
   There we shall see Him, there we shall sing.

468

PRAISE, my soul, the King of heaven;
   To His feet thy tribute bring;
Ransomed, healed, restored, forgiven,
   Who like thee His praise shall sing?
‖: Praise Him! praise Him! :‖
   Praise the everlasting King.

2 Praise Him for His grace and favor
   To our fathers in distress;
Praise Him still the same as ever,
   Slow to chide, and swift to bless;
‖: Praise Him! praise Him! :‖
   Glorious in His faithfulness!

3 Angels, help us to adore Him,
   Ye behold Him face to face;
Sun and moon, bow down before Him,
   Dwellers all in time and space:
||: Praise Him! praise Him! :||
   Praise with us the God of grace!

469

IN the hour when guilt assails me,
   On His gracious name I call,
Then I find the heavenly fullness,
   Christ, my righteousness, my all.

CHO.—All my song when standing yonder,
   Shall be Christ, my joy, my all,
||: This shall ever be my anthem,
   " Christ my glory, Christ my all.":||

2 In the night when sorrow clouds me,
   And the burning tear-drops fall,
Then I sing the song of patience,
   Christ, my Brother and my all.

3 In the day when this immortal
   Shall fling off its mortal thrall,
Then my song of resurrection
   Shall be Christ, my all in all.

470

THERE is a land of pure delight,
   Where saints immortal reign;
Eternal day excludes the night,
   And pleasures banish pain.

CHO.—O wondrous land beyond the sky,
   O land so bright and fair,
When shall we reach thy golden gates,
   And dwell forever there ?

2 There everlasting spring abides,
   And never-withering flowers;
Death, like a narrow sea, divides
   This heavenly land from ours.

3 Sweet fields beyond the swelling flood
    Stand dressed in living green;
So to the Jews old Canaan stood,
    While Jordan rolled between.

4 Could we but climb where Moses stood,
    And view the landscape o'er,
Not Jordan's stream, nor death's cold flood,
    Should fright us from the shore.

471

A S lives the flower within the seed,
    As in the cone the tree,
So, praise the God of truth and grace,
    His Spirit dwelleth in me.

Cho.—||: Christ liveth in me, :||
    O what a salvation this,
    That Christ liveth in me!

2 Once far from God and dead in sin,
    No light my heart could see;
But in God's word the light I found,
    Now Christ liveth in me.

3 As rays of light from yonder sun
    The flowers of earth set free,
So life and light and love came forth
    From Christ living in me.

4 With longing all my heart is filled,
    That like Him I may be,
As on the wondrous thought I dwell,
    That Christ liveth in me.

472

W E have felt the love of Jesus
    In our hearts with rapture glow;
Will that love forsake and leave us?
    Never, no! oh, never, no!
If on beds of pain we languish,
    Earthly friends may lightly go,
Will He leave us in our anguish?
    Never, no! oh, never, no!

2 Chosen not for our deservings,
  But that God His grace might show;
For our failures will He leave us?
  Never, no! oh, never, no!
'Tis in Christ the Father sees us,
  To His Son the love doth flow;
Will He turn away from Jesus?
  Never, no! oh, never, no!

3 Will He leave when care encroaches?
  When we're tempted will He go?
When the last dread hour approaches?
  Never, no! oh, never, no!
And when safely home in glory,
  When sad tears no longer flow,
Can we e'er forget the story?
  Never, no! oh, never, no!

473

SOON will come the setting sun,
  When our work will all be done,
And the weary heart at last be still;
  But the Lord with gentle cry,
  Will awake us by and by,
And we'll meet again on Zion's hill.

Cho.—We'll meet each other there,
  Yes, we'll meet each other there,
  And the Saviour's likeness bear,
  When we meet each other there;
  We'll meet each other there,
  Yes, we'll meet each other there,
  And His glory we shall share.

2 Deep the shadows in the vale,
  Fierce the howling of the gale,
Long and dark the storm around our door;
  But the Lord will make a way
  To the shining realms of day,
With the shadow and the storm no more.

3 Flood the heart with parting tears,
  Frost the head with passing years,
Let the days of earth be filled with care;

But the Lord at length will come,
In His love to take us home,
And we'll never know a sorrow there.

474

'TIS midnight; and on Olive's brow
  The star is dimmed that lately shone;
'Tis midnight; in the garden now
  The suffering Saviour prays alone.

2 'Tis midnight; and from all removed,
  The Saviour wrestles lone with fears;
Ev'n that disciple whom He loved
  Heeds not His Master's grief and tears.

3 'Tis midnight; and for others' guilt,
  The man of sorrow weeps in blood;
Yet He, who hath in anguish knelt,
  Is not forsaken by His God.

475

BLESSED Saviour, ever nearer
  I am drawing to Thy feet;
Thou hast borne my every sorrow,
  I am made in Thee complete;
For Thy love my soul is yearning,
  More and more its power impart;
I have heard Thy tender pleading,
  Come and dwell within my heart.

2 Blesséd Saviour, I would never,
  Never more Thy love reject;
At Thy feet I learn the lesson
  How Thine image to reflect;
There I go when all forsake me,
  When by foes I am oppressed;
Then I hear Thy loved voice saying,
  Come to me, I'll give you rest.

3 Blesséd Saviour, draw me nearer,
  Ever nearer to Thy heart,
When I'm weary, heavy-laden,
  And I feel the tempter's dart;
Oft I stumble, oft I falter,
  Oft I'm tossed on angry seas;

But I know that Thou wilt guide me,
   Through the storm, to endless peace.

4 Blesséd Saviour, let me linger
   Ever near Thy precious feet;
Till I hear that welcome summons,
   "Come," thy loved ones now to greet;
Oh, the joy that there awaits me,
   While I hope, and watch and pray!
For the morning light is dawning,
   Of the fair and endless day.

476

LOOK up! look up! ye weary ones,
      Whose skies are veiled in night,
For He who knows the path you tread
   Will yet restore the light;
Look up! and hail the dawning
Of hope's triumphant morning..

CHO.—Behold Him! behold Him!
         Your Saviour lives to-day;
      Behold Him! behold Him!
         The clouds have rolled away.

2 The gifts ye brought with loving hand
   Your Lord will not disown;
Their odors sweet to heaven shall rise
   Like incense 'round His throne;
Look up! and hail the dawning
Of joy's transcendent morning.

3 Rejoice! the grave is overcome,
   And lo! the angels sing;
The grandest triumph ever known
   Has come through Christ our King;
All heaven proclaims the dawning
Of love's all-glorious morning.

477

SAVIOUR, lead me, lest I stray,
      Gently lead me all the way;
I am safe when by Thy side,
I would in Thy love abide.

CHO.—Lead me, lead me,
  Saviour, lead me, lest I stray;
  Gently down the stream of time,
  Lead me, Saviour, all the way.

2 Thou, the refuge of my soul
 When life's stormy billows roll,
 I am safe when Thou art nigh,
 On Thy mercy I rely.

3 Saviour, lead me, till at last,
 When the storm of life is past,
 I shall reach the land of day,
 Where all tears are wiped away.

478

RETURN! return! O wanderer, now return!
 Return! return! And seek thy Father's face;
Those new desires which in thee burn
 ||: Were kindled by His grace. :||

2 Return! return! O wanderer, now return!
 Return! return! He hears thy humble sigh;
He sees thy burdened spirit mourn
 ||: When no one else is nigh. :||

3 Return! return! O wanderer, now return!
 Return! return! The Saviour bids thee live;
Come humbly to His feet and learn
 ||: How freely He'll forgive. :||

479

TURN thee, O lost one, care-worn and weary,
 Lo! the Good Shepherd is calling to-day;
Seeking to save thee, waiting to cleanse thee,
 Haste to receive Him, no longer delay.

CHO.—Tenderly calling, patiently calling,
  Hear the Good Shepherd calling to thee;
  Tenderly calling, patiently calling,
  Lovingly saying, "Come unto me!"

2 Still He is waiting, why wilt thou perish,
 Though thou hast wandered so far from the fold?
Yet, with His life-blood. He has redeemed thee,
 Wondrous compassion that cannot be told!

3 List to His message, think of His mercy!
    Sinless, yet bearing thy sins on the tree;
Perfect remission, life everlasting,
    Through His atonement, He offers to thee.

4 Come in the old way, come in the true way,
    Enter through Jesus, for He is the Door;
He is the Shepherd, tenderly calling,
    Come in thy weakness, and wander no more.

480

SEARCH me, O Lord, and try this heart of mine,
    Search me, and prove if I indeed am Thine;
Test by Thy word, that never changed can be,
My strength of hope and living faith in Thee.

2 Search me, O Lord, subdue each vain desire,
And in my soul a deeper love inspire;
Hide Thou my life, that I, supremely blest,
Beneath Thy wings in perfect peace may rest.

3 Search me, O Lord, and from the dross of sin,
Refine as gold, and keep me pure within;
Search Thou my thoughts whose springs Thine eyes
    can see,
From secret faults, O Saviour, cleanse Thou me.

4 Search me, O Lord, let faith through grace divine
Thyself reflect in every act of mine,
Till at Thy call my waiting soul shall rise,
Caught up with joy to meet Thee in the skies.

481

HEAR the blessèd invitation,
    Come, come, come;
To the fountain of salvation,
    Come, come, come;
Healing streams are flowing still;
Welcome, "whosoever will;"
Let him take the water of life freely."

Cho.—||: Let him take, let him take,
    Let him take the water of life freely. :||

2 'Tis the voice of Jesus saying,
  Come, come, come;
Now His blest command obeying,
  Come, come, come;
He will cleanse from every ill;
Welcome, " whosoever will;
Let him take the water of life freely."

3 'Tis the Holy Spirit calling,
  Come, come, come;
Ere the shades of death be falling,
  Come, come, come;
He the heart with peace will fill;
Welcome, " whosoever will;
Let him take the water of life freely."

4 Lo! the Spirit and the Bride say,
  Come, come, come;
And let him that heareth now say,
  Come, come, come;
And let him that is athirst
Come, and " whosoever will;
Let Him take the water of life freely."

482

———

SAFE upon the heavenly shore,
 Done with pain for evermore,
Weariness and weakness o'er, Up yonder;
O the calm and quiet rest
On the loving Saviour's breast;
It is better than earth's best, Up yonder.

2 Storms shall never reach us there,
No more sorrow, pain or care,
No more cross for us to bear, Up yonder;
Gain for them that suffered loss,
Crowns for them that bore the cross,
And a calm for hearts that toss, Up yonder.

3 Safe upon the heavenly shore,
Done with sin for evermore,
Weariness and weakness o'er, Up yonder;
Never more to know a fear,
Never more to shed a tear,
Better far than ever here, Up yonder.

483

IN the heavenly pastures fair,
'Neath the tender Shepherd's care,
Let us rest beside the living stream to-day;
Calmly there in peace recline,
Drinking in the truth divine,
As His loving call we now with joy obey.

CHO.—Glorious stream of life eternal,
Beauteous fields of living green,
Though revealed within the word
Of our Shepherd and our Lord,
By the pure in heart alone can they be seen.

2 Far from all the noise and strife
That disturb our daily life,
Let us pause awhile in silence and adore;
Then the sound of His dear voice
Will our waiting souls rejoice,
As He nameth us His own for evermore.

3 O how good and true and kind,
Seeking His stray sheep to find,
If they wander into danger from His side;
Ever closely may we tread
Where His holy feet have led,
So at last with Him in heaven we may abide.

———

484

MY heavenly home is bright and fair,
Nor pain, nor death can enter there:
It's glittering towers the sun outshine;
That heavenly mansion shall be mine.

CHO.—I'm going home, I'm going home,
I'm going home to die no more!
To die no more, to die no more,
I'm going home to die no more!

2 My Father's house is built on high,
Far, far above the starry sky;
When from this earthly prison free,
That heavenly mansion mine shall be.

3 Let others seek a home below,
   Which flames devour, or waves o'erflow;
   Be mine a happier lot to own
     A heavenly mansion near the throne.

485

WHEN I shall wake in that fair morn of morns,
   After whose dawning never night returns,
And with whose glory day eternal burns,
   I shall be satisfied, be satisfied.

REF.—||: I shall be satisfied,
     I shall be satisfied
When I shall wake in that fair morn of morns. :||

2 When I shall see Thy glory face to face,
When in Thine arms Thou wilt Thy child embrace,
When Thou shalt open all Thy store of grace,
   I shall be satisfied, be satisfied.

3 When I shall meet with those that I have loved,
Clasp in my arms the dear ones long removed,
And find how faithful Thou to me hast proved,
   I shall be satisfied, be satisfied.

4 When I shall gaze upon the face of Him
Who died for me, with eyes no longer dim,
And praise Him with the everlasting hymn,
   I shall be satisfied, be satisfied.

486

TAKE Thou my hand, and lead me—
   Choose Thou my way;
"Not as I will," O Father,
   Teach me to say;
What though the storms may gather?
   Thou knowest best;
Safe in Thy holy keeping,
   There I would rest.

2 Take Thou my hand, and lead me—
   Lord, I am Thine,
Fill with Thy Holy Spirit
   This heart of mine;

Then in the hour of trial
  Strong shall I be—
Ready to do or suffer,
  Dear Lord, for Thee.

3 Take Thou my hand and lead me,
    Lord, as I go;
Into Thy perfect image
  Help me to grow;
Still in Thine own pavilion
  Shelter Thou me;
Keep me, O Father, keep me,
  Close, close to Thee.

487

I AM waiting for the Master,
  Who will bid me rise and come
To the glory of His presence,
  To the gladness of His home.

Cho.—They are watching at the portal,
    They are waiting at the door;
Waiting only for my coming,
  All the loved ones gone before.

2 Many a weary path I've traveled,
    In the darkest storm and strife.
Bearing many a heavy burden,—
  Often struggling for my life.

3 Many friends that traveled with me
    Reached that portal long ago;
One by one they left me battling
  With the dark and crafty foe.

4 Yes, their pilgrimage was shorter,
    And their triumphs sooner won;
Oh, how lovingly they'll greet me
  When the toils of life are done.

488

FROM the Bethlehem manger-home,
  Walking His dear form beside,
We to Calvary's mount have come,
  Where our Lord was crucified.

CHO.—Sweet tones of love come down the ages through:
    "Father, forgive, they know not what they do."

2 Scornful words the soldiers fling;
    Wicked rulers Him deride,
Saying, If Thou be the King,
    Save Thyself, Thou Crucified.

3 Wondrous love for sinful men,
    Of the sinless One that died!
May we wound Thee not again,
    Thou, O Christ, the Crucified.

489

PASS along the invitation,
    Whosoever will may come;
Pass it on, pass it on,
Pass along the loving message
Unto every thirsty one;
    Pass it on, pass it on.

CHO.—Pass along the invitation,
        Pass along the word of God,
    Until every tribe and nation
        Shall have heard of Christ the Lord,
    Shall have heard, shall have heard,
        Shall have heard of Christ the Lord.

2 Pass along the cup of comfort
    That the Lord has given you;
        Pass it on, pass it on,
Other weary, troubled spirits
    Need to taste its sweetness too;
        Pass it on, pass it on.

3 Pass along each boon and blessing
    That may come to you through life;
        Pass it on, pass it on,
You may help the weary-hearted
    Who are faint amid the strife;
        Pass it on, pass it on.

4 Pass along the watchword, "Courage;"
    Soon the darkness will be o'er;

Pass it on, pass it on,
See, already dawn is breaking
On the bright celestial shore;
Pass it on, pass it on.

490

MORE of Jesus, More of Jesus,
'Tis the Christian's yearning cry;
More of Jesus, More of Jesus,
Only He can satisfy.

2 More of Jesus, More of Jesus,
While I tread earth's weary ways;
More of Jesus, More of Jesus,
Till in Heaven I hymn His praise.

3 More of Jesus, More of Jesus,
O to feel His love each hour!
More of Jesus, More of Jesus,
O to realize His power!

4 More of Jesus, More of Jesus,
In my weakness and my pain;
More of Jesus, More of Jesus,
He can turn my loss to gain.

5 More of Jesus, More of Jesus,
Sorely do I need His grace;
More of Jesus, Blessèd Jesus,
When shall I behold His face?

491

WHEN I survey the wondrous cross,
On which the Prince of glory died,
My richest gain I count but loss,
And pour contempt on all my pride.

Cho.—O wondrous cross where Jesus died,
And for my sins was crucified;
My longing eyes look up to Thee,
Thou blessèd Lamb of Calvary.

2 Forbid it, Lord, that I should boast,
Save in the death of Christ, my Lord;
All earthly things that charm me most,
I sacrifice them to His blood.

3 See, from His head, His hands, His feet,
    Sorrow and love flow mingled down;
Did e'er such love and sorrow meet,
    Or thorns compose so rich a crown?

4 Were all the realm of nature mine,
    That were a gift by far too small;
A love so great and so divine,
    Demands my soul, my life, my all.

492

JESUS, Thou Refuge of the soul,
    To Thy dear arms I flee;
From Satan's wiles, from self and sin,
    O make and keep me free.

2 Though clouds may rise, though tempests rage,
    Thou wilt my shelter be,
While with a steadfast heart and true,
    My trust is stayed on Thee.

3 No power on earth, or power below,
    Can tear me from Thy side,
If 'neath Thy sheltering wings of love,
    Dear Refuge, I abide.

4 Not death itself, that last dread foe,
    Can hold me with his chain;
Through Christ, who conquered Death, I rise
    And life eternal gain.

493

IN times of sorrow, God is near,
    His vigils never cease,—
His tender, loving voice I hear,
    "In me ye shall have peace."

CHO.—O blesséd peace! sweet boon of heaven!
        That bids our trouble cease;
    O precious word, divinely given,
        "In me ye shall have peace!"

2 Though long and weary is the night,
    And morn brings no relief,
Yet faith the promise still believes,
    "In me ye shall have peace."

3 His love we may not understand,
　　While trials here increase,
　But yet we know His word is sure,
　　" In me ye shall have peace."

4 Soon shall our eyes the land behold
　　Where pain and care shall cease;
　Till then we'll trust the promise sweet,
　　" In me ye shall have peace."

494

A M I a soldier of the cross—
　　A follower of the Lamb?
And shall I fear to own His cause,
　Or blush to speak His name?

CHO.—In the name of Christ the King,
　　Who hath purchased life for me,
　Through grace I'll win the promised crown,
　　Whate'er my cross may be.

2 Must I be carried to the skies,
　　On flowery beds of ease,
　While others fought to win the prize,
　　And sailed through bloody seas?

3 Are there no foes for me to face?
　　Must I not stem the flood?
　Is this vile world a friend to grace,
　　To help me on to God?

4 Since I must fight if I would reign,
　　Increase my courage, Lord!
　I'll bear the toil, endure the pain,
　　Supported by Thy word.

495

W HILE Thou, O my God, art my help and defender
　　No cares can o'erwhelm me, no terrors appall;
The wiles and the snares of the world will but render
　More lively my hope in my God and my all.

REF.—||: My God and my all, :||
　　　My treasure, my glory,
　　　My God and my all.

2 Yes, Thou art my refuge in sorrow and danger,
    My strength when I suffer, my hope when I fall;
My comfort and joy in this land of the stranger,
    My treasure, my glory, my God and my all.

3 And when Thou demandest the life Thou hast given,
    With joy will I answer Thy merciful call,
And quit this poor earth but to find Thee in heaven,
    My portion forever, my God and my all.

496

O I love to talk with Jesus, for it smooths the rugged
        road;
And it seems to help me onward, when I faint beneath my
        load;
When my heart is crushed with sorrow, and my eyes with
        tears are dim,
There is nought can yield me comfort like a little talk
        with Him.

2 Oft I tell Him I am weary, and I fain would be at rest;
That I'm daily, hourly, longing to repose upon His breast;
And He answers me so kindly, in the tenderest tones of
        love,
    "I am coming soon to take thee to My happy home
        above."

3 Though the way is long and dreary to that far-off distant
        clime,
    Yet I know that my Redeemer journeys with me all the
        time;
And the more I come to know Him, and His wondrous
        grace explore,
How my longing groweth stronger still to know Him more
        and more.

4 So I'll wait a little longer, till my Lord's appointed time,
    And along the upward pathway still my pilgrim feet shall
        climb;
Soon within my Father's dwelling, where the many man-
        sions be,
    I shall see my blesséd Saviour, and He then will talk with
        me.

497

"SING unto the Lord,
O ye saints of His, sing, sing,
Sing unto the Lord,
And at the remembrance of His holiness,
O give thanks unto the Lord."

1 O Lord, Thy loving kindness
    Doth compass all our ways,
And "Thy compassions fail not,"
    Through all the passing days;
To Thee, O great Jehovah,
    In "time of need" we cry;
And all who call upon Thee
    Shall find Thee ever nigh.

2 Thy goodness we remember,
    We praise Thy holiness,
We look to Thee, O Saviour,
    To save, and heal, and bless;
'Tis by Thy loving favor
    Thy trusting children stand,
Upheld, and kept, and guided,
    By Thy protecting hand.

3 Let saints recount His mercies,
    And fill His courts with praise;
Let all who know His goodness,
    Their hallelujahs raise,
Praise God, the loving Father,
    And Jesus Christ His Son,
With God the Holy Spirit,
    The glorious Three in One.

498

———

I WAIT for Thee, O Lord!
    Thy glorious face to see,
That holy face that once was marred,
    Was marred, O Lord, for me.

2 I wait for Thee, O Lord!
    Before Thy feet to fall,
To worship lowly and adore
    My Saviour, all in all.

3 I wait for Thee, O Lord!
   Thy loving hand to feel,
Whose tender touch can even now
   The wounded spirit heal.

4 I wait for Thee, O Lord!
   Thy rapture deep to know,
Of living evermore with Thee;
   Love cannot more bestow.

5 I wait for Thee, O Lord!
   But for a little while;
This night my longing eyes may meet
   Thy joyful, welcome smile.

499

HOW oft our souls are lifted up,
   When clouds are dark and drear,
For Jesus comes, and kindly speaks
   These loving words of cheer.

CHO.— "In my Father's house are many mansions;
   If it were not so I would have told you;
In my Father's house are many mansions,
   I go to prepare a place for you."

2 How oft amid our daily toil,
   With anxious care oppressed,
We hear again the precious word
   That tells of joy and rest.

3 O may our faith in Him be strong,
   Who feels our every care,
And will for us, as He hath said,
   A place in heaven prepare.

4 Then let us work, and watch and pray,
   Relying on the love
Of Him who now prepares a place
   For us in heaven above.

500

WE would see Jesus—for the shadows lengthen
   Across this little landscape of our life;
We would see Jesus, our weak faith to strengthen
   For the last weariness—the final strife.

2 We would see Jesus—the great Rock foundation,
    Whereon our feet were set with sovereign grace;
Not life, nor death, with all their agitation,
    Can thence remove us, if we see His face.

3 We would see Jesus—other lights are paling,
    Which for long years we have rejoiced to see;
The blessings of our pilgrimage are failing,
    We would not mourn them, for we go to Thee.

4 We would see Jesus—this is all we're needing,
    Strength, joy, and willingness come with the sight;
We would see Jesus, dying, risen, pleading;
    Then welcome, day! and farewell, mortal night!

501

PRAY, brethren, pray! The sands are falling;
    Pray, brethren, pray! God's voice is calling,
Yon turret strikes the dying chime;
    We kneel upon the verge of time:

    REF.—Eternity is drawing nigh!
Eternity is drawing nigh! (is drawing nigh!)

2 Praise, brethren, praise! The skies are rending!
Praise, brethren, praise! The fight is ending;
    Behold, the glory draweth near,
    The King Himself will soon appear:

3 Watch, brethren, watch! The years are dying:
Watch, brethren, watch! Old time is flying!
    Watch as men watch the parting breath,
    Watch as men watch for life or death:

4 Look, brethren, look! The day is breaking;
Hark, brethren, hark! The dead are waking:
    With girded loins all ready stand;
    Behold, the Bridegroom is at hand!

502

YOUNG men in Christ the Lord,
    Own Him your Saviour God,
    His name adore;
For by His wondrous sacrifice,
He paid the great redemption price,
That all might have eternal life,
    That come to God through Him.

2 Young men in Christ the Lord,
  Be mighty in His word,
    Its truths declare;
  And seek the Holy Spirit's power,
  By faith and persevering prayer,
  That ye may witness anywhere,
    That sinful men are found.

3 Young men in Christ the King,
  Your grateful tribute bring,
    Of love and praise;
  United in His royal name,
  With loyal hearts His words proclaim,
  Throughout the world to all Young Men,
    " Ye must be born again."

4 Young men in Christ the Friend,
  On Him all hopes depend,
    Of true relief;
  To every burdened soul you meet,
  His gracious, loving words, so sweet,
  " Come unto me," with love repeat,
    "And I will give you rest."

5 Young men in Christ, arise,
  The world before you lies,
    Enslaved in sin;
  Make haste to swell the mission band,
  Prepare to go at His command,
  To save lost men in every land,
    At any sacrifice.

6 Young men in Christ the Son,
  In Him we all are one;
    For this He prayed;
  Then let us join the heavenly throng,
  To sound His praise in endless song,
  For all we have and are belong
    To Christ, our Lord Divine.

503

WE are coming home to Jesus,
    We have heard His welcome voice;
We are trusting in His goodness,
  In His mercy we rejoice.

REF.—‖: We are coming home, :‖
We are coming from the darkness to the light;
‖: We are coming home, :‖
We are coming home to-night.

2 We are coming home to Jesus,
    For He died that we might live:
He is willing to receive us,
    He is waiting to forgive.

3 We are coming home to Jesus,
    By the cross, our only way;
There He finished our redemption,
    And we can no more delay.

504

AT even, ere the sun was set,
    The sick, O Lord, around Thee lay;
Oh, in what divers pains they met!
Oh, with what joy they went away!

2 Once more 'tis eventide; and we,
    Oppressed with various ills, draw near;
What if Thy form we cannot see!
    We know and feel that Thou art here.

3 O Saviour Christ, our woes dispel;
    For some are sick and some are sad,
And some have never loved Thee well,
    And some have lost the love they had.

4 And all, O Lord, crave perfect rest,
    And to be wholly free from sin;
And they who fain would serve Thee best,
    Are conscious most of sin within.

5 Thy touch has still its ancient power;
    No word from Thee can fruitless fall;
Here in this solemn evening hour,
    Lord, in Thy mercy heal us all.

505

O TENDER beseechings of Jesus!
    How sweetly they fall on the ear!
O gospel of grace and of kindness,
    God's love and compassion brought near!

CHO.—Is the Spirit of Jesus now striving?
    His warning, my brother, obey;
Resist not His gracious beseeching,
    O grieve not the Saviour away.

2 Beseeching in love for our Saviour,
    Unworthy we pray in His stead;
Believe in the word of forgiveness,
    Accept of the ransom He made.

3 Beseeching His blood-bought, His ransomed,
    Your bodies to Him gladly yield,
That, in you, and through you, and by you,
    His grace may be fully revealed.

4 Beseeching the saints to be holy,
    Filled always with meekness and love;
Like Jesus so gentle and lowly,
    Reflecting the light from above.

5 Beseeching that all for His coming
    Unshaken may ever remain,
And stand with the saved and the chosen,
    With Him in His glorious reign.

506

TROUBLED heart, thy God is calling!
    He is drawing very near;
Do not hide thy deep emotion,
    Do not check that falling tear.

CHO.—O, be saved, His grace is free!
    ||:O, be saved, He died for thee! :||

2 Come, the Spirit still is pleading,
    Come to Him, the meek and mild;
He is waiting now to save you,
    Wilt thou not be reconciled?

3 Art thou waiting till the morrow?
    Thou may'st never see its light;
Come at once! accept His mercy;
    He is waiting—come to-night.

4 Let the angels bear the tidings
    Upward to the courts of heaven!
Let them sing, with holy rapture,
    O'er another soul forgiven!

507

O LORD, my soul rejoiceth in Thee,
My tongue Thy mercy is telling;
I've found Thy love so precious to me,
My heart with its rapture is swelling.

REF.—Wonderful love! O wonderful love!
I'll sing of its fulness forever;
I've found the way that leadeth above,
The way to the life-giving river.

2 I came to Thee o'erburdened with care,
My guilt with sorrow confessing;
'Twas love, Thy love, that banished my fear,
And gave me for sadness a blessing.

3 To Thee, my hope and refuge divine,
My faith is fervently clinging;
And every hour some token of love
New joy to my spirit is bringing.

4 I look beyond this valley of tears,
Where Thou, a mansion preparing,
Wilt call me home forever with Thee,
The bliss of the glorified sharing.

508

ETERNAL life God's Word proclaims
To lost and dying men;
By it alone we know the Lord,
Unseen by mortal ken.

CHO.—O blesséd Word, O gracious Word,
We love it more and more;
O may it be our Strength and Sword
Till earthly strife is o'er.

2 God's grace is in His Holy Word;
We need it every day;
In all our conflicts, this the Sword,
Our every foe to slay.

3 By this same Word we know our work;
And how it should be done;
How we should live, and how through grace
The promised crown is won.

509

O COME to the merciful Saviour who calls you,
O come to the Lord who forgives and forgets;
Though dark be the fortune on earth that befalls you,
A bright home awaits you whose sun never sets.

Cho.—Come home, come home,
In darkness no longer to roam,
'Tis Jesus who tenderly calls you to-day,
Oh brother, my brother, come home.

2 O come then to Jesus whose arms are extended
To fold His dear children in closest embrace;
O come, and your exile shall shortly be ended,
And Jesus will show you the light of His face.

3 Then come to the Saviour, whose mercy grows brighter
The longer you look at the depths of His love;
O fear not, 'tis Jesus, and life's cares grow lighter
While thinking of home and the glory above.

510

I AM not skilled to understand
What God hath will'd, what God hath plann'd;
I only know at His right hand
Is One who is my Saviour!

2 I take Him at His word indeed:
"Christ died for sinners," this I read;
For in my heart I find a need
Of Him to be my Saviour!

3 That He should leave His place on high,
And come for sinful man to die,
You count it strange?—so once did I,
Before I knew my Saviour!

4 And O that He fulfilled may see
The travail of His soul in me,
And with His work contended be,
As I with my dear Saviour!

5 Yea, living, dying, let me bring
My strength, my solace from this spring,
That He who lives to be my King,
Once died to be my Saviour.

511

FOUNTAIN of purity opened for sin,
Here may the penitent wash and be clean;
Jesus, Thou blesséd Redeemer from woe,
Wash me and I shall be whiter than snow.

CHO.—Whiter than snow, whiter than snow,
Wash me, Redeemer,
And I shall be whiter than snow.

2 Though I have labored again and again,
All my self-cleansing is utterly vain;
Jesus, Redeemer from sorrow and woe,
Wash me and I shall be whiter than snow.

3 Cleanse Thou the thoughts of my heart, I implore,
Help me Thy light to reflect more and more;
Daily in loving obedience to grow,
Wash me and I shall be whiter than snow.

4 Whiter than snow! nothing further I need,
Christ is the Fountain; this only I plead;
Jesus my Saviour, to Thee will I go,
Wash me and I shall be whiter than snow.

————

512

I BRING to Thee, O Master,
My burden and my grief;
I do believe Thy promise,
Help Thou mine unbelief.

2 I bring my guilty nature,
For cleansing and for cure;
Oh, heal my sore diseases,
Restore and make me pure.

3 Thy mercy reaches lower
Than all the depths of sin;
As Thy compassions fail not,
Oh, give me peace within.

4 My faltering faith I bring Thee,
My weak and wavering will;
My spirit fails and falters:
Thy promises fulfill.

513

OUT on the desert, seeking, seeking;
   Sinner, 'tis Jesus seeking for thee;
Tenderly calling, calling, calling,
   Hither, thou lost one, O come unto Me.

Cho.—Jesus is calling, Jesus is calling;
      Why dost thou linger? why tarry away?
   Come to Him quickly, say to Him gladly,
      Lord, I am coming, coming to-day.

2 Still He is waiting, waiting, waiting;
   O what compassion beams in His eye!
Hear Him repeating, gently, gently,
   Come to thy Saviour, O why wilt thou die?

3 Lovingly pleading, pleading, pleading,
   Mercy, though slighted, bears with thee yet;
Thou canst be happy, happy, happy;
   Come ere the life-star forever shall set.

514

"GOD bless you!" from the heart we sing,
   God give to every one His grace;
Till He on high His ransomed bring
   To dwell with Him in endless peace.

Cho.—God bless you! God bless you!
      Bless and keep us all in Jesus' love;
   And, when our partings here are over,
      Take us to the joys above.

2 God bless you on your pilgrim way,
   Through storm and sunshine guiding still;
His presence guard you day by day,
   And keep you safe from every ill.

3 Gold bless you in this world of strife,
   When oft the soul would homeward fly,
And give the sweetness to your life,
   Of waiting for the rest on high.

4 God bless you, and the patience give
   To walk through life by Jesus' side;
For Him to bear, for Him to live,
   And then with Him be glorified.

5 God bless us all, and give us rest
  When Christ shall come and glory dawn;
Our sun is swinging toward the west,
  Life's little day will soon be gone.

— — —

515

IS thy cruse of comfort failing?
  Rise and share it with a friend,
And through all the years of famine
  It shall serve thee to the end.
Love divine will fill thy store-house,
  Or thy handful still renew;
||: Scanty fare for one will often
  Make a royal feast for two. :||

2 For the heart grows rich in giving;
    All its wealth is living grain;
Seeds, which mildew in the garner,
    Scattered, fill with gold the plain.
Is thy burden hard and heavy?
    Do thy steps drag wearily?
||: Help to lift thy brother's burden,
    God will bear both it and thee. :||

3 Lost and weary on the mountains,
    Wouldst thou sleep amidst the snow?
Chafe that frozen form beside thee,
    And together both shall glow.
Art thou wounded in life's battle?
    Many stricken round thee moan,
||: Give to them thy precious ointment,
    And that balm shall heal thine own. :||

4 Is thy heart a well left empty?
    None but God its void can fill;
Nothing but a ceaseless fountain
    Can its ceaseless longings still.
Is thy heart a living power?
    Self-entwined, its strength sinks low;
||: It can only live by loving,
    And by serving, love will grow. :||

516

L ORD, at Thy mercy-seat
    Humbly I fall;
Pleading Thy promise sweet,
    Lord, hear my call;
Now let Thy work begin,
Oh, make me pure within,
Cleanse me from every sin,
    Jesus, my all.

2 Tears of repentant grief
    Silently fall;
Help Thou my unbelief,
    Hear Thou my call;
Oh, how I pine for Thee!
'Tis all my hope and plea:
Jesus has died for me,
    Jesus, my all.

3 Still at Thy mercy-seat,
    Saviour, I fall;
Trusting Thy promise sweet,
    Heard is my call;
Faith wings my soul to Thee;
This all my song shall be,
Jesus has died for me,
    Jesus, my all.

517

C OME into His presence with singing,
    O worship the Lord with a song,
A tribute of gratitude bringing,
    To Him to whom praises belong;
But oh, while you join in thanksgiving,
    With voices in tuneful accord,
Remember, He watches your *living*,
    And sing with your hearts to the Lord.

Cho.—Singing, singing,
        This is true worship and love;
    Living, singing,
        This is accepted above.

2 Not yet, as the angels in heaven,
    May mortals their gratitude sing;

Not here upon earth is it given,
　　Perfection of service to bring;
But earnest and true adoration,
　　The heart in the hymn and the prayer,
Will be an accepted oblation,
　　And lighten life's burden and care.

3 Then come to His courts with rejoicing,
　　And join in the chorus of praise;
The prayer and the anthem but voicing
　　The thanks which your loving hearts raise;
With grace in your hearts even duty
　　Will change into pleasure ere long,
And seeing the King in His beauty,
　　Your life shall then be as a song.

518

TRUE-HEARTED, whole-hearted, faithful and loyal,
　　King of our lives, by Thy grace we will be;
Under the standard exalted and royal,
　　Strong in Thy strength we will battle for Thee.

Cho.—Peal out the watchword! silence it never!
　　Song of our spirits, rejoicing and free;
Peal out the watchword! loyal forever!
　　King of our lives, by Thy grace we will be.

2 True-hearted, whole-hearted, fullest allegiance
　　Yielding henceforth to our glorious King;
Valiant endeavor and loving obedience,
　　Freely and joyously now would we bring.

3 True-hearted, whole-hearted, Saviour all-glorious!
　　Take Thy great power and reign there alone,
Over our wills and affections victorious,
　　Freely surrendered and wholly Thine own.

519

BLEST Jesus, grant us strength to take
　　Our daily cross, whate'er it be,
And gladly, for Thine own dear sake,
　　In paths of duty follow Thee.

2 And day by day, we humbly ask
　　That holy memories of Thy cross
May sanctify each common task,
　　And turn to gain each earthly loss.

3 Help us, dear Lord, our cross to bear,
　Till at Thy feet we lay it down;
Win through Thy blood our pardon there,
　And through the Cross attain the Crown.

520

HOW sweet, O Lord, Thy word of grace
　Which bids a sinner seek Thy face,
||: And never seek in vain; :||
That face, once set so steadfastly
To meet Thy cross of agony,
||: Can never me disdain. :||

2 Thy visage, marred and crowned with thorn,
　Thou didst not hide from grief and scorn,
||: Nor from the dews of night; :||
Yet, in that face a love appears
Which scatters all my gloomy fears,
||: And fills my soul with light. :||

3 The heavens declare Thy power and love;
　In all Thy works, below, above,
||: Thy majesty I trace; :||
But mercy shines not in the skies,
And hope within my spirit dies,
||: Until I see Thy face. :||

4 The brightness of Thy glory, Lord,
　Fills heaven and earth and written Word
||: With beams of heavenly grace; :||
But all the hosts of heaven shine
With no such radiance divine
||: As Thy most blessèd face. :||

521

'TIS the hallowed hour of prayer,
　And we trustingly bring
All our doubtings and our fears
　To our Saviour and King;
For we know that He delights
　A glad welcome to give,
And the blessings that we ask for
　We shall fully receive.

Cho.—Precious hour of prayer!
   Hallowed hour of prayer!
   Sacred season of communion,
   It is sweet to be there!

2 'Tis the precious hour of prayer,
  And we humbly entreat:
Father, breathe the Spirit now,
  As we bow at Thy feet;
Touch our lips with power of song;
  Fill our souls with Thy love;
And bestow the benediction
  Of Thy peace from above.

3 'Tis the sacred hour of prayer,
  Calm as heaven above;
Soul to soul is breathing here
  The communion of love;
Every heart is sweetly filled
  With a peace most profound;
Oh, the place is like to heaven
  Where such true joys abound.

522

BEHOLD how plain the truth is made;
  Since Christ the ransom price has paid,
And all our sins on Him were laid,
  We must in Him be saved.

Cho.—If thou shalt confess with thy mouth,
   Confess with thy mouth the Lord Jesus,
   And believe in thine heart
   That God hath raised Him from the dead,
   ||: Thou shalt be saved.:||

2 The death of Christ upon the tree
  Was for the judgment due to thee;
He died that thou mightst ransomed be
  And live by faith in Him.

3 By raising Jesus from the dead
  Our blessèd God has surely said,
That He accepts the blood He shed
  As cleansing us from sin.

4 And now to God as sons brought nigh,
  We come and "Abba Father" cry,
  And seek the Spirit's full supply
  That we as sons may live.

523

THE Lord keep watch between us,
  The ever-present Friend;
No love like His so mighty,
  To keep and to defend.

CHO.—Mizpah! Mizpah!
  Keep watch in tenderest love,
  Until our praises mingle
  Around the throne above.

2 Though absent from each other,
  We are not far from Him;
  Let not our courage falter,
  Let not our faith grow dim.

3 Though time and space may sever
  The Master's servants here,
  'Tis only for a season,
  The meeting-time draws near.

4 The Lord Himself is watching,
  In tenderness and love;
  Let praises meet and mingle
  Around the throne above.

524

ENCAMPED along the hills of light,
  Ye Christian soldiers, rise,
And press the battle ere the night
  Shall veil the glowing skies;
Against the foe in vales below,
  Let all our strength be hurled;
Faith is the victory, we know,
  That overcomes the world.

CHO.—||: Faith is the victory! :||
  Oh, glorious victory,
  That overcomes the world.

2 His banner over us is love,
　Our sword the word of God;
We tread the road the saints above
　With shouts of triumph trod;
By faith, they like a whirlwind's breath,
　Swept on o'er every field;
The faith by which they conquered Death
　Is still our shining shield.

3 On every hand the foe we find
　Drawn up in dread array;
Let tents of ease be left behind,
　And onward to the fray;
Salvation's helmet on each head,
　With truth all girt about,
The earth shall tremble 'neath our tread,
　And echo with our shout.

4 To Him that overcomes the foe,
　White raiment shall be given;
Before the angels he shall know
　His name confessed in heaven;
Then onward from the hills of light,
　Our hearts with love aflame;
We'll vanquish all the hosts of night,
　In Jesus' conquering name.

525

GREAT Jehovah, mighty Lord,
　Vast and boundless is Thy word;
King of kings, from shore to shore
Thou shalt reign for evermore.

2 Jew and Gentile, bond and free,
　All shall yet be one in Thee;
All confess Messiah's name,
　All His wondrous love proclaim.

3 From her night shall China wake,
　Afric's sons their chains shall break;
Egypt, where Thy people trod,
　Shall adore and praise our God.

4 India's groves of palm so fair
  Shall resound with praise and prayer;
  Ceylon's isle with joy shall sing,
  Glory be to Christ our King.

5 North and South shall own Thy sway;
  East and West Thy voice obey;
  Crowns and thrones before Thee fall,
  King of kings and Lord of all.

526

SLEEP on, beloved, sleep, and take thy rest;
  Lay down thy head upon thy Saviour's breast;
We love thee well, but Jesus loves thee best—
    Good-night!   Good-night!   Good-night!

2 Calm is thy slumber as an infant's sleep;
  But thou shalt wake no more to toil and weep:
  Thine is a perfect rest, secure and deep—
      Good-night!

3 Until the shadows from this earth are cast,
  Until He gathers in His sheaves at last;
  Until the twilight gloom be overpast—
      Good-night!

4 Until the Easter glory lights the skies;
  Until the dead in Jesus shall arise,
  And He shall come, but not in lowly guise—
      Good-night!

5 Until, made beautiful by Love Divine,
  Thou, in the likeness of thy Lord shalt shine,
  And He shall bring that golden crown of thine—
      Good-night!

6 Only "Good-night," beloved—not "farewell!"
  A little while, and all His saints shall dwell
  In hallowed union indivisible—
      Good-night!

7 Until we meet again before His throne,
  Clothed in the spotless robe He gives His own,
  Until we know even as we are known—
      Good-night!

527

CHRIST hath risen! Hallelujah!
　　Blesséd morn of life and light;
Lo, the grave is rent asunder,
　　Death is conquered through His might.

CHO.—Christ is risen! Hallelujah!
　　Gladness fills the world to-day;
From the tomb that could not hold Him,
　　See, the stone is rolled away.

2 Christ hath risen! Hallelujah!
　　Friends of Jesus, dry your tears;
Through the vail of gloom and darkness,
　　Lo, the Son of God appears.

3 Christ hath risen! Hallelujah!
　　He hath risen, as He said;
He is now the King of glory,
　　And our great exalted Head.

528

THE living God, who by His might
　　Spake but the word and there was light,
Hath promised now to show His grace
　　To sinful men, in Jesus' face.

CHO.—In Jesus' face! in Jesus' face!
　　O wondrous sight! O wondrous grace!
The living God through sin concealed,
　　In Jesus' face is now revealed.

2 This mighty Christ, so strong and true,
　　Has come from God, His work to do;
He comes with power the soul to save,
　　To give the victory o'er the grave.

3 In Jesus' face our God we know,
　　And trust in Him to bear us through;
He will not leave us to defeat,
　　But make our victory complete.

4 When darkness gives the soul distress,
　　When sorrows on our pathway press,
One look at Him will clouds displace,
　　While comfort beams from Jesus' face.

5 Then come, ye weary ones, and rest;
  Come, sinful souls, and here be blessed;
Within your heart give Christ His place,
And see God's love in Jesus' face.

529

O SAVIOUR, precious Saviour,
    Whom, yet unseen, we love;
O Name of might and favor,
    All other names above.

CHO.—We worship Thee! we bless Thee!
      To Thee alone we sing!
    We praise Thee and confess Thee,
      Our Saviour, Lord and King,

2 O bringer of salvation,
    Who wondrously hast wrought,
  Thyself the revelation
    Of love beyond our thought.

3 In Thee all fulness dwelleth,
    All grace and power divine;
  The glory that excelleth,
    O Son of God, is Thine.

4 Oh, grant the consummation
    Of this our song, above,
  In endless adoration,
    And everlasting love.

530

BEYOND the light of setting suns,
    Beyond the clouded sky,
Beyond where starlight fades in night,—
    I have a home on high.

CHO.—A mansion there, not made with hands,
      A place prepared for me;
    And while God lives, and angels sing,
      That home my home shall be.

2 Beyond all pain, beyond all care,
    Beyond life's mystery,
  Beyond the range of time and change,—
    My home's reserved for me.

3 Swift-flying worlds, their nights that roll
 Far out on seas of light,
Will bring no darkness to my soul;
 My home's beyond the night.

4 My sins and sorrows, strifes and fears,
 I bid them all farewell,
High up amid th'eternal years,
 With Christ, my Lord, to dwell.

531

O DAY of rest and gladness,
 O day of joy and light;
O balm of care and sadness,
 Most beautiful, most bright;
On thee the high and lowly,
 Through ages joined in tune,
Sing " Holy, holy, holy,"
 To the great God Triune.

2 On thee, at the creation,
 The light first had its birth;
On thee, for our salvation,
 Christ rose from depths of earth;
On thee our Lord victorious,
 The Spirit sent from heaven;
And thus on thee, most glorious,
 A triple light was given.

3 New graces ever gaining
 From this our day of rest,
We reach the rest remaining
 To spirits of the blest;
To Holy Ghost be praises,
 To Father, and to Son;
The Church her voice upraises
 To Thee, blest Three in One.

---

532 " STRETCH forth thy hand," thy *palsied* hand,
 Fear not, it is thy Lord's command;
Seek not from Him to hide thy sin,
Confess, and ask to be made clean.

CHO. —"Stretch forth thy hand," on Christ believe,
  "Stretch forth thy hand," the power receive;
  He offers grace so full and free,
  "Stretch forth thy hand," He speaks to thee.

2 "Stretch forth thy hand," thy *empty* hand,
No gift of thine will God commend;
The empty hand that shows thy need,
Of this alone will He take heed.

3 "Stretch forth thy hand," thy *helpless* hand,
Upheld by God, thy soul shall stand;
Fight not in thine own strength the foe,
But trusting Jesus, onward go.

4 "Stretch forth thy hand," thy *dying* hand,
When thou shalt come to Jordan's strand;
Through all the billows Christ shall guide,
And bring thee safe to Canaan's side.

533

NOT now, but in the coming years,
  It may be in the better land,
We'll read the meaning of our tears,
  And there, sometime, we'll understand.

CHO.—Then trust in God through all thy days;
  Fear not! for He doth hold thy hand;
  Though dark thy way, still sing and praise:
  Sometime, sometime, we'll understand.

2 We'll catch the broken threads again,
  And finish what we here began;
Heaven will the mysteries explain,
  And then, ah then, we'll understand.

3 We'll know why clouds instead of sun
  Were over many a cherished plan;
Why song has ceased when scarce begun;
  'Tis there, sometime, we'll understand.

4 Why what we long for most of all,
  Eludes so oft our eager hand;
Why hopes are crushed and castles fall,
  Up there, sometime, we'll understand.

5 God knows the way, He holds the key,
  He guides us with unerring hand;
  Sometime with tearless eyes we'll see;
  Yes, there, up there, we'll understand.

534

FADING away like the stars of the morning,
  Losing their light in the glorious sun—
Thus would we pass from the earth and its toiling,
  Only remembered by what we have done.

REF.—Only remembered, only remembered,
  Only remembered by what we have done;
Thus would we pass from the earth and its toiling,
  Only remembered by what we have done.

2 Shall we be missed, though by others succeeded,
  Reaping the fields we in spring-time have sown?
No, for the sowers may pass from their labors,
  Only remembered by what they have done.

3 Only the truth that in life we have spoken,
  Only the seed that on earth we have sown;
These shall pass onward when we are forgotten,
  Fruits of the harvest and what we have done.

4 Oh, when the Saviour shall make up His jewels,
  When the bright crowns of rejoicing are won,
Then shall His weary and faithful disciples,
  All be remembered by what they have done.

535

WORK, for time is flying,
  Work with hearts sincere;
Work, for souls are dying,
  Work, for night is near;
In the Master's vineyard,
  Go and work to-day;
Be no useless sluggard
  Standing in the way.

2 In this glorious calling,
  Work till day is o'er;
Work, till evening falling;
  You can work no more;

Then your labor bringing
  To the King of kings,
Borne with joy and singing
  Home on angels' wings.

3 There where saints adore Him,
    Where the ransomed meet,
  Joy they show before Him,
    Bowing at His feet;
  Hear the Master saying,
    From His heavenly throne,
  When thy toil rewarding,
    "Laborer, well done!"

536

HAVE you sought for the sheep that have
    wandered,
  Far away on the dark mountains cold?
Have you gone, like the tender Shepherd,
  To bring them again to the fold?
Have you followed their weary footsteps?
  And the wild desert waste have you crossed,
Nor lingered till safe home returning,
  You have gathered the sheep that were lost?

2 Have you been to the sad and the lonely,
    Whose burdens are heavy to bear?
  Have you carried the name of Jesus,
    And tenderly breathed it in prayer?
  Have you told of the great salvation
    He died on the cross to secure?
  Have you asked them to trust in the Saviour
    Whose love shall forever endure?

3 Have you knelt by the sick and the dying,
    The message of mercy to tell?
  Have you stood by the trembling captive
    Alone in his dark prison cell?
  Have you pointed the lost to Jesus,
    And urged them on Him to believe?
  Have you told of the life everlasting
    That all, if they will, may receive?

4 If to Jesus you answer these questions,
    And to Him have been faithful and true,

Then behold, in the mansions yonder
　Are crowns of rejoicing for you;
And there from the King eternal
　Your welcome and greeting shall be,
"Inasmuch" as 'twas done for " my brethren,"
　Even so it was done "unto me."

537

WHEN morning gilds the skies,
　　My heart awaking cries,
May Jesus Christ be praised;
Alike at work and prayer,
To Jesus I repair;
May Jesus Christ be praised.

2 Does sadness fill my mind?
　A solace here I find,
May Jesus Christ be praised;
Or fades my earthly bliss?
My comfort still is this,
May Jesus Christ be praised.

3 Be this, while life is mine,
　My canticle divine,
May Jesus Christ be praised;
Be this th'eternal song,
Through all the ages long,
May Jesus Christ be praised.

538

THE call of God is sounding clear,
　O Christian, let it reach thine ear;
Endeavor now of souls to bring
A band to love and serve the King.

CHO.—Let us go forth, the call is clear,
　　Let us go forth, no tarrying here;
　　For Him to live, the Christ, the Lord,
　　A crown from Him, our high reward.

2 Let us go forth, as called of God,
　Redeemed by Jesus' precious blood;
His love to show, His life to live,
His message speak, His mercy give.

3 Let "Christ alone!" our watchword be—
The Son of God who made us free;
He bore our sins, He makes us pure,
For His name's sake we all endure.

4 The Christ of God to glorify,
His grace in us to magnify;—
His word of life to all make known,
Be this our work, and this alone.

539

I WILL lift up mine eyes unto the hills, from whence |
cometh my | help; ||
My help cometh from the Lord, which made | heaven and |
earth. ||

2 He will not suffer thy foot to be moved: He that keepeth
thee | will not | slumber; ||
Behold, He that keepeth Israel shall neither | slumber nor |
sleep. ||

3 The Lord is thy keeper: the Lord is thy shade upon thy |
right | hand; ||
The sun shall not smite thee by day, nor the | moon by |
night. ||

4 The Lord shall preserve thee from all evil: He shall pre- |
serve thy | soul. ||
The Lord shall preserve thy going out and thy coming in
from this time forth, and even for | ever- | more.
AMEN. ||

540

PRESS on, press on, O pilgrim,
Rejoicing in the Lord;
Believing in His promise,
And trusting in His word;
Fear not, for He is with us,
Whate'er the cross we bear;
And soon, beyond the swelling tide,
We'll gather over there.

REF.—||: Gather over there; :||
And soon, beyond the swelling tide,
We'll gather over there.

2 Press on, press on, O pilgrim,
　Along the heavenly way;
Remember God commands us
　To watch and work and pray;
He bids us all be faithful,
　And cast on Him our care;
And soon, beyond the swelling tide,
　We'll gather over there.

3 Press on, press on, O pilgrim,
　Though clouds and storms may rise;
The Light that never faileth
　Shines brightly in the skies;
Press on where crowns await us,
　In yonder mansions fair;
And soon, beyond the swelling tide,
　We'll gather over there.

541

THERE'S a wideness in God's mercy,
　Like the wideness of the sea:
There's a kindness in His justice,
　Which is more than liberty.

2 There is welcome for the sinner,
　And more graces for the good;
There is mercy with the Saviour;
　There is healing in His blood.

3 For the love of God is broader
　Than the measure of man's mind;
And the heart of the Eternal
　Is most wonderfully kind.

4 If our love were but more simple,
　We should take Him at His word;
And our lives would be all sunshine
　In the sweetness of our Lord.

542

O DAUGHTER take good heed,
　Incline, and give good ear;
Thou must forget thy kindred all,
　And father's house most dear.

Thy beauty to the King,
  Shall then delightful be:
And do thou humbly worship Him,
  Because thy Lord is He.

CHO.—With gladness and with joy,
      Thou all of them shalt bring,
    And they together enter shall
      The palace of the King,
    ||: The palace of the King; :||
    And they together enter shall
      The palace of the King.

2 The daughter then of Tyre
    There with a gift shall be,
  And all the wealthy of the land
    Shall make their suit to thee.
  The daughter of the King
    All-glorious is within;
  And with embroideries of gold
    Her garments wrought have been.

3 She cometh to the King
    In robes with needle wrought;
  The virgins that do follow her
    Shall unto Thee be brought.
  With gladness and with joy,
    Thou all of them shalt bring,
  And they together enter shall
    The palace of the King.

4 And in Thy fathers' stead,
    Thy children thou shalt take,
  And in all places of the earth
    Them noble princes make.
  I will show forth thy name
    To generations all:
  The people therefore evermore
    To Thee give praises shall.

543

O HAPPY day that fixed my choice
  On Thee, my Saviour and my God!
Well may this glowing heart rejoice,
  And tell its raptures all abroad.

CHO.—Happy day, happy day,
　　　When Jesus washed my sins away;
　　　He taught me how to watch and pray,
　　　And live rejoicing every day;
　　　Happy day, happy day,
　　　When Jesus washed my sins away.

2 O happy bond that seals my vows
　　To Him who merits all my love;
　Let cheerful anthems fill His house,
　　While to that sacred shrine I move.

3 'Tis done, the great transaction's done;
　　I am my Lord's and He is mine;
　He drew me, and I followed on,
　　Charmed to confess the voice divine.

4 Now rest, my long-divided heart,
　　Fixed on this blissful centre, rest;
　Nor ever from thy Lord depart,
　　With Him of every good possessed.

5 High heaven, that heard the solemn vow,
　　That vow renewed shall daily hear,
　Till in life's latest hour I bow,
　　And bless in death a bond so dear.

544

SPEED away! speed away on your mission of light,
　　To the lands that are lying in darkness and night:
'Tis the Master's command; go ye forth in His name,
The wonderful Gospel of Jesus proclaim;
Take your lives in your hand, to the work while 'tis day
Speed away! speed away! speed away!

2 Speed away, speed away with the life-giving Word,
To the nations that know not the voice of the Lord;
Take the wings of the morning and fly o'er the wave,
In the strength of your Master the lost ones to save;
He is calling once more, not a moment's delay,
Speed away! speed away! speed away!

3 Speed away, speed away with the message of rest,
To the souls by the tempter in bondage oppressed;
For the Saviour has purchased their ransom from sin,
And the banquet is ready, O gather them in;
To the rescue make haste, there's no time for delay,
Speed away! speed away! speed away!

545

HALLELUJAH! Hallelujah!
    Hearts to heaven and voices raise;
Sing to God a hymn of gladness,
    Sing to God a hymn of praise;
He who on the cross a victim
    For the world's salvation bled,
Jesus Christ the King of glory,
    Now is risen from the dead.

2 Christ is risen, Christ the first-fruits
    Of the holy harvest-field,
Which will all its full abundance,
    At His glorious advent, yield;
Then the golden ears of harvest
    Will before His presence wave,
Rising in His sunshine, joyous
    From the furrows of the grave.

3 Hallelujah! Hallelujah!
    Glory be to God above!
Hallelujah to the Saviour,
    Fount of life and source of love;
Hallelujah to the Spirit;
    Let our high ascriptions be,
Hallelujah, now and ever,
    To the blessèd Trinity.

546

"CAST thy bread upon the waters,"
    You who have but scant supply;
Angel eyes will watch above it,
    You shall find it by and by:
He who in His righteous balance,
    Doth each human action weigh,
Will your sacrifice remember,
    Will your loving deeds repay.

2 "Cast thy bread upon the waters,"
    Sad and weary, worn with care;
Often sitting in the shadow,—
    Have you not a crumb to spare?
Can you not to those around you
    Sing some little song of hope,

As you look with longing vision
Through faith's mighty telescope?

3 "Cast thy bread upon the waters,"
You who have abundant store;
It may float on many a billow,
It may strand on many a shore;
You may think it lost forever,
But, as sure as God is true,
In this life, or in the other,
It will yet return to you.

547

OH, list to the watchman crying,
Come, come away;
The arrows of death are flying,
Come, come to-day.

CHO.—||: Come, come away; :||
Jesus is gently calling,
Come, come to-day.

2 The Spirit of God is pleading,
Come, come away;
The Saviour is interceding,
Come, come to-day.

3 The mercy of God is calling,
Come, come away;
How sweetly the words are falling,
Come, come to-day.

4 The angels of God entreat you,
Come, come away;
The Father Himself will meet you,
Come, come to-day.

548

OH, hear the joyful message,
'Tis sounding far and wide;
Good news of full salvation,
Through Him, the Crucified;
God's Word is truth eternal;
Its promise all may claim,
Who look by faith to Jesus,
And call upon His name.

Cho.—‖: "Whosoever calleth, :‖
Whosoever calleth on His name shall be saved!
‖: Whosoever calleth, :‖
Whosoever calleth on the Lord shall be saved!"

2 Ye souls that long in darkness,
    The path of sin have trod,
Behold the light of mercy!
    Behold the Lamb of God;
With all your heart believe Him,
    And now the promise claim,
That none shall ever perish,
    Who call upon His name.

3 Ye weary, heavy-laden,
    Oppressed with toil and care,
He waits to bid you welcome,
    And all your burdens bear;
A precious gift He offers,
    A gift that all may claim,
Who look to Him believing,
    And call upon His name.

549

"THOUGH your sins be as scarlet,
    They shall be as white as snow;
Though they be red like crimson,
    They shall be as wool;"
‖: "Though your sins be as scarlet, :‖
‖: They shall be as as white as snow." :‖

2 Hear the voice that entreats you,
    Oh! return ye unto God!
He is of great compassion,
    And of wondrous love;
‖: Hear the voice that entreats you, :‖
‖: Oh, return ye unto God! :‖

3 He'll forgive your transgressions,
    And remember them no more!
"Look unto me, ye people,"
    Saith the Lord your God;
‖: He'll forgive your transgressions, :‖
‖: And remember them no more. :‖

550

HO, reapers in the whitened harvest!
　　Oft feeble, faint and few,
Come wait upon the blesséd Master,
　　Our strength He will renew.

CHO.—For "they that wait upon the Lord shall renew their
　　　　　　strength,
　　They shall mount up with wings, they shall mount
　　　　　up with wings as eagles;
　　　　‖: They shall run and not be weary,
　　　　　They shall walk and not faint." :‖

2 Too oft a-weary and discouraged,
　　We pour a sad complaint;
Believing in a *living* Saviour,
　　Why should we ever faint?

3 Rejoice, for He is with us alway,
　　Lo, even to the end!
Look up, take courage and go forward,
　　All needed grace He'll send.

551

"NEITHER do I condemn thee,"—
　　O words of wondrous grace;
Thy sins were borne upon the cross,
　　Believe, and go in peace.

CHO.—"Neither do I condemn thee,"
　　O sing it o'er and o'er;
　　"Neither do I condemn thee,
　　Go, and sin no more."

2 "Neither do I condemn thee,"—
　　For there is therefore now
No condemnation for thee,
　　As at the cross you bow.

3 "Neither do I condemn thee,"—
　　I came not to condemn;
I came from God to save thee,
　　And turn thee from thy sin.

4 "Neither do I condemn thee,"—
    O praise the God of grace;
  O praise His Son our Saviour,
    For this His word of peace.

552

HE lives and loves, our Saviour King;
    With joyful lips your tribute bring;
Repeat His praise, exalt His Name,
Whose grace and truth are still the same.

Cho.—His mercy flows, an endless stream,
        To all eternity the same;
        To all eternity, to all eternity,
        To all eternity the same.

2 His hand is strong, His word endures,
  His sacrifice our peace secures;
  From sin and death He doth redeem,
  His changeless love be all our theme.

3 Each day reveals His constant love,
  With "mercies new" from heaven above;
  Through ages past His word has stood;
  Oh, taste and see that He is good.

553

O THANK the Lord, the Lord of love,
    O thank the God all gods above;
  O thank the mighty King of kings,
  Whose arm hath done such wondrous things.

    Cho.—His mercy flows, etc.

2 Whose wisdom gave the heavens their birth,
  And on the waters spread the earth;
  Who taught yon glorious lights their way,
  The radiant sun to rule the day.

3 The moon and stars to rule the night,
  With radiance of a milder light;
  Who smote the Egyptians' stubborn pride,
  When in His wrath, their first-born died.

4 Who thought on us amidst our woes,
  And rescued us from all our foes;
  Who daily feeds each living thing;
  O thank the heaven's Almighty King.

554

WHEN morning lights the eastern skies.
Thy mercy, Lord, disclose;
And let Thy loving kindness rise;
On Thee my hopes repose.

CHO.—||: On Thee my hopes repose; :||
And let Thy loving kindness rise;
On Thee my hopes repose.

2 Teach me the way where I should go;
I lift my soul to Thee;
Redeem me from the raging foe;
To Thee, O Lord, I flee.

3 Because Thou art my God, I pray,
Teach me to do Thy will;
O lead me in the perfect way
By Thy good Spirit still.

4 Revive me, Lord, for Thy great name,
And, for Thy judgment's sake;
From all my woes, O Lord, reclaim,
My soul from trouble take.

555

O THOU my soul, bless God the Lord,
And all that in me is;
Be lifted up His holy name,
To magnify and bless.

CHO.—"Bless the Lord, bless the Lord,
Bless the Lord, O my soul,
And all that is within me,
Bless His holy name."

2 Bless, O my soul, the Lord thy God,
And not forgetful be
Of all His gracious benefits
He hath bestowed on thee.

3 All thy iniquities who doth
Most graciously forgive;
Who thy diseases all and pains
Doth heal, and thee relieve.

4 Who doth redeem thy life, that thou
  To death may'st not go down;
Who thee with loving kindness doth
  And tender mercies crown.

556

I'LL Thee exalt, my God, O King,
    Thy name I will adore;
I'll bless Thee every day, and praise
  Thy name for evermore.

2 The Lord is great, much to be praised,
    His greatness search exceeds;
Race unto race shall praise Thy works,
  And show Thy mighty deeds.

3 I of Thy glorious majesty
    The honor will record:
I'll speak of all Thy mighty works,
  Which wondrous are, O Lord.

4 Men, of Thine acts the might shall show,
    Thine acts that dreadful are;
And I, Thy glory to advance,
  Thy greatness will declare.

557

I CRIED to God, I cried, He heard;
    In day of grief I sought the Lord;
All night with hands stretched out I wept,
My soul no comfort would accept.

CHO.—Hath God forgotten to be kind?
        His tender love in wrath confined?
        My weakness this, yet faith doth stand
        Recalling years of God's right hand.

2 I thought of God, and was distressed:
  Complained, yet trouble round me pressed:
Thou holdest, Lord, my eyes awake;
So great my grief I cannot speak.

3 The days of old I called to mind,
  The ancient years when God was kind;
I called to mind my song by night;
My musing spirit sought for light.

4 Will God cast off for evermore?
His favor will He ne'er restore?
Has grace for ever passed away?
Or, doth His promise fall for aye?

558

IN Thy great loving kindness, Lord,
 Be merciful to me;
In Thy compassions great blot out
 All my iniquity.

Cho.—Wash Thou me, yes, wash Thou me,
 And then I shall be whiter than the snow,
 I shall be whiter than the snow.

2 O wash me thoroughly from sin;
 From all my guilt me cleanse;
For my transgressions I confess;
 I ever see my sins.

3 'Gainst Thee, Thee only have I sinned,
 Done evil in Thy sight,
That when Thou speak'st Thou may'st be just,
 And in Thy judging right.

4 Behold, I in iniquity
 My being first received;
And with a nature all corrupt
 My mother me conceived.

559

THEE will I love, O Lord, my strength,
 My fortress is the Lord;
My rock, and He that doth to me
 Deliverance afford.

Cho.—My God whom I will trust,
 A buckler unto me,
 The horn of my salvation, too,
 And my high tower is He.

2 The Lord is worthy to be praised,
 Upon His name I'll call;
And He from all my enemies
 Preserve me safely shall.

3 In my distress I called on God,
    Cry to my God did I;
He from His temple heard my voice,
    To His ears came my cry.

4 I therefore will to Thee, O Lord,
    In songs my thanks proclaim;
And I among the heathen will
    Sing praises to Thy name.

560

FAR from Thy sacred courts my tears
    Have been my food by night and day,
While constantly, with bitter sneers,
    "Where is thy God?" the scoffers say.

CHO.—As pants the hart for water brooks,
    So pants my soul, O God, for Thee:
For Thee it thirsts, to Thee it looks,
    And longs the living God to see.

2 These things I'll call to mind, and cry,
    When I shall tread the sacred way
To Zion, praising God on high,
    With throngs who keep the holy day.

3 O why art thou cast down, my soul?
    And what should so disquiet thee?
Still hope in God, and Him extol,
    Whose face brings saving health to me.

561

FROM the depths do I invoke Thee,
    O Jehovah, give an ear;
To my voice be Thou attentive,
    And my supplications hear.

CHO.—I am waiting, I am waiting,
    And my hope is in His word;
I am waiting, ever waiting,
    Yea, my soul waits for the Lord.

2 Lord, if Thou shouldst mark transgressions,
    Who before Thee, Lord, shall stand?
But with Thee there is forgiveness,
    That Thy name may fear command.

3 Israel, hope thou in Jehovah,
    Mercies great are found with Him;
He, abounding in redemption,
    Israel will from sin redeem.

562

O PRAISE our Lord, where rich in grace
    His presence fills His holy place;
Praise Him in yon celestial arch,
||: Where holds His power its glorious march. :||

CHO.—O praise Him, O praise Him for all His deeds of
        fame;
    O praise Him, O praise Him, O praise His mighty
        name;
    Let all that breathe with glad accord
    Lift up their voice, and praise the Lord.

2 O praise Him for His deeds of fame,
    O praise the greatness of His name;
O praise Him with the trumpet's sound,
||: With harp and psaltery answering round. :||

3 O praise Him with the notes of joy,
    And every harp in praise employ;
On cymbals loud, Jehovah praise,
||: On cymbals high His glory raise. :||

563

TO Thee I lift my soul, O Lord;
    My God, I trust in Thee;
O let me never be ashamed,
    Nor foes exult o'er me.

CHO.—Remember me, remember me,
        O Lord, remember me;
    In mercy for Thy goodness' sake,
        O Lord, remember me.

2 O Lord, let none be put to shame,
    Upon Thee who attend;
But make all those to be ashamed,
    Who causelessly offend.

3 Thy ways, Lord, show; teach me Thy paths;
   Lead me in truth, teach me;
   For of my safety Thou art God;
   All day I wait on Thee.

4 Let not the errors of my youth,
   Nor sins remembered be;
   In mercy, for Thy goodness' sake,
   O Lord, remember me.

564

DOWN in the valley with my Saviour I would go,
    Where the flowers are blooming and the sweet
       waters flow;
Everywhere He leads me I would follow, follow on.
Walking in His footsteps till the crown be won.

CHO.—Follow! follow! I would follow Jesus!
        Anywhere, everywhere, I would follow on!
        Follow! follow! I would follow Jesus!
        Everywhere He leads me I would follow on!

2 Down in the valley with my Saviour I would go,
   Where the storms are sweeping and the dark waters flow;
   With His hand to lead me I will never, never fear,
   Dangers cannot fright me if my Lord is near.

3 Down in the valley, or upon the mountain steep,
   Close beside my Saviour would my soul ever keep;
   He will lead me safely, in the path that He has trod,
   Up to where they gather on the hills of God.

565

JESUS knows thy sorrow,
   Knows thine every care;
Knows thy deep contrition,
   Hears thy feeblest prayer;
Do not fear to trust Him—
   Tell Him all thy grief;
Cast on Him thy burden,
   He will bring relief.

2 Trust the heart of Jesus,
   Thou art precious there;
Surely He would shield thee
   From the tempter's snare;

Safely He would lead thee
By His own sweet way,
Out into the glory
Of a brighter day.

3 Jesus knows thy conflict,
Hears thy burdened sigh;
When thy heart is wounded,
Hears thy plaintive cry;
He thy soul will strengthen,
Overcome thy fears;
He will send thee comfort,
Wipe away thy tears.

566

GATHER them in! for yet there is room
At the feast that the King has spread;
Oh, gather them in!—let His house be filled,
And the hungry and poor be fed.

CHO.—Out in the highway, out in the byway,
Out in the dark paths of sin,
Go forth, go forth, with a loving heart,
And gather the wanderers in!

2 Gather them in! for yet there is room;
But our hearts—how they throb with pain,
To think of the many who slight the call
That may never be heard again!

3 Gather them in! for yet there is room;
'Tis a message from God above;
Oh, gather them into the fold of grace,
And the arms of the Saviour's love!

567

COME, ye that love the Lord,
And let your joys be known,
||: Join in a song with sweet accord, :||
||: And thus surround the throne. :||

CHO.—We're marching to Zion,
Beautiful, beautiful Zion;
We're marching upward to Zion
The beautiful city of God.

2 Let those refuse to sing
   Who never knew our God;
‖: But children of the heavenly King, :‖
‖: May speak their joys abroad. :‖

3 The hill of Zion yields
   A thousand sacred sweets,
‖: Before we reach the heavenly fields, :‖
‖: Or walk the golden streets. :‖

4 Then let our songs abound,
   And every tear be dry;
‖: We're marching through Immanuel's ground, :‖
‖: To fairer worlds on high. :‖

568

HAVE you any room for Jesus,
   He who bore your load of sin;
As He knocks and asks admission,
   Sinner will you let Him in?

CHO.—Room for Jesus, King of glory!
   Hasten now His word obey!
   Swing the heart's door widely open,
   Bid Him enter while you may.

2 Room for pleasure, room for business,
   But for Christ the crucified;
Not a place that He can enter,
   In the heart for which He died?

3 Have you any room for Jesus,
   As in grace He calls again?
O to-day is time accepted,
   To-morrow you may call in vain.

4 Room and time now give to Jesus,
   Soon will pass God's day of grace;
Soon thy heart left cold and silent,
   And thy Saviour's pleading cease.

569

"ALMOST persuaded," Now to believe;
   "Almost persuaded," Christ to receive:
Seems now some soul to say,
   " Go, Spirit, go Thy way,

> Some more convenient day
> On Thee I'll call."

2 "Almost persuaded," Come, come to-day;
  "Almost persuaded," Turn not away;
  Jesus invites you here,
  Angels are lingering near,
  Prayers rise from hearts so dear:
  O wanderer come.

3 "Almost persuaded," Harvest is past!
  "Almost persuaded," Doom comes at last!
  "Almost" can not avail;
  "Almost" is but to fail!
  Sad, sad, that bitter wail—
  "Almost—but lost!"

570

THERE were ninety and nine that safely lay
In the shelter of the fold,
But one was out on the hills away,
Far-off from the gates of gold—
Away on the mountains wild and bare,
||: Away from the tender Shepherd's care. :||

2 "Lord, Thou hast here Thy ninety and nine:
  Are they not enough for Thee?"
But the Shepherd made answer; "This of mine
Has wandered away from me,
And, although the road be rough and steep,
||: I go to the desert to find my sheep." :||

3 But none of the ransomed ever knew
How deep were the waters crossed;
Nor how dark was the night that the Lord passed thro'
Ere He found His sheep that was lost.
Out in the desert He heard the cry—
||: Sick and helpless, and ready to die. :||

4 "Lord, whence are those blood-drops all the way
That mark out the mountain's track?"
"They were shed for one who had gone astray
Ere the Shepherd could bring him back,"
"Lord, whence are Thy hands so rent and torn?"
||: They are pierced to-night by many a thorn." :||

5 But all through the mountains, thunder-riven,
    And up from the rocky steep,
There arose a glad cry to the gate of heaven,
    " Rejoice! I have found my sheep!"
And the angels echoed around the throne.
||: " Rejoice for the Lord brings back His own!" :||

571

R EVIVE Thy work, O Lord!
    Thy mighty arm make bare;
Speak with the voice that wakes the dead,
    And make Thy people hear.

CHO.—Revive! revive!
    And give refreshing showers;
    The glory shall be all Thine own;
    The blessing shall be ours.

2 Revive Thy work, O Lord!
    Disturb this sleep of death;
Quicken the smouldering embers now
    By Thine Almighty breath.

3 Revive Thy work, O Lord!
    Create soul-thirst for Thee;
And hungering for bread of life,
    Oh, may our spirits be!

4 Revive Thy work, O Lord!
    Exalt Thy precious name;
And by the Holy Ghost, our love
    For Thee and Thine inflame.

572

I AM Thine, O Lord, I have heard Thy voice,
    And it told Thy love to me;
But I long to rise in the arms of faith,
    And be closer drawn to Thee.

CHO.—Draw me nearer, nearer, blesséd Lord,
    To the cross where Thou hast died;
    Draw me nearer, nearer, nearer, blesséd Lord,
    To Thy precious, bleeding side.

2 Consecrate me now to Thy service, Lord,
    By the power of grace divine;

Let my soul look up with a steadfast hope,
And my will be lost in Thine.

3 O, the pure delight of a single hour,
That before Thy Throne I spend,
When I kneel in prayer, and with Thee my God,
I commune as friend with friend.

4 There are depths of love that I cannot know
Till I cross the narrow sea,
There are heights of joy that I may not reach
Till I rest in peace with Thee,

573

———

WHEN peace, like a river, attendeth my way,
When sorrows like sea-billows roll;
Whatever my lot, Thou hast taught me to say,
It is well, it is well with my soul.

CHO.—It is well with my soul,
It is well, it is well with my soul.

2 Though Satan should buffet, though trials should come,
Let this blest assurance control,
That Christ hath regarded my helpless estate.
And hath shed His own blood for my soul.

3 My sin—oh, the bliss of this glorious thought—
My sin—not in part but the whole,
Is nailed to His cross and I bear it no more,
Praise the Lord, praise the Lord, O my soul!

4 And, Lord, haste the day when the faith shall be sight,
The clouds be rolled back as a scroll,
The trump shall resound, and the Lord shall descend,
"Even so"—it is well with my soul.

574

———

O SAFE to the Rock that is higher than I,
My soul in its conflicts and sorrows would fly;
So sinful, so weary, Thine, Thine would I be;
Thou blest "Rock of Ages," I'm hiding in Thee.

CHO.—Hiding in Thee, hiding in Thee,
Thou blest "Rock of Ages,"
I'm hiding in Thee.

2 In the calm of the moontide, in sorrow's lone hour,
  In times when temptation casts o'er me its power;
  In the tempests of life, on its wide, heaving sea,
  Thou blest "Rock of Ages," I'm hiding in Thee.

3 How oft in the conflict, when pressed by the foe,
  I have fled to my Refuge and breathed out my woe;
  How often when trials, like sea-billows roll,
  Have I hidden in Thee, O Thou Rock of my soul.

575

OH, where are the reapers that garner in
     The sheaves of the good from the fields of sin;
With sickles of truth must the work be done,
And no one may rest till the "harvest home."

CHO.—Where are the reapers! oh, who will come
   And share in the glory of the "harvest home?"
   Oh, who will help us to garner in
   The sheaves of good from the fields of sin.

2 Go out in the by-ways and search them all;
  The wheat may be there, though the weeds are tall;
  Then search in the highway, and pass none by,
  But gather from all for the home on high.

3 The fields all are ripening, and far and wide
  The world now is waiting the harvest tide:
  But reapers are few and the work is great,
  And much will be lost should the harvest wait.

4 So come with your sickles, ye sons of men,
  And gather together the golden grain;
  Toil on till the Lord of the harvest come,
  Then share ye His joy in the "harvest home."

576

TO the work! to the work! we are servants of God,
    Let us follow the path that our Master has trod;
With the balm of His counsel our strength to renew,
Let us do with our might what our hands find to do.

CHO.—||: Toiling on, toiling on, :||
   Let us hope, let us watch,
   And labor till the Master comes.

2 To the work! to the work! let the hungry be fed,
  To the fountain of Life let the weary be led;
  In the cross and its banner our glory shall be,
  While we herald the tidings, " *Salvation is free!*"

3 To the work! to the work! there is labor for all,
  For the kingdom of darkness and error shall fall;
  And the name of Jehovah exalted shall be
  In the loud swelling chorus, " *Salvation is free!*"

4 To the work! to the work! in the strength of the Lord,
  And a robe and a crown shall our labor reward;
  When the home of the faithful our dwelling shall be,
  And we shout with the ransomed " *Salvation is free!*"

577

I WILL sing of my Redeemer,
  And His wondrous love to me;
On the cruel cross He suffered,
  From the curse to set me free.

CHO.—Sing, oh, sing, of my Redeemer!
  With His blood He purchased me,
  On the cross He sealed my pardon,
  Paid the debt, and made me free.

2 I will tell the wondrous story,
  How my lost estate to save,
In His boundless love and mercy,
  He the ransom freely gave.

3 I will praise my dear Redeemer,
  His triumphant power I'll tell;
How the victory He giveth
  Over sin, and death, and hell.

4 I will sing of my Redeemer,
  And His heavenly love to me;
He from death to life hath brought me,
  Son of God, with Him to be.

578

THERE are lonely hearts to cherish,
  While the days are going by;
There are weary souls who perish,
  While the days are going by:

If a smile we can renew,
As our journey we pursue,
Oh, the good we all may do,
    While the days are going by

CHO.—‖: Going by, going by, :‖
    Oh, the good we all may do,
    While the days are going by.

2 There's no time for idle scorning,
    While the days are going by;
Let your face be like the morning,
    While the days are going by;
Oh, the world is full of sighs,
Full of sad and weeping eyes;
Help your fallen brother rise,
    While the days are going by.

3 All the loving links that bind us
    While the days are going by;
One by one we leave behind us,
    While the days are going by;
But the seeds of good we sow,
Both in shade and shine will grow,
And will keep our hearts aglow,
    While the days are going by.

579

SING them over again to me,
    Wonderful words of Life,
Let me more of their beauty see,
    Wonderful words of Life.
    Words of life and beauty,
    Teach me faith and duty;
‖: Beautiful words, wonderful words,
    Wonderful words of Life.:‖

2 Christ, the blesséd One gives to all
    Wonderful words of Life,
Sinner, list to the loving call,
    Wonderful words of Life.
    All so freely given,
    Wooing us to heaven.
‖: Beautiful words, wonderful words
    Wonderful words of Life. :‖

3 Sweetly echo the gospel call,
  Wonderful words of Life,
Offer pardon and peace to all,
  Wonderful words of Life.
    Jesus, only Saviour,
    Sanctify forever.
  ‖: Beautiful words, wonderful words,
    Wonderful words of Life. :‖

580

BEHOLD, what love, what boundless love
  The Father hath bestowed
On sinners lost, that we should be
Now called the sons of God!

Cho.—Behold, what manner of love!
What manner of love the Father hath bestowed upon us,
    That we—that we should be called,
    Should be called the sons of God.

2 No longer far from Him, but now
    By "precious blood" made nigh;
  Accepted in the "Well-belov'd,"
    Near to God's heart we lie.

3 What we in glory soon shall be,
    It doth not yet appear;
  But when our precious Lord we see,
    We shall His image bear.

4 With such a blessèd hope in view,
    We would more holy be,
  More like our risen, glorious Lord,
    Whose face we soon shall see.

581

SIMPLY trusting every day,
  Trusting through a stormy way;
Even when my faith is small,
Trusting Jesus that is all.

Cho.—Trusting as the moments fly,
    Trusting as the days go by:
    Trusting Him whate'er befall,
    Trusting Jesus, that is all.

Brightly doth His Spirit shine
Into this poor heart of mine;
While He leads I cannot fall,
Trusting Jesus, that is all.

3 Singing, if my way is clear;
Praying, if the path is drear;
If in danger, for Him call;
Trusting Jesus, that is all.

4 Trusting Him while life shall last,
Trusting Him till earth is past;
Till within the jasper wall,
Trusting Jesus, that is all.

582

YIELD not to temptation,
For yielding is sin,
Each victory will help you
Some other to win;
Fight manfully onward,
Dark passions subdue,
Look ever to Jesus,
He'll carry you through.

CHO.—Ask the Saviour to help you,
Comfort, strengthen, and keep you,
He is willing to aid you,
He will carry you through.

2 Shun evil companions,
Bad language disdain,
God's name hold in reverence,
Nor take it in vain;
Be thoughtful and earnest,
Kind-hearted and true,
Look ever to Jesus,
He'll carry you through.

3 To him that o'ercometh
God giveth a crown,
Through faith we shall conquer,
Though often cast down;

He who is our Saviour,
　　Our strength will renew;
Look ever to Jesus,
　　He'll carry you through.

583

WHAT a friend we have in Jesus,
　　All our sins and griefs to bear;
What a privilege to carry
　　Everything to God in prayer.
Oh, what peace we often forfeit,
　　Oh, what needless pain we bear—
All because we do not carry
　　Everything to God in prayer.

2 Have we trials and temptations?
　　Is there trouble anywhere?
We should never be discouraged;
　　Take it to the Lord in prayer.
Can we find a Friend so faithful,
　　Who will all our sorrows share?
Jesus knows our every weakness,
　　Take it to the Lord in prayer.

3 Are we weak and heavy-laden,
　　Cumbered with a load of care?
Precious Saviour, still our Refuge,—
　　Take it to the Lord in prayer.
Do thy friends despise, forsake thee?
　　Take it to the Lord in prayer;
In His arms He'll take and shield thee,
　　Thou wilt find a solace there.

584

I'VE found a Friend; oh, such a Friend!
　　He loved me ere I knew Him;
He drew me with the cords of love,
　　And thus He bound me to Him;
And 'round my heart still closely twine
　　Those ties which naught can sever,
For I am His, and He is mine,
　　Forever and forever.

2 I've found a Friend; oh, such a Friend!
　　He bled, He died to save me;
And not alone the gift of life,
　　But His own self He gave me.
Nought that I have my own I call,
　　I hold it for the Giver:
My heart, my strength, my life, my all,
　　Are His, and His forever.

3 I've found a Friend; oh, such a Friend!
　　All power to Him is given;
To guard me on my onward course,
　　And bring me safe to heaven.
Th'eternal glories gleam afar,
　　To nerve my faint endeavor;
So now to watch, to work, to war,
　　And then to rest forever.

4 I've found a Friend; oh, such a Friend!
　　So kind, and true, and tender,
So wise a Counsellor and Guide,
　　So mighty a Defender!
From Him, who loves me now so well,
　　What power my soul can sever?
Shall life, or death, or earth, or hell?
　　No; I am His forever.

585

_____

PASS me not, O gentle Saviour,
　　Hear my humble cry;
While on others Thou art smiling,
　　Do not pass me by.

CHO.—Saviour, Saviour, hear my humble cry,
　　While on others Thou art calling,
　　　Do not pass me by.

2 Let me at a throne of mercy
　　Find a sweet relief;
Kneeling there in deep contrition,
　　Help my unbelief:

3 Trusting only in Thy merit,
　　Would I seek Thy face;
Heal my wounded, broken spirit,
　　Save me by Thy grace.

4 Thou the Spring of all my comfort,
More than life to me,
Whom have I on earth beside Thee?
Whom in heaven but Thee?

586

MY Jesus, I love Thee, I know Thou art mine!
For Thee all the follies of sin I resign;
My gracious Redeemer, my Saviour art Thou,
If ever I loved Thee, my Jesus, 'tis now.

2 I love Thee, because Thou hast first lovéd me,
And purchased my pardon on Calvary's tree;
I love Thee for wearing the thorns on Thy brow;
If ever I loved Thee, my Jesus, 'tis now.

3 I will love Thee in life, I will love Thee in death,
And praise Thee as long as Thou lendest me breath:
And say when the death-dew lies cold on my brow,
If ever I loved Thee, my Jesus, 'tis now.

4 In mansions of glory and endless delight,
I'll ever adore Thee in heaven so bright;
I'll sing with the glittering crown on my brow,
If ever I loved Thee, my Jesus, 'tis now.

587

COME, every soul by sin oppressed,
There's mercy with the Lord,
And He will surely give you rest,
By trusting in His word.

CHO.—Only trust Him, only trust Him,
Only trust Him now;
He will save you, He will save you,
He will save you now.

2 For Jesus shed His precious blood
Rich blessings to bestow;
Plunge now into the crimson flood
That washes white as snow.

3 Yes, Jesus is the Truth, the Way;
That leads you into rest;
Believe in Him without delay,
And you are fully blest.

4 Come then, and join this holy band,
　　And on to glory go,
　　To dwell in that celestial land
　　　Where joys immortal flow.

588

I HEAR the Saviour say—
　　Thy strength indeed is small;
Child of weakness, watch and pray,
　Find in Me thine all in all.

Cho.—Jesus paid it all,
　　　All to Him I owe;
　　Sin had left a crimson stain;
　　　He washed it white as snow.

2 Lord, now indeed I find
　　Thy power, and Thine alone,
　Can change the leper's spots,
　　And melt the heart of stone.

3 For nothing good have I
　　Whereby Thy grace to claim—
　I'll wash my garments white
　　In the blood of Calvary's Lamb.

4 When from my dying bed
　　My ransomed soul shall rise,
　Then "Jesus paid it all!"
　　Shall rend the vaulted skies.

5 And when before the throne
　　I stand in Him complete,
　I'll lay my trophies down,
　　All down at Jesus' feet.

589

I HAVE a Saviour, He's pleading in glory,
　A dear, loving Saviour tho' earth-friends be few,
And now He is watching in tenderness o'er me,
　But oh, that my Saviour were your Saviour too.

Cho.—For you I am praying,
　‖: For you I am praying, :‖
　　I'm praying for you.

2 I have a Father: to me He has given
   A hope for eternity, blesséd and true;
   And soon will He call me to meet Him in heaven,
   But oh, that He'd let me bring you with me too!

3 I have a robe: 'tis resplendent in whiteness,
   Awaiting in glory my wondering view;
   Oh, when I receive it all shining in brightness,
   Dear friends, could I see you receiving one too!

4 I have a peace: it is calm as a river—
   A peace that the friends of this world never knew;
   My Saviour alone is its Author and Giver,
   And oh, could I know it was given to you!

5 When Jesus has found you, tell others the story,
   That my loving Saviour is your Saviour too;
   Then pray that your Saviour may bring them to glory,
   And prayer will be answered—'twas answered for you

590

SOUL of mine, in earthly temple,
   Why not here content abide?
Why art thou forever pleading?
   Why art thou not satisfied?

CHO.—‖: I shall be satisfied,
         I shall be satisfied,
   When I awake in His likeness. :‖

2 Soul of mine, my heart is clinging
   To the earth's fair pomp and pride;
Ah, why dost thou thus reprove me?
   Why art thou not satisfied?

3 Soul of mine, must I surrender,
   See myself as crucified;
Turn from all of earth's ambition,
   That thou may'st be satisfied.

4 Soul of mine, continue pleading;
   Sin rebuke, and folly chide;
I accept the cross of Jesus,
   That thou may'st be satisfied.

591

SAVIOUR! Thy dying love
   Thou gavest me,
Nor should I aught withhold,
   Dear Lord, from Thee;
In love my soul would bow,
   My heart fulfill its vow,
Some offering bring Thee now,
   Something for Thee.

2 O'er the blest mercy-seat,
   Pleading for me,
My feeble faith looks up,
   Jesus, to Thee:
Help me the cross to bear,
   Thy wondrous love declare,
Some song to raise, or prayer,
   Something for Thee.

3 Give me a faithful heart—
   Likeness to Thee—
That each departing day
   Henceforth may see
Some work of love begun,
   Some deed of kindness done,
Some wanderer sought and won,
   Something for Thee.

4 All that I am and have—
   Thy gifts so free—
In joy, in grief, through life,
   Dear Lord, for Thee!
And when Thy face I see,
   My ransomed soul shall be,
Through all eternity,
   Something for Thee.

592

RESCUE the perishing,
   Care for the dying,
Snatch them in pity from sin and the grave;
   Weep o'er the erring one,
   Lift up the fallen,
Tell them of Jesus the mighty to save.

CHO.—Rescue the perishing,
 Care for the dying;
 Jesus is merciful,
 Jesus will save.

2 Though they are slighting Him,
 Still He is waiting,
Waiting the penitent child to receive;
 Plead with them earnestly,
 Plead with them gently:
He will forgive if they only believe.

3 Down in the human heart,
 Crushed by the tempter,
Feelings lie buried that grace can restore:
 Touched by a loving heart,
 Wakened by kindness,
Chords that were broken will vibrate once more

4 Rescue the perishing,
 Duty demands it;
Strength for thy labor the Lord will provide;
 Back to the narrow way
 Patiently win them;
Tell the poor wanderer a Saviour has died.

593

SAVIOUR, more than life to me,
 I am clinging, clinging close to Thee;
Let Thy precious blood applied,
Keep me ever, ever near Thy side.

REF.—Every day, every hour,
 Let me feel Thy cleansing power;
 May Thy tender love to me
 Bind me closer, closer, Lord, to Thee.

2 Through this changing world below,
Lead me gently, gently as I go;
Trusting Thee, I cannot stray,
I can never, never lose my way.

3 Let me love Thee more and more,
Till this fleeting, fleeting life is o'er;
Till my soul is lost in love,
In a brighter, brighter world above.

594

MORE holiness give me,
      More strivings within;
More patience in suffering,
      More sorrow for sin;
More faith in my Saviour,
      More sense of His care;
More joy in His service,
      More purpose in prayer.

2 More gratitude give me,
      More trust in the Lord;
More pride in His glory,
      More hope in His word;
More tears for His sorrows,
      More pain at His grief;
More meekness in trial,
      More praise for relief.

3 More purity give me,
      More strength to o'ercome;
More freedom from earth-stains,
      More longings for home;
More fit for the kingdom,
      More used would I be;
More blessèd and holy,
      More, Saviour, *like Thee.*

595

I HEAR Thy welcome voice
      That calls me, Lord, to Thee;
For cleansing in Thy precious blood
      That flowed on Calvary.

CHO.—I am coming Lord!
      Coming now to Thee!
Wash me, cleanse me, in the blood
      That flowed on Calvary.

2 Though coming weak and vile,
      Thou dost my strength assure;
Thou dost my vileness fully cleanse,
      Till spotless all and pure.

3 'Tis Jesus calls me on
    To perfect faith and love,
To perfect hope, and peace, and trust,
    For earth and heaven above.

4 Tis Jesus who confirms
    The blesséd work within,
By adding grace to welcomed grace,
    Where reigned the power of sin.

5 And He the witness gives
    To loyal hearts and free,
That every promise is fulfilled,
    If faith but brings the plea.

6 All hail, atoning blood!
    All hail, redeeming grace!
All hail, the Gift of Christ. our Lord,
    Our Strength and Righteousness!

526

'TIS the blesséd hour of prayer, when our hearts lowly
    bend,
And we gather to Jesus, our Saviour and Friend;
If we come to Him in faith, His protection to share,
What a balm for the weary! O how sweet to be there!

CHO.—Blesséd hour of prayer, blesséd hour of prayer;
        What a balm for the weary! O how sweet to be there!

2 'Tis the blesséd hour of prayer, when the Saviour draws
        near,
With a tender compassion His children to hear;
When He tells us we may cast at His feet every care,
What a balm for the weary! O how sweet to be there!

3 'Tis the blesséd hour of prayer, when the tempted and tried
To the Saviour who loves them their sorrow confide:
With a sympathizing heart He removes every care;
What a balm for the weary! O how sweet to be there!

4 At the blesséd hour of prayer, trusting Him we believe
That the blessings we're needing we'll surely receive,
In the fulness of this trust we shall lose every care;
What a balm for the weary! O how sweet to be there!

597

I NEED Thee every hour,
  Most gracious Lord;
No tender voice like Thine
  Can peace afford.

REF.—I need Thee, oh! I need Thee;
  Every hour I need Thee;
O bless me now, my Saviour!
  I come to Thee.

2 I need Thee every hour;
  Stay Thou near by;
Temptations lose their power
  When Thou art nigh.

3 I need Thee every hour;
  In joy or pain;
Come quickly and abide,
  Or life is vain.

4 I need Thee every hour;
  Teach me Thy will;
And Thy rich promises
  In me fulfil.

5 I need Thee every hour,
  Most Holy One;
Oh, make me Thine indeed,
  Thou blesséd Son.

598

JESUS, keep me near the Cross,
  There a precious fountain
Free to all—a healing stream,
  Flows from Calvary's mountain.

CHO.—In the Cross, in the Cross,
  Be my glory ever;
Till my raptured soul shall find
  Rest beyond the river.

2 Near the Cross, a trembling soul,
  Love and mercy found me;
There the Bright and Morning Star
  Shed its beams around me.

3 Near the Cross! O Lamb of God,
  Bring its scenes before me;
Help me walk from day to day,
  With its shadows o'er me.

4 Near the Cross I'll watch and wait,
  Hoping, trusting ever,
Till I reach the golden strand,
  Just beyond the river.

599

THOU my everlasting portion,
  More than friend or life to me,
All along my pilgrim journey,
  Saviour, let me walk with Thee.

REF.—||: Close to Thee, close to Thee; :||
  All along my pilgrim journey,
  Saviour, let me walk with Thee

2 Not for ease or worldly pleasure,
  Nor for fame my prayer shall be;
Gladly will I toil and suffer,
  Only let me walk with Thee.

REF.—||: Close to Thee, close to Thee; :||
  Gladly will I toil and suffer,
  Only let me walk with Thee.

3 Lead me through the vale of shadows,
  Bear me o'er life's fitful sea;
Then the gate of life eternal,
  May I enter, Lord, with Thee.

REF.—||: Close to Thee, close to Thee; :||
  Then the gate of life eternal,
  May I enter, Lord, with Thee.

600

I GAVE My life for thee,
  My precious blood I shed,
That thou might'st ransomed be,
  And quickened from the dead;
I gave, I gave My life for thee,
  What hast thou given for Me?

2 My Father's house of light,—
    My glory-circled throne
I left, for earthly night,
    For wanderings sad and lone;
I left, I left it all for thee,
    Hast thou left aught for Me?

3 I suffered much for thee,
    More than my tongue can tell,
Of bitterest agony,
    To rescue thee from hell;
I've borne, I've borne it all for thee,
    What hast thou borne for Me?

4 And I have brought to thee.
    Down from My home above,
Salvation full and free.
    My pardon and My love;
I bring, I bring rich gifts to thee,
    What hast thou brought to Me?

601

THERE is a green hill far away,
    Without a city wall;
Where the dear Lord was crucified,
    Who died to save us all.

CHO.—Oh dearly, dearly has He loved,
    And we must love Him too;
And trust in His redeeming blood,
    And try His works to do.

2 We may not know, we cannot tell
    What pains He had to bear;
But we believe it was for us
    He hung and suffered there.

3 He died that we might be forgiven
    He died to make us good,
That we might go at last to heaven,
    Saved by His precious blood.

4 There was no other good enough,
    To pay the price of sin;
He only could unlock the gate
    Of heaven and let us in.

602

Beyond the smiling and the weeping,
    I shall be soon, I shall be soon;
Beyond the waking and the sleeping,
Beyond the sowing and the reaping,
    I shall be soon, I shall be soon.

Ref.—Love, rest and home!
        Sweet, sweet home!
        Lord, tarry not,
        Lord tarry not, but come.

2 Beyond the blooming and the fading,
    I shall be soon, I shall be soon;
Beyond the shining and the shading,
Beyond the hoping and the dreading,
    I shall be soon, I shall be soon.

3 Beyond the parting and the meeting,
    I shall be soon, I shall be soon;
Beyond the farewell and the greeting,
Beyond the pulse's fever beating,
    I shall be soon, I shall be soon.

4 Beyond the frost-chain and the fever,
    I shall be soon, I shall be soon;
Beyond the rock-waste and the river,
Beyond the ever and the never,
    I shall be soon, I shall be soon.

603

Oh, the clanging bells of Time!
    Night and day they never cease;
We are wearied with their chime,
    For they do not bring us peace;
And we hush our breath to hear,
And we strain our eyes to see
If thy shores are drawing near,—
    Eternity! Eternity!

2 Oh, the clanging bells of Time!
    How their changes rise and fall,
But in undertone sublime,
    Sounding clearly through them all.

Is a voice that must be heard,
    As our moments onward flee,
And it speaketh, aye, one word,—
        Eternity! Eternity!

3 Oh, the clanging bells of Time!
    To their voices, loud and low,
In a long, unresting line
    We are marching to and fro;
And we yearn for sight or sound,
    Of the life that is to be,
For thy breath doth wrap us round,—
        Eternity! Eternity!

4 Oh, the clanging bells of Time!
    Soon their notes will all be dumb,
And in joy and peace sublime,
    We shall feel the silence come;
And our souls their thirst will slake,
    And our eyes the King will see,
When thy glorious morn shall break,—
        Eternity! Eternity!

804

WE shall meet beyond the river,
    By and by, by and by;
And the darkness shall be over,
    By and by, by and by;
With the toilsome journey done,
And the glorious battle won,
We shall shine forth as the sun,
    By and by, by and by.

2 We shall strike the harps of glory,
    By and by, by and by;
We shall sing redemption's story
    By and by, by and by;
And the strains for evermore
Shall resound in sweetness o'er
Yonder everlasting shore,
    By and by, by and by.

3 We shall see and be like Jesus,
    By and by, by and by;

Who a crown of life will give us,
    By and by, by and by;
And the angels who fulfil
All the mandates of His will
Shall attend, and love us still,
    By and by, by and by.

4 There our tears shall all cease flowing,
    By and by, by and by;
And with sweetest rapture knowing,
    By and by, by and by;
All the blest ones, who have gone
To the land of life and song,—
We with shoutings shall rejoin,
    By and by, by and by.

605

CHRIST is coming! let creation
    From her groans and travail cease;
Let the glorious proclamation
    Hope restore and faith increase:

CHO.—‖: Christ is coming! Christ is coming!
    Come, Thou blessèd Prince of peace! :‖

2 Earth can now but tell the story
    Of Thy bitter cross and pain;
She shall yet behold Thy glory,
    When Thou comest back to reign.

3 Though once cradled in a manger,
    Oft no pillow but the sod;
Here an alien and a stranger,
    Mocked of men, disowned of God.

4 Long Thy exiles have been pining,
    Far from rest, and home, and Thee;
But, in heavenly vesture shining,
    Soon they shall Thy glory see.

5 With that "blessèd hope" before us,
    Let no harp remain unstrung;
Let the mighty ransomed chorus
    Onward roll from tongue to tongue.

606

JOY to the World! the Lord is come;
  Let earth receive her King;
Let every heart prepare Him room,
  And heaven and nature sing.

2 Joy to the world! the Saviour reigns;
  Let men their songs employ;
While fields and floods, rocks, hills, and plains,
  Repeat the sounding joy.

3 He rules the world with truth and grace,
  And makes the nations prove
The glories of His righteousness,
  And wonders of His love.

607

I AM far frae my hame, an' I'm weary aftenwhiles,
  For the langed-for hame-bringin', an' my Faither's
    welcome smiles
An' I'll ne'er be fu' content, until my een do see
The gowden gates o' heav'n an' my ain countrie.
The earth is fleck'd wi' flowers, mony-tinted, fresh an' gay
The birdies warble blithely, for my Faither made them sae
But these sichts an' these soun's will as naething be to me
When I hear the angels singin' in my ain countrie.

2 I've His gude word o' promise that some gladsome day
    the King
To His ain royal palace His banished hame will bring;
Wi' een an' wi' hert rinnin' owre we shall see
The King in His beauty, in oor ain countrie.
My sins hae been mony, an' my sorrows hae been sair;
But there they'll never vex me, nor be remembered mair;
For His bluid has made me white, an' His han' shall dry
    my e'e,
When He brings me hame at last, to my ain countrie.

3 Sae little noo I ken, o' yon blessèd, bonnie place,
I only ken it's Hame, whaur we shall see His face;
It wad surely be eneuch for ever mair to be
In the glory o' His presence, in oor ain countrie.

Like a bairn to its mither, a wee birdie to its nest,
I wad fain he gangin' noo, unto my Saviour's breast,
For He gathers in His bosom witless, worthless lambs like
    me,
An' carries them Himsel', to His ain countrie.

4 He is faithfu' that hath promised, an' He'll surely come
    again,
He'll keep His tryst wi' me,—at what oor I dinna ken;
But He bids me still to wait, an' ready aye to be,
To gang at ony moment to my ain countrie;
Sae I'm watchin' aye, and singin' o' my hame, as I wait
For the soun'in' o' His futfa' this side the gowden gate;
God gie His grace to ilka ane wha' listens noo to me,
That we a' may gang in gladness to oor ain countrie.

608

I'VE reached the land of corn and wine,
    And all its riches freely mine;
Here shines undimmed one blissful day,
For all my night has passed away.

CHO.—O Beulah land, sweet Beulah land,
    As on thy highest mount I stand,
    I look away across the sea,
    Where mansions are prepared for me,
    And view the shining glory shore,
    My heaven, my home for evermore.

2 The Saviour comes and walks with me,
    And sweet communion here have we;
He gently leads me with His hand,
For this is heaven's border-land.

3 A sweet perfume upon the breeze
Is borne from ever vernal trees,
And flowers that never fading grow
Where streams of life forever flow.

4 The zephyrs seem to float to me,
Sweet sounds of heaven's melody,
As angels, with the white-robed throng,
Join in the sweet redemption song.

609

SOWING in the morning, sowing seeds of kindness,
　　Sowing in the noontide and the dewy eve;
Waiting for the harvest, and the time of reaping,
　　We shall come, rejoicing, bringing in the sheaves.

CHO.—‖: Bringing in the sheaves,
　　　　Bringing in the sheaves,
　　　　We shall come rejoicing,
　　　　Bringing in the sheaves. :‖

2 Sowing in the sunshine, sowing in the shadows,
　　Fearing neither clouds nor winter's chilling breeze;
By and by the harvest, and the labor ended,
　　We shall come, rejoicing, bringing in the sheaves.

3 Going forth with weeping, sowing for the Master,
　　Though the loss sustained our spirit often grieves;
When our weeping's over, He will bid us welcome,
　　We shall come, rejoicing, bringing in the sheaves.

610

DEPTH of mercy! can there be
　　Mercy still reserved for me?
Can my God His wrath forbear?
‖: Me, the chief of sinners, spare? :‖

2 I have long withstood His grace;
Long provoked Him to His face;
Would not hearken to His calls,
‖: Grieved Him by a thousand falls. :‖

3 Now, incline me to repent;
Let me now my sins lament;
Now my foul revolt deplore,
‖: Look, believe, and sin no more. :‖

611

OUR Lord is now rejected,
　　And by the world disowned,
By the *many* still neglected,
　　And by the *few* enthroned,
But soon He'll come in glory,
　　The hour is drawing nigh,
For the crowning day is coming by and by.

CHO.—Oh, the crowning day is coming,
 Is coming by and by,
When our Lord shall come in "power,"
 And "glory" from on high.
Oh, the glorious sight will gladden,
 Each waiting, watchful eye,
In the crowning day that's coming by and by.

2 The heavens shall glow with splendor,
 But brighter far than they
The saints shall shine in glory,
 As Christ shall them array,
The beauty of the Saviour,
 Shall dazzle every eye,
In the crowning day that's coming by and by.

3 Our pain shall then be over,
 We'll sin and sigh no more,
Behind us all of sorrow,
 And naught but joy before.
A joy in our Redeemer,
 As we to Him are nigh,
In the crowning day that's coming by and by.

4 Let all that look for, hasten
 The coming joyful day,
By earnest consecration,
 To walk the narrow way.
By gathering in the lost ones,
 For whom our Lord did die,
For the crowning day that's coming by and by.

312

OH, tender and sweet was the Master's voice
 As He lovingly called to me,
"Come over the line, it is only a step—
I am waiting, My child, for thee."

REF.—"Over the line," hear the sweet refrain,
 Angels are chanting the heavenly strain:
"Over the line,"—Why should I remain
 With a step between me and Jesus.

2 But my sins are many, my faith is small,
   Lo! the answer came quick and clear;
" Thou needest not trust in thyself at all,
   Step over the line, I am here."

3 But the flesh is weak, I tearfully said,
   And the way I cannot see;
I fear if I try I may sadly fail,
   And thus may dishonor Thee.

4 Ah, the world is cold, and I cannot go back,
   Press forward I surely must;
I will place my hand in His wounded palm,
   Step over the line, and *trust*.

Ref.—" Over the line," hear the sweet refrain,
   Angels are chanting the heavenly strain:
   " Over the line,"—I *will not* remain,
   I'll cross it and go to Jesus.

613

HOW firm a foundation, ye saints of the Lord!
   Is laid for your faith in His excellent word!
What more can He say, than to you He hath said,—
||: To you, who for refuge to Jesus have fled? :||

2 Fear not, I am with thee, oh, be not dismayed,
For I am thy God; I will still give thee aid;
I'll strengthen thee, help thee, and cause thee to stand,
||: Upheld by My gracious omnipotent hand. :||

3 " When through the deep waters I call thee to go,
The rivers of sorrow shall not overflow;
For I will be with thee thy trouble to bless,
||: And sanctify to thee thy deepest distress. :||

4 " The soul that on Jesus hath leaned for repose,
I will not —I will not desert to His foes;
That soul—though all hell should endeavor to shake,
||: I'll never—no never—no never forsake!" :||

614

GLORY be to the Father, and to the Son, and to the Holy
   Ghost;
As it was in the beginning, is now, and ever shall be, world
   without end. Amen, Amen.

615

STAND up!—stand up for Jesus!
  Ye soldiers of the cross;
Lift high His royal banner,
  It must not suffer loss:
From victory unto victory
  His army shall He lead,
Till every foe is vanquished,
  And Christ is Lord indeed.

2 Stand up!—stand up for Jesus!
    The trumpet call obey;
  Forth to the mighty conflict,
    In this His glorious day:
  "Ye that are men, now serve Him,"
    Against unnumbered foes;
  Let courage rise with danger,
    And strength to strength oppose.

3 Stand up!—stand up for Jesus!
    Stand in His strength alone;
  The arm of flesh will fail you—
    Ye dare not trust your own:
  Put on the gospel armor,
    And, watching unto prayer,
  Where duty calls, or danger,
    Be never wanting there.

4 Stand up!—stand up for Jesus!
    The strife will not be long;
  This day, the noise of battle,
    The next, the victor's song:
  To him that overcometh,
    A crown of life shall be;
  He with the King of glory
    Shall reign eternally!

616

THE morning light is breaking:
  The darkness disappears!
The sons of earth are waking
  To penitential tears;
Each breeze that sweeps the ocean
  Brings tidings from afar,
Of nations in commotion,
  Prepared for Zion's war.

2 See heathen nations bending
  Before the God we love,
And thousand hearts ascending
  In gratitude above;
While sinners, now confessing,
  The gospel call obey,
And seek the Saviour's blessing—
  A nation in a day.

3 Blest river of salvation!
  Pursue thine onward way;
Flow thou to every nation,
  Nor in thy richness stay:
Stay not till all the lowly
  Triumphant reach their home:
Stay not till all the holy
  Proclaim—" The Lord is come!"

617

SOMETIMES a light surprises
  The Christian while He sings;
It is the Lord who rises
  With healing in His wings:
When comforts are declining,
  He grants the soul again
A season of clear shining,
  To cheer it after rain.

2 In holy contemplation,
  We sweetly then pursue
The theme of God's salvation,
  And find it ever new:
Set free from present sorrow,
  We cheerfully can say,
Let the unknown to-morrow
  Bring with it what it may.

3 It can bring with it nothing,
  But He will bring us through;
Who gives the lilies clothing,
  Will clothe His people too:
Beneath the spreading heavens,
  No creature but is fed;
And He who feeds the ravens,
  Will give His children bread.

4 Though vine nor fig-tree neither
     Their wonted fruit shall bear;
   Though all the fields should wither,
     Nor flocks, nor herds be there;
   Yet God the same abiding,
     His praise shall tune my voice,
   For while in Him confiding,
     I cannot but rejoice.

618

"WHOSOEVER heareth," shout, shout the sound!
     Send the blesséd tidings all the world around,
   Spread the joyful news wherever man is found:
     "Whosoever will, may come."

CHO.—"Whosoever will, whosoever will,"
     Send the proclamation over vale and hill;
   'Tis a loving Father calls the wanderer home:
     "Whosoever will, may come."

2 "Whosoever cometh need not delay,
   Now the door is open, enter while you may;
   Jesus is the true, the only Living Way:
     "Whosoever will, may come."

3 "Whosoever will," the promise secure,
   "Whosoever will," forever must endure;
   "Whosoever will," 'tis life for evermore:
     "Whosoever will, may come."

619

LOOK, ye saints, the sight is glorious;
     See the "Man of sorrows" now;
   From the fight returned victorious,
     Every knee to Him shall bow.

REF.—‖: Crown Him, crown Him, angels crown Him,
         Crown the Saviour "King of kings." :‖

2 Crown the Saviour, angels, crown Him;
     Rich the trophies Jesus brings;
   In the seat of power enthrone Him,
     While the vault of heaven rings.

3 Sinners in derision crowned Him,
　Mocking thus the Saviour's claim;
Saints and angels crowd around Him,
　Own His title, praise His name.

4 Hark! the bursts of acclamation!
　Hark! these loud triumphant chords;
Jesus takes the highest station,
　Oh, what joy the sight affords.

620

JESUS Christ is passing by,
　Sinner, lift to Him thine eye;
As the precious moments flee,
Cry, "be merciful to me!"

2 Lo! He stands and calls to thee,
　"What wilt thou then have of Me?"
Rise, and tell Him all thy need;
Rise, He calleth thee indeed.

3 "Lord, I would Thy mercy see;
Lord, reveal Thy love to me;
Let it penetrate my soul,
All my heart and life control."

4 Oh, how sweet the touch of power
Comes,—and is salvation's hour;
Jesus gives from guilt release,
"Faith hath saved thee, go in peace!"

621

I KNOW not the hour when my Lord will come
　To take me away to His own dear home;
But I know that His presence will lighten the gloom,
　And that will be glory for me.

CHO.—And that will be glory for me,
　Oh, that will be glory for me;
But I know that His presence will lighten the gloom,
　And that will be glory for me.

2 I know not the song that the angels sing,
I know not the sound of the harps' glad ring;
But I know there'll be mention of Jesus our King,
　And that will be music for me.

CHO.—And that will be music for me,
Oh, that will be music for me;
But I know there'll be mention of Jesus our King
And that will be music for me.

3 I know not the form of my mansion fair,
I know not the name that I then shall bear;
But I know that my Saviour will welcome me there,
And that will be heaven for me.

CHO.—And that will be heaven for me,
Oh, that will be heaven for me;
But I know that my Saviour will welcome me there,
And that will be heaven for me.

622

RING the bells of heaven! there is joy to-day,
For a soul returning from the wild;
See! the Father meets him out upon the way,
Welcoming His weary, wandering child.

CHO.—Glory! glory! how the angels sing;
Glory! glory! how the loud harps ring;
'Tis the ransomed army, like a mighty sea,
Pealing forth the anthem of the free.

2 Ring the bells of heaven! there is joy to-day,
For the wanderer now is reconciled;
Yes, a soul is rescued from his sinful way,
And is born anew a ransomed child.

3 Ring the bells of heaven! spread the feast to-day,
Angels, swell the glad triumphant strain!
Tell the joyful tidings! bear it far away!
For a precious soul is born again.

623

GOD loved the world of sinners lost
And ruined by the fall;
Salvation full, at highest cost,
He offers free to all.

CHO.—Oh, 'twas love, 'twas wondrous love!
The love of God to me;
It brought my Saviour from above,
To die on Calvary.

2 E'en now by faith I claim Him mine,
    The risen Son of God;
Redemption by His death I find,
    And cleansing through the blood.

3 Love brings the glorious fulness in,
    And to His saints makes known
The blessèd rest from inbred sin,
    Through faith in Christ alone.

4 Believing souls, rejoicing go;
    There shall to you be given
A glorious foretaste, here below,
    Of endless life in heaven.

5 Of victory now o'er Satan's power
    Let all the ransomed sing,
And triumph in the dying hour
    Through Christ the Lord our King.

824

JESUS shall reign where'er the sun
    Does his successive journeys run,
His kingdom spread from shore to shore,
Till moons shall wax and wane no more.

2 To Him shall endless prayer be made,
    And praises throng to crown His head:
His name, like sweet perfume, shall rise
With every morning sacrifice.

3 People and realms of every tongue,
    Dwell on His love with sweetest song;
And infant voices shall proclaim
    Their early blessings on His name.

4 Blessings abound where'er He reigns
    The prisoner leaps to loose His chains;
The weary find eternal rest,
    And all the sons of want are blest.

5 Let every creature rise, and bring
    Peculiar honors to our King:
Angels descend with songs again,
    And earth repeat the loud Amen

625

SO let our lips and lives express
The holy gospel we profess;
So let our works and virtues shine;
To prove the doctrine all divine.

2 Thus shall we best proclaim abroad
The honors of our Saviour God;
When His salvation reigns within,
And grace subdues the power of sin.

3 Religion bears our spirits up,
While we expect that blessed hope,—
The bright appearance of the Lord:
And faith stands leaning on His word.

626

THE whole world was lost in the darkness of sin,
The Light of the world is Jesus;
Like sunshine at noonday His glory shone in,
The Light of the world is Jesus.

CHO.—Come to the Light, 'tis shining for thee;
Sweetly the Light has dawned upon me,
Once I was blind but now I can see:
The Light of the world is Jesus.

2 No darkness have we who in Jesus abide,
The Light of the world is Jesus;
We walk in the Light when we follow our Guide,
The Light of the world is Jesus.

3 Ye dwellers in darkness with sin-blinded eyes,
The Light of the world is Jesus;
Go, wash, at His bidding, and light will arise.
The Light of the world is Jesus.

4 No need of the sunlight in heaven, we're told,
The Light of that world is Jesus;
The Lamb is the light in the City of Gold,
The Light of that world is Jesus.

627

COME home! come home!
You are weary at heart,
For the way has been dark,
And so lonely and wild;

O prodigal child!
Come home! oh, come home!

CHO.—Come home!　Come, oh come home!

2 Come home! come home!
For we watch and we wait,
And we stand at the gate,
While the shadows are piled;
O prodigal child!
Come home! oh come home!

3 Come home! come home!
From the sorrow and blame,
From the sin and the shame,
And the tempter that smiled,
O prodigal child!
Come home, oh come home!

4 Come home! come home!
There is bread and to spare,
And a warm welcome there;
Then, to friends reconciled,
O prodigal child!
Come home, oh, come home!

628

NOT now, my child,—a little more rough tossing,
A little longer on the billow's foam;
A few more journeyings in the desert darkness,
And then, the sunshine of thy Father's Home!

2 Not now; for I have wanderers in the distance,
And thou must call them in with patient love;
Not now; for I have sheep upon the mountains,
And thou must follow them where'er they rove.

3 Not now; for I have loved ones sad and weary;
Wilt thou not cheer them with a kindly smile?
Sick ones, who need thee in their lonely sorrow;
Wilt thou not tend them yet a little while?

4 Not now; for wounded hearts are sorely bleeding,
And thou must teach those widowed hearts to sing;
Not now; for orphans' tears are quickly falling,
They must be gathered 'neath some sheltering wing.

5 Go, with the name of Jesus, to the dying,
    And speak that Name in all its living power;
Why should thy fainting heart grow chill and weary?
    Canst thou not watch with Me one little hour?

6 One little hour! and then the glorious crowning,
    The golden harp-strings, and the victor's palm;
One little hour! and then the hallelujah!
    Eternity's long, deep, thanksgiving psalm!

329

THE great Physician now is near,
    The sympathizing Jesus;
He speaks the drooping heart to cheer,
    Oh, hear the voice of Jesus.

CHO.—"Sweetest note in seraph song,
        Sweetest name on mortal tongue,
        Sweetest carol ever sung,
        Jesus, blessèd Jesus."

2 Your many sins are all forgiven,
    Oh, hear the voice of Jesus;
Go on your way in peace to heaven,
    And wear a crown with Jesus.

3 All glory to the dying Lamb!
    I now believe in Jesus;
I love the blessèd Saviour's name,
    I love the name of Jesus.

4 His name dispels my guilt and fear,
    No other name but Jesus;
Oh, how my soul delights to hear
    The precious name of Jesus.

630

TO-DAY the Saviour calls;
    Ye wanderers, come;
O ye benighted souls,
    Why longer roam?

CHO.—‖: Come home, come home,
        The Saviour calls, come home. :‖

2 To-day the Saviour calls;
　　O hear Him now;
　Within these sacred walls
　　To Jesus bow.

3 To-day the Saviour calls;
　　For refuge fly;
　The storm of justice falls,
　　And death is nigh.

4 The Spirit calls to-day;
　　Yield to His power;
　O grieve Him not away,
　　'Tis mercy's hour.

631

WHERE is my wandering boy to-night—
　　The boy of my tenderest care,
　The boy that was once my joy and light,
　　The child of my love and prayer?

Cho.—||: O where is my boy to-night? :||
　My heart o'erflows, for I love him, he knows;
　　O where is my boy to-night?

2 Once he was pure as morning dew,
　　As he knelt at His mother's knee;
　No face was so bright, no heart more true,
　　And none was so sweet as he.

3 O could I see you now, my boy,
　　As fair as in olden time,
　When prattle and smile made home a joy
　　And life was a merry chime!

4 Go for my wandering boy to-night;
　　Go, search for him where you will;
　But bring him to me with all his blight,
　　And tell him I love him still.

632

IT passeth knowledge, that dear love of Thine,
　My Jesus! Saviour! yet this soul of mine
Would of that love, in all its depth and length,
Its height, and breadth, and everlasting strength,
　Know more and more.

2 It passeth telling! that dear love of Thine!
  My Jesus! Saviour! yet these lips of mine
  Would fain proclaim to sinners far and near
  A love which can remove all guilty fear,
            And love beget.

3 It passeth praises! that dear love of Thine!
  My Jesus! Saviour! yet this heart of mine
  Would sing a love so rich, so full, so free,
  Which brought an undone sinner, such as me,
            Right home to God.

4 But ah! I cannot tell, or sing, or know,
  The fulness of that love whilst here below;
  Yet my poor vessel I may freely bring;
  O Thou who art of love the living spring,
            My vessel fill.

5 I am an empty vessel! scarce one thought
  Or look of love to Thee I've ever brought;
  Yet, I may come, and come again to Thee
  With this—the contrite sinner's truthful plea—
            "Thou lovest me."

6 Oh, fill me, Jesus, Saviour, with Thy love!
  May woes but drive me to the fount above;
  Thither may I in childlike faith draw nigh.
  And never to another fountain fly,
            But unto Thee!

7 And when my Jesus! Thy dear face I see,
  When at the lofty throne I bend the knee,
  Then of Thy love, in all its breadth and length,
  Its height. and depth, and everlasting strength,
            My soul shall sing.

633

COME, Thou Fount of every blessing,
   Tune my heart to sing Thy grace;
Streams of mercy, never ceasing,
   Call for songs of loudest praise;
Teach me some melodious sonnet,
   Sung by flaming tongues above;
Praise the mount—I'm fixed upon it!
   Mount of Thy redeeming love.

2 Here I'll raise my Ebenezer,
　　Hither by Thy help I'm come;
And I hope, by Thy good pleasure,
　　Safely to arrive at home;
Jesus sought me when a stranger,
　　Wandering from the fold of God;
He, to rescue me from danger,
　　Interposed His precious blood.

3 Oh, to grace how great a debtor,
　　Daily I'm constrained to be!
Let Thy goodness, as a fetter,
　　Bind my wandering heart to Thee;
Prone to wander, Lord, I feel it—
　　Prone to leave the God I love—
Here's my heart, oh, take and seal it,
　　Seal it for Thy courts above.

634

SWEET hour of prayer! sweet hour of prayer!
　　That calls me from a world of care,
And bids me at my Father's throne
Make all my wants and wishes known:
In seasons of distress and grief,
My soul has often found relief;
‖: And oft escaped the tempter's snare,
By thy return, sweet hour of prayer! :‖

2 Sweet hour of prayer! sweet hour of prayer!
Thy wings shall my petition bear
To Him whose truth and faithfulness
Engage the waiting soul to bless:
And since He bids me seek His face,
Believe His word, and trust His grace,
‖: I'll cast on Him my every care,
And wait for thee, sweet hour of prayer! :‖

3 Sweet hour of prayer! sweet hour of prayer!
May I thy consolation share,
Till, from Mount Pisgah's lofty height,
I view my home and take my flight;
This robe of flesh I'll drop, and rise
To seize the everlasting prize;
‖: And shout, while passing through the air,
Farewell, farewell, sweet hour of prayer! :‖

635

THERE is life for a look at the Crucified One,
 There is life at this moment for thee;
Then look, sinner, look unto Him and be saved,
 Unto Him who was nailed to the tree.

REF.—Look! look! look and live!
 There is life for a look at the Crucified One,
 There is life at this moment for thee.

2 Oh, why was He there as the Bearer of sin,
 If on Jesus thy guilt was not laid?
Oh, why from His side flowed the sin-cleansing blood,
 If His dying thy debt has not paid?

3 It is not thy tears of repentance, and prayers,
 But the *blood*, that atones for the soul;
On Him, then, who shed it, thou mayest at once
 Thy weight of iniquities roll.

4 Then doubt not thy welcome, since God has declared
 There remaineth no more to be done;
That once in the end of the world He appeared,
 And completed the work He begun.

4 Then take with rejoicing from Jesus at once
 The life everlasting He gives;
And know with assurance thou never canst die,
 Since Jesus thy righteousness, lives.

636

COME to the Saviour, make no delay:
 Here in His word He's shown us the way;
Here in our midst He's standing to-day,
 Tenderly saying, "Come!"

CHO.—Joyful, joyful will the meeting be,
 When from sin our hearts are pure and free;
 And we shall gather, Saviour, with Thee,
 In our eternal home.

2 "Suffer the children!" Oh, hear His voice,
Let every heart leap forth and rejoice,
And let us freely make Him our choice;
 Do not delay, but come.

3 Think once again, He's with us to-day;
   Heed now His blest commands, and obey;
   Hear now His accents tenderly say,
       " Will you, my children, come ? "

637

HE leadeth me! oh! blesséd thought,
    O words with heavenly comfort fraught;
Whate'er I do, where'er I be,
Still 'tis God's hand that leadeth me.

REF.—He leadeth me! He leadeth me!
        By His own hand He leadeth me;
        His faithful follower I would be,
        For by His hand He leadeth me.

2 Sometimes 'mid scenes of deepest gloom,
   Sometimes where Eden's bowers bloom,
   By waters still, o'er troubled sea—
   Still 'tis God's hand that leadeth me.

3 Lord, I would clasp Thy hand in mine,
   Nor ever murmur nor repine,
   Content, whatever lot I see,
   Since 'tis my God that leadeth me.

4 And when my task on earth is done,
   When, by Thy grace, the victory's won,
   E'en death's cold wave I will not flee,
   Since God through Jordan leadeth me.

638

WHEN He cometh, when He cometh
    To make up His jewels,
All His jewels, precious jewels,
His loved and His own.

CHO.—Like the stars of the morning,
        His bright crown adorning,
        They shall shine in their beauty,
        Bright gems for His crown.

2 He will gather, He will gather
   The gems for His kingdom;
   All the pure ones, all the bright ones,
   His loved and His own.

3 Litttle children, litttle children,
   Who love their Redeemer,
   Are the jewels, precious jewels,
   His loved and His own.

—————

539

LORD, I hear of showers of blessing
   Thou art scattering full and free—
Showers the thirsty land refreshing;
   Let some droppings fall on me—
      Even me, even me,
      Let Thy blessing fall on me.

2 Pass me not, O gracious Father,
   Sinful though my heart may be;
Thou might'st leave me, but the rather
   Let Thy mercy fall on me—

3 Pass me not, O tender Saviour!
   Let me love and cling to Thee;
I am longing for Thy favor;
   Whilst Thou'rt calling; oh, call me—

4 Pass me not, O mighty Spirit!
   Thou canst make the blind to see;
Witnesser of Jesus' merit,
   Speak the word of power to me—

5 Love of God, so pure and changeless;
   Blood of Christ, so rich and free;
Grace of God, so strong and boundless,
   Magnify them all in me—

6 Pass me not! Thy lost one bringing,
   Bind my heart, O Lord, to Thee;
While the streams of life are springing,
   Blessing others, oh, bless me—

—————

640

HARK! the voice of Jesus crying,—
   "Who will go and work to-day?
Fields are white, and harvest waiting;
   Who will bear the sheaves away?"

Loud and strong the Master calleth,
Rich reward He offers thee;
Who will answer, gladly saying,
"Here am I; send me, send me!"

4 If you cannot cross the ocean,
And the heathen lands explore,
You can find the heathen nearer,
You can help them at your door.
If you cannot give your thousands,
You can give the widow's mite;
And the least you do for Jesus,
Will be precious in His sight.

3 If you cannot speak like angels,
If you cannot preach like Paul,
You can tell the love of Jesus,
You can say He died for all.
If you cannot rouse the wicked
With the judgment's dread alarms,
You can lead the little children
To the Saviour's waiting arms.

4 If you cannot be the watchman,
Standing high on Zion's wall,
Pointing out the path to heaven,
Offering life and peace to all;
With your prayers and with your bounties
You can do what heaven demands;
You can be like faithful Aaron,
Holding up the prophet's hands.

5 If among the older people,
You may not be apt to teach,
"Feed my lambs," said Christ, our Shepherd,
"Place the food within their reach."
And it may be that the children
You have led with trembling hand,
Will be found among your jewels,
When you reach the better land.

6 Let none hear you idly saying,
"There is nothing I can do,"
While the souls of men are dying,
And the Master calls for you.

Take the task He gives you, gladly,
Let His work your pleasure be;
Answer quickly when He calleth,
"Here am I; send me, send me!"

641

NOTHING but leaves! The Spirit grieves
O'er years of wasted life;
O'er sins indulged while conscience slept,
O'er vows and promises unkept,
And reap from years of strife—
Nothing but leaves! Nothing but leaves!

2 Nothing but leaves! No gathered sheaves
Of life's fair ripening grain:
We sow our seeds; lo! tares and weeds,—
Words, *idle* words, for earnest deeds—
Then reap, with toil and pain,
Nothing but leaves! Nothing but leaves!

3 Nothing but leaves! Sad memory weaves
No veil to hide the past:
And as we trace our weary way,
And count each lost and misspent day,
We sadly find at last—
Nothing but leaves! Nothing but leaves!

4 Ah, who shall thus the Master meet,
And bring but withered leaves?
Ah, who shall, at the Saviour's feet,
Before the awful judgment-seat,
Lay down, for golden sheaves,
Nothing but leaves? Nothing but leaves?

642

"YET there is room!" The Lamb's bright hall
of song,
With its fair glory, beckons thee along;
REF.—Room, room, still room! oh, enter, enter now!

2 Day is declining, and the sun is low;
The shadows lengthen. light makes haste to go:
Room, room, still room! oh, enter, enter now!

3 The bridal hall is filling for the feast:
Pass in! pass in! and be the Bridegroom's guest:
Room, room, still room! oh, enter, enter now!

4 It fills, it fills, that hall of jublilee!
Make haste, make haste; 'tis not too full for thee:
Room, room, still room! oh, enter, enter now!

5 Yet there is room! Still open stands the gate,
The gate of love; it is not yet too late:
Room, room, still room! oh, enter, enter now!

6 Pass in, pass in! That banquet is for thee;
That cup of everlasting love is free:
Room, room, still room! oh, enter, enter now!

7 All heaven is there, all joy! Go in, go in;
The angels beckon thee the prize to win:
Room, room, still room! oh, enter, enter now!

8 Ere night that gate may close, and seal thy doom:
Then the last, low, long cry:—"No room, no room!"
No room, no room;—oh, woful cry, "No room!"

643

Do you see the Hebrew captive kneeling,
　　At morning, noon and night, to pray?
In his chamber he remembers Zion,
　　Though in exile far away.

Cho.—Are your windows open toward Jerusalem,
　　Though as captives here a "little while" we stay?
For the coming of the King in His glory,
　　Are you watching day by day?

2 Do not fear to tread the fiery furnace,
　　Nor shrink the lion's den to share;
For the God of Daniel will deliver,
　　He will send His angel there.

3 Children of the living God, take courage,
　　Your great deliverance sweetly sing;
Set your faces toward the hill of Zion,
　　Thence to hail your coming King!

644

SOON shall we see the glorious morning,
    Saints arise! Saints arise!
Sinners, attend the notes of warning;
    Saints arise! Saints arise!
The resurrection day draws near,
The King of Saints shall soon appear,
And high His royal standard rear;
    Saints arise! Saints arise!

2 Hear ye the trump of God resounding,
    Saints arise! Saints arise!
Through all the vaults of death rebounding;
    Saints arise! Saints arise!
To meet the Bridegroom, haste, prepare!
Put on your bridal garments fair,
And hail your Saviour in the air;
    Saints arise! Saints arise!

3 The Saints who sleep, with joy awaken,
    All arise! all arise!
Their beds of death are quick forsaken,
    All arise! all arise!
Not one of all the faithful few
Who here on earth the Saviour knew,
But starts with bliss his Lord to view;
    All arise! all arise!

4 Fast by the throne of God behold them
    Crowned at last! crowned at last!
See in His arms the Saviour folds them,
    Crowned at last! crowned at last!
With wreaths of glory round their head,
No tears of sorrow now are shed,
To joy's full fountain all are led,
    Crowned at last! crowned at last!

645

"MAN of Sorrows," what a name
    For the Son of God, who came,
Ruined sinners to reclaim!
    Hallelujah, what a Saviour!

2 Bearing shame and scoffing rude,
  In my place condemned He stood;
  Sealed my pardon with His blood;
    Hallelujah! what a Saviour!

3 Guilty, vile and helpless, we;
  Spotless Lamb of God was He:
  "Full atonement!" can it be?
    Hallelujah! what a Saviour!

4 Lifted up was He to die,
  "It is finished," was His cry,
  Now in heaven exalted high:
    Hallelujah! what a Saviour!

5 When He comes, our glorious King,
  All His ransomed home to bring,
  Then anew this song we'll sing;
    Hallelujah! what a Saviour!

546

HO! reapers of life's harvest,
    Why stand with rusted blade,
Until the night draws round thee,
    And day begins to fade?
Why stand ye idle, waiting
    For reapers more to come?
The golden morn is passing,
    Why sit ye idle, dumb?

2 Thrust in your sharpened sickle,
    And gather in the grain,
The night is fast approaching,
    And soon will come again;
The Master calls for reapers,
    And shall He call in vain?
Shall sheaves lie there ungathered,
    And waste upon the plain?

3 Mount up the heights of Wisdom,
    And crush each error low;
Keep back no words of knowledge
    That human hearts should know.

Be faithful to thy mission,
In service of thy Lord,
And then a golden chaplet
Shall be thy just reward.

647

FADE, fade, each earthly joy,
Jesus is mine!
Break, every tender tie;
Jesus is mine!
Dark is the wilderness,
Earth has no resting-place,
Jesus alone can bless,
Jesus is mine!

2 Tempt not my soul away;
Jesus is mine!
Here would I ever stay;
Jesus is mine!
Perishing things of clay,
Born but for one brief day,
Pass from my heart away,
Jesus is mine!

3 Farewell, ye dreams of night;
Jesus is mine!
Lost in this dawning light;
Jesus is mine!
All that my soul has tried,
Left but a dismal void,
Jesus has satisfied,
Jesus is mine!

4 Farewell, mortality;
Jesus is mine!
Welcome, eternity;
Jesus is mine!
Welcome, O loved and blest,
Welcome, sweet scenes of rest,
Welcome, my Saviour's breast,
Jesus is mine!

648

KNOCKING, knocking, who is there?
　　Waiting, waiting, oh, how fair!
'Tis a Pilgrim, strange and kingly,
　　Never such was seen before;
Ah! my soul, for such a wonder
　　Wilt thou not undo the door?

2 Knocking, knocking, still He's there,
　　Waiting, waiting, wondrous fair;
But the door is hard to open,
　　For the weeds and ivy-vine,
With their dark and clinging tendrils,
　　Ever round the hinges twine.

3 Knocking, knocking,—what! still there?
　　Waiting, waiting, grand and fair!
Yes, the piercéd hand still knocketh,
　　And beneath the crownéd hair
Beam the patient eyes, so tender,
　　Of thy Saviour, waiting there.

649

I heard the voice of Jesus say,
　　"Come unto me and rest;
Lay down, thou weary one, lay down
　　Thy head upon my breast."

2 I came to Jesus as I was—
　　Weary, and worn, and sad;
I found in Him a resting place,
　　And He has made me glad.

3 I heard the voice of Jesus say,
　　"Behold, I freely give
The living water—thirsty one,
　　Stoop down, and drink, and live."

4. I came to Jesus, and I drank
　　Of that life-giving stream;
My thirst was quenched, my soul revived,
　　And now I live in Him.

5 I heard the voice of Jesus say,
　　"I am this dark world's Light;
Look unto me, thy morn shall rise,
　　And all thy day be bright."

6 I looked to Jesus, and I found
In Him my Star, my Sun;
And in that light of life I'll walk
'Till traveling days are done.

650

REPEAT the story o'er and o'er,
Of *grace* so full and free;
I love to hear it more and more,
Since grace has rescued me.

Cho.—‖: The half was never told, :‖
Of *grace* divine, so wonderful,
The half was never told.

2 Of *peace* I only knew the name,
Nor found my soul its rest,
Until the sweet-voiced angel came
To soothe my weary breast.

Cho.—‖: The half was never told, :‖
Of *peace* divine, so wonderful,
The half was never told.

3 My highest place is lying low
At my Redeemer's feet;
No real *joy* in life I know,
But in His service sweet.

Cho.—‖: The half was never told, :‖
Of *joy* divine, so wonderful,
The half was never told.

4 And oh, what rapture will it be,
With all the host above,
To sing through all eternity
The wonders of His *love!*

Cho.—‖: The half was never told, :‖
Of *love* divine, so wonderful,
The half was never told.

651

IT may be at morn, when the day is awaking,
When sunlight thro' darkness and shadow is breaking,
That Jesus will come in the fullness of glory,
To receive from the world "His own."

CHO.—O Lord Jesus, how long? how long
    Ere we shout the glad song?
  Christ returneth; Hallelujah! hallelujah!
    Amen, Hallelujah! Amen.

2 It may be at midday, it may be at twilight,
  It may be, perchance, that the blackness of midnight
  Will burst into light in the blaze of His glory,
    When Jesus receives "His own."

3 While its hosts cry Hosanna, from heaven descending,
  With glorified saints and the angels attending,
  With grace on His brow, like a halo of glory,
    Will Jesus receive "His own."

4 Oh, joy! oh, delight! should we go without dying,
  No sickness, no sadness, no dread and no crying,
  Caught up through the clouds with our Lord into glory,
    When Jesus receives "His own."

652

STANDING by a purpose true,
  Heeding God's command,
Honor them, the faithful few!
  All hail to Daniel's Band!

CHO.—Dare to be a Daniel,
    Dare to stand alone!
    Dare to have a purpose firm!
    Dare to make it known!

2 Many mighty men are lost,
  Daring not to stand,
Who for God had been a host,
  By joining Daniel's Band.

3 Many giants, great and tall,
  Stalking through the land,
Headlong to the earth would fall,
  If met by Daniel's Band.

4 Hold the gospel banner high!
  On to victory grand!
Satan and his hosts defy,
  And shout for Daniel's Band.

653

ARISE, my soul, arise;
     Shake off thy guilty fears;
The bleeding sacrifice
     In my behalf appears;
Before the throne my Surety stands,
My name is written on His hands.

2 He ever lives above,
     For me to intercede;
His all redeeming love,
     His precious blood to plead;
His blood atoned for all our race,
And sprinkles now the throne of grace.

3 Five bleeding wounds He bears,
     Received on Calvary;
They pour effectual prayers,
     They strongly plead for me;
Forgive him, oh, forgive, they cry,
Nor let that ransomed sinner die.

4 My God is reconciled;
     His pardoning voice I hear;
He owns me for His child;
     I can no longer fear;
With confidence I now draw nigh,
And "Father, Abba, Father!" cry.

654

MY hope is built on nothing less
     Than Jesus' blood and righteousness;
I dare not trust the sweetest frame,
But wholly lean on Jesus' name.

CHO.—On Christ, the Solid Rock, I stand;
     All other ground is sinking sand.

2 When darkness veils His lovely face,
I rest on His unchanging grace;
In every high and stormy gale,
My anchor holds within the vail.

3 His oath, His covenant, His blood,
Support me in the whelming flood;
When all around my soul gives way,
He then is all my hope and stay.

4 When He shall come with trumpet sound,
   O, may I then in Him be found;
   Clothed in His righteousness alone,
   Faultless to stand before the throne!

655

THERE'S a beautiful land on high,
   To its glories I fain would fly,
When by sorrows pressed down,
   I long for my crown
In that beautiful land on high.

CHO.—In that beautiful land I'll be,
      From earth and its cares set free;
         My Jesus is there,
         He's gone to prepare
      A place in that land for me.

2 There's a beautiful land on high,
   I shall enter it by and by;
      There with friends hand in hand,
      I shall walk on the strand,
   In that beautiful land on high.

3 There's a beautiful land on high;
   Then why should I fear to die,
      When death is the way
      To the realms of day
   In that beautiful land on high?

4 There's a beautiful land on high,
   And my kindred its bliss enjoy;
      And methinks I now see
      Them waiting for me,
   In that beautiful land on high.

5 There's a beautiful land on high,
   Where we never shall say "good-bye;"
      Where the righteous will sing,
      And their chorus will ring,
   In that beautiful land on high.

656

OH! do not let the Word depart,
   And close thine eyes against the light;
Poor sinner, harden not thy heart;
   Thou would'st be saved—Why not to-night?

Cho.—Why not to-night? Why not to-night?
　　　Thou would'st be saved—Why not to-night?

2 To-morrow's sun may never rise,
　　To bless thy long deluded sight;
　　This is the time!　Oh, then be wise!
　　Thou would'st be saved—Why not to-night?

3 The world has nothing left to give—
　　It has no new, no pure delight;
　　Oh, try the life which Christians live!
　　Thou would'st be saved—Why not to-night?

4 Our blessed Lord refuses none
　　Who would to Him their souls unite;
　　Then be the work of grace begun!
　　Thou would'st be saved—*Why not to-night?*

857

SHE only touched the hem of His garment
　　As to His side she stole,
Amid the crowd that gathered around Him,
　　And straightway she was whole.

Cho.—Oh, touch the hem of His garment!
　　　And thou, too, shalt be free;
　　　His saving power this very hour
　　　Shall give new life to thee.

2 She came in fear and trembling before Him,
　　She knew her Lord had come;
　　She felt that from Him virtue had healed her,
　　The mighty deed was done.

3 He turned with "Daughter, be of good comfort,
　　Thy faith hath made thee whole;"
And peace that passeth all understanding
　　With gladness filled her soul.

658

I AM coming to the cross;
　　I am poor, and weak, and blind;
I am counting all but dross,
　　I shall full salvation find.

Cho.—I am trusting, Lord, in Thee,
　　　Elesséd Lamb of Calvary;
　　　Humbly at Thy cross I bow,
　　　Save me, Jesus, save me now.

2 Long my heart has sighed for Thee,
    Long has evil reigned within;
  Jesus sweetly speaks to me,—
    " I will cleanse you from all sin."

3 Here I give my all to Thee,
    Friends, and time, and earthly store;
  Soul and body Thine to be,—
    Wholly Thine for evermore.

4 In the promises I trust,
    Now I feel the blood applied:
  I am prostrate in the dust,
    I with Christ am crucified.

5 Jesus comes! He fills my soul!
    Perfected in Him I am;
  I am every whit made whole:
    Glory, glory to the Lamb.

659

WHEN Jesus comes to reward His servants,
    Whether it be noon or night,
Faithful to Him will He find us watching,
    With our lamps all trimmed and bright !

REF.—Oh, can we say we are ready, brother?—
        Ready for the soul's bright home?
    Say, will He find you and me still watching,
        Waiting, waiting when the Lord shall come

2 If at the dawn of the early morning,
    He shall call us one by one,
  When to the Lord we restore our talents,
    Will He answer thee—" Well done!"

3 Have we been true to the trust He left us?
    Do we seek to do our best?
  If in our hearts there is naught condemns us,
    We shall have a glorious rest.

4 Blesséd are those whom the Lord finds watching,
    In His glory they shall share;
  If He shall come at the dawn or midnight,
    Will He find us watching there?

660

SAVIOUR, like a shepherd lead us,
   Much we need Thy tend'rest care;
In Thy pleasant pastures feed us,
   For our use Thy folds prepare.
Bléssed Jesus,   Bléssed Jesus,
   Thou hast bought us, Thine we are.

2 We are Thine, do Thou befriend us,
   Be the Guardian of our way;
Keep Thy flock, from sin defend us,
   Seek us when we go astray.
Bléssed Jesus,   Bléssed Jesus,
   Hear, O hear us, when we pray.

3 Thou hast promised to receive us,
   Poor and sinful though we be;
Thou hast mercy to relieve us,
   Grace to cleanse, and power to free.
Bléssed Jesus,   Bléssed Jesus,
   We will early turn to Thee.

661

COME, ye disconsolate! where'er ye languish,
   Come to the mercy-seat, fervently kneel:
Here bring your wounded hearts, here tell your anguish
   Earth has no sorrow that heaven cannot heal.

2 Joy of the desolate! light of the straying,
   Hope of the penitent, fadeless and pure!
Here speaks the Comforter, tenderly saying,
   Earth has no sorrow that heaven cannot cure.

3 Here see the bread of life: see waters flowing
   Forth from the throne of God, pure from above:
Come to the feast of love; come, ever knowing,
   Earth has no sorrows but heaven can remove.

662

SOWING the seed by the daylight fair,
   Sowing the seed by the noonday glare,
Sowing the seed by the fading light,
Sowing the seed in the solemn night;
   Oh, what shall the harvest be?

CHO.—Sown in the darkness, or sown in the light,
Sown in our weakness or sown in our might
Gathered in time or eternity,
Sure, ah, sure will the harvest be.

2 Sowing the seed by the wayside high,
Sowing the seed on the rocks to die,
Sowing the seed where the thorns will spoil,
Sowing the seed in the fertile soil:
Oh, what shall the harvest be?

3 Sowing the seed of a lingering pain,
Sowing the seed of a maddened brain,
Sowing the seed of a tarnished name,
Sowing the seed of eternal shame;
Oh, what shall the harvest be?

4 Sowing the seed with an aching heart
Sowing the seed while the tear-drops start,
Sowing in hope till the reapers come
Gladly to gather the harvest home:
Oh, what shall the harvest be?

663

TAKE my life and let it be
Consecrated, Lord, to Thee;
Take my hands and let them move
At the impulse of Thy love.

2 Take my feet and let them be
Swift and beautiful for Thee;
Take my voice and let me sing
Always—only—for my King.

3 Take my moments and my days,
Let them flow in endless praise;
Take my intellect, and use
Every power as Thou shalt choose.

4 Take my will, and make it Thine;
It shall be no longer mine;
Take my heart, it is Thine own,
It shall be Thy royal throne.

5 Take my love, my God, I pour
At Thy feet its treasure-store;
Take myself, and I will be
Ever, only, all for Thee.

664

O word of words the sweetest,
    O words, in which there lie
All promise, all fulfillment,
    And end of mystery;
Lamenting or rejoicing,
    With doubt or terror nigh,
I hear the " Come!" of Jesus,
    And to His cross I fly.

REF.—Come, oh, come to me,
        Come, oh, come to me,
        Weary, heavy-laden,
        Come, oh, come to me.

2 O soul! why shouldst thou wander
    From such a loving Friend?
Cling closer, closer to Him,
    Stay with Him to the end;
Alas! I am so helpless,
    So very full of sin,
For I am ever wandering,
    And coming back again.

3 O, each time draw me nearer,
    That soon the " Come " may be,
Naught but a gentle whisper,
    To one, close, close to Thee;
Then, over sea and mountain,
    Far from, or near my home,
I'll take Thy hand and follow,
    At that sweet whisper "Come!"

665

MY days are gliding swiftly by,
    And I, a pilgrim stranger,
Would not detain them as they fly,
    Those hours of toil and danger.

CHO.—For, oh! we stand on Jordan's strand;
        Our friends are passing over:
        And, just before, the shining shore
        We may almost discover.

2 Should coming days be cold and dark,
   We need not cease our singing;
That perfect rest naught can molest,
   Where golden harps are ringing.

3 Let sorrow's rudest tempest blow,
   Each cord on earth to sever;
Our King says—"Come!"—and there's our home,
   For ever, oh! for ever!

666

I AM now a child of God,
   For I'm washed in Jesus' blood;
I am watching and I'm longing while I wait.
   Soon on wings of love I'll fly,
   To my home beyond the sky,
To my welcome, as I'm sweeping through the gate.

Ref.—In the blood of yonder Lamb,
   Washed from every stain I am;
   Robed in whiteness, clad in brightness,
   I am sweeping through the gate.

2 Oh! the blessèd Lord of light,
   He upholds me by His might;
And His arms enfold, and comfort while I wait.
   I am leaning on His breast,
   Oh! the sweetness of His rest,
Hallelujah, I am sweeping through the gate.

3 I am sweeping through the gate
   Where the blessèd for me wait;
Where the weary workers rest for evermore;
   Where the strife of earth is done,
   And the crown of life is won;
Oh, the glory of that city just before!

4 Burst are all my prison bars;
   And I soar beyond the stars,
To my Father's house, the bright and blest estate.
   Lo! the morn eternal breaks,
   And the song immortal wakes,
Robed in whiteness I am sweeping through the gate.

667

WOULD we be joyful in the Lord?
　　Then count the riches o'er,
Revealed to faith within His word,
　　And note the boundless store.

CHO.—There is pardon, peace, and power,
　　　And purity, and Paradise;
　　With all of these in Christ for me,
　　　Let joyful songs of praise to Him arise!

2 For every sin, by grace divine
　　A *pardon* free bestowed;
And with the pardon *peace* is mine,
　　The peace in Jesus' blood.

3 Of grace to break the power of sin,.
　　He gives a full supply,
The Holy Ghost, tne heart within,
　　From sin doth *purify*.

4 The *power* to win a soul to God,
　　The Spirit, too, imparts;
And He, the gift of Christ our Lord,
　　Dwells *now* in all our hearts.

5 These blessings we by faith receive,
　　By simple childlike trust;
In Christ, 'tis God's delight to *give;*
　　He promised, and He must.

668

COME souls that are longing for pleasure,
　　Our Saviour has pleasures to give;
Come find in His love the rare treasure,
　　That makes every true pleasure live.

CHO.—Come *now* saith the Lord, let us reason,
　　　Come *now* and your purpose declare;
　　Is it pleasures of sin for a season,
　　　Or pleasures the glorified share?

2 The pleasures of sin are deceiving,
　　They've nothing for yesterday's pain,
But hope of to-morrow receiving,
　　And then, its—*To-morrow*—again.

3 The pleasures of sin are all fleeting,
   They vanish with life's passing morn;
Like dew-drops the morning sun greeting,
   They glisten and then they are gone.

4 Then all who are longing for pleasure,
   Ye weary and all who are worn;
Come find in the Lord a sure treasure,
   That from you shall never be torn.

5 Of Jesus, thy choice be now making,
   Redeemer, and Saviour, and Lord;
And soon in the glory awaking,
   You'll share in the Saint's blest reward.

669

SHALL we gather at the river;
   Where bright angel-feet have trod;
With its crystal tide for ever
   Flowing by the throne of God?

CHO.—Yes, we'll gather at the river;
   The beautiful, the beautiful river—
   Gather with the saints at the river,
   That flows by the throne of God.

2 On the margin of the river,
   Washing up its silver spray,
We will walk and worship ever,
   All the happy, golden day.

3 Ere we reach the shining river,
   Lay we every burden down;
Grace our spirits will deliver,
   And provide a robe and crown.

4 At the smiling of the river,
   Mirror of the Saviour's face,
Saints, whom death will never sever,
   Lift their songs of saving grace.

5 Soon we'll reach the silver river,
   Soon our pilgrimage will cease;
Soon our happy hearts will quiver,
   With the melody of peace.

670

COME, ye sinners, poor and needy,
    Weak and wounded, sick and sore;
Jesus ready stands to save you,
    Full of pity, love and power:
        He is able,
    He is willing: doubt no more.

2 Now, ye needy, come and welcome;
    God's free bounty glorify;
True belief and true repentance,—
    Every grace that brings you nigh,—
        Without money,
    Come to Jesus Christ and buy.

3 Let not conscience make you linger;
    Nor of fitness fondly dream:
All the fitness He requireth
    Is to feel your need of Him:
        This He gives you,—
    'Tis the Spirit's glimmering beam.

4 Come, ye weary, heavy-laden,
    Bruised and mangled by the fall;
If you tarry 'till you're better,
    You will never come at all;
        Not the righteous,—
    Sinners, Jesus came to call.

671

GOD is love; His mercy brightens
    All the path in which we rove;
Bliss He wakes, and woe He lightens,
    God is wisdom, God is love.

2 Time and change are busy ever;
    Man decays, and ages move;
But His mercy waneth never;
    God is wisdom, God is love.

3 E'en the hour that darkest seemeth
    Will His changeless goodness prove;
From the gloom His brightness streameth,
    God is wisdom, God is love.

4 He with earthly cares entwineth
   Hope and comfort from above;
Everywhere His glory shineth;
   God is wisdom, God is love.

672

FROM all that dwell below the skies,
   Let the Creator's praise arise;
Let the Redeemer's name be sung,
Through every land, by every tongue.

2 Eternal are Thy mercies, Lord;
Eternal truth attends Thy word:
Thy praise shall sound from shore to shore,
Till suns shall rise and set no more.

673

IN the Christian's home in glory,
   There remains a land of rest;
There my Saviour's gone before me,
   To fulfil my soul's request.

CHO.—There is rest for the weary,
   There is rest for the weary,
     There is rest for you.
   On the other side of Jordan,
   In the sweet fields of Eden,
   Where the tree of life is blooming
     There is rest for you.

2 He is fitting up my mansion,
   Which eternally shall stand,
For my stay shall not be transient,
   In that holy, happy land.

3 Sing, oh! sing, ye heirs of glory!
   Shout your triumph as you go;
Zion's gate will open for you,
   You shall find an entrance through.

674

SUN of my soul, Thou Saviour dear,
   It is not night if Thou be near;
Oh, may no earth-born cloud arise,
To hide Thee from Thy servant's eyes

2 When the soft dews of kindly sleep
  My wearied eye-lids gently steep,
  Be my last thought—how sweet to rest
  Forever on my Saviour's breast.

3 Abide with me from morn till eve,
  For without Thee I cannot live;
  Abide with me when night is nigh,
  For without Thee I dare not die.

4 If some poor wandering child of Thine
  Have spurned to-day the voice divine—
  Now, Lord, the gracious work begin;
  Let him no more lie down in sin.

675

COME every joyful heart,
    That loves the Saviour's name,
Your noblest powers exert,
    To celebrate His fame;
Tell all above, and all below,
    The debt of love to Him you owe.

2 He left His starry crown,
    And laid His robes aside;
  On wings of love came down,
    And wept, and bled, and died;
  What He endured no tongue can tell,
    To save our souls from death and hell.

3 From the dark grave He rose—
    The mansion of the dead;
  And thence His mighty foes
    In glorious triumph led:
  Up through the sky the Conqueror rode
    And reigns on high the Saviour God.

4 From thence He'll quickly come—
    His chariot will not stay—
  And bear our spirits home
    To realms of endless day;
  There shall we see His lovely face,
    And ever be in His embrace.

676

MY soul, be on thy guard,
    Ten thousand foes arise;
The hosts of sin are pressing hard,
    To draw Thee from the skies.

2 O watch, and fight, and pray;
    The battle ne'er give o'er;
Renew it boldly every day,
    And help divine implore.

3 Ne'er think the victory won,
    Nor lay thine armor down:
The work of faith will not be done,
    Till thou obtain the crown.

677

AWAKE, my soul, stretch every nerve,
    And press with vigor on;
A heavenly race demands thy zeal,
    And an immortal crown.

2 A cloud of witnesses around
    Hold thee in full survey;
Forget the steps already trod,
    And onward urge thy way.

3 'Tis God's all-animating voice,
    That calls thee from on high,
'Tis His own hand presents the prize
    To thine aspiring eye.

4 Blest Saviour, introduced by Thee
    Have I my race begun;
And, crowned with victory, at Thy feet
    I'll lay my honors down.

678

THE Lord's my Shepherd, I'll not want:
    He makes me down to lie
In pastures green; He leadeth me
    The quiet waters by.

2 My soul He doth restore again;
    And me to walk doth make
Within the paths of righteousness,
    E'en for His own name's sake.

3 Yea, though I walk in death's dark vale,
  Yet I will fear none ill;
For Thou art with me; and Thy rod
  And staff me comfort still.

4 My table Thou hast furnished
  In presence of my foes;
My head Thou dost with oil anoint,
  And my cup overflows.

5 Goodness and mercy all my life
  Shall surely follow me;
And in God's house for evermore
  My dwelling-place shall be.

679

MAJESTIC sweetness sits enthroned
  Upon the Saviour's brow;
His head with radiant glories crowned,
  His lips with grace o'erflow.

2 He saw me plunged in deep distress,
  And flew to my relief;
For me He bore the shameful cross,
  And carried all my grief.

3 To heaven, the place of His abode,
  He brings my weary feet;
Shows me the glories of my God,
  And makes my joys complete.

4 Since from Thy bounty I receive
  Such proofs of love divine,
Had I a thousand hearts to give,
  Lord! they should all be Thine.

680

AMAZING grace, how sweet the sound.
  That saved a wretch like me!
I once was lost, but now am found,
  Was blind, but now I see.

2 'Twas grace that taught my heart to fear,
  And grace my fears relieved;
How precious did that grace appear,
  The hour I first believed.

3 Through many dangers, toils, and snares,
   I have already come;
'Tis grace that brought me safe thus far,
   And grace will lead me home.

4 Yes, when this heart and flesh shall fail,
   And mortal life shall cease,
I shall possess, within the vail,
   A life of joy and peace.

681

COME, Holy Spirit, Heavenly Dove!
   With all Thy quickening powers;
Kindle a flame of sacred love
   In these cold hearts of ours.

2 Dear Lord! and shall we ever live
   At this poor dying rate?
Our love so faint, so cold to Thee,
   And Thine to us so great?

3 Come, Holy Spirit, Heavenly Dove,
   With all Thy quickening powers:
Come, shed abroad a Saviour's love,
   And that shall kindle ours.

682

JUST as I am, without one plea,
   But that Thy blood was shed for me,
And that Thou bidd'st me come to Thee,
   O Lamb of God! I come, I come!

2 Just as I am, and waiting not
   To rid my soul of one dark blot,
To Thee, whose blood can cleanse each spot,
   O Lamb of God! I come, I come!

3 Just as I am, though tossed about,
   With many a conflict, many a doubt,
Fightings and fears within, without,
   O Lamb of God! I come, I come!

4 Just as I am, poor, wretched, blind,
   Sight, riches, healing of the mind,
Yea, all I need, in Thee to find,
   O Lamb of God! I come, I come!

5 Just as I am; Thou wilt receive,
　　Wilt welcome, pardon, cleanse, relieve;
　　Because Thy promise I believe,
　　　O Lamb of God! I come, I come!

683

COME, said Jesus' sacred voice,
　　Come, and make My paths your choice;
I will guide you to your home,
　　Weary pilgrim, hither come!

2 Thou who, homeless, sole, forlorn,
　　Long hast borne the proud world's scorn,
　　Long hast roamed the barren waste,
　　Weary pilgrim, hither haste.

3 Ye who, tossed on beds of pain,
　　Seek for ease, but seek in vain,
　　Ye, by fiercer anguish torn,
　　In remorse for guilt who mourn;—

4 Hither come! for here is found
　　Balm that flows for every wound,
　　Peace that ever shall endure,
　　Rest eternal, sacred, sure.

684

WHILE life prolongs its precious light
　　Mercy is found, and peace is given;
But soon, ah, soon, approaching night
　　Shall blot out every hope of heaven.

2 While God invites, how blest the day!
　　How sweet the Gospel's charming sound!
Come, sinners, haste, O haste away
　　While yet a pardoning God is found.

3 Soon, borne on time's most rapid wing,
　　Shall death command you to the grave,—
Before His bar your spirits bring.
　　And none be found to hear or save.

4 In that lone land of deep despair,
　　No Sabbath's heavenly light shall rise,—
No God regard your bitter prayer,
　　No Saviour call you to the skies.

5 Now God invites; how blest the day:
    How sweet the Gospel's charming sound!
Come, sinners, haste, O haste away,
    While yet a pard'ning God is found.

685

FROM every stormy wind that blows,
    From every swelling tide of woes,
There is a calm, a sure retreat;
'Tis found beneath the mercy-seat.

2 There is a place where Jesus sheds
    The oil of gladness on our heads;
A place than all besides more sweet,—
    It is the blood-bought mercy-seat.

3 There is a scene where spirits blend,
    Where friend holds fellowship with friend;
Though sundered far, by faith we meet
Around one common mercy-seat.

686

ONCE I was dead in sin,
    And hope within me died;
But now I'm dead to sin—
    With Jesus crucified.

CHO.—And can it be that "He loved me,
    And gave Himself for me?"

2 Oh height I cannot reach,
    Oh depth I cannot sound,
Oh love, O boundless love,
    In my Redeemer found!

3 O cold, ungrateful heart
    That can from Jesus turn,
When living fires of love
    Should on His altar burn.

4 I live—and yet, not I,
    But Christ that lives in me;
Who from the law of sin
    And death hath made me free.

687

O Holy Spirit, come,
  And Jesus' love declare;
Oh, tell us of our heavenly home,
  And guide us safely there.

2 Our unbelief remove
  By Thine almighty breath;
Oh, work the wondrous work of love,
  The mighty work of faith.

2 Come with resistless power,
  Come with almighty grace,
Come with the long-expected shower,
  And fall upon this place.

688

I LOVE Thy kingdom, Lord,
  The house of Thine abode,
The Church our blest Redeemer saved
  With His own precious blood.

2 I love Thy church, O God!
  Her walls before Thee stand,
Dear as the apple of Thine eye,
  And graven on Thy hand.

3 For her my tears shall fall;
  For her my prayers ascend;
To her my cares and toils be given,
  Till toils and cares shall end.

4 Beyond my highest joy
  I prize her heavenly ways;
Her sweet communion, solemn vows,
  Her hymns of love and praise.

5 Sure as Thy truth shall last,
  To Zion shall be given
The brightest glories earth can yield,
  And brighter bliss of heaven.

689

N OT all the blood of beasts
  On Jewish altars slain,
Could give the guilty conscience peace,
  Or wash away the stain.

2 But Christ, the heavenly Lamb,
   Takes all our sins away;
A sacrifice of nobler name
   And richer blood than they.

3 My faith would lay her hand
   On that dear head of Thine,
While like a penitent I stand,
   And there confess my sin.

4 My soul looks back to see
   The burden thou didst bear,
While hanging on th'accursèd tree,
   And knows here guilt was there.

590

HOW solemn are the words,
   And yet to faith how plain,
Which Jesus uttered while on earth—
   "Ye must be born again!"

2 *"Ye must be born again!"*
   For so hath God decreed;
No reformation will suffice—
   'Tis *life* poor sinners need.

3 *"Ye must be born again!"*
   And life *in Christ* must have;
In vain the soul may elsewhere go—
   'Tis He *alone* can save.

4 *"Ye must be born again!"*
   Or never enter heaven;
'Tis only blood-washed ones are there,
   The ransomed and forgiven.

591

LORD, bless and pity us,
   Shine on us with Thy face:
That th'earth Thy way, and nations all
   May know Thy saving grace.

2 Let people praise Thee, Lord!
   Let people all Thee praise!
Oh, let the nations all be glad,
   In songs their voices raise!

3 Thou'lt justly people judge,
   On earth rule nations all;
Let people praise Thee, Lord! let them
   Praise Thee, both great and small!

4 The earth her fruit shall yield,
   Our God shall blessing send;
God shall us bless: men shall Him fear
   Unto earth's utmost end.

692

AWAKE, and sing the song
   Of Moses and the Lamb;
Wake, every heart and every tongue,
   To praise the Saviour's name.

2 Sing of His dying love;
   Sing of His risen power;
Sing how He intercedes above
   For those whose sins He bore.

3 Ye pilgrims, on the road
   To Zion's city, sing;
Rejoice ye in the Lamb of God—
   In Christ, th'eternal King.

4 There shall each raptured tongue
   His endless praise proclaim;
And sweeter voices tune the song
   Of Moses and the Lamb.

693

WHILE shepherds watched their flocks by
     night,
All seated on the ground,
The angel of the Lord came down,
   And glory shone around.

2 "Fear not," said he,—for mighty dread
   Had seized their troubled mind,—
"Glad tidings of great joy I bring,
   To you and all mankind.

3 "To you, in David's town, this day,
   Is born of David's line,
The Saviour, who is Christ, the Lord,
   And this shall be the sign;—

4 "The heavenly babe you there shall find,
    To human view displayed,
All meanly wrapped in swathing bands,
    And in a manger laid."

5 Thus spake the seraph—and forthwith
    Appeared a shining throng
Of angels, praising God, who thus
    Addressed their joyful song:—

6 "All glory to God on high,
    And to the earth be peace;
Good-will henceforth from heaven to men
    Begin, and never cease! '

894

SALVATION! O the joyful sound!
    What pleasure to our ears;
A sovereign balm for every wound
    A cordial for our fears.

2 Salvation! let the echo fly
    The spacious earth around,
While all the armies of the sky
    Conspire to raise the sound.

3 Salvation! O Thou bleeding Lamb;
    To Thee the praise belongs;
Salvation shall inspire our hearts,
    And dwell upon our tongues.

895

SPIRIT of truth, O let me know
    The love of Christ to me;
Its conquering, quickening power bestow,
    To set me wholly free.

2 I long to know its depth and height,
    To scan its breadth and length;
Drink in its ocean of delight,
    And triumph in its strength.

3 It is Thine office to reveal
    My Saviour's wondrous love;
Oh, deepen on my he rt Thy seal,
    And bless me from bove.

4 Thy quickening power to me impart,
  And be my constant Guide;
With richer gladness fill my heart;
  Be Jesus glorified.

696

O MY soul, bless thou Jehovah,
  All within me, bless His name;
Bless Jehovah, and forget not
  All His mercies to proclaim.

2 Who forgives all thy transgressions,
  Thy diseases all who heals:
Who redeems thee from destruction,
  Who with thee so kindly deals.

3 Who with tender mercies crowns thee,
  Who with good things fills thy mouth,
So that even like the eagle
  Thou hast been restored to youth.

4 In His righteousness, Jehovah
  Will deliver those distressed;
He will execute just judgment
  In the cause of all oppressed.

697

J ESUS only, when the morning
  Beams upon the path I tread;
Jesus only, when the darkness
  Gathers round my weary head.

2 Jesus only, when the billows
  Cold and sullen o'er me roll;
Jesus only, when the trumpet
  Rends the tomb and wakes the soul

3 Jesus only, when in judgment
  Boding fears my heart appall;
Jesus only, when the wretched
  On the rocks and mountains call.

4 Jesus only, when adoring,
  Saints their crowns before Him bring;
Jesus only, I will, joyous,
  Through eternal ages sing

698

IN the cross of Christ I glory,
  Towering o'er the wrecks of time;
All the light of sacred story,
  Gathers round its head sublime.

2 When the woes of life o'ertake me,
  Hopes deceive and fears annoy,
Never shall the cross forsake me;
  Lo! it glows with peace and joy.

3 When the sun of bliss is beaming
  Light and love upon my way,
From the cross the radiance streaming,
  Adds new luster to the day.

4 Bane and blessing, pain and pleasure,
  By the cross are sanctified;
Peace is there, that knows no measure,
  Joys that through all time abide.

699

WE are waiting by the river,
  We are watching by the shore,
Only waiting for the boatman,
  Soon he'll come to bear us o'er.

2 Though the mist hangs o'er the river,
  And its billows loudly roar,
Yet we hear the song of angels,
  Wafted from the other shore.

3 And the bright celestial city,—
  We have caught such radiant gleams
Of its towers like dazzling sunlight,
  With its sweet and peaceful streams.

4 He has called for many a loved one,
  We have seen them leave our side;
With our Saviour we shall meet them
  When we too, have crossed the tide.

5 When we've passed the vale of shadows,
  With its dark and chilling tide,
In that bright and glorious city
  We shall evermore abide.

700

SAVIOUR! visit Thy plantation;
　Grant us, Lord, a gracious rain;
All will come to desolation,
　Unless Thou return again.

2 Keep no longer at a distance;—
　Shine upon us from on high,
Lest for want of Thine assistance,
　Every plant should droop and die.

3 Let our mutual love be fervent,
　Make us prevalent in prayers;
Let each one, esteemed Thy servant,
　Shun the world's enticing snares.

4 Break the tempter's fatal power;
　Turn the stony heart to flesh;
And begin from this good hour,
　To revive Thy work afresh.

701

JESUS, hail! enthroned in glory,
　There for ever to abide;
All the heavenly hosts adore Thee,
　Seated at Thy Father's side.

2 There for sinners Thou art pleading,
　There Thou dost our place prepare;
Ever for us interceding,
　Till in glory we appear.

3 Worship, honor, power and blessing
　Thou art worthy to receive:
Loudest praises, without ceasing,
　Meet it is for us to give.

4 Help, ye bright angelic spirits!
　Bring your sweetest, noblest lays,
Help to sing our Saviour's merits,—
　Help to chant Immanuel's praise.

702

JESUS wept! those tears are over
　But His heart is still the same,
Kinsman, Friend and Elder Brother,
　Is His everlasting name.
Saviour, who can love like Thee,
　Gracious One of Bethany.

2 When the pangs of trial seize us,
   When the waves of sorrow roll,
I will lay my head on Jesus,
   Pillow of the troubled soul.
Surely, none can feel like Thee,
   Weeping One of Bethany.

3 Jesus wept! and still in glory
   He can mark each mourner's tears;
Living to retrace the story
   Of the hearts He solaced here:
Lord, when I am called to die,
   Let me think of Bethany.

4 Jesus wept! those tears of sorrow
   Are a legacy of love;
Yesterday, to-day, to-morrow,
   He the same doth ever prove,
Thou art all in all to me,
   Living One of Bethany.

703

I WAITED for the Lord my God,
   And patiently did bear;
At length to me He did incline
   My voice and cry to hear.

2 He took me from a fearful pit,
   And from the miry clay,
And on a rock He set my feet,
   Establishing my way.

3 He put a new song in my mouth,
   Our God to magnify;
Many shall see it, and shall fear,
   And on the Lord rely.

4 O blessèd is the man whose trust
   Upon the Lord relies;
Respecting not the proud, nor such
   As turn aside to lies.

704

JESUS! and shall it ever be,
   A mortal man ashamed of Thee?
Ashamed of Thee, whom angels praise,
Whose glories shine through endless days?

2 Ashamed of Jesus! sooner far
   Let evening blush to own a star;
He sheds the beams of light divine
   O'er this benighted soul of mine.

3 Ashamed of Jesus! that dear friend
   On whom my hopes of heaven depend!
No, when I blush, be this my shame,
   That I no more revere His Name.

4 Ashamed of Jesus! yes, I may,
   When I've no guilt to wash away,
No tear to wipe, no good to crave,
   No fear to quell, no soul to save.

5 Till then—nor is my boasting vain,
   Till then, I boast a Saviour slain;
And O, may this my glory be,
   That Christ is not ashamed of me.

705

HOW sweet the name of Jesus sounds
   In a believer's ear;
It soothes his sorrows, heals his wounds,
   And drives away his fear.

2 It makes the wounded spirit whole,
   And calms the troubled breast;
'Tis manna to the hungry soul,
   And to the weary, rest.

3 Dear Name, the Rock on which I build
   My Shield and Hiding-place;
My never-failing Treasure, filled
   With boundless stores of grace.

4 Jesus my Shepherd, Saviour, Friend
   My Prophet, Priest and King,
My Lord, my Life, my Way, my End
   Accept the praise I bring.

5 I would Thy boundless love proclaim
   With every fleeting breath;
So shall the music of Thy name
   Refresh my soul in death.

706

SAVE, Jesus, save!
  Thy blessing now we crave;
For every anxious sinner here,
  Oh, let Thy mercy now appear,
Lord Jesus, save, Lord Jesus, save.

2 Save, Jesus, save!
  Thy banner o'er us wave,
    Of love eternal and divine;
    Oh, Lord, let each one here be Thine,
Lord Jesus, save, Lord Jesus, save.

3 Save, Jesus, save!
  Thou conqueror o'er the grave,
    Give every fettered soul release,
    And to the troubled, whisper "Peace."
Lord Jesus, save, Lord Jesus, save.

4 Save, Jesus, save!
  And Thou alone shalt have
    The glory of the work divine,
    Yea, endless praises shall be Thine!
Lord Jesus, save, Lord Jesus, save.

707

O FOR a faith that will not shrink,
  Though pressed by every foe,
That will not tremble on the brink
  Of any earthly woe.

2 That will not murmur or complain
  Beneath the chastening rod,
But, in the hour of grief or pain,
  Will lean upon its God;—

3 A faith that shines more bright and clear
  When tempests rage without;
And when in danger knows no fear,
  In darkness feels no doubt.

4 Lord, give us such a faith as this,
  And then, whate'er may come,
We'll taste e'en here the hallowed bliss
  Of an eternal home.

708

A H, this heart is void and chill,
　　'Mid earth's noisy thronging;
For my Father's mansion, still
　　Earnestly I'm longing.

REF.—Looking home, looking home,
　　　T'ward the heavenly mansion,
　　Jesus hath prepared for me,
　　　In His Father's kingdom.

2 Soon the glorious day will dawn,
　　Heavenly pleasures bringing;
Night will be exchanged for morn,
　　Sighs give place to singing.

3 Oh, to be at home, and gain,
　　All for which we're sighing,
From all earthly want and pain
　　To be swiftly flying.—

4 Blesséd home! oh, blesséd home!
　　There no more to sever;
Soon we'll meet around the throne
　　Praising God forever.

709

W HEN I survey the wondrous cross
　　On which the Prince of Glory died,
My richest gain I count but loss,
　　And pour contempt on all my pride.

2 Forbid it, Lord, that I should boast,
　　Save in the death of Christ my God:
All the vain things that charm me most,
　　I sacrifice them to His blood.

3 See! from His head, His hands, His feet,
　　Sorrow and love flow mingled down!
Did e'er such love and sorrow meet,
　　Or thorns compose so rich a crown?

4 Were the whole realm of nature mine,
　　That were an offering far too small:
Love so amazing, so divine,
　　Demands my soul, my life, my all.

710

WHAT various hindrances we meet,
In coming to the mercy-seat!
Yet who that knows the worth of prayer,
But wishes to be often there?

2 Prayer makes the darkened clouds withdraw;
Prayer climbs the ladder Jacob saw,
Gives exercise to faith and love,
Brings every blessing from above.

3 Restraining prayer, we cease to fight;
Prayer makes the Christian's armor bright;
And Satan trembles when he sees
The weakest saint upon his knees.

711

FAITH is a living power from heaven
Which grasps the promise God has given;
Securely fixed on Christ alone,
A trust that cannot be o'erthrown.

2 Faith finds in Christ whate'er we need,
To save and strengthen, guide and feed;
Strong in His grace it joys to share
His cross, in hope His crown to wear.

3 Faith to the conscience whispers peace,
And bids the mourner's sighing cease;
By faith the children's right we claim,
And call upon our Father's name.

4 Such faith in us, O God, implant,
And to our prayers Thy favor grant,
In Jesus Christ, Thy saving Son,
Who is our fount of health alone.

712

BLEST be the tie that binds
Our hearts in Christian love;
The fellowship of kindred minds
Is like to that above.

2 Before our Father's throne
We pour our ardent prayers;
Our fears, our hopes, our aims are one,
Our comforts and our cares.

3 We share our mutual woes,
　　Our mutual burdens bear;
And often for each other flows
　　The sympathizing tear.

4 When we asunder part,
　　It gives us inward pain;
But we shall still be joined in heart,
　　And hope to meet again.

713

DID Christ o'er sinners weep,
　　And shall our cheeks be dry?
Let floods of penitential grief
　　Burst forth from every eye.

2 The Son of God in tears
　　The wondering angels see;
Be thou astonished, O my soul!
　　He shed those tears for thee.

3 He wept that we might weep;
　　Each sin demands a tear;
In heaven alone no sin is found,
　　And there's no weeping there.

714

HASTEN, sinner, to be wise!
　　Stay not for the morrow's sun;
Wisdom, if you still despise,
　　Harder is it to be won.

2 Hasten, mercy to implore!
　　Stay not for the morrow's sun;
Lest thy season should be o'er
　　Ere this evening's stage is run.

3 Hasten, sinner, to return!
　　Stay not for the morrow's sun,
Lest thy lamp should fail to burn
　　Ere salvation's work is done.

4 Hasten, sinner, to be blest!
　　Stay not for the morrow's sun,
Lest perdition thee arrest
　　Ere the morrow is begun.

715

COME, Thou almighty King,
 Help us Thy name to sing,
Help us to praise:
Father! all-glorious,
O'er all victorious,
Come, and reign over us,
 Ancient of Days!

2 Come, Thou incarnate Word,
Gird on Thy mighty sword;
 Our prayer attend;
Come, and Thy people bless,
And give Thy word success;
Spirit of holiness!
 On us descend.

3 Come, Holy Comforter,
Thy sacred witness bear
 In this glad hour:
Thou, who almighty art,
Now rule in every heart,
And ne'er from us depart,
 Spirit of power!

4 To the great One in Three,
The highest praises be,
 Hence evermore!
His sovereign majesty
May we in glory see,
And to eternity
 Love and adore.

716

SOUND, sound the truth abroad
 Bear ye the word of God
Through the wide world:
Tell what our Lord has done,
Tell how the day is won,
And from His lofty throne
 Satan is hurled.

2 Speed on the wings of love,
Jesus, who reigns above,
 Bids us to fly;

They who His message bear
Should neither doubt nor fear,
He will their Friend appear,
    He will be nigh.

3 Ye who, forsaking all,
At your loved Master's call,
    Comforts resign;
Soon will your work be done;
Soon will the prize be won;
Brighter than yonder sun
    Then shall ye shine.

RISE, glorious Conqueror, rise
    Into Thy native skies,
Assume Thy right;
And where in many a fold
The clouds are backward rolled—
Pass through those gates of gold,
    And reign in light!

2 Victor o'er death and hell!
Cherubic legions swell
    Thy radiant train:
Praises all heaven inspire;
Each angel sweeps his lyre,
And waves his wings of fire,—
    Thou Lamb once slain!

3 Enter, incarnate God!—
No feet but Thine, have trod
    The serpent down:
Blow the full trumpets, blow!
Wider yon portals throw!
Saviour triumphant—go,
    And take Thy crown!

4 Lion of Judah—Hail!
And let Thy name prevail
    From age to age;
Lord of the rolling years!
Claim for Thine own the spheres,
For Thou hast bought with tears
    Thy heritage.

5 And then was heard afar
  Star answering to star—
      "Lo! these have come
  Followers of Him who gave
  His life their lives to save;
  And now their palms they wave,
      Brought safely home."

718

MY faith looks up to Thee,
    Thou Lamb of Calvary,
      Saviour divine;
Now hear me while I pray,
Take all my guilt away,
O, let me from this day
    Be wholly Thine.

2 May Thy rich grace impart
  Strength to my fainting heart,
      My zeal inspire;
  As Thou hast died for me,
  Oh may my love to Thee
  Pure, warm, and changeless be
      A living fire.

3 While life's dark maze I tread,
  And griefs around me spread,
      Be Thou my Guide;
  Bid darkness turn to day,
  Wipe sorrow's tears away,
  Nor let me ever stray
      From Thee aside.

4 When ends life's transient dream,
  When death's cold, sullen stream
      Shall o'er me roll—
  Blest Saviour! then, in love,
  Fear and distrust remove;
  Oh, bear me safe above—
      A ransomed soul.

719

NEARER, my God, to Thee,
    Nearer to Thee,

E'en though it be a cross
　　That raiseth me,
Still all my song shall be—
Nearer, my God, to Thee!
　　Nearer to Thee!

2 Though, like the wanderer,
　　The sun gone down,
Darkness be over me,
　　My rest a stone,
Yet in my dreams I'd be—
Nearer, my God, to Thee!
　　Nearer to Thee!

3 There let the way appear,
　　Steps unto heaven;
All that Thou sendest me,
　　In mercy given;
Angels to beckon me—
Nearer, my God, to Thee!
　　Nearer to Thee!

4 Then with my waking thoughts,
　　Bright with Thy praise,
Out of my stony griefs,
　　Bethel I'll raise;
So by my woes to be—
Nearer, my God, to Thee!
　　Nearer to Thee!

5 Or if, on joyful wing,
　　Cleaving the sky,
Sun, moon, and stars forgot,
　　Upward I fly.
Still all my song shall be—
Nearer, my God, to Thee!
　　Nearer to Thee!

───────

720

COME to Jesus, come to Jesus,
　Come to Jesus just now,
Just now come to Jesus,
　Come to Jesus just now.

2 He will save you, He will save you, etc.

3 He is able, He is able, etc.

4 He is willing, He is willing, etc.

5 He is waiting, He is waiting, etc.

6 He will hear you, He will hear you, etc.

7 He will cleanse you, He will cleanse you, etc.

8 He'll renew you, He'll renew you, etc.

9 He'll forgive you, He'll forgive you, etc.

10 If you'll trust Him, if you'll trust Him, etc.

11 He will save you, He will save you, etc.

721

JESUS, Lover of my soul,
 Let me to Thy bosom fly,
While the nearer waters roll,
 While the tempest still is high;
Hide me, O my Saviour, hide,
 Till the storm of life is past;
Safe into the haven guide,
 Oh, receive my soul at last.

2 Other refuge have I none,
 Hangs my helpless soul on Thee;
Leave, oh, leave me not alone,
 Still support and comfort me:
All my trust on Thee is stayed,
 All my help from Thee I bring;
Cover my defenceless head
 With the shadow of Thy wing.

3 Thou, O Christ, art all I want;
 More than all in Thee I find:
Raise the fallen, cheer the faint,
 Heal the sick, and lead the blind:
Just and holy is Thy name,
 I am all unrighteousness;

Vile, and full of sin I am,
  Thou art full of truth and grace.

4 Plenteous grace with Thee is found—
    Grace to cover all my sin:
  Let the healing streams abound;
    Make me, keep me, pure within.
  Thou of life the Fountain art,
    Freely let me take of Thee:
  Spring Thou up within my heart,
    Rise to all eternity.

722

SINNERS, turn, why will ye die?
  God, your Maker, asks you—Why:
God, who did your being give,
Made you with Himself to live;
He the fatal cause demands,
Asks the work of His own hands,—
Why, ye thankless creatures, why
Will ye cross His love and die?

2 Sinners, turn, why will ye die?
  God, your Saviour, asks you—Why:
He who did your souls retrieve,
Died Himself that ye might live!
Will ye let Him die in vain?
Crucify your Lord again?
Why, ye ransomed sinners, why
Will ye slight His grace, and die?

3 Sinners, turn, why will ye die?
  God, the Spirit, asks you—Why;
He, who all your lives hath strove,
Urged you to embrace His love;
Will ye not His grace receive?
Will ye still refuse to live?
Why, ye long-sought sinners! why
Will ye grieve your God, and die?

723

SUFF'RING Saviour, with thorn-crown,
  Bruis'd and bleeding, sinking down;
Heavy-laden, weary-worn,
Fainting, dying, crushed and torn—
  All for me, yes, all for me.

2 Jesus, Saviour, pure and mild,
 Let me ever be Thy child;
 So unworthy though I be,
 Thou did'st suffer this for me—
  All for me, yes, all for me.

3 Fain would I to Thee be brought,
 Blesséd Lord forbid it not;
 In the kingdom of Thy grace,
 Give Thy wandering child a place;
  Oh, bless me, yes, even me.

724

JESUS loves me! this I know,
 For the Bible tells me so:
Little ones to Him belong;
They are weak, but He is strong.

CHO.—Yes, Jesus loves me! Yes, Jesus loves me!
 Yes, Jesus loves me! The Bible tells me so!

2 Jesus from His throne on high,
 Came into this world to die;
 That I might from sin be free,
 Bled and died upon the tree.

3 Jesus loves me! He who died
 Heaven's gate to open wide!
 He will wash away my sin,
 Let His little child come in.

4 Jesus, take this heart of mine;
 Make it pure, and wholly Thine:
 Thou hast bled and died for me,
 I will henceforth live for Thee.

725

GLORY to God on high!
 Let heaven and earth reply,
 "Praise ye His name!"
His love and grace adore,
Who all our sorrows bore;
Sing loud for evermore,
 "Worthy the Lamb."

2 While they around the throne
  Cheerfully join in one,
    Praising His name—
  Ye who have felt His blood,
  Sealing your peace with God,
  Sound His dear name abroad,
    "Worthy the Lamb!"

3 Join, all ye ransomed race,
  Our Lord and God to bless;
    Praise ye His name—
  In Him we will rejoice,
  And make a joyful noise,
  Shouting with heart and voice,
    "Worthy the Lamb!"

4 Soon must we change our place,
  Yet will we never cease
    Praising His name;
  To Him our songs we bring;
  Hail Him our gracious King;
  And, through all ages sing,
    "Worthy the Lamb!"

726

M Y God I have found
    The thrice blesséd ground,
Where life, and where joy, and true comfort abound.

CHO.—Hallelujah! Thine the glory!
      Hallelujah! Amen!
      Hallelujah! Thine the glory!
      Revive us again.

2 'Tis found in the blood
  Of Him who once stood
My refuge and safety, my surety with God.

3 He bore on the tree
  The sentence for me,
And now both the surety and sinner are free

4 And though here below
  'Mid sorrow and woe,
My place is in heaven with Jesus I know.

5 And this I shall find
    For such is His mind,
" **He'll not be in glory and leave me behind.**"

---

727   (*See Number 721.*)

728

STAY, Thou insulted Spirit, stay,
    Though I have done Thee such **despite,**
Cast not the sinner quite away,
    Nor take Thine everlasting flight.

2 Though I have most unfaithful been
    Of all who e'er Thy grace received;
Ten thousand times Thy goodness seen,
    Ten thousand times Thy goodness **grieved.**

3 Yet O, the chief of sinners spare,
    In honor of my great High Priest;
Nor in Thy righteous anger swear
    I shall not see Thy people's rest.

4 O Lord, my weary soul release,
    Upraise me by Thy gracious hand;
Guide me into Thy perfect peace,
    And bring me to the promised land.

729

ALL hail the power of Jesus' **name!**
    Let angels prostrate fall;
Bring forth the royal diadem,
    And crown Him Lord of all.

2 Let every kindred, every tribe,
    On this terrestrial ball,
To Him all majesty ascribe,
    And crown Him Lord of all.

3 Oh, that with yonder sacred **throng**
    We at His feet may fall;
We'll join the everlasting song,
    And crown Him Lord of all.

730

O FOR a thousand tongues to sing
   My great Redeemer's praise;
The glories of my God and King,
   The triumphs of His grace.

2 My gracious Master, and my God,
   Assist me to proclaim,—
To spread, through all the earth abroad,
   The honors of Thy Name.

3 Jesus!—the name that charms our fears,
   That bids our sorrows cease;
'Tis music in the sinners ears,
   'Tis life, and health, and peace.

4 He breaks the power of cancelled sin,
   He sets the prisoner free;
His blood can make the foulest clean,
   His blood availed for me.

———

731

A SK ye what great thing I know
   That delights and stirs me so?
What the high reward I win?
Whose the name I glory in?
   Jesus Christ, the Crucified.

2 What is faith's foundation strong?
What awakes my lips to song?
He who bore my sinful load,
Purchased for me peace with God,
   Jesus Christ, the Crucified.

3 Who defeats my fiercest foes?
Who consoles my saddest woes?
Who revives my fainting heart,
Healing all its hidden smart?
   Jesus Christ, the Crucified.

4 Who is life in life to me?
Who the death of death will be?
Who will place me on His right
With the countless hosts of light?
   Jesus Christ, the Crucified.

5 This is that great thing I know;
    This delights and stirs me so;
Faith in Him who died to save,
Him who triumphed o'er the grave,
    Jesus Christ, the Crucified.

132

LORD, dismiss us with Thy blessing,
    Fill our hearts with joy and peace;
Let us each, Thy love possessing,
    Triumph in redeeming grace;
O, refresh us,   O, refresh us,
    Traveling through this wilderness,

2 Thanks we give, and adoration,
    For Thy gospel's joyful sound;
May the fruits of Thy salvation
    In our hearts and lives abound;
Ever faithful,   Ever faithful,
    To the truth may we be found.

3 So, whene'er the signal's given
    Us from earth to call away,
Borne on angel's wings to heaven,'
    Glad the summons to obey,
May we ever,   May we ever
    Reign with Christ in endless day!

133

THERE is a fountain filled with blood,
    Drawn from Immanuel's veins;
And sinners plunged beneath that flood,
    Lose all their guilty stains.

REF.—Lose all their guilty stains;
    And sinners plunged beneath that flood
    Lose all their guilty stains.

2 The dying thief rejoiced to see
    That fountain in his day;
And there may I, though vile as he,
    Wash all my sins away.

3 Dear dying Lamb, Thy precious blood
    Shall never lose its power,
Till all the ransomed church of God
    Be saved to sin no more.

4 E'er since, by faith, I saw the stream
    Thy flowing wounds supply,
Redeeming love has been my theme,
    And shall be, till I die.

5 Then in a nobler, sweeter song,
    I'll sing Thy power to save,
When this poor lisping, stammering tongue
    Lies silent in the grave.

734

BY faith I view my Saviour dying,
    On the tree, On the tree;
To every nation He is crying,
    Look to Me! Look to Me!
He bids the guilty now draw near,
Repent, believe, dismiss their fear:
Hark, hark what precious words I hear,
    Mercy's free! Mercy's free!

2 Did Christ, when I was sin pursuing,
    Pity me, Pity me?
And did He snatch my soul from ruin,
    Can it be, Can it be?
O, yes! He did salvation bring;
He is my Prophet, Priest, and King;
And now my happy soul can sing,
    Mercy's free, Mercy's free.

3 Jesus my weary soul refreshes:
    Mercy's free, Mercy's free,
And every moment Christ is precious
    Unto me, Unto me;
None can describe the bliss I prove,
While through this wilderness I rove,
All may enjoy the Saviour's love,
    Mercy's free, Mercy's free.

4 Long as I live, I'll still be crying,
    Mercy's free,   Mercy's free,
And this shall be my theme when dying,
    Mercy's free,   Mercy's free,
And when the vale of death I've passed,
When lodged above the stormy blast,
I'll sing, while endless ages last,
    Mercy's free,   Mercy's free.

735

O FOR a heart to praise my God,
    A heart from sin set free;—
A heart that always feels Thy blood,
    So freely shed for me:—

2 A heart resigned, submissive, meek,
    My great Redeemer's throne;
Where only Christ is heard to speak,—
    Where Jesus reigns alone.

3 O for a lowly, contrite heart,
    Believing, true, and clean;
Which neither life nor death can part
    From Him that dwells within:—

4 A heart in every thought renewed,
    And full of love divine;
Perfect, and right, and pure, and good,
    A copy, Lord, of Thine.

736

WAIT, my soul, upon the Lord,
    To His gracious promise flee,
Laying hold upon His word
    "As thy days thy strength shall be."

2 If the sorrows of thy case,
    Seem peculiar still to Thee,
God has promised needful grace
    "As thy days thy strength shall be."

3 Days of trial, days of grief
    In succession thou may'st see,
This is still thy sweet relief
    "As thy days thy strength shall be."

4 Rock of Ages, I'm secure,
   With Thy promise full and free,
Faithful, positive, and sure—
   "As thy days thy strength shall **be.**"

737

COME, my soul, thy suit **prepare,**
   Jesus loves to answer **prayer;**
He Himself has bid thee pray,
   Therefore will not say thee nay.

2 Thou art coming to a King,
   Large petitions with thee **bring,**
For His grace and power are such,
   None can ever ask too much.

3 With my burden I begin,
   Lord, remove this load of sin;
Let Thy blood for sinners spilt,
   Set my conscience free from **guilt.**

4 Lord, I come to Thee for rest,
   Take possession of my breast,
There Thy blood-bought right **maintain,**
   And without a rival reign.

738

MY country, 'tis of thee,
   Sweet land of **liberty,**
Of thee I sing;
Land where my fathers died,
Land of the pilgrim's pride,
From every mountain side
   Let freedom ring.

2 My native country, thee,
   Land of the noble free,
   Thy name I love;
I love thy rocks and rills,
Thy woods and templed **hills;**
My heart with rapture **thrills**
   Like that above.

3 Let music swell the breeze,
  And ring from all the trees
        Sweet freedom's song:
  Let mortal tongues awake,
  Let all that breathe partake,
  Let rocks their silence break,
        The sound prolong.

4 Our fathers' God, to Thee,
  Author of liberty,
        To Thee we sing:
  Long may our land be bright,
  With freedom's holy light;
  Protect us by Thy might,
        Great God, our King.

739

THE Lord bless thee, and keep thee!
    The Lord make his face shine upon **thee**,
        And be gracious unto thee:
The Lord lift up his countenance upon **thee**,
    And give thee peace.   AMEN.

INDEX.

Y

WOLVES

WOLVES

Written by Shaun Ellis
Photography by Monty Sloan

Bath · New York · Singapore · Hong Kong · Cologne · Delhi
Melbourne · Amsterdam · Johannesburg · Auckland · Shenzhen

This edition published by Parragon in 2011

Parragon
Queen Street House
4 Queen Street
Bath BA1 1HE, UK

Copyright © Parragon Books Ltd 2006

Designed, produced, and packaged by
Stonecastle Graphics Limited

Text and captions by Shaun Ellis
Photographs © Monty Sloan
Edited by Maggie Lofts
Designed by Sue Pressley and Paul Turner

ISBN: 978-1-4454-3425-4

Printed in China

The Author

Fascinated by wolves from a very early age, Shaun Ellis dreamed
of living alongside them in the wilderness. Little did he know
that he would one day turn his dream into reality. As a young
man living in the country, Shaun first developed an interest in
foxes and spent many hours observing their behavior. This
eventually spurred him on to leave England and go to North
America to live with and study wolves. He learned to mimic the
wolves' sounds and soon became accepted by the pack. This
privilege enabled him to discover intimate details about their
lives and gain a rare insight into their world.

The Photographer

Monty Sloan finds something deeply inspirational and intriguing
about wolves. Having studied geology at the University of
California, Berkeley, he developed a fascination for wildlife – in
particular wolves and their behavior. Studies of wolf social behavior,
coupled with his hobby as a photographer, quickly turned to a
photographic career – a passion to capture every aspect of wolf
life on film. But wild wolves are elusive, wary, and often difficult
to observe – let alone to photograph – on an intimate and
personal level. Monty found that working with socialized wolves
was the answer. He became a wolf behaviorist and photographer
at Wolf Park, near Battle Ground, Indiana, USA, where nearly
two decades of working with captive wolves have enabled him
to create the world's largest collection of wolf images. His work
has been published in numerous books and magazines
throughout Europe, as well as North and South America.

CONTENTS

Photograph © Angela Curtis

KINDRED SPIRITS

I grew up in a farming community where there were few other children, and so I made friends with the wildlife in the surrounding countryside. I felt at home in woodland at night, and I learned to use my senses of smell and hearing to find my way around. I bonded with the badgers and foxes who were fearless and relaxed in my presence. For many years, I was privileged to be able to watch their family groups and study their behavior.

So how did a young man from rural England end up at the foot of the Rocky Mountains in Idaho studying wolves under the guidance of the Nez Perce Native Americans? It was mostly due to hard work, perseverance and a chance encounter with a Native American biologist at a wolf seminar, who I persuaded to take me on as a volunteer. Working with him and fellow students by day, and studying the wolves on my own by night, I slowly earned the respect of the amazing Nez Perce people.

It was here in two to three feet of snow that I realized the best way to learn about wolves was to return to the ways of my childhood and live alongside them. And a few years later, I decided to try to join a wild pack not as a leader but as a low-ranking member, because I understood that only in this position would the wolves be prepared to teach me about their society.

I now work with captive wolves at Wolf Pack Management, Combe Martin, Devon, England and through the in-depth study of their behavior, my colleagues and I are constantly discovering new sides to these fascinating animals. I hope that I can use this knowledge to help protect wolves for future generations to study and admire.

Shaun Ellis
AUTHOR

Photograph © Paul Herbert

WOLVES IN FOCUS

Though I studied geology at university, wolves soon took over from rocks as a source of inspiration, and I started to focus on these fascinating animals. An interest in photography grew into a career: I have been taking pictures of wolves in color and black and white since 1984 and have accumulated an extensive library of wolf images.

Despite decades of research, both in captivity and in the field; despite success in recovery programs in the upper Midwest and Northern Rockies; despite growing public support for wolves and predators in general; despite the fact that you are far more likely to be killed by a toaster than a wild predator, especially a wolf; this animal remains in peril, or has already become locally extinct in many parts of the world.

So since 1988 to help conserve and promote the wolf, I have been working as a handler, lecturer, researcher, and photographer at Wolf Park in Indiana, USA. Wolf

Park is home to several packs of gray wolves, and part of the proceeds from my photographic sales go to the park to support education initiatives. Working with captive wolves has allowed me to get really close to my subjects, and I've been able to capture intimate behavior that would have been extremely difficult to shoot in the wild. I also design and maintain various websites, most of which are dedicated to wolf conservation.

Field studies, especially those conducted in Yellowstone National Park, have shown the importance of the wolf as a key species in the ecosystem – yet the wolf still remains a maligned, feared, and misunderstood predator. I can only hope that we can now come to accept the wolf for what it is, rather than live in fear for what it is not.

Monty Sloan
PHOTOGRAPHER

SPIRIT OF THE WOLF

Throughout history, wolves have been a constant source of fascination to humans as well as awakening some of our deepest fears. Featured in myths, legends, fables, and folklore, the relationship between humans and wolves is both ancient and complex. From the unsettling children's bedtime story *Little Red Riding Hood* to frightening tales of humans becoming werewolves when the moon is full, we are familiar with the traditional image of the wolf as both a cunning predator and an evil supernatural monster, but is there any truth in these popular myths?

And what of the gentler side of the wolf's nature? Tales of lost children being raised by wolves exist in many cultures, and these ancient stories, together with more recent ones, such as Rudyard Kipling's *The Jungle Book*, suggest that wolves possess superior parental skills. In fact, today the parenting skills of wolves are highly respected by zoologists and animal behaviorists who consider that, within the entire animal kingdom, only humans and some other primates can equal the care and education they offer to their young.

One of the earliest and best known legends of wolves and human children is the fourth-century story of the Roman twins Romulus and Remus. These sons of Mars and Rhea Silvia, a vestal virgin, were thrown into the River Tiber in a basket by Amulius, who saw them as a threat to his rule of Alba Longa. When they floated ashore, a "she-wolf" heard their cries and suckled them. After being found and brought up by a royal shepherd, the twins later became the founders of Rome.

Wolf mythology is filled with stories about wolves raising orphaned or lost children, and these tales represent a positive attitude toward the wolf and its relationship with human society. Sadly, however, myths also portray the wolf in a negative light, helping to create a climate of fear among the people of Europe, in

particular, who throughout history have set about hunting the wolf almost to extinction.

For example, the legendary beast of Gévaudan, said to be a giant wolf, reportedly killed about 100 people, over a three-year period, in the Auvergne region of France in the mid-eighteenth century. Such was its ferocity that King Louis XV called out his troops to hunt it down. Even though a large wolf was killed, the attacks continued until two more wolves were slaughtered, both of which were thought to be the beast.

The wolf's association with evil is still fueled today by horror movies, which portray wolf-like creatures transformed by a full moon and driven by a thirst for human blood. So this insatiable interest in the wolf's traditional reputation as a fierce killer continues today. Interestingly, a recent survey, which sought children's attitudes toward the wolf, highlighted that more young people are afraid of the wolf's howl than of the animal itself, which has become familiar to them through modern documentary television programs and natural history books.

In fact, proven attacks by a healthy wild wolf on people are almost non-existent. Wolves that act aggressively toward humans are usually suffering from an illness, such as rabies, and in captivity, attacks are more likely to occur if animals have been poorly handled by their keepers.

Native American legends tell of a sacred pact between wolves and humans to respect each other's families and land. Arguably, the wolf has honored its side of the agreement, but, sadly, we have not, instead we have systematically eradicated the wolf from much of its former habitat.

Today, the dedicated work of conservationists and animal behaviorists has helped us to understand the nature of the wolf and its vital role in the natural world. As ever more wilderness is destroyed due to increased

development and the destruction of natural habitat, nature reserves have allowed the wolf to survive in areas where its very existence was gravely threatened.

This book offers us the privileged opportunity to learn about the secret world of the wolf through the eyes of Shaun Ellis, who was shown the mystical ways of the

wolf by the Nez Perce Native Americans, and who has lived with wolves and studied them for many years.

With stunning photography by Monty Sloan, whose unique viewpoint enables us to glimpse the fascinating world of the wolf from within the pack, this book offers a remarkable insight into the spirit of the wolf.

Natural balance

Top predators, such as the wolf, help to maintain a balanced environment. In wooded areas, deer kill trees by stripping and eating bark, and so by controlling deer numbers, wolves help conserve trees, which are an essential habitat for birds and other wildlife.

White Protector

According to Native American legend, if a white wolf is seen either in a dream or reality, it has been sent to protect you. The Native Americans respected the wolf's strong family values, among other qualities.

On the brink

Wild wolves live on the brink of starvation for most of their lives, but the adult wolves always return with food for their pups, realizing the importance of the next generation in increasing pack numbers and ensuring hunting success.

The parenting skills of wolves are highly respected by zoologists and animal behaviorists who consider that, within the entire animal kingdom, only humans and some other primates can equal the care and education they offer to their young.

Pup school

Young wolves receiving lessons in life from their nanny. The nanny is selected by the alpha female before the birth of her pups to continue their care and education once they are weaned at four to six weeks of age. This enables the alpha female to devote herself once more to leading her pack.

Dangerous game

There is a constant risk of injury for wolves when hunting large quarry. A kick from a bison or a stab from a deer stag's antlers could be fatal. Adult wolves use the antlers and legs of dead prey during play to teach the young wolves avoidance techniques.

The stuff of myth

Images such as this, with a wolf howling at a full moon, have fueled the human imagination, and horror stories often portray the wolf as a vicious killer with a taste for human blood.

A recent survey, which sought

children's attitudes toward the wolf,

highlighted that more young people are

afraid of the wolf's howl than of

the animal itself.

WOLF MYTHOLOGY

From the northern Rockies of North America to the Carpathian Mountains in Europe, wherever there were wolves, human societies have surrounded them with folklore and superstitions, some of which have led to the demise of the wolf in many areas. Other cultures, however, such as Native American ones, have revered wolves and granted them an almost God-like status.

NATIVE AMERICAN CULTURE

One Native American tribe – the Shoshone – believed that coyotes and wolves had created the world and that after death the spirit of a tribal member was taken to the land of the coyote. The wolf guarded the path walked by the dead, and it would first awaken and then wash a human soul in the river. The newly cleaned spirit could then gain entry into the Promised Land.

As human populations increased, wolves began to seek sanctuary in the remote mountainous regions. As a result, Native Americans bestowed even greater mystic importance on the wolf, and they studied the animal in an effort better to understand it and learn from its wisdom. They say that the wolf taught them about co-operation for living together in extended families, and they learned the importance of social structure – they respected their chieftains in the same way that wolves respect the decision-making role of alphas.

Because of its ability to discover new places and find its way around its huge territory, the wolf became known as The Pathfinder. Native hunters often found elk and bison by following the wolves, whose sharp senses of smell and hearing enabled them to detect prey long before their human counterparts. The Native hunters never killed without leaving some meat as a thank you for their wolf helpers. The Native American tribes of the Great Plains believed that they could become great warriors by observing the wolf's hunting

skills. The sign for the Pawnee, one of the most feared tribes on the plains, was the same as the sign for wolf. And the Lakota tribes respected and honored the wolf's loyalty to its mate and family, and before hunting they would smear red dye on their mouths to mimic a feeding wolf.

The Native Americans and the wolf had a pact to support each other, but when Europeans began to colonize North America huge numbers of wolves were killed. Many tribes felt that the pact had been broken, and the Blackfoot and Lakota believed that a gun used to kill a wolf would never shoot straight again.

Native Americans have many stories that tell of shape-shifting: the ability to change from human to a different animal form. According to one old legend, a Native American woman found a wolf pup while out collecting wood for her tribe. The animal was alone, starving and close to death. She carried the wolf back to her camp where she fed him and kept him warm in her tepee. He grew quickly and they became inseparable friends. One morning they went to the river to drink, and in the soft mud the woman saw their tracks from the previous evening; human and wolf footprints turned into two sets of wolf tracks. Confused by what she saw, the woman sought advice from the old chief who told her that as recompense for the tiny life she had saved the wolf had given her the gift of existing in two forms: human and wolf. That evening she sat by the water with her wolf companion and looked at her reflection, and a female wolf looked back at her.

Spiritual cleaner

The wolf's natural love of water inspired some Native American folklore. The wolf was believed to guard the path walked by the dead, where it would wash the human soul in water before the newly cleaned spirit gained entry to the Promised Land.

EUROPEAN CULTURE

The wolf has for centuries captured the imagination of different cultures and features strongly in the complex body of European folklore and mythology. Several of Aesop's fables (c.600 BC) refer to the wolf's cunning; "The Boy Who Cried Wolf" is one of the best known. After the shepherd boy had sounded many false alarms, his cries of "A wolf!" are ignored by the townspeople. To the boy's dismay, his sheep are attacked by wolves and he is left helpless. Similarly, *Little Red Riding Hood*, a children's fairy story which originated in the seventeenth century, reinforces this perception of the wolf as a cunning predator.

Not only are there such stories of wolves dressing up as humans, but there are also ones in which humans turn into wolves. A number of cultures have "were" creatures, often inspired by the most dangerous animal found in the area. There were "were-tigers" in India, "were-leopards" in Africa, and "were-wolves" in medieval Europe. The term "were" is taken from the old English word "wer," meaning "man," thus werewolves or man-wolves were believed to be half-human and half-wolf.

Humans who became werewolves of their own free will were supposed to have made a pact with the devil. Most werewolf transformations took place at night when the moon was full; the werewolf attacked, killed and often ate people and animals, returning to human form at daybreak. On the other hand, people could sometimes inherit the condition. In Greece, for instance, anyone suffering from epilepsy was thought to be a werewolf.

There are various possible explanations for the origin of werewolf myths. A person living in one of the vast European forests 700 to 800 years ago could very easily have been mistaken for a wolf or werewolf. Receding and bleeding gums, sometimes coupled with excessive hair growth, are signs of severe malnutrition, which

would have been common at that time among the poor. Village outcasts trying to scavenge a living might have moved like wolves or mimicked their hunting behavior in an effort to feed themselves. And the wearing of animal skins – often wolfskins because of their outstanding insulating qualities – afforded protection from the cold. Another theory suggests that the poor conditions in which grain was stored at the time might have led to a variety of hallucinogenic

Safe routes

Wolves often use well-worn paths when moving around their territories. With daily scent-marking, these paths become safe areas where attacks from rival packs are unlikely.

reactions. So perhaps something as ordinary as a slice of bread, which might have contained bad rye seed, could have induced a werewolf sighting.

Today we also recognize the existence of a condition known as lycanthropy, which is a form of schizophrenia during which a patient believes that he or she is a wild animal, often a wolf or a werewolf. Sufferers have been observed making growling and snarling noises and chewing on furniture as if it were prey. In other non-European countries, characteristics of similarly powerful beasts common to the region, such as tigers in India, for example, are displayed by patients.

One of the most famous wolf stories is that of St Francis and the wolf of Gubbio, which can be found in *The Little Flowers of St Francis*, an anonymous fourteenth-century source of St Francis stories. The story tells of how St Francis tamed a large wolf that was terrorizing the good people of Gubbio, a town in

Under cover of darkness

The wolf's nocturnal habits added to its mystery, fueling numerous legends and horror stories. The wolf is, in fact, an intelligent, shy animal that avoids interaction with humans.

Umbria, Italy. While St Francis was staying in the town he was told of a wolf that had become so ravenous that it was not only killing and eating their livestock but also people.

The inhabitants of Gubbio became afraid to go outside the town walls, and so St Francis took pity not only on the people but on the wolf, too, and decided to go out and meet the animal. The townspeople desperately tried to warn St Francis of the danger, but he insisted that God would protect him. One brave friar and several peasants accompanied him outside the town gates, but soon after leaving, the peasants became terrified and refused to go any further. St Francis and the friar walked on, and suddenly the wolf charged at them from the forest, its jaws wide open. St Francis made the sign of the cross at the wolf and it immediately slowed down, and closed its mouth. St Francis then called out

to the wolf: "Come to me Brother Wolf, I wish you no harm," and at once the wolf lowered its head and laid down at the feet of St Francis. He asked why the wolf had been killing the people of Gubbio and their animals. "Brother Wolf", said St Francis, "I would like you to make peace with the townspeople, they will harm you no more and you must no longer harm them, all your past wrongs will be forgiven."

The wolf displayed its agreement by moving its body and nodding its head. In front of the crowd that had gathered, St Francis asked the wolf to make a pledge. He extended his hand and the wolf in turn extended its paw to seal the peace pact. St Francis then invited the wolf to follow him into the town. By the time they reached the square, everyone had gathered to witness the miracle. He then offered the townspeople peace on behalf of the wolf. The townsfolk promised to feed the animal, and St Francis asked the wolf if it could live under these terms. The wolf lowered its head and twisted its body in agreement. This convinced everyone that the wolf was willing to accept the pact. The animal once more placed its paw in St Francis's hand.

From that day the wolf and the townspeople kept their pact. The wolf went from house to house and was given food. When it finally died of old age, the people of Gubbio were sad. The wolf's peaceful ways had been a constant reminder to them of the tolerance and holiness of St Francis, and they had seen it as a living symbol of the providence of God. St Francis had educated them to accept the wolf and, in return, the wolf had accepted them.

Native respect

The Native Americans respected all animals and believed that each one had special qualities and skills that they could learn from: none more so than the bison and the wolf.

The wolf has for centuries captured the imagination of different cultures and features strongly in the complex body of European folklore and mythology.

Relative differences
European wolves (above) are generally smaller than their North American counterparts (left), and tend to be shorter, darker and more thickly set.

Wherever there were wolves, human societies have surrounded them with folklore and superstitions.

Bedtime stories
Children's fairy stories, such as *Little Red Riding Hood*, which originated in Europe in the seventeenth century, reinforced the perception of the wolf as a cunning predator.

THE PACK

Wolves originated in the New World about five million years ago. During the Pleistocene epoch (the last ice age), the dire wolf was the largest known species of wolf ever to exist. But it was a much smaller species that crossed into Siberia from Alaska, and this species eventually developed into the larger gray wolf *Canis lupus* of today. It settled in Eurasia and also migrated back to North America where it populated much of what is now known as Canada and the United States, except for one small region in the south-eastern US, which was home to a smaller wolf known as the red wolf *Canis rufus*.

Thanks to many detailed studies by biologists in the wild, we now know much more about the behavior of gray wolves, including the complex ways they use sound, smell, and posture, which are all specific to a particular rank, to communicate with each other.

The close-knit pack, usually consisting of eight to 12 animals, comprises a pair of high-ranking individuals known as the alpha male and alpha female. These two animals lead the pack but, contrary to previous supposition, are not always the largest wolves. They make all the necessary decisions to protect the pack and its territory, and in return they are usually the only two animals that will breed.

VISUAL COMMUNICATION

The muzzle is one of the most important parts of the wolf's body for communication and to kill prey. The alpha male and female are usually easy to recognize within the family because, among other characteristics, their muzzles are clearly highlighted with bold lines and colors, which act as a clear visual deterrent to members of other packs who will instantly register their status.

It is often said that a direct stare into a wolf's or dog's eyes represents a challenge. But rather than our eyes, it

now seems that it is more likely to be our teeth that convey dominance. Adult wolves teach pups to avert their muzzles when approaching adults in the pack by snapping into the air near the pups' heads to make them turn or lower their heads. Having learned this at an early age, adult wolves lower their heads as a mark of respect to a more dominant pack member.

The head position adopted by each animal depends on its position within the social order. For example, a mid- to high-ranking animal would show respect to a higher family member by moving its muzzle horizontally to either the right or left. If respect is not shown, the dominant animal is entitled to move its own muzzle to either the right or left of the offender's muzzle. This intimidation is usually all that is needed to gain a demonstration of respect, but if more pressure is required, the higher-ranked animal will issue a low, throaty growl, with increasing intensity if necessary, backed up by facial expressions. A snap into the air just to the side of the muzzle will be the final warning before the use of physical force.

The wolf's ear positions also play a vital role in communication. They can be splayed sideways (resembling outstretched wings) to indicate defence, or extended and pointed forward to gain respect by drawing attention to the muzzle.

The hackles are sometimes raised around the neck and shoulders to give the impression of increased size during defensive situations. A dominant animal has a continuous bold line that extends from the neck all the way along the spine to the tip of the tail, the bolder and more continuous the line, the higher the rank of the animal.

One as yet unproven theory among biologists is that the different types of food eaten by the specific ranks within the pack affect their color and markings as well as their scent patterns. An ageing alpha will be demoted when there is a suitable younger candidate in the pack, and the older animal will no longer be able to consume the best parts of the kill. Photographic evidence has recorded a change in the markings and color of demoted individuals sometime after this, suggesting direct links between food, markings and rank.

SCENT-MARKING

The dominant alpha male and female are recognized just as easily by their smell as by their appearance. As the highest-ranking wolves, they will consume the best quality food from each kill: essential organs, such as heart, liver, kidneys, and the best fresh meat, along with possibly the brain, which will give them a stronger smell than any other pack member. Each rank within the pack is allowed to consume a different part of the carcass, ensuring that each emits a different scent.

The strong scent of the alpha pair is essential for defending the pack's territory as rival packs will avoid trespassing into another pack's territory only if the invisible scent barrier is strong and powerful. The alphas will lay scent down in a variety of different patterns – by urinating, defecating and rubbing around trees on the borders of their territory – designed to send different messages either to rival packs or to lone wolves operating within the buffer zones between established families. Raised-leg urination is used only by the alpha wolves as this enables them to spray their strong-smelling urine to a much higher level on trees and bushes, which is essential for marking and defending their territory.

Seasonal changes affect the variety and intensity of scent patterns, continually altering the level of potential threat from neighboring packs. It is the responsibility of the dominant male, as the protector of his family, to maintain and reinforce the scent patterns that define their territory, and it is vital for this purpose that he consumes the best parts from each kill.

Leader of the pack

This alpha wolf can be identified by both its posture and bold coat markings – note the difference in color to the wolf on the left. Alphas are not always the biggest and boldest animals in the pack, but they do have a piercing stare and bold attitude.

A snap into the air just to the side of the muzzle will be the final warning before the use of physical force.

VOCAL COMMUNICATION

Growls, yips, yaps, and whines are vocalisations used at close range in combination with body language. The howl is a long-range method of communicating with pack members who are out of sight, or with rival wolves, in which case it is used as a way of avoiding conflict and can be heard several miles away. Each animal has a different sound depending on its pack status. The alpha pair's howl is low in tone, and they can also be identified by the length of the pauses between howls. It may not be the alpha wolves which initiate the howling, but they will quickly assume control of the situation once vocal contact is made with, for example, a neighboring pack, a lone wolf, or a family member that has become lost while hunting. If the alpha wolves consider that the pack needs to prolong its calls, they will offer encouragement to howl by repeating a long, deep howl or if they want to stop the pack, a series of two or three cut-off howls in quick succession.

THE BETAS

Second in rank to the alpha pair are the betas, which are also usually a pair of animals, where numbers permit, which hold disciplinary positions within the family. Betas are easy to recognize because they are often the biggest and boldest animals in the pack; they rely on their strength to establish pack rules passed down by the alpha pair. The beta's role is that of enforcer, deflecting much of the potential danger away from the valuable alphas. Their spine markings, though quite bold, are broken, in contrast to the strong and continuous lines of the alphas.

The betas are vocally quite low in tone: not as low as the alphas but lower than the remaining pack members. They howl for approximately three to four times longer than the alphas, adding strength and continuity to the pack calls.

Top marks

An alpha wolf can also be recognized by its bold facial markings, in particular on the muzzle, ears, and around the eyes, which distinguish it from the other wolves. It will also have a very strong scent.

Alpha line

The alpha's hackles have a bold outline, and a dark line continues down the body, creating the outline of a saddle on its back, and runs right to the base of the tail.

THE LOWER RANKS

Lower in rank than the betas is a group known as the mid-ranking wolves, which are usually led by a pair of more dominant wolves: the female teaches and disciplines subordinate females and the male performs the same role with the male wolves. These animals receive information from the alpha pair via the betas. In large packs of wolves with up to 15 animals, this line of communication is vital in order for the alpha pair to retain control.

The main duty of the mid-ranking wolves is to create the illusion that there are more wolves in the pack than there actually are. This is done in several ways and helps the pack defend its territory. The mid-ranking wolves vary their diet so that their scent-markings never remain the same, thus giving the illusion of a larger number of wolves. And during howling, the mid-ranking wolves use a variety of sounds – yips, yaps, barks, whines, howls, and growls – to make it hard for packs in neighboring territories to identify exactly how many wolves are in the pack. Mid-ranking wolves are naturally suspicious and are always aware of anything new or unfamiliar. The alpha and beta wolves rely on them to alert the pack to any danger.

The pack is completed by the specialists: the hunters, the nannies and the much misunderstood omega wolves. Hunters are often female as they are 20-25 percent smaller than the males and therefore much faster. This gives them the ability to catch the prey or cut off the escape route of the intended quarry. But males

A dominant animal has a continuous bold line that extends from the neck all the way along the spine to the tip of the tail, the bolder and more continuous the line, the higher the rank of the animal.

Under exposure

This wolf (opposite) is showing respect by exposing its light underside. It is also showing that it trusts the dominant animal because it has exposed the most vulnerable parts of its body; a single bite to these areas could kill.

Marks of respect

An alpha wolf's bold outlines can be seen from some distance and are used in conjunction with body posture, scent, and sound to gain respect from fellow or rival pack members.

Alpha and beta
The bold markings of the alpha wolf (left) clearly distinguish it from the beta wolf on the right.

Strong second
The beta wolves (opposite) are the biggest and boldest wolves in the pack. They are responsible for enforcing the wishes of the alpha pair and are sent forward to do a recce in times of danger.

are also required for their strength, particularly when hunting large prey such as bison. The female hunter may separate the quarry from the herd and tire it, but she would need the assistance of the larger male hunter to pull the animal down.

Nannies are specialist female or male wolves selected by the alpha female to care for and educate her pups once they are weaned, when she returns to her duties as leader of the pack.

Omega wolves are essential to the survival of the wolf pack. They are responsible for defusing tension within the pack and minimizing injury. From the age of two to three weeks, the omega pup is always at the center of constant bouts of quarreling among its litter-

mates. The omega learns very quickly how to attract attention toward itself by playing games and acting like a "court jester" or clown. Then by using a series of instinctive and learned behaviors, ranging from body postures, facial expressions, and vocal sounds, the omega is able to calm a situation, avoid injury, and restore harmony.

The omega wolf has often been labeled as the "Cinderella wolf" because it was assumed to be low-ranking and mistreated. This could be because when a wolf pack is feeding, the omega has been seen to be chased away, often repeatedly, from the carcass. One possible explanation for this behavior is to allow the high-ranking animals to change position at the carcass

without fighting. This ensures that they get the select parts and the right amount of food for their rank. Hungry wolves could seriously injure each other without the distraction provided by the omega. Once the other wolves have fed, the omega is rewarded by being allowed access to some high-quality food that has been saved for it specifically by a beta wolf. So it is probable that, despite appearances, the omega holds a high-ranking specialist position which is valued within the pack.

The omega howl is the most tuneful in the pack, reaching both high and low notes, and by bringing harmony to a bout of howling, it can help to calm the pack when it is on the defensive.

The main duty of the mid-ranking wolves is

to create the illusion that there are more wolves

in the pack than there actually are.

Remaining flexible

The mid-ranking animals have quite neutral markings, which allow them to change their rank if necessary. When a wolf dies, they may be required to fill a high-ranking or a specialist position.

Pack hierarchy

These pictures show how a low-ranking wolf is expected to turn its muzzle away when a dominant member of the pack approaches. If it fails to do this, the dominant wolf will resort to "mouthing" on the muzzle or neck areas to command respect.

The strong scent of the alpha pair is essential for defending the pack's territory.

Staying high

Scent-rolling helps to maintain a high position in the pack. Fish is often used because of its strong smell. The wolf rolls on the fish and rubs its scent onto its nose, head, back, and tail.

Bonding sessions

Close family bonds are reinforced by frequent rubbing of scent against pack members. Other bonding activities include grooming and play.

Rival packs will avoid trespassing into another pack's territory

only if the invisible scent barrier is strong and powerful.

Membership application

A lone wolf howls frequently to gain information from surrounding packs. It can tell if a rank is absent from the response and can then decide whether to try to enroll.

Howling from on high

Wolves often prefer to howl from an elevated position in order to project the sound further. They can also be seen standing in a semicircle during howling to project their sound in different directions.

Alpha duet

A breeding alpha pair often indicates their breeding rights by howling. When the alpha female comes into season, there will be visible spots of blood in her urine. By urinating over it, the alpha male is proclaiming his right to mate with her.

Sound disguise

The wolf pack howls for a variety of reasons including defence. It relies on the mid-ranking animals vocally to create the illusion that there are many more individuals within the pack.

The howl is a way of communicating with pack members close by or out of sight, or with rival wolves, in which case it is used as a way of avoiding conflict.

Howling lessons

Communication through howling is taught to the young wolves at an early age, and they are rewarded with food and praise. Each pup learns the howl relevant to its own rank.

Vocal flare

A wolf away from its pack will often call them using a rallying or locating howl. This wolf doesn't expect to get a reply but is just sending out a vocal beacon so the pack can find him or her again.

Low equals high

The alpha howl is low in tone which is a sign of its high status
in the pack. It howls for short periods and then stops to listen
to any response so he or she can decide whether the pack as
a whole should continue or stop.

Wolf gazing

The wolf's eyesight is poor in comparison to its other senses. Its lingering stare has often been likened to a human gaze and was said to be why the Native Americans referred to the animal as "brother wolf."

Sensitive hearing

Wolves can hear rival packs up to 10 miles away on open ground. The mid-ranking animals are naturally suspicious and often hear things before the rest of the pack, alerting them to any danger with a warning bark.

Pack jesters

Omega wolves were once wrongly thought to be the lowest ranking in the pack, but they are, in fact, highly respected and allowed to feed on good-quality meat as their reward for defusing tension in volatile situations, such as during feeding.

By using a series of instinctive and learned behaviors, ranging from body postures, facial expressions, and vocal sounds, the omega is able to calm a situation, avoid injury, and restore harmony.

Omega wolves are essential to the survival of the wolf pack. They are responsible for defusing tension within the pack and minimizing injury.

Peace-keepers

An omega wolf (right) uses its posture and vocal tones to calm a hostile situation. This is a vital role in all wolf packs.

Meet and greet
After time apart, pack bonds are re-established with licking and tail wagging. This behavior

Means of communication

Body postures make up a large percentage of the wolf's communication at short distance, and this is reinforced with facial expressions, ear and tail positions, use of hackles, and vocal sounds.

Thanks to many detailed studies by biologists in the wild, we now know much more about the behavior of wolves, including the complex ways they use sound, smell, and posture, which are all specific to a particular rank, to communicate with each other.

Size constraints

A wolf's territory can range from just a few to several hundred miles. This, together with the availability of food, determines the size of the pack.

The Magnificent Seven

A wolf pack varies in size from as few as three to twenty animals. Generally, a pack consists of the alpha pair and their young, betas, mid-ranking wolves, and the specialists, such as the omegas.

Wisdom of age

In most wolf packs there are ageing animals that are valued for their knowledge and life experience, like grandparents in human society. These wolves are often selected as nannies and take part in educating and teaching the pups.

The head position adopted by each

animal depends on its position within

the social order.

Variety packs

Pack size depends on the amount of available habitat and how many wolves are needed
to defend and hunt within it. European packs (above) now usually occupy small territories
unlike North American wolves (right), which inhabit vast areas of open plains and forest.

Cleaning contract
It is the right of an alpha to both groom and be groomed by other pack members. Grooming helps the pack to bond and removes dirt and parasites from their fur.

Dual-purpose coat

During winter, the wolf develops a thick fur coat (right) to
keep it warm. This is divided into two layers: the top layer of
fur, called guard hair, keeps the animal dry in snow and rain,
and the layer of soft fur underneath keeps it warm. The thick
winter coat is molted in the spring months ready for warmer
summer temperatures (above).

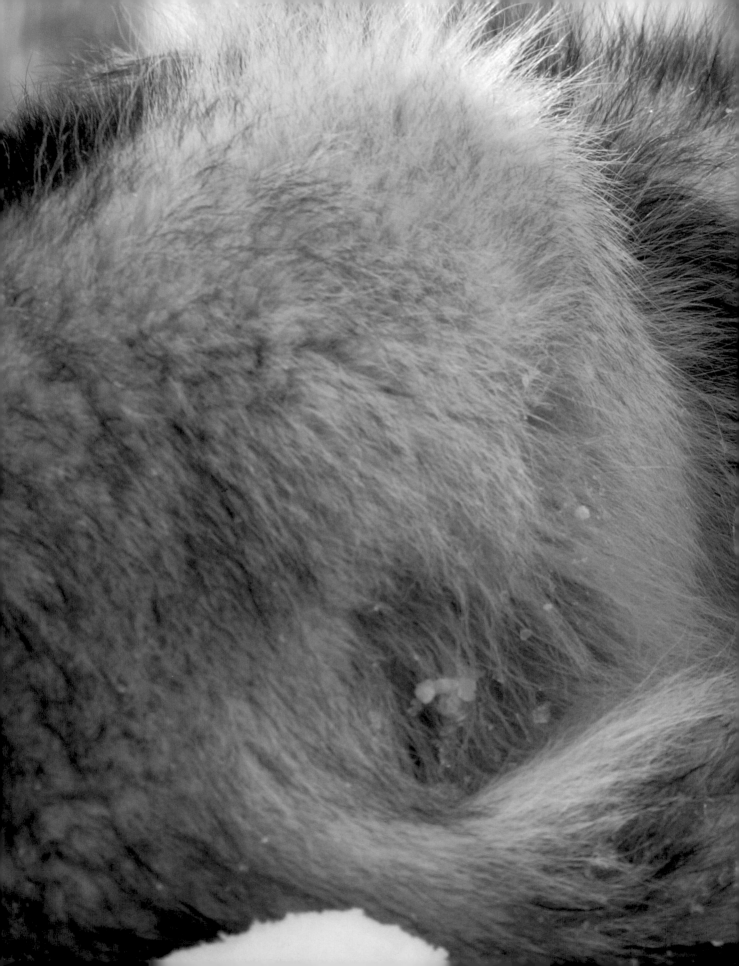

Winter warmers

During the winter, wolves always appear much larger as they have developed their thick, thermal winter coats, which help them survive in harsh weather conditions and low temperatures.

Wolf's clothing
The varied coloration and markings on the wolf's coat allow it to blend into its natural surroundings. Camouflage is vital for hiding from both predator and prey.

No wolf's land

A lone wolf passing through a strange territory will often urinate in water to remain undetected. This wolf has no territory of its own but operates in the buffer zone, a neutral area between existing packs where it is usually safe to travel.

Smelly feet

Wolves can strengthen territorial boundaries by means of scent glands in their feet. A beta wolf will also leave scratch-marks as a visual deterrent along with its scent.

Liquid asset

A wolf pack's territory will usually contain a water source, ranging from lakes to streams.
Wolves need large quantities of water after feeding and during pregnancy.

Natural swimmers

Wolves, with their large feet and long legs, are good swimmers, and they can easily cross lakes and rivers in their territory. Though they catch and eat fish in shallow water, they rarely follow large prey into water.

Fleet of foot

Hunters are specialist animals and tend to be smaller and quicker than other pack members. They therefore tend to be females, but the strength of the males will also be needed to help bring down large prey.

Speed merchants
The maximum speed that a wolf can run is between 30 and 40mph, and this can be maintained for up to an hour if necessary, either to escape danger or during a hunt.

Long-distance runners

Wolves prefer to trot or lope at about 4 to 6mph and
can cover 100 miles in a day in search of food.

Quick thinking

The wolf is very intelligent: its brain is 30 percent larger than the domestic dog's. Captive wolves learn after short periods of observation how to undo simple latches and get to the food rewards behind gates.

THE HUNT

Native Americans have always considered the wolf to be one of the finest and most successful of all hunters, even when it was in direct competition with them for food. Early North American settlers were also in awe of the wolf's strength and power – wolves have been known to track prey for up to 100 miles a day and bring down quarry 10 times their own size. Behavioral studies have revealed what actually happens before, during and after a kill and the high level of collective skill and co-operation involved in hunting as a pack.

TEAM-BUILDING
Much of the wolf's hunting success as a pack is based on careful preparations before the hunt. Individuals constantly revise their skills and practice techniques so that every member is ready to play their part.

The hunter, like the omega, is a specialist animal and is usually female. Females are smaller than the males by approximately 20-25 percent, which usually means they are faster and more agile. There are often one or two wolves within the pack that can sprint like a greyhound – fast enough to catch, turn, or run their quarry into an ambush. The hunter may not always be the alpha female in a large pack because she is too valuable to risk getting injured. She will, however, direct operations from the sidelines and will keep control of the lower-ranking wolves during the hunt. As this is a difficult task, she often initiates a practice session just before the hunt.

First, by adjusting the position of her tail, she excretes an odor which tells the pack which way to turn. She also uses her body to push them either to one side or the other. Second, she lets them know which species is going to be hunted. The alpha female will select the kind of prey most appropriate to the pack's seasonal needs: in winter, often large animals with a high fat content, such as bison, elk, and wild boar, and in summer,

smaller animals such as mountain goats or young deer. She indicates her chosen prey by digging up cached food – such as a piece of hoof – which has been buried for later consumption or for use in training sessions. In summer, food is usually buried around lakes and ponds or along riverbanks where the cool mud just above the waterline acts as a refrigerator.

Having shown the hunters and the rest of the pack which food she wants them to hunt, she must now demonstrate the movements that the prey animal would make while being chased. She usually does this while carrying the food object in her mouth. The alpha male will be allowed to take the food from her and act as if to defend it, showing that he will have control once the kill has been made and the pack begins to feed.

Sometimes a wolf may hunt alone, and it is then more cautious, tending to catch small prey such as rodents, birds, rabbits, and fish.

ON THE SCENT

Wolves have an exceptional sense of smell. Scientists have proved that domestic dogs have a sense of smell ten thousand times more sensitive than our own, and although it has not yet been scientifically calculated, the wolf's sense of smell is far superior to that of the dog. However, it has been suggested that it is one hundred thousand times more sensitive than that of humans. The wolf can detect potential prey, using the wind direction to its advantage, at a distance of nearly $1^3/4$ miles.

Hunt rehearsal

The alpha female (center) uses her body to push and steer the other wolves to the left or right to follow the scent of the prey. In doing this she prepares them for the hunt and asserts her dominance as a decision-maker.

Hunting practice

The alpha female instigates a game of tag in which the young wolves will be shown how to catch and bring down their prey by practicing on each other.

When wolves are tracking the movements of quarry, they can follow the scent of the animal's hoofprints, urine and droppings and can also smell any hair, skin particles or parasites in its tracks. They are also able to smell the tooth decay (from chewed vegetation) of an old animal. Indeed, so honed are the wolf's information-gathering skills that it can tell if the quarry is in poor condition, sick, old or injured and how far ahead it is.

Successful hunting requires various techniques, depending on the size of the quarry. Stalking in long grass or ambush are used to catch smaller animals. During an ambush the pack splits into two or more groups, and one will chase the animal toward the remaining pack members, camouflaged in the trees or

bushes. Wolves have been seen to pick up snow in their mouths so that their breath will not be visible to their prey. Once the prey is caught, one bite around the neck and a few shakes will quickly kill the animal.

Another technique is intimidation. Wolves single out their prey and try to get it to run – there is less danger from hooves and horns when the animal moves away from them and cannot turn to defend itself. Wolves have been known to move at a top speed of between 30 and 40 miles per hour, and they can maintain this pace for an hour if they need to. Or, if they are chasing a large, healthy ungulate, such as elk or moose, they can stay the course and deny their quarry food, water, rest and herd security for up to two weeks. The wolves wound their quarry by snapping at it from time to time,

The alpha female will often initiate a practice session

just before the hunt.

and eventually the larger animals will collapse from loss of blood and exhaustion.

TASTE OF SUCCESS

Once the prey has been killed, the pack feeds in an orderly and controlled manner. The alphas do not always feed first but they decide exactly what each wolf is to eat and when. Larger wolves such as the betas need to retain their strength to act as enforcers and will be allowed more food than lower-ranking wolves.

Each wolf is capable of consuming between 5lb and 20lb of meat in one go because it could be several days or even weeks before the pack feeds again. If there is more food than they can eat, wolves have been seen caching the surplus and then marking the spot with

urine so that they can locate when food is scarce.

After feeding, the wolf pack relaxes and indulges in play and grooming sessions to ensure that valuable bonds are renewed after the tension and risks of the hunt (wolves make a kill only once in every ten hunts). And then the wolves rest in order to aid digestion. They always remain alert, however, and, if they need to run to escape danger, have been known to regurgitate the contents of their stomachs. Running on a full stomach would not only be uncomfortable and reduce speed, but could cause twisted gut, a potentially fatal condition.

After the hunt and initial feast, the wolf pack often howls to defend its hard-earned meal from other predators. Scavengers such as ravens, eagles, foxes, or coyotes will eventually polish off the leftovers.

By adjusting the position of her tail, the alpha female excretes

an odor which tells the pack which way to turn.

Nose to tail
Here the alpha female uses her lifted tail to release a scent and
to act as a sign for the other wolves to follow her. She will
practice a change of direction when she is some distance ahead
of them.

The deer hunters

The alpha female indicates
her intention to hunt deer by
using a previously cached leg
to teach the pack what to
look for, and how to catch it.
If the wolves approach her
from the front, she will
demonstrate potential
dangers by turning her head
from side to side, and by
hitting them with the leg to
simulate a kick.

Tracking techniques

Wolves find their prey in three ways: by scent, using their fantastic sense of smell; by following tracks; and by chance encounters.

Winning by a nose

The wolf's sense of smell is so sensitive that they have the ability to smell disease and decay in elderly or injured prey from the tracks they leave in the snow.

When wolves are tracking the movements of quarry, they can follow the scent of the animal's hoofprints, urine and droppings and can also smell any hair, skin particles or parasites in its tracks.

Poised for action
This wolf raises himself onto his hind legs as he smells, hears, and finally sees the rest of his pack directing the prey toward him ready for an ambush. This is one of the many techniques used during hunting.

One in ten chance
Wolf packs have a one in ten success rate for catching prey. They compete with both other predators, such as bears and cougars, as well as human hunters.

The alpha female will select the kind of prey most appropriate
to the pack's seasonal needs: in winter, often large animals with a
high fat content, such as bison, elk, and wild boar.

Survival of the fittest

Wolves often test ungulate herds for old, weak, or vulnerable individuals. By hunting these animals, wolves keep deer or bison populations healthy because only the fittest animals will go on to breed.

Wolf intimidation
A wolf intimidates a bison to try to make him run. During the hunt, following large prey as it runs away is less risky than confronting it.

Risky business

A kick from a large animal, such as a bison, could be fatal. Male bison often lead and protect their herd and can be very bold and aggressive. They are not easily intimidated by the wolves.

Deflecting danger
The wolf is most at risk of injury when its prey is charging toward it, and so it circles its prey to try to turn the animal away from him.

Staying the pace

The wolf's slender body and long legs are ideally adapted for the tight twists and turns required when hunting. Moving with a fluid motion, wolves also have stamina over long distances.

Closing in

Having chased this bison for many hours, the wolves will finally pull it down by its nose or rump. Once it has fallen, the wolves close in for the kill.

Once the prey is caught, one bite around the neck and

a few shakes will quickly kill the animal.

Flesh, bone and fur

Large, hoofed animals, including deer, make up a high percentage of the prey in the wolf's varied diet. As well as flesh, wolves also consume bone, which provides calcium and phosphorus, and fur to coat the bone to prevent sharp fragments doing any internal damage.

Mobile menu

Herd animals have been known to destroy large areas of vegetation during continuous grazing. The wolf, however, helps to maintain good quality grass by hunting the prey and consequently moving the herds around.

Snowpaws

When traveling long distances in deep snow, wolves will frequently switch places so the animal in the lead does not tire. The slight webbing between the wolf's toes helps it to travel on snow and ice with ease.

Slippery end

During the winter, wolves sometimes chase their prey onto frozen lakes to speed up the kill. Hoofed animals find it difficult to run and stay upright on the ice and will often slip and fall without the wolves having to risk injury by pulling them down.

Prey sensors
Wolves are able to detect their prey up to 3ft under
the snow. They use their acute sense of smell and
can even hear the heart beat of small animals.

The sound of success
After hunting, the wolves defend both their food and their
territory over long distances by using a low defensive howl.
Increased scenting will also occur to back this up, in and
around the edge of the territory.

Food defence

Ears lowered to the sides, head down and baring of teeth indicate that a wolf is defending something. Adult wolves teach the pups to defend their food by stealing it, and then when the pups approach and try to get it back the adults show their teeth and growl. The pups soon learn that they must do the same to keep their food.

Howl of triumph

After a kill has been made, defending territory is just as important as defending the food. The wolves will howl periodically throughout the night to advertise their kill and their intention to defend it.

Cut above the rest

After a kill, the alpha wolves defend their food by baring their teeth and flicking their tongues. These wolves have the right to consume the vital organs such as heart, liver, and kidneys, which will give them the strongest scent.

Sharp warnings

Feeding can appear to be a volatile time, but often the bared teeth and growls are just used to defend a wolf's share of the carcass. The omega wolf is vital in calming such situations and often plays the fool.

Smell of success

This older wolf knows from experience the value in hunting and eating particular prey species to increase his scent. His knowledge is respected and used to teach younger members of the pack. Fish is particularly pungent and may be abundant in some wolf territories.

Hunter-gatherer

In times of extreme hardship the wolf will consume fruit, berries, and nuts to survive. The adult wolves will teach the pups how to avoid sharp thorns; once they've been pricked, they soon learn to be cautious.

Wolves have been known to track prey for
up to 100 miles a day and bring down quarry
10 times their own size.

Wolf watching

Most wild wolf sightings occur in winter when prey
is most active and the pack has to travel further.
Generally, wolves will smell humans and hide away
long before we catch a glimpse of them.

Light snacks

For many years scientists did not know how wolves survived in areas
where large ungulates were in decline. The stomach contents of dead
wolves, however, revealed that the animals survived on small prey such
as rodents, squirrels and birds when larger prey was scarce.

Sometimes a wolf may hunt alone, and it is then more cautious, tending to catch small prey such as rodents, birds, rabbits, and fish.

Fast food

Though European wolves (above) also hunt and kill prey up to 10 times their own body weight, they regularly eat much smaller animals such as mice and frogs. The wild boar still exists in areas of Europe and is a good source of food for them.

Lone ranger

Packs of wolves can bring down large quarry by co-operative hunting, but the lone wolf must search for small prey, such as rabbits, rodents, and birds, until he or she can join a pack or meet another lone wolf of the opposite gender.

Larger wolves, such as the betas, need to retain their strength to act as enforcers and will be allowed more food than lower-ranking wolves.

Tell-tail signs

Tail posture signifies a wolf's position within the pack and where and when it can feed. Each rank of wolf is allowed to eat certain parts of the prey which will give it the correct scent for its place in the hierarchy.

Meatwinner

This wolf (opposite) may be carrying food back to the safety of her own territory before consuming it. Or she may be returning to feed her pups and the nanny she has left to look after them.

Food storage

Burying food for consumption at a later stage. Often this is done close to water or in a riverbank so that the food is refrigerated and kept fresh until needed.

Eating for others

Because the betas rely on their strength and are often the largest animals in the pack, they have huge appetites. They are allowed to consume more food than the other wolves because they protect the pack.

Bone-breaking bite

The wolf has a bite pressure of 1,500lb per 1 sq in which enables them to bite through and remove the limbs of prey. Many years ago when human limbs were broken and reset in hospitals, 400lb per 1 sq in of pressure was all that was required.

Aid to digestion

Sometimes, like the domestic dog, the wolf eats grass and other vegetation to add fiber to its diet and help with digestion. Low-ranking wolves already have more fiber in their diet because they eat their prey's stomach, which contains digested grass.

Twig toothpicks

When naturalists first saw wolves chewing twigs and branches, they thought they were sharpening their teeth before hunting; it is now thought that they are cleaning their teeth after a feed.

After feeding, the wolf pack relaxes and indulges in play and grooming sessions to ensure that valuable bonds are renewed after the tension and risks of the hunt.

Light relief
Hunting can stretch and test pack relationships. After hunting and feeding, these European wolves enjoy playing together and grooming, which help to establish their bonds with each other again.

Replete

Wolves consume as much meat as they can in one feed – between 5lb and 20lb – because the next meal could be two days or two weeks away. After such a large feed, resting is essential for digestion.

Waking sleep

Wolves have been known to rest for up to 18 hours a day, but they remain constantly alert to their surroundings and can spring into action if predators, prey or rival packs enter their territory.

In the twilight hours
The wolf has adapted its hunting patterns and now prefers to catch its food at dusk and dawn to avoid human conflict.

Night vision
Though poor in comparison to its other senses, the wolf's eyesight is good at night, allowing it to pick up movement in particular.

Queuing for the kill

Scavengers, such as foxes, often live close to wolves and, though rodents and small mammals naturally form the bulk of their diet, they also feed on the leftovers from a wolf kill.

Canid competitor

Wolves and coyotes often live close to each other. The wolves will chase and kill coyotes because they see them as competition for food. The name coyote comes from an Aztec word *coyotl*, meaning "barking dog" and describes the calls of these smaller canids.

Rich pickings

Scraps of food left by the wolves are cleaned up by birds of prey, such as eagles. They can often be seen and heard circling above a wolf kill and will come down to feed once the wolves have left the carcass.

Big competition

Bears and wolves often live in the same areas and compete for food. The adults rarely fight but will attack and kill each other's young as they are seen as competition for food. Together with humans, bears are responsible for a large percentage of wolf-pup fatalities. An adult bear can easily chase away any guarding nannies and dig out a den of young pups.

BREEDING

Breeding in North America takes place from January to April. Wolves in the southern regions of their territorial range tend to breed earlier than those in the north because food is available earlier. The Ethiopian wolf, for example, which lives only a few degrees north of the equator, breeds anytime from August through to December.

The female wolf reaches sexual maturity at two years old and comes into oestrus only once a year. There are records in some subspecies of females breeding in their first season, but they are usually too young to be able to cope successfully with pups, and the chances of survival are very poor. Females have been known to continue to produce young up to their tenth year, but this is exceptional as wolves rarely live beyond six or seven years in the wild. Although the alpha female is usually the only animal to breed in a pack, subordinate females sometimes produce multiple litters possibly because significant pack members, such as the alpha female, have been killed, which causes the remaining animals to panic breed to reclaim vacant pack positions or territory.

Scientists are researching whether the type of food the pack eats enables the alpha female to predetermine seven or eight months before her breeding season the number and gender of pups she will have, depending on whether their purpose in life will be to stay with the pack or to move away and establish a new pack in a neighboring territory. Without other wolf packs on the borders of the alpha female's territory, prey is often lost as it escapes into areas where there are no wolves. Wolf packs flush out and drive prey back and forth between territories, so an unoccupied adjacent territory represents potential loss of food.

Adult courtship begins during late winter and early spring, but well before this the alpha female will start to suppress all other potential breeding females by

reminding them of her dominant position in the pack. She does this by constantly wrestling with them and by preventing them from moving in a certain direction by "T-ing," where she blocks their path, thus demonstrating her dominance .

The alpha female also selects nannies who will look after and educate her pups shortly after they have been weaned onto solid food at about four to six weeks, allowing her to get back to her decision-making duties as pack leader. Despite the name, nannies can be of either gender and are selected by the alpha female for their experience and ability to teach pack etiquette to the youngsters. The alpha female employs a complex selection process and initiates play behavior among pack members to determine which wolves are the most balanced and patient and best suited to looking after her pups.

As the female's receptive period approaches, she will increase her suppression of the lower-ranking females to prevent them coming into season at the same time. By growling and snarling and constantly pushing another female around, she can even cause miscarriage.

During mating, the alpha male mounts the female from the rear, and this usually locks them together in a copulatory tie, which happens when a gland in the male's penis swells and the female's vaginal muscles tighten. The tie can last from five to thirty-five minutes; they can even run together for a while if they need to until the tie breaks.

PUPS JOIN THE PACK

The gestation period for wolves is between 60 and 63 days, and birth, from January to April, is usually timed to coincide with the arrival of young prey species to provide the new mother with plentiful food.

For the first four to five weeks of their lives, the wolf pups only have contact with their mother. She suckles them in the den, offering food, security and warmth: the

Peak time
Constant checking of the alpha female's condition is essential near her receptive time. Courtship behavior at this time involves a lot of sniffing and licking.

three vital components they need for survival. These components form the basis of all their future education and are either offered as rewards for good behavior or denied to teach them a lesson.

During the first early weeks in the den, the alpha female will start to introduce the scent of other pack members to the pups. When the mother leaves the den she rubs her face and underside around the other adults and nannies to pick up their scent so that the pups will become familiar with them. She will begin to teach the pups, even at this early stage, what type of respect is required for each rank of wolf. For example, if she has the scent of a dominant member on her muzzle, she will take a young pup's head or neck gently in her mouth and turn the pup over to show the submissive

position required in greeting this member of the pack.

The higher-ranking pups quickly discover that the middle teats have better quality milk, and they will begin to show early signs of dominance over their litter-mates by maintaining this position when feeding.

When the pups' hearing and sight are more developed at about four to five weeks, the alpha female brings them above ground for the first time to meet the pack and the nannies who will continue their education and care. When weaning takes place, a similar-ranking adult will regurgitate solid food for a pup, helping it identify the correct food for his or her rank. Once the pups have moved onto solid chunks of meat, the nannies often steal food from the pups to teach them how to defend their food.

The young wolf's education involves vital lessons in communication, social interaction and hunting. Young wolves join in with the hunt at about six to seven months, and lessons taught by older, more experienced members of the wolf family are essential for the youngsters' survival and for the successful future of the pack and of the wolf as a species.

The first six to nine months of the young wolf's life are the most crucial. Many do not survive due to starvation, human persecution or loss to other predators such as bears, cougars, or large birds of prey. Sadly, humans are responsible for a large number of pup deaths either directly through shooting, poisoning and trapping or indirectly through logging and general loss of wolf habitat.

Preparing for pups

Getting ready for the arrival of wolf pups often begins seven to eight months before the alpha female comes into season.

Up close and personal

The alpha male remains close to the alpha female during her season. Her scent will change dramatically when she comes into her short receptive period, and he must be the first male to mate with her to ensure his genes are passed on.

Early maturity

Female wolves are usually sexually active during their second year or season; males become active at 22 months. Wolves can breed for their entire life if they stay free from injury.

As the female's receptive period approaches, she will increase her suppression of the lower-ranking females to prevent them coming into season at the same time.

Staying on top

The alpha male and female suppress the other wolves to ensure that they are the only pair to breed, thus keeping strong genes in the pack. The alpha female dominates the other females to prevent them coming into season.

Selection tests
Choosing the right wolves to act as nannies is vitally important. Here an adult wolf is being tested; if selected, it will be responsible for the pups' education from the age of four to five weeks.

Adult courtship begins during late winter and early spring, but well before this the alpha female will start to suppress all other potential breeding females by reminding them of her dominant position in the pack.

Mating season
Wolf mating usually takes place between January and March depending on the species or subspecies of wolf. A tie between the male and the female has to take place to ensure mating is successful. Even though the wolves are quite vulnerable at this time, they can still run together if the need arises.

Paired for life

The strong bond between the alpha pair keeps them safe and healthy, and they will usually stay together for life. If one of them dies or is killed, however, the remaining alpha will select a new mate.

Fleetingly fertile

The alpha female, unlike many domestic dogs, has only one season a year lasting between seven and twenty-one days. The receptive period when mating takes place is even shorter and lasts four to seven days.

Domestic bliss

During courtship the alpha pair spends long periods of time resting together. This pair of European wolves (above) rest together in woodland. The North American pair (left) are joined on the ice by a potential nanny for their future pups.

Waterfront homes

Wolves always live close to water, and the alpha female often digs her den close to a water source, fully aware that she will need to increase her liquid intake during pregnancy and while feeding her pups.

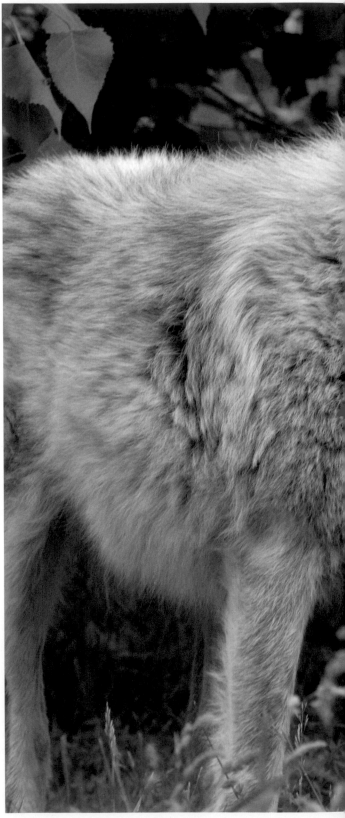

Conserving energy

The gestation period for a wolf is between 60 and 63 days. Toward the end of this period, the alpha female can be seen resting more frequently, saving energy for the weeks to come.

Social climbing

During the alpha female's gestation period, the pack is on its best behavior. Each wolf tries to impress the alpha pair in an attempt to get the job as a nanny.

Infanticide
Rival packs are fiercely territorial, and in an attack pups are seen as future competitors for territory and are usually killed. But some packs have been known to raise orphaned pups in order to boost their own numbers.

Safe haven

The selection of a den site is essential for the survival of the pups, particularly as most of their predators can dig them out. This is why the den is usually positioned under a hard surface, such as a rock, or at the base of a tree to provide extra protection.

Pups as prey

Smaller predators, such as coyotes, pose no threat to adult wolves but would not hesitate in killing a wolf pup or even a whole litter if they found one unguarded.

Adult education

Alphas give refresher lessons in, for example, balance and trust, to make sure every wolf knows how to behave around the young impressionable wolf pups.

For the first four to five weeks of their lives, the wolf pups only have contact with their mother. She suckles them in the den, offering food, security and warmth: the three vital components they need for survival.

Blind beginning

Young wolf pups are born both blind and deaf; they find their way to their mother's teats using their sense of smell. At 10-13 days, the pups open their eyes which start blue and later change to golden brown.

Sneak preview

Sometimes the nanny's curiosity gets the better of her and she attempts to take a quick look at her new charges when the alpha female is away from the den. She is taking a risk in doing this because the alpha mother does not tolerate any interaction with her pups until she is ready to hand them over.

Full-time nanny

During the first few weeks spent below ground both the pups and their mother are watched over by a nanny. These animals are totally dedicated to the safety and training of their future charges and won't leave until dismissed by the alpha female.

First outside view

At four to five weeks, the pups venture to the entrance to the den. Their development rate is so fast that in another two weeks they will be exploring up to half a mile away from the den.

The mouth test

The young wolf pup explores its surroundings by tasting
everything and is always on the look out for a potential meal.
The adult wolves will observe and give guidance when required.

Choir practice

The pups listen with interest to the pack howling and will usually attempt to join in with the chorus at three to four weeks. Perfecting the art of howling is essential for a young wolf pup. Usually it's the more dominant pups that howl first, but it's not long before all the pups join in the family howls.

Etiquette lessons

The alpha female introduces her pups to the scent of the other pack members while they are still in their den. She shows them how to respond correctly to the adults depending on their rank.

Early days

For the first four to five weeks
of their lives, the pups only
have contact with their mother.

Semi-solids

When the young wolf pups are weaned, they receive regurgitated food from the adults after they have fed. This will be replaced by solid meat as the pups' teeth develop.

Once the pups have moved onto solid chunks of meat, the nannies often steal food from the pups to teach them how to defend their food.

What not to eat

These young pups soon establish a feeding routine based on the right food for each rank. They have been taught how to defend their food using body posture and growls.

Hunting howl

Wolves are active and often howl on the night of a full moon. Rather than calling up the devil, it is more likely that the alpha instigates howling because the moonlight increases the pack's chances of a successful hunt.

Defensive techniques
The young wolves learn to
defend their food both at the
kill, with body postures,
growls, and snarls, and, longer
range, by using a deep howl.

The first six to nine months of the young wolf's life are the most crucial. Many do not survive due to starvation, human persecution or loss to other predators such as bears, cougars, or large birds of prey.

Test of strength

Three wolf pups practice their skills in a tug of war. The beta pup has the advantage of strength during this game, but the smaller pups are usually quicker and will often run off with the toy if the beta lets go.

Playing chase

When wolf pups play together, mock hunting is one of their favorite games. Chasing and biting the backs of each other's legs, and running in front of one another are rehearsals for catching prey in the future. Here the nanny is involved in the boisterous play.

Serious play

Constant play-fights help young wolves to learn about pack survival. These sessions teach different hunting techniques, such as the ambush, where some animals hide in the trees and jump out on the other wolves as they approach.

Educational games
Play is used for teaching
purposes and to maintain
family bonds. Bones or sticks
are sometimes picked up and
used in chasing games of tag
and relay.

CONSERVATION

The gray wolf once had the largest distribution of any mammal, apart from humans, ranging from the Northwest Territories of Canada to Mexico and across much of Eurasia. By the time it was finally protected by the US Endangered Species Act of 1973, it had been wiped out from the lower 48 states except for a few hundred in Minnesota and a few on Isle Royale, Michigan. Similarly, during the nineteenth and twentieth centuries, wolves were exterminated from central and northern European countries.

Governments played a significant part in the decline of the wolf by introducing bounties for dead animals. As early as 600 BC, Greek local government officials paid a bounty of five silver drachmas for each dead male wolf. England introduced wolf bounties in the 1500s, Sweden, in 1647 and Norway, in 1730. The first wolf bounty in North America was issued by the Massachusetts Bay Colony in 1630.

Wolf bounties and legal culls were widespread throughout Europe, Canada and the US. Though culling is an attempt to control wolf numbers, more often than not it has quite the opposite effect, causing what's left of a pack to panic breed.

The gray wolf is now classified as vulnerable by the IUCN (The World Conservation Union) Red List and endangered in the US (lower 48 states) except Minnesota where it is listed as threatened. Despite continued persecution in some countries, such as Russia, the species is now protected by the Endangered Species Act in the US and by the Bern Convention in Europe, which also protects its habitat.

Wolves are now gradually gaining ground in western Europe, with small populations in France, Germany, Norway, Sweden, Finland, Greece, and Italy. There is also now a viable population of about 2,000 Iberian wolves, a gray wolf subspecies, in Spain and Portugal.

Apart from the wolves in Portugal, most of the rest live near highly populated areas in northern Spain, though recent forest fires have destroyed large areas of their natural habitat.

Gray wolves are still found in about 90 percent of their original range in Canada and number between 52,000 and 60,000. In the US, wolf populations have been increasing and there are now about 2,700 wolves in the lower 48 states and between 6,000 and 8,000 in Alaska. Various reintroduction schemes have helped to boost wolf numbers in the US: the red wolf *Canis rufus*, a distinct species which had become extinct in the south-eastern US by 1980, has been returned to parts of its former range and now numbers more than 100; there are now 11 packs of Mexican wolves *Canis lupus baileyi* in New Mexico and Arizona; populations of eastern timber wolves, another gray wolf subspecies, have been augmented in Minnesota and now also roam Michigan and Wisconsin; and there are increasing numbers of gray wolves in the Northern Rocky Mountains, spanning Montana, Idaho and Wyoming. These reintroductions have not been trouble free as some wolves have attacked livestock and have had to be removed by the US Fish and Wildlife Service.

We now know that the alpha female will deliberately produce pups to occupy vacant territories and start new packs in order to cut off the escape route of prey and so increase her own pack's chances of survival. Research shows that it is often the dispersing wolves that are the ones that become a problem to livestock because in seeking vacant territory they sometimes approach farms or ranches.

Dispersing animals also help to prevent inbreeding. In the past, when wolf-pack territories covered several hundred square miles, co-operative pairing of offspring between adjacent packs would create slight but beneficial genetic variation. Now the wolf

often has as little as 30 to 40 square miles of territory, and it is much harder to ensure genetic variety for future generations.

With ever more behavioral studies constantly improving our knowledge about the way wolves live and interact, we are developing a clearer picture of their world and their extreme level of intelligence. Only by

using this knowledge will be able to devise sophisticated techniques to manage the co-existence of wolf and human populations.

Most of our current methods to prevent wolves from taking livestock have been unsuccessful. Simple gate closures can be opened by wolves after only a short period of observation. Electric fencing can be disabled

Fishing wolf

The rapid expansion of towns and farmland diminishes the wolf's habitat and causes a corresponding decrease in its natural prey. So the animal is forced to try alternative food sources, such as fish. Unfortunately, if eaten in excessive amounts, this can dramatically affect a pack's social order.

by snow and guard dogs have been tricked by the wolf's cunning. Wolf packs have been known to send a female wolf forward who will act as if she's in season and whimper to attract the dog. The rest of the pack then appears and kills the animal to get to the livestock.

A guard dog would be a more effective deterrent if it had visual traits such as upright, well-marked ears, a strongly marked muzzle, and a long tail and hackles. Also if the dog were trained to socialize and mingle with the sheep or cattle, the wolf might then regard it as the equivalent of the herd's alpha male.

Ecotourism is a modern phenomenon which raises funds from tourists who wish to observe or photograph wild wolves in their natural habitat. In organizing and running ecologically-supportive holidays, local people can generate a sustainable income by protecting their indigenous wildlife. The positive financial benefits of a tourist-based industry could provide a valuable alternative income for local hunters.

So the wheel of fortune does seem to be turning at last in favor of the wolf, not least in part due to the efforts of numerous organizations worldwide in promoting the survival of this species. Some wolf centers house captive-bred and rescued animals for study and educational purposes, and raise money for conservation and reintroduction schemes.

Yellowstone National Park, where wolves were reintroduced from Canada in 1995, now has 16 packs of wolves, and a positive "wolf-effect" on the whole ecosystem is being noted by scientists. The out-of-control elk population has been halved by the wolves, and this has allowed trees, such as willow and aspen, to regenerate. Beavers have, in turn, been attracted back to the area by a healthy food supply, and wolf kills have pulled in scavengers, such as grizzly bears, ravens and birds of prey. It will be fascinating to see what other effects the wolf, as a predator at the top of the food

chain, will have over time on the park's ecosystem.

The Yellowstone to Yukon Conservation Initiative was launched in 1996 and is an ambitious long-term project which aims to connect wildlife parks and wild areas by conservation corridors all along the Rocky Mountains of Canada and the northern US. It will eventually allow wildlife the space to roam, to interbreed and will create a vast, interconnected mountain ecosystem.

And perhaps one day in the UK, if the Wolf Trust is successful in its campaign for wolves to be reintroduced to Scotland, visitors to the Scottish glens will once more thrill to the call of the wolf.

Losing ground

With the ever-increasing loss of their habitat and continual logging, wolves are sometimes forced to turn their attention to catching cattle or sheep on ranches and open farmland.

Critically endangered

The red wolf *Canis rufus* (above), the world's most endangered canid, was hunted to extinction. In 1980, just before it was declared extinct in the wild, 14 wolves were rounded up by the US Fish and Wildlife Service to be bred in captivity. By the end of 1987 enough animals had been bred to start a reintroduction program, and there are now about 100 red wolves in the wild.

There are now 11 packs of Mexican wolves in New Mexico and Arizona.

European survivors

Wolves prefer to live as far away from humans as possible. But as human populations have increased and as wolf territories and their prey species have decreased, wolves are sometimes forced into European towns and cities to look for food. The territories of European wolves (opposite) are much smaller than North American wolves, and so their pack size also tends to be smaller. European wolves have managed to survive only in the most remote, densely forested or mountainous regions.

Mexican stronghold

The Mexican wolf (*Canis lupus baileyi*) was originally found in the mountainous regions of central Mexico. Now recognized as an endangered species, captive-bred wolves have been released and allowed to disperse into western New Mexico.

Worth more alive than dead?

Though a protected species in most European countries, some hunters see no need to stop killing the wolf for sport and will pay large sums of money for the privilege. But with the advent of ecotourism, money can now be generated by people who wish to visit countries to watch wolves, and this has helped to fund conservation work and show local businesses the value of keeping the wolf alive.

Ecotourism is a modern phenomenon which raises funds from tourists who wish to observe or photograph wild wolves in their natural habitat.

Return of the native

The gray wolf (left) became extinct in England in about 1486 and was exterminated in Scotland in 1743. Wolves survived in Ireland until about 1773. The species also vanished from other Western European countries, but now populations can be found in about nine of them.

INDEX